POSTWAR

RICHARD MAYNE

POSTWAR

The Dawn of Today's Europe

SCHOCKEN BOOKS
NEW YORK

To Bill

First American edition published by Schocken Books 1983
10 9 8 7 6 5 4 3 2 1   83 84 85 86
© 1983 Thames and Hudson Ltd, London
All rights reserved
Published by agreement with Thames and Hudson Ltd, London

Library of Congress Cataloging in Publication Data
Mayne Richard.
Postwar, the dawn of today's Europe.
Bibliography: p.
Includes index.
1. Europe—History—1945–   . I. Title.
D1051.M39   1983   940.5   83–42720

Manufactured in the United States of America
ISBN 0–8052–3864–6

Contents

Acknowledgments

My grateful acknowledgments are due to the following for use of copyright verse material, some of it in my own translation. Chapter 1—for 'The White Cliffs of Dover': © MCMXLI Renewed by Shapiro Bernstein & Co Inc., 10 East 53rd St., New York, New York 10022, International Copyright Secured, All Rights Reserved Including Public Performance for Profit. Used by permission; reproduced by permission of EMI Music Publishing Ltd. Chapter 2—for 'Milano, agosto 1943' by Salvatore Quasimodo (transl. R.M.): Arnoldo Mondadori Editore; for 'Ich hab' es nicht gewollt' (transl. R.M.): Felix Berner, Stuttgart. Chapter 5—for their translation of 'Russia' by Aleksandr Blok: Jon Stallworthy and Peter France. Chapter 7—for lines from 'La vie en rose': Noel Gay Music Co Ltd. Chapter 8—for 'Family Matters' by Günter Grass: to the author, the translator (Michael Hamburger), and Martin Secker & Warburg, publishers of Grass's *Selected Poems*; for the quotation from his 'verteidigung der wölfe gegen die lämmer' (transl. R.M.): Hans Magnus Enzensberger; for his 'Etwas kündigt sich an' (transl. R.M.): Albert Arnold Scholl. Chapter 10—for the quotation from 'The Volunteer' by C. Day Lewis: The Executors of the Estate of C. Day Lewis, Jonathan Cape Ltd, and the Hogarth Press.

1

Great Expectations

History takes us unawares: our own lives colour our memories of events too momentous to grasp.

When World War II ended in Europe, I was in an army camp at Catterick, Yorkshire. It was a fine, dry evening. A group of soldiers and ATS girls stood on the parade-ground, an expanse of well-battered asphalt among the Nissen huts and red-brick barrack-rooms. To us, this was only a respite: we were still expecting to be sent on 'the banana boat', to the war in the Pacific. But for the moment the flags were flying, and we crowded round the victory bonfire. The unit dance-band, led by a wily Signals man with steel spectacles and a soft moustache, played its signature tune, *I'm confessing*, then a string of other popular numbers. Some people danced. Most of us simply stood there, eyeing the fire and the girls. In our heads rang the tinsel lyrics of one of the songs:

> There'll be blue birds over
> The white cliffs of Dover
>   Tomorrow, just you wait and see.
> There'll be love and laughter
> And peace ever after
>   Tomorrow, just you wait and see.

> The shepherd will tend his sheep,
>   The valley will bloom again,
> And Jimmy will go to sleep
>   In his own little room again . . .

Paltry as the words now sound, they were poignant then. They spoke of deep longings, partly contradictory: the ache for a safe, imagined rural past; the nostalgia for home and childhood; the insistent dream that tomorrow, soon, eventually, some day, everything would be different – a happy issue out of all our afflictions, a halcyon future to match the sacrifice so many had made.

As the daylight faded, the lights came on. It was an astonishing sight. For six years, all over Europe, people had groped their way through the blackout. The night sky had been lit only by searchlights, explosions, and incendiary flares. Now, at last, Europe's cities began to sparkle like jewels.

In London, the skyline was suddenly floodlit. Landmarks that had survived Hitler's bombs stood out like a stage set: the Tower, the Mansion House, Westminster Abbey, Buckingham Palace. Amid the ruins of the City, the dome of St Paul's Cathedral still upheld the Cross. From private houses, lights were streaming; curtains had been opened, blinds rolled up, frames of black paper put away. All around, as the crowds surged in Trafalgar Square, down Whitehall, and along the Mall, bonfires reddened the sky as the Blitz had done. Fireworks parodied the sound of guns.

In Paris, rivalling the fireworks, multi-coloured flares were dropped from aircraft, and people in cars shot pistols into the night sky. Here, too, crowds thronged the floodlit landmarks – the Arc de Triomphe, the Opéra, the Place de la Concorde. Shimmering like liquid fireworks, fountains played.

In Rome, the buildings glowed red-ochre, and all over the city the bells rang out, from St Peter's and a hundred other churches. For a full ten minutes, the air-raid sirens sounded a last 'All Clear'.

Even in German cities there was rejoicing of a sort. In Berlin, still hazy with smoke from the burning buildings and dust from streets encumbered with rubble and road-blocks, the victors celebrated with flags, speeches, singing, champagne, and vodka. In Marburg, where suburban villas were still smouldering, some of the Nazis' newly freed slave-girls gave themselves to all comers on mattresses piled in the open streets.

Lights, bonfires, bells, sirens, flags, flowers, confetti, music, drink, kisses, and dancing – jubilation everywhere had its repertoire. In Brussels, the crowds danced in front of a huge portrait of King Leopold, recently released from captivity. In the Netherlands, RAF aircrew were showered with tulips, and even the windmills flew flags. In Oslo, barely liberated, Nazi soldiers were jostled by Norwegians singing the National Anthem. In Moscow, thousands of people filled Red Square and the broad streets round the Kremlin, past St Basil's Cathedral to the bridge and the river banks, and away towards Theatre Square, where there was a bandstand for dancing – one of more than a hundred throughout the city. Some of the Moscow revellers stopped foreign cars, embraced their inhabitants, and dragged them out to be carried shoulder-high. Outside the US Embassy, there were cries of 'Long live America!'

The euphoria was typical; but so, too, was some of the confusion.

Not all the celebrations coincided. Some began early, before the war was officially over. In the West, 'VE Day' – for 'Victory in Europe' – was 8 May 1945, the day after the Nazi surrender in Rheims to the Allied Supreme Commander, General Dwight D. Eisenhower. In the East, it was 9 May, date of the official surrender to all the Allies in Berlin. In years to come, the discrepancy would look ominous. At the time, it merely seemed to confirm what one of Eisenhower's aides noted in his diary: 'I've learned the hard way that it is much easier to start a war than to stop one.'

Civilian bureaucrats would have agreed with him. In several cities, the bonfires got out of hand. In Glasgow, the emergency services had to answer some seventy calls; in Plymouth, police had to stop the crowd feeding a giant blaze with municipal deckchairs. In Belfast, a new hotel burned down, apparently by accident. In Sunderland, a ship in the River Wear endangered the population by firing off live 20-millimetre shells.

Surprisingly, there were few serious disorders: but official celebrations could scarcely contain the saturnalian mood. The British Prime Minister Winston Churchill, speaking to the London crowds from the balcony of the Ministry of Health in Whitehall, summoned up resounding, unrepentant patriotism:

We were the first, in this ancient land, to draw the sword against Germany. After a while we were left alone against the most tremendous military power that has been seen. We were all alone for a whole year. There we stood. Did anyone want to give in? Were we downhearted? ['No!' roared the crowd.]
The lights went out, and the bombs came down, but every man, woman and child in this country had no thought of quitting the struggle. London could take it. So we came back after long months, back from the jaws of death, out of the mouth of hell, while all the world wondered.
When shall the reputation and faith of this generation of English men and women fail? I say that in the long years to come not only the people of this island, but from all over the world, wherever the bird of freedom chirps in human hearts, they will look back to what we have done, and they will say, 'Don't despair, don't yield to violence and tyranny. March straight forward, and die, if need be, unconquered.'

Not everyone in Europe could share that surpassing pride; and alongside the formal solemnities, with their brass bands and national anthems, popular feeling welled up in humbler ways, potentially more subversive. When millions were rejoicing, it was their tastes that called the tune – often from Tin Pan Alley. For future social historians, a telling sight on the evening of VE day in London was that of Humphrey Lyttelton, an Old Etonian subaltern in a Guards regiment, playing *High Society* at the head of an impromptu jam session parading in the Mall.

World War II had in fact been a people's war. Unlike previous conflicts, it had also been ideological – a struggle against dictatorship and cruelty as much as against national aggression. As the British writer and critic V.S. Pritchett put it in 1944:

We have felt that our war is a war to defend civilization, even when we are not reading official propaganda; and we have felt this not because we are especially clear about what our civilization is, but because we have thought that this war and the kind of society that produced it, was a conspiracy against man.

Nor was the feeling confined to the British and their allies. Thoughtful Germans and Italians were just as appalled at Nazi and Fascist barbarity. Konrad Adenauer, the gaunt elderly Rhinelander who was to become West Germany's first postwar Chancellor, wrote from bitter experience: 'I had seen where an atheistic dictatorship could bring mankind.' And Giordano Cavestro, an eighteen-year-old student from Parma, shot by the Fascists on 4 May 1944, spoke for all his Resistance comrades when he declared on that last day: 'The great beacon of freedom will arise upon our graves.'

The task of the survivors was to honour that pledge. How they tried, and how far they succeeded, is the subject of this book: how in thirteen years they built postwar Europe – the chequered, tarnished, but still hopeful Europe that we know today.

For many, a first priority was to ensure that evil was rooted out. It involved a purge that was bound to be imperfect – exemplary punishment for some but not all of the guilty, inadequate screening of others, and an effort to ingraft new habits on sometimes tainted stock. 'There'll Always Be an England' ran the refrain of one popular wartime song. Would there always be a Deutschland – and if so, of what kind?

Elsewhere, and especially among the Allies, the overwhelming urge was for 'business as usual' – to return to civilian life, find a home, found a family, resume a normal career. One effect of war, in fact, was a great wave of nostalgia. Like many such emotions, it was thwarted: the wave broke against the hard realities of the postwar world.

One such reality was what came to be called 'interdependence'. Battered, exhausted, and impoverished, the countries of Western Europe soon discovered that they could no longer stand alone. They needed, in fact, to look Westward – not only to the new network of agencies set up by the United Nations, but also, more directly, to partnership with the United States.

This was partly because another postwar hope was to prove illusory: the hope of a united world. The Yalta and Potsdam Conferences of 1945 marked the high tide of East-West co-operation; it soon gave way to suspicion, hostility, and fear. Stalin, in particular, broke his pledge to foster free elections in the countries close to the Soviet Union, and Europe found itself facing 'lost horizons' to the East.

To the West, peace brought 'economic miracles' – prosperity without precedent, created by industries on an international scale. The repercussions were unexpected. They involved a new breed of corporate manager, a new role for the labour unions, and a new relationship with government which itself threw down a challenge to democracy.

Europe's eagerness to enjoy its new wealth may seem in retrospect greedy and superficial – an arrogant conviction that everyone could now live on 'Easy Street'. At the time, it was perfectly natural. For millions long excluded from middle-class plenty, and for a whole generation deprived by war and its aftermath, the aim of 'Prosperity for All' was not to be scorned as 'materialistic': it was a worthy human ideal.

At the same time, 'the affluent society' involved disconcerting change. When the survivors of World War II looked up from the labour of rebuilding their cities, linking them with highways, modernizing farms and factories, creating new wealth and spreading it more widely, they suddenly found that there were 'strangers in their midst'. Some of the strangers were their children – a new sub-culture, listening to new music, speaking a new language, voicing new doubts and protests, acknowledging allegiance to a new international tribe. Others were philosophers and artists, questioning and challenging, the eloquent prophets of disquiet.

And some of the strangers came from outside Europe. In art and music especially, external influence had long been at work. What was new now was the end of Europe's overseas empires – and the reflex and reflux that followed. 'Decolonization' was another of the postwar generation's lasting achievements. With resettlement and immigration, it proved far less easy than many had thought.

Gradually stripped of overseas possessions, peaceful and prosperous, but uneasy and overshadowed in a divided world of mutually hostile super-powers, Europeans came to realize that their future must lie in greater unity

– however hard it might be to achieve. Spurred by a handful of statesmen from half-a-dozen countries, they set out on 'the road to Rome'. It was there, on 25 March 1957, that they signed the Treaty establishing a European Economic Community. Its subject-matter might seem humdrum – the achievement of a 'common market': but to the pioneers who had struggled to create it, this was the founding charter of the United States of Europe for which many had already died.

Not all Europe's 'great expectations' were to be fulfilled. But one underlay all the others: the sense of solidarity that so many had glimpsed during the war. Acknowledged or not, it informed most of men's efforts to build a better world, a better Europe, and a better society – more equal, less rigid, less hierarchical, and freed from the artificial barriers that World War II had swept aside.

War had been a crucible for change. In the services or in Resistance circuits, millions had learned how to fight, destroy, conspire, and kill. Civilians, too, as the saying went, had been 'in the front line'. Many had been ruled by the dictators. Many more had suffered invasion, defeat, and occupation. Many had been deported. Almost everyone had been bombed.

Europe had become a melting-pot. In six years, 27 million people had left their own countries – transported, exiled, or as refugees. I myself, like countless others, had trained and served with several nationalities, including Belgians and Norwegians; I had shared military hospitals with Frenchmen, Russians, and Poles. To me, and to millions, the experience had been what the Russian-born French novelist Romain Gary called *Une éducation européenne*. Early or late in the war, Belgians, Luxembourgers, Frenchmen, Dutchmen, Italians, and Germans had seen their frontiers overrun, their governments set aside, and their independence violated. When peace came, their view of 'national sovereignty' was more realistic than in countries like Britain, whose physical frontiers had remained intact.

Throughout Europe, including Britain, class as well as national barriers had felt the impact of war. Evacuated from the cities, some urban slum children had seen the countryside or the sea for the first time in their lives, and discovered such luxuries as sheets to sleep in or a table to eat at. Their new hosts had been horrified. In September 1939, seeing the first pinched and ragged evacuees from London, Prime Minister Neville Chamberlain had written in a private letter: 'I never knew that such conditions existed, and I feel ashamed of having been so ignorant of my neighbours.'

In the services, others from middle-class homes and schools had been no
less astonished by their first close contact with factory-workers or farmhands
– men with strange accents who called each other 'mate', 'Mensch', or 'mon
p'tit pote', seemed to swear incessantly, slept in vests and underpants, and
had milk-white bodies that belied their weatherbeaten faces. In conscript
barrack-rooms, precarious camaraderie spanned social differences; in battle
or captivity, the old order was swept aside. As in J.M. Barrie's 1902 play *The
Admirable Crichton*, where after a shipwreck the family butler took charge,
leaders in wartime emerged from the ranks. Manual skills – including safe-
cracking – were suddenly vital, and men had to prove themselves if they
aspired to command. At the end of *The Admirable Crichton*, the butler
reverted to domestic service. At the end of World War II, innumerable new
Crichtons demanded social change.

At its simplest, the mood was caught by a British member of the Allied
Military Government in Germany, describing the first trade union meetings
held in the Aachen coalmining area:

After a few words of thanks for their liberation (we were still liberators in
those days) the speakers launched a tirade against their former bosses, many
of whom had been Nazis and had by then disappeared. They were not,
however, after their blood, nor did they even want to see them sent to prison.
They merely wanted to see them take their coats and collars off and do some
real work, by which they apparently meant manual labour. I always knew
when a speech was veering round to an attack on the bosses, as the passage
invariably started with the words: 'Let them take a pick and shovel . . .' and
the rest was usually drowned in applause.

Others were more systematic. 'From Resistance to Revolution' was the
slogan that most sharply summarized their aims. For more than twenty years,
it was to appear under the masthead of *Combat*, the left-wing Paris daily.
Founded in 1941 by the Resistance circuit of the same name, *Combat* had
been edited first by the brilliant but unassuming Pascal Pia, then by the
novelist Albert Camus. On 21 August 1944, while Paris was in the throes of
insurrection and liberation, the paper was published openly for the first time
– a mere two-page sheet bearing the proud legend '4th Year, No. 59'.
Alongside its editorial, the new *Combat* carried an unsigned article, in all
probability written mainly by Camus, which took the slogan as its title:

It required five years of silent and stubborn fighting for a newspaper, born of
the resistance spirit, published without a break throughout the dangers of the
underground movement, to be able to appear at last in broad daylight in a
Paris liberated from its shame.

Those years were not wasted. The people of France, who entered them
with the simple urge to redeem their honour, are emerging from them with

deeper understanding. They now know that they must prize above all things intelligence, courage, and the truth of the human heart. They know too that this imperative, general as it may seem, imposes on them specific moral and political obligations. To speak clearly – in 1940 they had only faith: in 1944 they have a policy, in the noblest sense of the word. What they began as resistance they mean to complete by revolution.

Combat accordingly championed what it called a 'people's and workers' democracy' – a new, more libertarian Constitution, an end to the power of capital and 'the trusts', and a foreign policy loyal to all the Allies alike, including the Soviet Union. 'In the present state of affairs,' it claimed, 'this may be termed a Revolution.'

It sounded like the rhetoric of Communism, whose spokesmen seemed to express most forcefully the social ideals for which many had fought the war. Anyone who had come into contact with such Communist-led Resistance groups as the Garibaldi brigades in Italy or the French *Francs-tireurs et partisans* knew how ruthlessly some of them had pursued party-political ends: but their dedication and bravery were beyond dispute. It was little wonder that in the first postwar elections throughout Western Europe, the national Communist parties won a combined total of nearly 13 million votes, including about a quarter of those in Italy and France.

But for Camus and many others, Communism was too despotic a creed. As a young man in Algeria, he had for two years been a member of the Party, but had been expelled from it in November 1937. Now, despite wartime rapprochements, he distanced himself from it sooner and more decisively than his then friend and associate Jean-Paul Sartre. As early as November 1945, he defended General de Gaulle from Communist attacks, and remarked to Sartre's companion Simone de Beauvoir: 'General de Gaulle at least doesn't look like M. Jacques Duclos' – the old-style Communist leader whom one Socialist deputy described as 'small and fat and ugly as a toad'.

Camus and *Combat* were not alone in their disillusion with the traditional parties. In Italy, the Action Party, *Il Partito d'Azione*, felt similar impatience. In March 1944, some of its partisans issued a typical manifesto, proclaiming themselves 'the resolute advance-guard of a movement of renewal, of a revolutionary process that is at work on the country's whole political and social structure.' Although its name harked back to Giuseppe Mazzini and Italy's nineteenth-century struggle for liberation and unity, the Action Party had begun as an underground movement in 1942. Its early adherents included Count Carlo Sforza, one of his country's most illustrious exiles, and Ugo La Malfa, later to head the Republican Party; but its leader,

Ferruccio Parri, was no traditional politician. A scholar who had turned man of action in revolt against Mussolini, he had been imprisoned and maltreated by the Fascists. Now 52 years old, with his thick spectacles and a shock of hair prematurely white, he still looked very much the academic: but under his wartime alias 'General Maurizio' he was a fearless partisan leader. In late 1944, he was captured by the SS. Released not long afterwards, in 1945 he became Prime Minister of Italy's first postwar coalition government – largely as a compromise between its Left and Right wings.

The Action Party's programme was radical, but not Marxist. It championed regional autonomy and worker participation against 'over-mighty subjects' – the landed aristocracy, big business, the army, and the church. What it sought was a 'liberal revolution'. What it did was to fall between two stools. Before long, it had split into dogmatic collectivists and pragmatic democrats – the former eager to align with Pietro Nenni's Left-wing Socialists and perhaps with the Communists, the latter unable to woo either workers or middle-class idealists. Perhaps naïvely, Parri had hoped to recruit and reconcile two sections of Italian society which had seldom before made common cause: manual workers, and the smaller bourgeoisie. Both were under-privileged; but both were politically volatile. Wooed in the past by the Fascists, many of them now turned to a short-lived populist party, *L'Uomo Qualunque*, 'The Common Man', founded in 1945 by the journalist and playwright Guglielmo Giannini with the curious slogan 'We were better off when we were worse off.' In the 1946 election for a Constituent Assembly, *L'Uomo Qualunque* cleared more than a million votes. It disappeared thereafter, leaving as its only legacy the derogatory adjective 'qualunquist'. And by the time of that same 1946 election, the Action Party had disappeared too. Parri, Sforza, La Malfa and others had become Republicans; most of their left-wing colleagues had joined the Italian Socialists.

But the Action Party's most serious rival was another grouping that consciously set out to break the mould of traditional politics. This was Christian Democracy – a Europe-wide movement whose roots stretched back into the nineteenth century and beyond, but which had only latterly grown into a political force. In Italy, its immediate forebear had been the *Partito Popolare*, or Popular Party, founded in 1919 by Don Luigi Sturzo, a Sicilian priest. Its leader now was an austere, bespectacled 64-year-old Catholic who looked like a strict and incisive music-teacher. His name was Alcide De Gasperi. His party, *Democrazia Cristiana*, was to dominate Italian politics for more than thirty-five years.

Born of humble parents in the mountain region of the Trentino, then part
of Austria, De Gasperi had clashed with Mussolini as early as 1909. As
Sturzo's successor in the 1920's, he was continually harassed and eventually
arrested. On his release from prison after the 1929 pacts between the
Church and the Fascist State, De Gasperi and others took refuge in Vatican
City, now an independent Papal territory in the heart of Rome. By day, he
was employed there to catalogue the library; by night, he translated books
from German to earn extra money for his family. Gradually, he made
stealthy contact with other Catholic anti-Fascists in Milan, Florence, and
elsewhere. By the time that Mussolini's regime collapsed, the Christian
Democrat movement had developed a national underground network. From
1933 onwards, moreover, De Gasperi had been writing political commentaries for the Vatican's bimonthly *Illustrazione Vaticana*, patiently spelling out
a programme for Christian Democracy after the war.

The party in Italy paid particular attention to re-integrating Church and
State: but its main concern everywhere was that Christian values should
permeate society. Like the Action Party, it called for worker participation
and agrarian reform. It was firmly anti-Fascist and critical of the power of big
business; yet, unlike the traditional Left, it rejected class conflict and purely
material aims. Its ideal was an organic, united society – neither ruthlessly
competitive nor starkly collectivist. Central to all its ideals was a Christian
vision of mankind. As the French Confederation of Christian Trade Unions
put it in 1945:

Man is not a tool of production, nor may he be reduced to a mere servant of
society. He is a free and reasonable being, endowed by God with an eternal
destiny, and equipped to that end with a supreme value as a person, with
inalienable rights and high responsibilities.

Potentially, therefore, Christian Democracy was even more radical than its
secular left-wing rivals. Characteristic of its appeal in postwar Europe was
the call of the Christian-inspired *Volksbeweging* or People's Movement in the
Netherlands, urging everyone to join in 'the common task: the necessary
thoroughgoing renovation of our people's life – economically, socially,
politically, spiritually'.

Nowhere was the appeal more heartfelt than in Germany. Meeting in
Berlin in June 1945, the Christian Democratic Union declared:

From the chaos of guilt and shame into which the idolization of a criminal
adventurer threw us, an order of democratic freedom can grow only if we
return to the cultural, moral, and intellectual forces of Christianity, and open
up this source of strength more and more for our people.

In the same spirit, Konrad Adenauer called for 'a great Party with its roots in the Western Christian tradition and the principles of Christian ethics.' He recruited Protestants as well as Catholics into the party leadership, and he deliberately welcomed left-wing and trade-union representatives. By 1949, however, when he became Chancellor, the main threat to democracy seemed no longer to be Nazism, but atheistic Communism. Christian Democracy in Germany, therefore, despite its moral convictions, was in practice more conservative than elsewhere.

In France, by contrast, the Christian-Democratic *Mouvement républicain populaire* or MRP was very clearly a Catholic party of the Left. Its early theorist, the Lyons student Gilbert Dru, was shot by the Nazis in 1944; but a year before he died he had circulated a memorandum to the movement's founders – Resistance colleagues like Pierre-Henri Teitgen, Georges Bidault, and François de Menthon. Communism, he had recognized, would play an important role in postwar French politics.

Nevertheless, if it declares itself to be the *only* revolutionary movement in our country, this would be a regrettable slur on the integrity of the French spirit which is so diverse and so rich with potentiality. Its very presence, which is both real and justified, demands the formation of a powerful movement capable of counterbalancing it and of collaborating with it.

'Revolutionary' or not, the French MRP enjoyed immediate postwar success. In the 1945 and 1946 elections, it won about a quarter of the votes. But, unlike *Democrazia Cristiana* in Italy or the *Christlich-Demokratische Union* in Germany, it soon afterwards lost ground. Within five years, the MRP's electoral support had slumped from nearly 5 million to fewer than 2½ million. The reasons were complex: but three at least were clear. In France, the Church was less powerful than in Italy. The Soviet threat seemed less immediate than in Germany. And, above all, the MRP faced a formidable rival in the person of General Charles de Gaulle.

Solitary, proud, and stubborn, De Gaulle had symbolized and led the wartime 'Free French'. His broadcasts from London had been moving and inspiring: in contrast to Marshal Philippe Pétain's faded eloquence from Vichy, they had also been vigorous and caustic. On 25 August 1944, while Nazi snipers were still at large on the Paris rooftops, De Gaulle had marched in triumph down the Champs-Elysées; on 13 November 1945, the Assembly had unanimously elected him President of the Provisional Government of France. Yet within ten weeks he had resigned – formally in protest at a left-wing attempt to cut the military budget, actually in disgust at party-political squabbling, and in hopes of installing a more presidential regime. If he had expected a plea to return on his own terms, he was disappointed: it was the start of a twelve-year exile from power. But in April 1947, De Gaulle once more entered politics, founding a new and ostentatiously 'non-party' movement, the *Rassemblement du peuple français*.

It was instantly popular. By 1951, about half of the Christian-Democrat MRP's original voters had rallied to De Gaulle; and most of them never returned. Some were disillusioned with MRP-dominated governments. Many were attracted by De Gaulle's personal prestige. Many, too, were shifting to the Right. But the paradox was that the Gaullist *Rassemblement* itself used 'progressive' rhetoric. 'I am not Bonaparte! I am not Boulanger!' De Gaulle thundered, trying to exorcise the shades of both 1804 and 1889, and prove that he planned neither coronation nor *coup d'état*. But if he was by no means to be compared with the vain, resentful, and latterly royalist General Boulanger, De Gaulle certainly shared with Napoleon a degree of reforming zeal. To the end of his life he saw himself as anything but conservative. Both he and his Gaullist followers vilified the old, divisive party system, promised greater social justice, and dreamed of a new, lasting partnership to unite capital, labour, and high technology. In the aftermath of war, even Gaullism espoused the doctrine of change.

Across the Channel, Britain had no Gaullists, no Christian Democrats, no Action Party born of Resistance, and relatively few open Communists. But, even in Britain, World War II had encouraged political dissentients – partly because of the Labour Party's wartime alliance with the Conservatives, a 'Grand Coalition' foreshadowing the 1966 alliance of German Socialists and Christian Democrats. Rather as the *Grosse Koalition* sparked off 'extra-parliamentary opposition', so Britain's wartime coalition compelled protesters to seek other outlets for their complaints. When the war was going badly for the Allies, the British Government found itself attacked at parliamentary by-elections. Between the Spring of 1941 and the end of 1942, 47 seats fell vacant, 19 of them previously held by Labour MPs and 28 by Conservatives. Of the Labour seats, only two were contested; but the Conservatives had to fight 19, and three of these they actually lost.

Not all the contestants were impressive. Noel Pemberton Billing, an advocate of reprisal bombing, toured Hornsey in a yellow Rolls-Royce. Reg Hipwell, founder of the soldiers' pin-up magazine *Reveille*, confessed in Scarborough: 'I only came up here for a holiday – something to make a change.' Both, nonetheless, preached popular doctrines: full employment in peacetime – 'Equal Opportunity, not Old School Tie'. And the three by-elections which the Government lost were all won by former Labour activists, whatever labels they subsequently wore. Denis Kendall, a live-wire engineering manager elected at Grantham in March 1942, urged the State to take over inefficient firms – although his own was later accused of taking excess profits. W. J. Brown, a maverick trade-unionist and popular broadcaster, went much further: he called for 'a non-party approach to postwar reconstruction', the abolition of unemployment, the ending of the slums, and the banishing of economic insecurity. He was elected for Rugby at the end of April, 1942; and on the same day the cheerful, diminutive journalist George Reakes won Wallasey with a majority of 6,000 votes after a campaign centred on a call for more housing and effective price control.

In more senses than one, these individuals could all be regarded as 'sports'. A more organized campaign for change was mounted by an entirely new left-wing party established in July 1942. Its name was Common Wealth, and its leading light was Sir Richard Acland, a tall, thin, bespectacled 36-year-old baronet and landowner educated at Rugby and Balliol. Earnest and idealistic, Acland had been Liberal MP for Barnstaple since 1935; but in the House of Commons his speeches had turned more and more into sincere but slightly incongruous calls for a Christian and bloodless 'socialist revolution'. In 1940, parodying Hitler, he had published *Unser Kampf*, followed by *The Forward March* in 1941. 'Forward March', indeed, was the name he gave to his band of disciples, eager to turn the war into a crusade against economic egotism. At the Wallasey by-election, they had supported George Reakes, who was described as looking like Sancho Panza to Acland's Don Quixote. Two months later, on 25 June 1942, 'Forward March' joined forces with another such group to form Common Wealth.

The new partner in Common Wealth was the '1941 Committee' of left-wing intellectuals headed by the novelist J.B. Priestley, well known for his broadcast 'Postscripts' to the BBC's Nine O'Clock News. Priestley's Yorkshire accent had startled and in many cases pleased those accustomed to the Southern English elocution of Broadcasting House; and his often inspiring messages, full of feeling for ordinary people's hopes and worries, had sometimes disconcerted the authorities. His associates on the '1941 Committee', apart from Acland himself, included Kingsley Martin, editor of the *New Statesman*; Sir Edward Hulton and Tom Hopkinson, respectively publisher and editor of the illustrated weekly *Picture Post*; the economist Thomas Balogh; the journalist J.L. Hodson; and the 'Independent Progressive' MP for Bridgwater, the author and radical journalist Vernon Bartlett.

The political programme of Common Wealth was essentially idealistic and ethical: it could be summed up in the slogan used by one of its candidates – 'Human Fellowship, not Inhuman Competition; Service to the Community, not Self Interest; the Claims of Life, not the Claims of Property.' Characteristically, Acland made over his own estates to the National Trust, and his outdoor recreation was not hunting, shooting, or fishing, but the far less lethal pursuit of sailing. 'The most important thing to understand about Common Wealth is this,' he told the party conference in 1943. 'When we say that we have come to the end of an age and that a new society must emerge from the present world chaos WE MEAN IT.' To publicize its views, Common Wealth needed a magazine. Unable to create one of its own, owing to wartime paper restrictions, it bought an existing publication, *Town and Country Planning*. The title was appropriate to the party's aims and clientele. Its organizing secretary, R.W.G. ('Kim') Mackay, was Australian by birth, a lawyer by training, and a likeably maverick figure on the Left of British politics: after the war, as a Labour MP, he passionately argued for a united Europe. The historian of the movement, Angus Calder, has described the typical Common Wealth member as 'a comfortably off schoolteacher living in one of the pleasanter suburbs of Liverpool, who had never been active in politics before, and quite likely would never be active in them again.' At its height, the party had no more than 15,000 supporters, and only four representatives in the House of Commons: Acland, and three MPs who had defeated Conservatives at by-elections in April 1943, January 1944, and April 1945. But if Common Wealth made no great impact on its own account, it was a significant pointer to wartime and postwar opinion. In the words of another historian, Paul Addison, 'Like a violinist playing in a brass band, it took up in a more sensitive rendering the basic wartime theme of "fair shares for all".'

The crescendo came on 5 July 1945. On that day, with the war in Europe at last behind them, the British went to the polls. And not only in Britain – 1,700,653 postal and proxy votes were cast by men and women in the services. The postal votes caused a delay: the result of the election was not announced until 26 July.

The Conservatives had placed their hopes on Winston Churchill. 'Help Him Finish the Job' proclaimed the posters; and on his triumphal tour of the country at the end of June he had been almost continually cheered.

Mistaken rumour had it that he might remain in office whichever way the election went. On the Left, only Ernest Bevin, the burly Devonian 'dockers' KC' who had been Minister of Labour in the wartime coalition, had anything like Churchill's popular appeal. The Labour Party leader Clement Attlee, however crisp and effective, seemed to many people colourless and prim. Perhaps it was natural, therefore, that the Labour Party's campaign stressed measures rather than men. Characteristic of it was a *Daily Mirror* cartoon by Philip Zec, showing a plump, supercilious shopkeeper in an apron inscribed 'Tory Peace Stores (very limited)'. In the shop are a tired-looking middle-aged man and woman. The man thumps angrily on the counter. 'What do you mean – you're out of stock?' he exclaims: 'I've paid twice for those goods – once in 1914 and again in 1939!' Concealed under the counter like black-market provisions are packages labelled 'The Fruits of Victory – reserved for the rich and privileged: decent schools, good homes, jobs, proper medical attention.' The wordiness, like the depth of feeling, was typical of the time.

Right up to the end, the Conservative press predicted victory for Churchill: but by midday on 26 July 1945, it was clear that Labour had swept the board. Already halfway through the morning, Harold Macmillan was known to have lost at Stockton-on-Tees; and as the hours went by, Conservative strongholds went on falling – Dover, Winchester, Buckingham, St Albans, even Wimbledon. Twenty-nine Conservative ministers in Churchill's 'caretaker' Government were defeated, including L.S. Amery, Brendan Bracken, Sir James Grigg, Leslie Hore-Belisha, and Duncan Sandys. Altogether, the Conservatives and their allies lost 203 seats, and Labour gained 227. With 394 MPs in the House against 212 for the Conservatives, 12 for the Liberals, and 22 others, Labour had an absolute majority of 148. In Churchill's own constituency of Woodford, the Labour and Liberal parties had agreed not to oppose him; but a little-known local farmer, standing as an Independent, took more than a quarter of the votes.

That afternoon, Churchill's doctor Lord Moran complained of the people's 'ingratitude'. 'Oh no,' said Churchill, depressed but still generous. 'I wouldn't call it that. They have had a very hard time.' At 7 p.m., he went to Buckingham Palace in his chauffeur-driven Rolls-Royce, to hand to the King his resignation as Prime Minister. Fifteen minutes later, Attlee and his wife drove there, through cheering crowds, in their modest Standard 10. At last, Labour was in office. A new age seemed to have begun.

Most of the planks in the new Government's platform had been shaped in wartime – some of them by its political rivals. The Conservative R.A. Butler had steered his Education Act past right-wing opposition in 1944; and the author of the immensely influential Beveridge Report on social security, published in 1942, actually stood as a Liberal in 1945. In common with most of his party, Sir William Beveridge was beaten at the election: but it was a Pyrrhic defeat. Something very like the Beveridge recommendations was a central feature of Labour's own manifesto, *Let Us Face the Future*. This also pledged the Labour Government to nationalize the Bank of England, fuel and power, iron and steel, and inland waterways; it promised to implement Butler's Education Act, and to establish a National Health Service; and it called for physical controls to allocate raw materials, keep down food prices, provide homes, and direct the location of industry.

All over Western Europe, similar reforms were being proposed. What they implied was not just greater equality, fairer shares, and better social conditions – full employment, higher pay, fairer taxes, more rights for trade unions, anti-trust laws, and land reform. To achieve these ends would mean a vast expansion in the role of governments. In earlier centuries, and in some cases up to 1939, the authorities' main tasks had been to defend the realm and keep the peace – 'holding the ring', as it were, for the free play of private initiative and market forces, leaving employers, workers, and consumers to fight it out as best they could. War had changed all that. In various ways, most European countries had undergone what the Germans called '*Kriegs-sozialismus*', or 'wartime socialism'. Now, rising expectations were to make greater demands; and even the least socialist of postwar governments were to embark on what might be called *Nachkriegskeynesianismus*, applying the interventionist policies urged by John Maynard Keynes. The 'Welfare State' tasted and promised in wartime would involve precisely what the French called it: '*l'état-providence*', providing benefits and assuming responsibilities in many fields hitherto private, and thereby enormously increasing governmental power.

In most of the countries of Western Europe, total government expenditure soon ranged between 20 and 30 percent of national wealth. Of total national investments, governments directly controlled some 40–60 percent, compared with only 20 percent in the United States. And while the United States Government spent less than 10 percent of the national wealth on social security, many West European countries now began to spend between 11 and 16 percent.

In some of them, social security was the most notable postwar innovation. It ranged from the full contributory state system of welfare benefits established in Britain to the much more limited services offered in Spain, Portugal, and Greece; but in France, Germany, Italy, Austria, the Netherlands, Belgium, Luxembourg, and most of Scandinavia, a combination of state and private insurance now provided security on a far more generous and comprehensive scale than before the war.

In several countries, moreover, postwar governments began to play a direct role in the economy. Throughout most of Western Europe, rail, air, and urban transport and telecommunications were now publicly owned. France and Britain nationalized their coal industries. Britain nationalized steel and long-distance road haulage: France extended government ownership or control to the oil industry, the Renault motor works, and several leading banks. In Italy, the *Istituto di Ricostruzione Industriale* (IRI) tightened the state's already firm grip.

IRI's avowed aim was to 'plan' the economy; and in France and Britain in particular, 'planning' was now a key word. Like most words, it was ambiguous. To some, it meant statutory controls of the type that had been used in wartime – rationing, the direction of labour, import and currency restrictions, the allocation of investments and raw materials to specific areas and industries. In Britain, these powers were used quite widely in the first years after the war. In France, by contrast, 'planning' took on a different connotation: it came to mean 'indicative planning' as practised by the small, dynamic team of technocrats headed by the extraordinary Jean Monnet.

Monnet looked like a well-to-do French peasant – upright and stocky, with a small brisk moustache and hooded but twinkling eyes. In fact, he was a native of Cognac in the Charente, where his family had a brandy firm: as a very young man, he had been his father's salesman in Britain, Canada, and the United States. In World War I, at the age of 26, he had had the nerve to tell the French Prime Minister that France and Britain were failing to co-ordinate their overseas supplies. He was promptly given the job of ensuring that they did. After World War I, he had helped to set up the League of Nations, and had become its deputy Secretary-General; later, he had returned to the family business and to a career in banking that had led him as far afield as San Francisco and Shanghai. With World War II looming, he had helped to secure, for France, American aircraft that were subsequently used to defend Britain; and in 1939 he had taken on his old task of co-ordinating Franco-British supplies. In 1940, he had even proposed Franco-

British union in order to keep France in the war. Then, when France had fallen, Monnet became a British civil servant. He worked with the British Supply Council in the United States, and played an important part in launching President Roosevelt's 'Victory Program' of aircraft production. In 1943, Roosevelt sent him to Algiers to help heal the breach between the American-backed General Henri Giraud and the London-based General de Gaulle. In Algiers, Monnet became a member of De Gaulle's Provisional Government, and was later assigned as a special Commissioner to deal among other things with American economic aid. De Gaulle's talk of French greatness irked him: France would only be great, he pointed out, if her industry were modernized. De Gaulle agreed. And so, in 1946, in an old four-storey rabbit-warren of a house on the Left Bank in Paris, at No. 18 rue de Martignac, Monnet established the grandly-named Commissariat-General of the French Modernization and Investment Plan.

Deliberately, Monnet kept his planning staff small. There were few more than a hundred all told, including secretaries and doormen; and Monnet's own central team was only four or five. Its strength lay in the people it brought together: government officials, employers, and workers' representatives from all the major industries of France. At the time, such 'participation' was unheard-of: never before had civil servants, managers, and trade unionists sat down together at the same table to discuss investment and production plans. But, as Monnet tirelessly insisted, the essence of the French Plan was to involve everyone in a collective effort. The aim was very practical: to agree on realistic production targets in the priority sectors, and lay the basis for ordered recovery and future growth. It was not 'planning' in the sense of state control: but it was none the less effective. The Commissariat-General, attached to the Prime Minister's office and not to any particular minister or government, weathered countless political crises, and survives to this day. Its methods have been copied in many countries, including Britain. It certainly put down the foundations for the postwar prosperity of France.

Armed with high ideals, their resolve strengthened by war, Europe's postwar planners had a noble vision of the world they wanted to build. Yet, when they looked about them, the immediate prospects were bleak. 'My heart ached,' wrote Monnet, 'to see how impoverished and exhausted people were, once the excitements of the Liberation had passed.'

Paris itself bore few physical scars: walls chipped by bullets or home-made petrol bombs during the Liberation, a shattered pillar – oddly, the 'fifth column' – on the façade of the Hotel Crillon. Rome, Brussels, and Prague were likewise more or less unscathed. But many of Europe's finest cities were dusty moonscapes of destruction, with gaping craters where buildings had once stood, and mountains of rubble blocking the pitted streets. Whole areas of Vienna, London, Coventry, St-Nazaire, Toulon, Trieste, and Lübeck had been laid waste. Rotterdam, Le Havre, Cologne, Warsaw, and Budapest lay in ruins. Dresden, Stuttgart, and other German towns had been cremated by fire storms. Some, like Hanover, Nuremberg, and Düsseldorf, had been virtually obliterated. Berlin, as one visitor remarked, 'was like a city of the dead.'

Death had claimed 15 million Europeans – more than half of them on the battlefields, but many in air-raids, and at least six million in extermination camps. Many of those who survived were ill, emaciated, disabled: there were two million cripples in West Germany alone. In the Netherlands, in the last year of the war, some adults were existing on 900 calories a day – little more than half of what was needed for a six-year-old child. One young British officer described a trip through Germany:

Crowds of people throng round all the troop trains at each station. Wherever there is any sort of habitation, the railway track is lined by children. The sight of them, perfectly spaced out along our route, many crippled, many barefoot, and all of them mechanically waving at our train, with their cries of 'Schokolade', remains the most vivid memory of the journey. Outside Karlsruhe, this amazing formation persisted for miles into the country. Nobody with any humane feelings can possibly resist the natural impulse to throw out all the food one can. To see the children fighting for the food was like watching animals being fed at the zoo.

The troop trains themselves were makeshift. I remember one 48-hour journey through France in the depths of winter with no heating – and no windows. Civilian travel was worse. For thousands of kilometres, railway lines were out of action – 4,000 kilometres in France, 12,000 in north-west Germany, two-thirds of the whole network in Yugoslavia and Greece. Viaducts were down, bridges impassable, rolling stock derailed and often destroyed. Half of Germany's locomotives were out of commission; three-fifths of those in Belgium and Poland; three-quarters in the Netherlands; five-sixths in France. Fewer than a quarter of French goods wagons were still serviceable – in part a tribute to the skill of the railway Resistance.

The waterways of Europe were almost paralysed, with locks damaged, canals and rivers blocked by sunken barges, bridges down, and much of the cargo fleet destroyed. Of the major ports, only Antwerp and Bordeaux were still working. Hamburg and Toulon were obstructed by foundered and scuttled ships.

The roads had suffered less; but many were blocked. Seventy-seven percent of West Germany's main river bridges were closed. All the Rhine bridges were down; so were most of those across the Seine and the Loire. In Sicily, there were no permanent bridges left on the main road between Catania and Palermo, and a journey of ten miles on the map might mean a drive of more than twenty across country. Much of the countryside itself was charred and churned by battle; and many roads were a mosaic of potholes. Vehicles were scarce and unreliable. Ninety percent of French trucks were unusable, partly for want of spares. Supplies of oil, tyres, and gasoline were desperately short.

Straggling along Europe's roads with knapsacks, prams, and cardboard suitcases, or herded into camps for 'displaced persons', were innumerable refugees. Weary, hungry, bewildered, resentful, they came from more than fifty ethnic groups and spoke a medley of languages, including the universal '*Lagerdeutsch*' and polyglot slang – '*Alles kaputt*', '*finito*', '*nix OK*'. World War II had uprooted sixty million European civilians. Twenty-seven million had left their own countries, voluntarily or otherwise; four-and-a-half million had been deported for slave labour by the Nazis; many thousands had been sent to Siberia by Stalin's regime in the USSR. Many had had to move more than once. Now, at the end of the war, two-and-a-half million Poles and Czechs were transferred to Soviet Russia, and more than twelve million Germans fled or were expelled to the West. At one time, in 1945, they were pouring into north-west Germany at the rate of 40,000 a week. And as well as displaced persons, the Allies had to cope with seven million prisoners of war.

The human maelstrom seemed universal. So, too, did the moral confusion. In the occupied countries, everyone had faced cruel choices. Was it honourable to go about one's business, earn money for one's family, teach, or write, or paint, or publish – or even play *boules* – when such 'normal' activities seemed to condone foreign tyranny? The Resistance itself had wrought havoc with values and loyalties, turning citizens into outlaws and making it hard to know whom to trust. Criminals as well as heroes had fought the oppressor: lawbreaking, sabotage, and killing had become legitimate. And while Fascist and Nazi atrocities had plumbed the depths of evil, the hardest to forgive were those committed by compatriots who had changed sides. Small wonder that the Liberation involved orgies of vengeance; but, rumour to the contrary, these were limited in scope. More pervasive was the general atmosphere of lawlessness and alienation, most tellingly caught in such films as Vittorio De Sica's *Sciuscia*, about street children in newly liberated Rome, and Roberto Rossellini's *Germania Anno Zero*, or in Curzio Malaparte's anguished novel of postwar Naples, *La Pelle*. As Malaparte put it, 'All of us in Europe...are more or less Neapolitan.' What he meant was put less tendentiously by the Belgian statesman Paul-Henri Spaak:

We were people all of whose countries had been occupied or had been (in the case of the Germans, and Italy) under a fascist government. It had been the patriotic duty of everybody during the War in those countries to oppose the government, to oppose authority, to lie, to cheat, to do everything which it was your patriotic duty not to do. Suddenly to reverse it, suddenly, when the enemy was defeated, to get out of the way of lying and cheating, withholding taxes, engaging in black-market activities and all that – it was a tremendous moral crisis in our countries.

The crisis was worsened by hunger, hardship, and envy. For those who could afford it, the black market in goods sold off the ration became a virtual necessity: but the prices – and the social cost – were high. In Rome in 1945, children and old women snatched food from the tables of open-air black-market restaurants. Elsewhere in Italy at that time, bread was being sold by the slice. The Allied armies added to the injustice. They had been welcomed as liberators; but now, in the midst of penury, some of them lived like kings. In Austria in 1946, a single cigarette could be sold for as much as a schilling; and every British soldier in the occupation army received fifty free cigarettes a week. In Italy shortly afterwards, Allied servicemen could buy a hundred cigarettes from the NAAFI stores for 200 lire, and sell them on the black market for five times as much. The same black-market traders charged seventy lire for a packet of soap which before the war might have cost one or two. For a time, in Italy and Germany especially, cigarettes, soap, and chocolate virtually replaced the official currency. Barter was the last resort in an economy that had collapsed.

How great the collapse had been was soon apparent to the planners. In Paris, Jean Monnet and his team found that in real terms France's national income in 1945 was less than half of what it had been in 1929. In Italy, production had fallen to less than a quarter of the peacetime figure; in Belgium, the Netherlands, Greece, Yugoslavia, and Poland, it was one-fifth, and in southern Germany only about one-twentieth. European coal production – a vital key to recovery – was down to two-fifths of its prewar level.

With so little being produced, prices naturally rocketed – nowhere more so than in Greece and Hungary, where the currencies were totally submerged. In November 1944, the Greek Government had to devalue the drachma at the rate of 50,000 million to one; and when the Hungarian Government introduced a new currency, the old pengo had sunk to 11×10^{27} against the US dollar.

In Britain, the effects of war were less obvious: but their economic impact was no less profound. During the war, government expenditure had risen to five times its prewar level, while exports had fallen by three-fifths. To fill part of the gap, Britain had sold off £1,118 million worth of overseas assets; but this still left foreign debts of more than £3,000 million. The world's greatest creditor had become the world's biggest debtor. At home, much of industry had suffered as it had on the continent. For six years, raw materials, energy, and manpower had been diverted to produce weapons of destruction: a large number of firms had had to be run down. What was more, although Britain had escaped invasion, many industrial towns had been subjected to heavy bombing, latterly by 'pilotless planes' and V2 rockets. By the end of the war, the Government estimated, air raids had destroyed or damaged some four million homes.

If 'planning', then, was the general aspiration, the urgent priority was 'rebuilding'. This too was a word with special resonance. In 1928, in his first published book of poems, W.H. Auden had called for 'new styles of architecture, a change of heart'; and for most of the Thirties and Forties these two notions had tended to be linked. Popular books on town planning and modern design had excoriated 'clutter', 'disorder', 'suburbia', 'speculative builders', 'the wedding-cake tradition', 'ostentation', 'pretence', 'imitation', 'Victorian acquisitiveness and display'. They had praised 'clean lines', 'fitness for function', 'order', 'simplicity', 'honesty', 'twentieth-century buildings for twentieth-century man'. Their vision of the future was both architectural and social – dazzling white palaces for the people, set in parkland: a glass, steel, and concrete utopia for a society reborn.

Perhaps its clearest expression was in a play by J.B. Priestley, *They Came to a City*, produced on the London stage in 1943 and filmed by Basil Dearden in the following year. I remember my parents dismissing it as 'Socialistic propaganda': but the anonymous theatre critic of John Lehmann's left-wing *Penguin New Writing* held that

The interest in this charming play lies in the lucidity of its argument: Socialism is not a Utopia but a real possibility. The characters react to the wonderful city, where equality reigns and no man can exploit another, in different ways. Some turn their backs on it in disgust and outrage, some remain to live and work there. The two main characters leave it only in order to tell its story and struggle back to it from the dark world outside. The weakness of the play lies in its form. It is a realistic, down-to-earth argument, but it is played in a setting of fantasy. Because of this, some people in the audience, fed for years on the mystical hereafter and might-have-been play formulas, incline to misunderstand this excellent and thoughtful contribution to the drama from sheer force of habit. They confuse the city where Socialism works with Heaven, and believe all the characters to be dead.

Although today this reads sardonically, no irony was intended at the time. The characteristic tone was serious, idealistic, and rather paternalist, preaching what Henry Wallace, Progressive Party candidate for the US presidency in 1948, called 'the Century of the Common Man'. If the phrase caused shudders then among an older generation, its high-minded condescension may evoke different shudders now. Many spokesmen for the common man were far from ordinary themselves – including Wallace, who had been a well-to-do editor and a distinguished plant geneticist before becoming Roosevelt's Secretary of Agriculture and Vice-President of the United States. As well as a left-wing proselytizer, he was a religious and health fanatic who liked to hold forth on the virtues of garlic eaten raw.

In Britain, the new Labour Prime Minister, Clement Attlee, was a sincere and practical idealist whose Socialist convictions had been strengthened by fourteen years of social work in the East End of London. But he was the product of a middle-class, Christian, and Conservative home. A barrister, educated at Haileybury and Oxford, he had served as a major in World War I. Throughout his life, he was a stickler for good manners: he rebuked his ebullient Welsh colleague Aneurin Bevan for wearing a lounge suit to a royal banquet, and was said to be uneasy if the port was passed anti-clockwise. Equally remarkable was Attlee's first Chancellor of the Exchequer, Hugh Dalton, an Old Etonian whose country walking parties with fellow Labour stalwarts were a further reminder that British Socialism had roots in Charles Kingsley's 'muscular Christianity'.

On the continent, too, some of the prophets of change were equally the children of privileged tradition. Jean Monnet himself may have looked like a peasant, but his style and assumptions were partly those of the 1910's – brandy of course, but also cigars, first-class carriages, and chauffeur-driven cars. Outside politics, the most notable instance of all was the film director Luchino Visconti, Marxist scion of a noble Italian family whose very name was part of the history of Milan. His 1948 film about poor Sicilian fishermen, *La Terra Trema*, based on part of Giovanni Verga's classic novel *I Malavoglia*, was long mistakenly regarded as belonging to the documentary 'neo-realist' school of De Sica and Rossellini. In fact, its most striking feature is its loving, picturesque photography – human suffering turned into Old Master art.

To point out such paradoxes is not to impugn the motives of patricians who championed reform. Their upbringing made leadership natural; and the better life they sought for everyone would not be brought about spontaneously or haphazardly. It had to be worked for; and there was an immense amount to be done. To feed the hungry, clothe and shelter them, repatriate refugees, repair roads and railways, rebuild houses and factories, locate and if necessary commandeer supplies – all these emergency tasks demanded administration; and the administrative model that lay to hand was the military machine. Service experience haunted postwar Europe. Welfare officials from the United Nations Relief and Rehabilitation Administration (UNRRA) even looked like soldiers in their jeeps and uniforms; and such early organizations as the International Ruhr Authority, set up by the Allies to deal with German heavy industry, shared with the military the assumption of decision-making from above.

Paternalism was perhaps most evident in the rebuilding of Europe's cities. Modern techniques and materials, making possible glass walls and huge spans of ferro-concrete, had already given designers an exciting and dangerous new freedom. A whole generation of architects and town-planners had been reared on the international styles pioneered by giants like Walter Gropius and Le Corbusier, suited to what one chronicler typically called 'a century of masses and science'. Before the war, that generation had made its mark in isolated ventures. Now was its chance to work a general transformation. Some of the results were strikingly beautiful: but many were also cold, impersonal, and collectivist – deeply out of tune with the tastes of many ordinary people, who detested Le Corbusier's '*béton brut*', or unadorned grey ferro-concrete, preferred houses to flats, wanted private back-gardens, and – in Britain – actually liked suburban mock-Tudor (later, mock-Georgian) semi-detached villas. Perhaps there was poetic justice in the fact that some of Le Corbusier's most ambitious housing developments proved too expensive for their intended working-class tenants. More to the point was the way in which the less gifted postwar planners, architects, and accountants were to impose on some of Europe's cities a bleak inhumanity all the more saddening in that it enshrined altruistic ideals.

In one respect, however, altruism evoked an overwhelming response. The 'better life' that Europeans were seeking was not simply a life of greater abundance, or less penury – food, housing, clothes, transport, and so on: there was also a great hunger of the mind. 'Where are the war poets?' was the quizzical title of a wartime poem by Cecil Day-Lewis, parodying the politicians' appeal for propagandist versifiers: but the answer to his question might well have been 'in France'. There, the intensity of wartime experience and wartime privations – including imprisonment and torture – distilled poetry from people who had no thought of being 'writers'. Everywhere, in fact, war had revealed similar needs. In Britain, the blackout had boosted the sales of long novels like *War and Peace*. Long stretches of waiting, in the services and elsewhere, had encouraged the habit of reading, and persuaded some non-professionals to write. Serious music was another consolation. Middle-aged Londoners have fond memories of the lunch-time piano recitals in the National Gallery begun by Dame Myra Hess in October 1939. I myself recall a suburban cinema packed out to hear the London Symphony Orchestra on an unprecedented tour. And when the war ended, it became clear that in Italy and Germany too there was a new and eager public for the arts. There, but especially in Germany, books had been among the casualties of dictatorship: 'decadent' foreign literature had been banned. Now, huge quantities of once forbidden fruit were waiting to be tasted. In Germany, because of paper rationing, translations of some American novels were first published in the form of newspapers. Readers still seized them eagerly, and passed them on to their friends. Some families travelled long distances, in appalling conditions, to see for the first time a play by Jean-Paul Sartre. In the devastated cities, some audiences paid in coal, not cash, to hear orchestras and theatre companies playing to capacity in all kinds of makeshift auditoriums. One *avant-garde* production, staged in the hall of a lunatic asylum, was actually interrupted by an inmate. The audience thought that he was part of the show.

So great was the demand that public authorities at all levels felt obliged to help meet it. In France, the State gave subsidies to provincial theatres; in Germany, the cities continued the old tradition of princely patronage for the arts. In Britain, government aid had been the exception, although official 'war artists' had been appointed in World War I, and similar arrangements were made in World War II. In the winter of 1939–40, however, a major change occurred. Prompted by Lord De La Warr, President of the Board of

Education, and the Minister of Information, Lord Macmillan, the Government approved a bold, if roundabout, plan. It persuaded the Pilgrim Trust, established in 1930 by the American millionaire Edward Harkness, to put up £25,000 to help form CEMA, the Council for the Encouragement of Music and the Arts, and matched this private donation with an equal grant from public funds. It was partly through CEMA's encouragement that Tennent Plays Ltd staged J.B. Priestley's *They Came to a City*. By 1945, when CEMA became the Arts Council of Great Britain, the Government's annual contribution to the arts had increased to £235,000.

A still more significant innovation took place in 1946. On 29 September, the BBC started up its nightly 'Third Programme', uncompromisingly devoted to the 'highbrow' arts – an idea soon copied in various forms throughout much of Western Europe. The Third Programme's first Controller, George Barnes, was related to the 'Bloomsbury' set: his mother was a Strachey, and E.M. Forster a personal friend; and the network bore traces of the 'Bloomsbury' ethos. When it began, it carried no news bulletins, and deliberately set out to treat the arts as autonomous. In this respect, it was an aural counterpart of *Horizon*, the magazine founded by Cyril Connolly in January 1940 with the proclamation 'Our standards are aesthetic, and our politics are in abeyance.' In practice, although both were predictably criticized as 'escapist', neither *Horizon* nor the Third Programme could totally ignore current affairs. Nevertheless, the whole tone of the network reflected one facet of the immediate postwar mood – an understandable longing to turn from reality towards the imagination or the past.

Already, one month after the war had ended in Europe, and while it still continued in the Far East, Sadler's Wells Theatre had re-opened in London. Without CEMA, it would probably never have survived. Now, on 7 June 1945, it presented the world première of a new work by a brilliant 32-year-old. A work of Socialist realism? The harbinger of a brave new world? Hardly. The central figure was certainly a man of the people – an East Coast fisherman; but the tale was from 135 years earlier, and the production was grand opera. It was Benjamin Britten's *Peter Grimes*. Musically, it marked an epoch. But it was also a reminder that, for many people, ending the war meant 'getting back to normal' in a world purged of guilt.

2

There'll Always be a Deutschland

'Everywhere there was a strange silence, as though people were stunned.'

So wrote one woman UNRRA worker, crossing from France into Germany in 1945. To many, like the English poet Stephen Spender, the wasteland cities recalled Carthage or Pompeii – 'scenes of a collapse so complete that it already has the remoteness of all final disasters.'

Nuremberg was no exception. Once, it had been a picture-postcard embodiment of Bavarian grandeur and *Gemütlichkeit*: an imperial city walled and moated, with towers and gateways, a huddle of steep roofs, and a medieval castle perched upon a rock. Its greatest son was Albrecht Dürer, whose masterly woodcuts and engravings had married Renaissance influence with Gothic themes. Dürer's father had been a goldsmith; and four centuries later the city was still famous for its *objets d'art* in metal and ivory, its carved wooden toys and clocks. As the biggest hop market in Europe, only a hundred miles north-west of Munich, it was also involved with that other Bavarian speciality, beer. To many visitors in days gone by, Nuremberg had stood for the old, traditional Germany of Grimm's fairy tales, *'Tannenbaum'*, *'Ach du lieber Augustin'*, steins full of foaming *Münchner*, plump men in *Lederhosen*, and local brass bands.

Now, the old town lay in ruins – 'decayed and jagged,' wrote Harold Nicolson, 'like some old jawbone of a camel in the desert.' Dürer's reddish house still stood, held up by its central beam; but its roof, like hundreds of others, was open to the sky. A mere half-hour's bombing on Sunday 7 January 1945 had gutted the city and killed more than five thousand people. Many were still buried beneath their houses; the graves of others were simple mounds of stone and splintered wood. There was no drinkable water. The air stank of death and disinfectant.

Only the bleak new suburbs and a few isolated buildings remained intact. Along streets still strewn with rubble, a few tramcars threaded their way, linked together in threes and crowded to suffocation with pale, cowed, angry people, mostly middle-aged, who turned away when they passed American or British soldiers. At hourly intervals, the bell tolled from the tower of the bombed cathedral.

To the south of the city, one of the few monuments still standing was the *Heldenfeld* or stadium, renamed by the Americans, in big blue lettering, 'Soldiers' Field'. Its stone plinth now showed scars of brick, where a huge eagle and swastika had been torn down. It was here that Adolf Hitler had staged his vast, precision-drilled Nazi rallies. Each September, amid forests of flags and banners and smoking torches, under a lattice of searchlights, thousands of men in uniform had marched and wheeled and stood stock-still, row upon row of them, to salute their Führer. The fearsome mechanical ballet had been frozen on film, the year after Hitler's accession, in Leni Riefenstahl's *Triumph of the Will*. Its images still convey some of the hypnosis that Hitler exerted – and to which he succumbed. But now Hitler was dead, and his impresario Josef Goebbels, and the dreaded Heinrich Himmler. After little more than a decade, the 'Thousand-year Reich' had crumbled, leaving desolation behind. From the Führer's rostrum, GIs were taking snapshots of each other giving mock Nazi salutes.

Also intact in Nuremberg was the Grand or Palast Hotel Fürstenhof, with its Hitlerian guest-house next door. For a time, it was the only building in the city that still had electric light. Once the resort of visitors to the Nazi rallies, the hotel had been requisitioned. In front, instead of black Daimlers and Mercedes limousines, there now stood camouflaged jeeps, PUs, and 15-cwt. trucks. Inside, in the Marble Room, men and women in Allied uniforms danced to the rather wooden music of the hotel orchestra – a brittle contrast with the darkness, cold, hunger, and bereavement elsewhere.

But the real focal point of Nuremberg was another undestroyed monument some distance away in the Fürtherstrasse: a tall grey sandstone building with massive squat round pillars and endless wide stone corridors – the Palace of Justice. Behind it was a long, twisting, covered wooden passage with an echoing duckboard floor. Two-thirds of the way down, a gate led into an exercise yard; but at the far end of the passage was a heavy door, with a bell to summon the armed guard who opened it. This led into the prison, a star-shaped building with four cell-blocks, each of three storeys, linked by a spiral staircase. On either side there were numbered cells, thirteen foot by nine, each with a steel bed fastened to the floor, a flimsy table, and a chair that was removed at night. In the corner by the door, just out of sight of the guards' peephole, was a water-closet with fixed wooden slats for a seat. Each cell had a washbasin with running water. In the fifth wing of the prison there was a hospital on the ground floor with a chapel above. On the wall of the prison gymnasium was a scrawled sign: 'VD walks the streets'.

Smelling of lavatories and stale food, resounding to guards' shouts and whistles, the rattle of keys, and the scrape and clang of containers dragged on metal floors, it was like prisons the world over. At present, it housed twenty-two men who were soon to be on trial for their lives. They were no ordinary criminals. For the past five years, they had lorded it over Europe as rich and powerful representatives of Adolf Hitler's murderous regime.

Not surprisingly, security was stringent. Outside, the courthouse was guarded daily by five Sherman tanks with 76-millimetre guns. To forestall any possible rescue attempt, there were squads of United States infantry; nearby, at Fürth, there were fighter planes and anti-aircraft guns. In the courtyard and the corridors, soldiers with machine-guns were stationed behind sandbag barricades; in the prison block, there was an air-raid siren and the sentries were armed with automatic pistols. All visitors had to check in: once, the President of the Court himself forgot to show his pass and was halted by an abrupt 'Hey, you!' To begin with, there was one guard for every four cells; but then a mishap occurred.

Among the prisoners was Robert Ley, a former Storm-trooper General and head of the Nazi Labour Front or 'Strength Through Joy' movement. Now, instead of *Sturmabteilung* uniform, he wore an American field jacket, ill-fitting khaki trousers, and felt boots. For years he had been an alcoholic: it had left him bleary, red-eyed, and ranting. 'Stand us against the wall and shoot us! You are the victors!' he shouted. He was never tried. On the evening of 24 October 1945, he hooked the zipper of his GI jacket to the lever of the lavatory cistern in his cell, and attached it to the hem of a wet towel tied in a noose. He tore up his underpants, and stuffed them in his mouth to stifle any noise. Then he hanged himself.

After that, a permanent guard was stationed outside every cell door, with a lamp to shine through the peep-hole.

One month later, on 20 November, the trial began. It was held in a sombre, old-fashioned courtroom, its walls panelled in dark wood, with heavy green marble round the doors. Above the main entrance was a large sculpture depicting original sin. But the Wilhelm II decor had been modernized. The windows were tightly curtained, and covered outside with wire netting. The room now had overhead slit-lights, and was fitted with functional court furniture which made it seem crowded and small.

At one end were galleries for reporters and, above them, the public, with embrasures for cine-cameramen and photographers. Facing them was a wide blank wall for maps and diagrams and, on occasion, a cinema screen; below it, slightly to the right, was a movable witness-stand. On the far left of that wall was a glass booth housing two rows of interpreters. The court was equipped with an IBM simultaneous-translation system: there was a microphone for each speaker, with warning lights to slow him down if need be, a pair of headphones for everyone present, and a dial by each seat, with which to select the original language on position 1, English on 2, Russian on 3, French on 4, and German on 5 – a sequence not without point. Familiar as it all grew later, to visitors at the time it seemed strange. The English novelist Evelyn Waugh was struck by the 'faint continuous chatter' coming from the glass booth. 'One had the curious illusion', he wrote, 'of seeing two men bullyragging and seeming to hear their own voices in the piping American accents of the girl interpreter.'

In the well of the court sat the lawyers and stenographers; to the right, on a raised platform under the Allied flag, the Judges were ranged along the bench. Their President, sitting in front of the central door, was Lord Justice Lawrence. In private life he was a countryman, a connoisseur of old china and proud of his Wiltshire dairy herd. In Nuremberg, he arrived each morning in a shiny black limousine, wearing a long dark overcoat and bowler hat, a wing collar, and a black coat and striped trousers. On the bench, in a black gown, with his reading glasses perched on his nose, and his lips calm and precise, he looked like a figure out of Dickens or Galsworthy, courteous, shrewd, and formal, bowing slightly to counsel as he took his seat. All that was missing was a judicial wig: except for their headphones, the judges were bare-headed.

To the left of Lord Justice Lawrence sat his Alternate, Sir Norman Birkett, six foot three inches tall, lean-faced and bespectacled, with slightly ruffled reddish hair. A brilliant advocate with a mordant wit, Birkett frankly admitted that he would have liked Lawrence's job. So would the President's neighbour on his other side, the 59-year-old American Judge Francis Biddle, until recently US Attorney-General – bronzed, neat, dynamic, and incisive, with piercing eyes, dark eyebrows, and a trim emphatic moustache. His Alternate, John J. Parker, looked and behaved like a large, bluff, wise, and fatherly judge from some reassuring Hollywood film. To Parker's right, and almost always silent though very attentive, were the two French members of the Tribunal, in gowns with white jabots and ruffles. Henri Donnedieu de Vabres looked very much the Sorbonne professor with his heavy spectacles and drooping moustache; his Alternate, Robert Falco, small, dark, and birdlike, was well-named.

The Soviet judges, perhaps appropriately, sat on the far left of the bench as seen from the court: Major-General of Jurisprudence I.T. Nikitchenko and Colonel Alexander Fedorovich Volchkov. Both, as their rank implied, wore dress uniform instead of black gowns. Nikitchenko was small and round-faced, with cold nervous eyes behind his pince-nez, and his hair brushed straight back. On closer acquaintance he was less forbidding: he had a keen sense of humour, was fond of a drink, and enjoyed playing tennis with the daughters of Lord Justice Lawrence. Colonel Volchkov was less genial. A 'People's Commissar for Justice', he was said to be a professor of international law; but his long grey face and hard mouth seemed to fit him better for the role of an NKVD officer. Persistent rumour at Nuremberg alleged that he was at least close to the Soviet secret police.

'Quiet, please! Take your seats!' The Marshal of the Court's command was the signal for the British justices' clerks to enter. A further call of 'Attention!' brought everyone to his feet. The Judges filed in.

'This trial', declared Lord Justice Lawrence, 'is unique in the history of the jurisprudence of the world, and of supreme importance to millions of people all over the globe.' It had to judge on four counts: the Nazis' 'common plan or conspiracy', 'crimes against peace', 'war crimes', and 'crimes against humanity'. The first two concerned the preparation and pursuit of what was then called 'aggressive war', engulfing most of Europe and involving most of the world. The third count covered such violations of the Geneva Convention as the use of slave labour or the torture and murder of prisoners and hostages. But it was the fourth accusation, 'crimes against humanity', that contained the explosive force of the world's horror and anger. Only five months earlier, the British and the Americans had liberated Belsen and Buchenwald, concentration camps that had turned into 'bone-mills', where those still alive – skeletal, diseased scarecrows in striped prison clothing – looked scarcely different from the dead in ragged heaps in the compound, or bulldozed into stinking collective graves. Even worse, if comparisons were possible, had been the true extermination camps like Auschwitz, Bełżec, Chełmno, Sobibór, or Treblinka, where 'the final solution' to 'the Jewish problem' had made genocide an industry and dispatched at least six million men, women, and children.

Who had been responsible? At one level, several thousand underlings, many of whom escaped trial. At the top, Adolf Hitler, who had shot himself through the mouth on the afternoon of 30 April 1945. Next day, Goebbels had followed him. Heinrich Himmler, former head of the SS had lived a little longer: shaving off his moustache, he had put on a black eye-patch and dressed as an army private. Caught at a British control point, he had been stripped and searched; but on 23 May he had bitten a cyanide capsule concealed in his gum. Twelve minutes later, he too was dead.

Now, twenty-one survivors from Hitler's entourage faced their judges at Nuremberg. Without the trappings of office, they looked almost insignificant – pale, drab, waxen figures crowded into the long wooden dock. They sat in two rows on the left of the court, opposite the bench, with seven white-helmeted US guards standing behind them under the modernistic clock, and three more at the side and in front. As the trial proceeded, journalists in the gallery took to using black army binoculars, and even mother-of-pearl opera glasses, to scan the prisoners one by one.

Furthest away, on the far right of the back row, a youngish figure in a crumpled civilian suit, with dark receding hair and a sharp alert face, was Hans Fritzsche, known to some as 'his master's voice'. Head of the radio division in the Nazis' propaganda ministry, he was said to have owed his job to the fact that he sounded like Goebbels. Next to him sat Constantin von Neurath, the one-time Foreign Minister, later Reich Protector for Bohemia and Moravia – a dapper 73-year-old with a neat moustache and a polite, waiterly diplomat's smile. Then came Albert Speer, still only 40, tall, dark, and rather handsome. Highly intelligent, forthright, and apparently straight-forward, he spoke excellent English and even cracked sardonic jokes. As Minister for Armaments, he had master-minded the Third Reich's war production, and had indirectly employed slave labour; but towards the end of the war he had told Hitler that all was lost and had tried, he said, to kill him.

Speer's next neighbour, Dr Artur Seyss-Inquart, was in complete contrast. A Viennese lawyer and politician, Seyss-Inquart had been the first of the quislings: he had helped Hitler to annexe Austria. Later, as Commissioner for the Occupied Netherlands, he had imposed a reign of terror. Now, his cold eyes looked frightened behind their thick spectacles; his whole manner was resentful and withdrawn. Still more aloof was his co-conspirator in the Anschluss, Franz von Papen, Hitler's Vice-Chancellor and later Minister to Austria – silver-haired, bony-faced and vulpine, very much the ex-ambassador in his blue pinstriped suit.

Beside him, in field-grey uniform without badges of rank, sat General Alfred Jodl, 55 years old, a faithful professional soldier. As a member of the High Command, he had planned the invasion of Russia, and sanctioned not only the recruitment of forced labour, but also the execution of British commandos and the summary shooting of civilians. Although he had sometimes argued with Hitler about military matters, he had remained loyal to the very end. Trim, erect, and bony, with a long neck, pink cheeks, fierce blue eyes and a bare skull, he seemed to one British officer at Nuremberg, Major Airey Neave, 'like a Leech cartoon of a Victorian coachman'.

Sitting slightly apart from Jodl was Fritz Sauckel, who had risen from the ranks to become the boss of the Nazis' five million slave labourers. Foreign workers, he had decreed, were 'to be treated in such a way as to exploit them to the highest possible extent at the lowest conceivable degree of expenditure.' In court, he looked no more than a nervous little man with piggy brown eyes, a round bald head, and a small Hitler moustache. If Jodl seemed to shrink from him, so did Sauckel's neighbour on the gallery side, Baldur von Schirach, the 38-year-old former leader of the Hitler Youth and Gauleiter of Vienna, plump, soft, and elegant in a pale-grey suit.

On the left of the back row sat two admirals, both looking resigned and disillusioned. The retired Grossadmiral Erich Raeder had built up Hitler's navy in violation of the Versailles peace treaty, and had planned the invasion of Norway. His colleague Karl Doenitz, with small features, bright grey eyes, neat lips, and a smart blue suit, had been Hitler's official successor. As naval Commander-in-Chief, he was accused of responsibility for the death of commando prisoners.

The front row of the dock held eleven prisoners. On the far right was the Führer's one-time banker and Minister of Economics, Hjalmar Horace Greeley Schacht. Imprisoned by Hitler in the wake of the 20 July 1944 assassination plot, Schacht was now nearly 70 – tall, stiff, and upright in his high collar, with short white hair and a prim moustache. Behind his heavy spectacles, he looked cross and supercilious; he had a prominent nose, a small chin, and a neck like an angry ostrich. In the dock he tended to sit sideways, with his back to the interpreters' booth: his whole bearing expressed resentment at being cooped up with vulgar Nazis. His intelligence quotient was 143, the highest of all the defendants' scores – but he would sometimes scream with rage. He complained bitterly at the noise the gum-chewing GIs made in the prison, with their radios playing 'Don't Fence Me In'. Once, he threw his coffee over a photographer.

Schacht's neighbour in the dock was his successor as Minister of Economics, Walther Funk, a pale, bald, miserable, flabby-faced 55-year-old whom Schacht disparaged as a 'harmless homosexual'. When President of the Reichsbank, Funk had stored in its vaults the gold from spectacle frames, teeth, and fillings taken by the SS from victims of the death camps.

Next to Funk was the 60-year-old Julius Streicher, Hitler's scurrilous Jew-baiter – stocky, coarse, and blustering, with a receding forehead and sharp, greedy eyes. In prison, he boasted of his sexual appetites: the British writer Rebecca West thought he looked like 'the sort of old man who gives trouble in parks'. As a spokesman of the master race he was unimpressive: at 106, his IQ was the lowest of all among the accused. Only slightly more attractive was his neighbour Wilhelm Frick. With shaggy eyebrows, hair *en brosse*, and a fawn tweed jacket, Frick looked like a retired farmer or horse-breeder; but his rugged appearance was belied by his pedantic, high-pitched, bleating voice. As Hitler's Minister of the Interior he had drafted, signed, and ruthlessly administered countless laws against the Church, the trade unions, and the Jews. Although well aware that sick, insane, and aged people – 'useless eaters' – were being systematically put to death, he had done nothing to stop the murders, which in the end totalled seventy or eighty thousand.

Next to Frick sat another of Hitler's complaisant lawyers, Hans Frank, in 1933 Minister of Justice (in a Nazi uniform and jackboots), later – as Governor-General – 'the butcher of Poland'. 'We must annihilate the Jews wherever we find them and wherever possible,' he had written. Of the Poles he had said: 'We must not be squeamish when we hear the figure 17,000 shot.' At the end of the war, he had rejoined the Catholic Church, and made many confessions: shortly after being captured by Allied troops, he had tried to cut his throat. Now, in the dock, he often wore dark glasses, which hid his narrowed eyes. His face was pale and heavy under sparse black hair. When he spoke, his voice had rich courtroom resonance, and his full lips could still twist in a one-sided smile.

There were few smiles from Alfred Rosenberg, chief philosopher of Nazism and Reich Minister for the Eastern Occupied Territories. Throughout the trial he looked glum, shrunken, and bilious, with sharp beady eyes, and a quiff of hair pushed up now and then by the band of his headphones. Even before the war, a British Foreign Office official had dismissed him as 'a ponderous lightweight'. Stripped of power, his timid mediocrity matched his quavering voice. His neighbour in the dock towered above him physically.

This was Ernst Kaltenbrunner, who as chief of Himmler's Security Headquarters had supervised among other things 'the final solution'. His voice was soft, with a gentle Austrian accent: but he was a giant of a man with huge hands, a long gaunt deeply-scarred face, and gaps in teeth long discoloured by drink and by smoking a hundred cigarettes a day.

Kaltenbrunner sometimes looked more military than the Wehrmacht officer sitting next to him, Field-Marshal Wilhelm Keitel, Chief of Staff of the High Command. In his rankless field-grey uniform, with a general officer's red-striped breeches and field boots, Keitel sat erect and 'soldierly' – a favourite adjective. For a soldier, he kept repeating, orders were orders: but his had included the murder of fifty to a hundred hostages in Eastern Europe for every soldier attacked by civilians. 'Human life', he had commented, 'is less than nothing in the East.' Yet, despite his rough, soldier's complexion, cropped hair, and small moustache, Keitel looked confused and stupid, a weak man doing his best – quite bravely – to be strong.

The three last defendants in the front row of the dock were perhaps the best known. Joachim von Ribbentrop, who had succeeded von Neurath as Foreign Minister in 1938, had long been involved in Hitler's expansionist policies; and in September 1942 he had actually ordered the Third Reich's representatives in occupied countries to speed up the deportation of the Jews. In his heyday, Ribbentrop had been elegant and supercilious. Now, at 52, he merely looked old. His face was tired and ill-tempered, with baggy eyes under wispy hair; and although in the course of the trial he showed bursts of angry energy, his performance in the witness-stand was poor. 'Ribbentrop', wrote Evelyn Waugh,

was like a seedy schoolmaster being ragged, who knows he doesn't know the lesson, knows that the boys know, knows he has done the sum wrong on the blackboard, knows he has nothing to hope for at the school, but still hopes he can hold out to the end of term to get a 'character' for another post. He lied instinctively and without apparent motive.

Still more enigmatic was Ribbentrop's neighbour, Rudolf Hess. As the Führer's original deputy, he had played his part in plans for the attacks on Austria, Czechoslovakia, and Poland; but on 10 May 1941, then aged 46, he had taken off in a Messerschmitt-110 fighter plane and landed in Scotland on an abortive one-man peace mission. Always unpredictable, Hess now seemed to live in a world of his own. Beetle-browed, with burning eyes in deep sockets, he glared theatrically if anyone looked at him: his face was like a Hallowe'en skull. He was very thin, and constantly afraid that his food was poisoned. In court, he wore a grey tweed jacket and Luftwaffe flying boots; in his cell, he read crime novels. He claimed to have lost his memory. To many, he seemed half out of his mind.

Last of all, and first of all, hunched in his dove-grey uniform in the front corner seat with his elbow on the side of the dock and an army blanket across his knees like a travelling rug, was Hermann Göring, the cruel, falsely jovial fat boy of the Nazi court. Reichsmarschall, head of the Luftwaffe, President of the Reichstag, Plenipotentiary of the Four-Year Plan, Göring had played many roles: commander of Nazi storm-troopers, adviser and agent of Hitler, founder of the Gestapo, creator of the first concentration camps, organizer of purges, ringleader in the Anschluss, persecutor of Jews, conniver at slave labour, spoliator of conquered territories, collector of stolen art treasures, with a corrupt Roman emperor's greedy passion for medals and jewels.

In captivity, Göring had lost weight: he was now 15 stone – 210 pounds – instead of 20 (280). He was being weaned from his morphine addiction with the aid of paracodeine. His face was brown, his eyes a hard blue, and at 53 he still had thick dark hair. His broad cheekbones curved down to a thin, menacing mouth. To Janet Flanner of *The New Yorker*,

Of all the Nazis' hierarchy whose faces were already famous when they appeared at the big *Parteitag*, his has since changed the least. Then it looked like the face of an aging, fat tenor; now it looks like the face of a middle-aged, fleshy contralto (but in either case a star).

Göring certainly behaved like a star. In his cell, he smoked a big Bavarian pipe. He refused at first to touch his morning porridge, because 'a person of culture' could not eat with a lavatory under his nose. He had his trousers pressed daily by the prison tailor; and in the visiting room he used the glass partition and his lawyer's dark suit as a mirror to help him smooth his hair. He continually asked for a private interpreter. He gloated at not having to clean his own cell after a medical check on his heart. In the dock, he exchanged winks and glances with his fellow-prisoners. He might despise most of them – he was pleased to come near the top in the IQ test – but he valued an audience, even so late in the day.

The former Reichsmarschall provided some of the trial's few moments of overt drama. For the most part it was quiet, subdued, and clinical, with long legal arguments, diagrams, historical maps, and countless documents to be read into the record: memoranda, minutes, lists, decrees, official reports and diaries. The SS files alone filled eight freight cars – a bureaucratic record of barbarity. Nazi evil had above all been pedantic, calculation without human feeling. Characteristically, Rudolf Hoess, the Commandant of Auschwitz, corrected one of his captors:

No, you don't figure it right. The killing itself took the least time. You could dispose of 2,000 head in a half-hour, but it was the burning that took all the time.

Hoess had been responsible for the death of two-and-a-half million Jews.

The court proceedings went on for nine months – 284 days. The transcript filled twenty million duplicated sheets: the English version alone contained six million words, in 42 published volumes. The total cost was estimated at $4½ million. So long a process unavoidably grew monotonous: the local newspaper, the *Nürnberger Nachrichten*, had to be pressed by the Allies to give the trial more coverage. Newsworthy scenes were rare.

One occurred on the afternoon of 29 November 1945, ten days after the inaugural session. In the morning, for once, there had been laughter in the dock, at transcripts of Göring's telephone calls, glorying in the conquest of Austria. Then the prosecution showed a film of the concentration camps – a barn full of prisoners burned alive, bunks crowded with the sick and dying, crematorium ovens, naked corpses thrown into a pit, a doctor describing experiments on female inmates, a lampshade made of tattooed human skin. In the light of the film projector, the Nuremberg defendants sat transfixed. Schacht folded his arms and turned away, refusing to look at the screen. Von Neurath sat with his head bowed: Funk covered his eyes, and so did Ribbentrop: Keitel and Sauckel mopped their foreheads: Doenitz buried his head in his hands. By the end of the film, at least two of them were in tears. Streicher looked terrified, and even Göring coughed and bit his lips. In gloomy silence, they all filed out.

Later, they became more hardened. On 19 February 1946, shown a Soviet film of Nazi atrocities, some tried to dismiss it as propaganda – although Fritzsche, on the verge of breakdown, said he felt he was 'drowning in filth'.

Meanwhile, another film had provided a piquant contrast. Official footage of a Nazi trial had shown the judge yelling and almost screaming at the accused: 'You beast! You brute! You traitor!' When the film stopped and the lights went up, Lord Justice Lawrence said gently to Schacht's defence counsel: 'Please continue your examination, Dr Dix.'

Courtesy proved to be a deadly weapon. When Göring strode to the witness-stand on the afternoon of 13 March 1946, he looked confident, powerful, and aggressive in his vast grey jacket and breeches and his high maroon boots, with a thick sheaf of documents under his arm. Sitting back from the microphone, gripping the sides of the witness-box with his big, soft, white hands, he began to address the court in his strong, reedy, slightly rasping baritone. It was a bravura performance. It lasted twenty-one hours, spread over four days – a masterful, malicious account of Nazism from the inside. Göring concluded with what he claimed was a quotation from Churchill: 'In a struggle for life and death there is no legality.'

Then, on 18 March, came his cross-examination. 'This', wrote one British lawyer, 'will be a duel to the death between the representative of all that is worthwhile in civilization and the last important surviving protagonist of all that was evil.'

The American prosecutor was Robert H. Jackson, a determined, passionate, and eloquent lawyer, tough and ambitious, a Justice of the US Supreme Court. At the outset of the trial, he had made a brilliant speech, affirming with conviction and truth:

That four great nations, flushed with victory and stung with injury, stay the hand of vengeance and voluntarily submit their captive enemies to the judgment of the law is one of the most significant tributes that Power has ever paid to Reason.

Confronted with Göring, he was less effective. Even his courtroom manner was unfortunate: as an American observer wrote, 'He unbuttoned his coat, whisked it back over his hips, and, with his hands on his back pockets, spraddled and teetered like a country lawyer.' Within ten minutes he was in difficulties, fumbling with his documents, while Göring mockingly offered to help. Next day, still in trouble, Jackson appealed to the Judges. Göring's long, elaborate answers to simple questions, he said, were 'unresponsive and a waste of time'. Later, he threw down his headphones. 'This man', he declared, 'is adopting in the dock and the witness-stand an arrogant and contemptuous attitude toward a tribunal which is giving him a trial which he never gave to a living soul.' Lord Justice Lawrence adjourned the court. Göring strutted back to the dock. 'Jackson is not up to me,' he told his lawyer. To his fellow-defendants he remarked: 'If you all handle yourselves half as well as I did, you will do all right.'

Nemesis was on its way. On the following morning, 21 March 1946, Göring faced the British chief prosecutor, Sir David Maxwell Fyfe. A burly, heavy-faced Scot, 45 years old, balding slightly, with dark eyebrows above piercing eyes, he may have looked like a bulldog, but he acted like a rapier. Impeccably dressed in the style of the London law courts, he was polished and silkily polite. 'I want to be perfectly fair,' he would say, before some lethal thrust. In cross-examination, he usually called the prisoner 'witness'. By skilful questioning, he proved that Göring had acquiesced in the murder of RAF officers after 'the great escape' from Sagan prisoner-of-war camp on 24 March 1944. Cornered, Göring clenched his fists and turned crimson. At the lunch break, Airey Neave – himself an escaped POW – congratulated Maxwell Fyfe: 'You've got him.' 'I know how you must feel,' he replied.

From that point onward, Göring lost prestige with his fellow-prisoners. Three times he asked the prison psychologist: 'I didn't cut a *petty* figure, did I?' Later, through his counsel, he tried to intimidate one of Schacht's witnesses.

Visibly, the defence was falling apart. One by one, the prisoners gave evidence, were cross-examined, contradicted each other, and tried to exculpate themselves, pleading either that they had obeyed orders or that they had been too senior to know how their underlings had behaved. At length, after hard deliberation during August and September, the Judges came back to the courtroom on 1 October 1946, to deliver their verdicts and sentences. Three of the accused they acquitted: Schacht, von Papen, and Fritzsche. For fear of reprisals, these three stayed in custody for several days at their own request. Seven of the defendants received prison sentences: ten years for Doenitz, fifteen for von Neurath, twenty for Speer and von Schirach, life for Funk, Raeder, and Hess. The other eleven – as well as the missing Martin Bormann, Hitler's secretary, tried *in absentia* – were sentenced to be hanged. The executions were carried out by a US Master-Sergeant in the prison gymnasium, just after 1 a.m. on 17 October 1946.

The announcement of Göring's sentence had seen one last moment of ghastly comedy. While it was being pronounced, he had waved his arms and laughed – the interpretation system had broken down. When he finally heard his fate, he removed his headphones, turned, and marched out of the court in silence. He still had a final secret. Long ago, a routine search had revealed a potassium cyanide capsule hidden under his clothes; another had been found in a pot of his face cream. Perhaps they were both decoys. Somewhere, possibly under the lavatory rim, Göring had concealed yet a third capsule: it may have been smuggled in. He bit it, and died, shortly before he was due to be hanged.

At 4 a.m. that same night, in heavy rain, two lorries took the bodies to Dachau, where they were cremated. The ashes, under fictitious names, were scattered in the waters of the Conwentz, a ten-foot-wide brook flowing two hundred feet below the US mortuary at Heilmannstrasse 25, Munich-Solln.

Retribution assuaged a universal need. It could not be total. Justice was imperfect. Not all the guilty were identified or punished. No punishment could match the crime or bring back the victims. Even so, the Nuremberg Trial was revealing in at least four ways. It exposed crimes against humanity which no one, henceforth, could plausibly deny. It unmasked the perverse mediocrity of most of the criminals. It demonstrated the frailty of human judgement. And, as a reflection of powerful, complex, and conflicting feelings towards the German people, it prefigured the mould in which postwar Germany was to be shaped.

The trials in Nuremberg had parallels elsewhere. Before they began, France had arraigned the 89-year-old Marshal Philippe Pétain, head of the collaborationist Vichy Government. On 15 August 1945, the court condemned him to death, but recommended mercy. For the last six years of his life, he was imprisoned on the Ile d'Yeu in the Bay of Biscay. On 4 October, Pétain's unprepossessing Chief Minister Pierre Laval was brought to justice; found guilty, and revived after an attempt at suicide, he was shot on 24 October. In Norway, meanwhile, on 10 September, after a three-week hearing, sentence of death had been passed on Vidkun Quisling, the vain and bemused 'Minister-President' whose name had come to signify treacherous collaboration with the invader. Co-incidentally, Quisling faced a firing-squad on the same day as Laval.

Two lesser quislings evaded justice. Frits Clausen, the brutal, drunken leader of the Danish Nazi party, died of a heart attack while awaiting trial. In Belgium, the moon-faced, slit-eyed 'rexist' Léon Degrelle had been sentenced to death *in absentia* as early as December 1944; but he had long since escaped to Spain. Others were less fortunate. The Dutch collaborator Anton Mussert, fleshy 'Shadow Führer' under Seyss-Inquart, was charged with high treason in November 1945 and sentenced to death on 12 December. After both an appeal and a plea for mercy had been rejected, he was shot at Scheveningen on 7 May 1946. In the Soviet Union, the lean, bespectacled General Andrei Andreievich Vlasov, who had gone over to the enemy after his capture in 1942, was executed with eleven others some time before 2 August 1946, when *Pravda* published a discreet announcement to that effect.

Less prominent collaborators also faced judicial retribution. In Western Europe outside France, it was most extensive in Belgium, where 100,000 people were arrested. Of these, 87,000 were tried and 77,000 convicted. Although only 230 were finally executed, no fewer than 4,170 were condemned to death and some 16,000 received long prison terms. In Norway, 90,000 suspects were investigated: 18,000 were imprisoned, and a further 18,000 were punished in lesser ways. Thirty received death sentences, of which all but five were carried out. In the Netherlands, although between 120,000 and 150,000 people were arrested, only 96,044 of them were still in prison by October 1945. Some 60,000 lost their Dutch citizenship – and their property; military collaborators were imprisoned. In Denmark, 15,724 people were arrested and 14,449 convicted. The death sentence, abolished between the wars, was revived: it was carried out in 46 cases, although pronounced in 112.

Britain, having escaped invasion, had very few native quislings. The best-known of them alleged – when brought to trial – that he was not British at all. This was William Joyce, the son of an Irish-born naturalized American. Before the war, although born in the United States, Joyce had been a fierce British patriot and a follower of Sir Oswald Mosley's Blackshirts. On 6 July 1933, falsely claiming to have been born in the British Isles, he had applied for and obtained a British passport. On 24 August 1939, he had renewed it and gone to Nazi Germany, becoming a German citizen on 26 September 1940. His wartime propaganda broadcasts, beamed at Britain, had earned him the nickname 'Lord Haw-Haw'. 'This is Jairmany calling, Jairmany calling. Here are the Reichsender Hamburg, Station Bremen, and Station DXB, on the 31-metre band...' No one who heard him could forget those sneering, nasal, stage-villain's tones.

On 17 September 1945, Joyce came to trial at London's Central Criminal Court. Morally, he was guilty without a doubt. Legally, the case hinged on whether or not he owed allegiance to Britain: on appeal, it went as far as the House of Lords, which decided that he did. He was hanged at Wandsworth Prison in south London on the morning of 3 January 1946. Similar sentences were passed on John Amery, who had invented the renegade 'British Free Corps' to fight alongside the Nazis, Walter Purdy, an informer, and Thomas Haller Cooper, who had joined the SS. Penal servitude was reserved for smaller fry – deluded junior members of Amery's traitor corps, and Joyce's fellow-broadcaster Norman Baillie-Stewart, né Wright.

France was also an exception, although in a different sense. Here, at the Liberation, at least 5,000 people faced 'summary execution', at best after trial by kangaroo courts. A further 2,071 were sentenced to death after due process of law, as well as some 4,400 condemned *in absentia*; but in the end only 768 were executed. General de Gaulle automatically commuted capital sentences passed on women and minors.

Those executed in France included several journalists – men like Jean Luchaire, Paul Chack, or Georges Suarez – and one well-known critic and novelist, the round-faced, round-spectacled Robert Brasillach, who looked a little like a wettened owl. His first novel, *Le voleur d'étincelles*, published in 1932 when he was 23, had set the tone for Brasillach's moody obsession with Youth, Beauty, and Destiny. In Italy before the war he had admired the children's holiday camps with their youth leaders and Fascist songs; at the 1937 Nuremberg rally, he had been enraptured by the silent 'cathedral of light' that had greeted Hitler's emergence on the rostrum. 'If the Jews bother you,' he had written on 2 June 1941, 'prevent them from speaking. I know one camp at least where this is done and it is good.' On 6 February 1945, at 9.38 in the morning, Brasillach himself was silenced by a firing-squad at Montoire. Bookish as he looked, he showed courage at the end. Several artists and writers, including Albert Camus and François Mauriac, had petitioned De Gaulle for clemency, but in vain. Explaining his reasons, the General alluded to Brasillach's admiration for the classical tragic heroes of Pierre Corneille. 'Brasillach would have wished it thus,' he declared.

Other French writers accused of collaboration were spared Brasillach's fate. The novelist Drieu la Rochelle, who had been a member of the late Jacques Doriot's national-socialist party, and who under the Occupation had edited the once illustrious *Nouvelle Revue Française*, killed himself while awaiting trial. 'Yes, I am a traitor,' he had written: 'I demand death.' Jacques Benoist-Méchin, the historian of the German Army who had become a Vichy minister, was himself condemned to death, but had his sentence commuted. Lucien Rebatet, who in 1942, in *Les décombres*, had savagely celebrated France's defeat and decadence, and who had not only denounced anti-Nazis but allegedly helped the Gestapo hunt them down, was lucky to escape with a term in prison. There, on concealed scraps of lavatory paper, he wrote a remarkably fine and tender novel, *Les deux étendards*. Another talented novelist, also deeply tainted, took refuge in Denmark. This was Louis-Ferdinand Destouches, otherwise Céline, the scurrilous and obsessive anti-semite best known for his scorching first novel, *Voyage au bout de la nuit*, published in 1932.

These and other writers compromised during the Occupation, like the boulevard playwright Sacha Guitry and the novelist Henry de Montherlant,

were blacklisted for a time by the *Comité National des Ecrivains*, a body close
to the Resistance, in word if not always in deed. Its members included not
only André Malraux, who had actually fought both in Spain and in World
War II, but also François Mauriac, Jean-Paul Sartre, and the Left-wing poet
Louis Aragon. Partly owing to their efforts, works by the authors incrimi-
nated became hard to find. Some were not reprinted; some reappeared in
Switzerland. Not until years later were some of them republished in France,
enabling younger readers to judge, say, Drieu and Brasillach at their real,
rather modest worth.

Even Britain felt a touch of blacklist fever. In 1940, the humorist P.G.
Wodehouse, creator of 'Jeeves', had been living in Le Touquet. When
France was invaded, he was captured and imprisoned, later being transferred to Belgium and then to Germany. Like other such internees, he was
released as he neared the age of sixty, in 1941. Shortly afterwards, anxious
to get into touch with American readers who had been agitating for his
release, he recorded five radio talks from Berlin, describing his time in
captivity – and raised an almighty storm. 'Of course,' he wrote later, 'I ought
to have had the sense to see that it was a loony thing to do to use the German
radio for even the most harmless stuff, but I didn't. I suppose prison life saps
the intellect.' In fact, the talks were good-humoured, stiff-upper-lip, but
quite outspoken accounts of unpleasant treatment: but in wartime Britain –
partly at official instigation – they were bitterly and inaccurately denounced.
After the Liberation of Paris, Wodehouse was arrested. Investigated by
British Intelligence – in the person of his fellow-writer Malcolm Muggeridge – he was quickly exonerated and released; but, as he remarked later,
'You need dynamite to dislodge an idea that has got itself firmly rooted in the
public mind,' and for many people he long remained under a cloud. He
never again lived in Britain, and died in 1975 in the United States at the age
of 93, a few weeks after receiving a belated knighthood. Thirty years earlier,
one of his most eloquent defenders had been George Orwell, author of
Animal Farm and *Nineteen Eighty-Four*. 'In the desperate circumstances of
the time,' wrote Orwell, 'it was excusable to be angry at what Wodehouse
did, but to go on denouncing him three or four years later – and more, to let
an impression remain that he acted with conscious treachery – is not
excusable.'

Orwell had consistently opposed the idea of a postwar witch-hunt – even
against the Nazis. 'What is important', he had written in 1943, in the left-
wing weekly *Tribune*, 'is not that these political gangsters should be made to

suffer, but that they should be made to discredit themselves.' His feeling was confirmed two years later when he visited a prisoner-of-war camp in southern Germany, and saw a former SS man savagely kicked:

Quite apart from the scrubby, unfed, unshaven look that a newly captured man generally has, he was a disgusting specimen. But he did not look brutal or in any way frightening: merely neurotic and, in a low way, intellectual. His pale, shifty eyes were deformed by powerful spectacles. He could have been an unfrocked clergyman, an actor ruined by drink, or a spiritualist medium. I have seen very similar people in London common lodging houses, and also in the Reading Room of the British Museum. Quite obviously he was mentally unbalanced – indeed, only doubtfully sane, though at this moment sufficiently in his right mind to be frightened of getting another kick.... So the Nazi torturer of one's imagination, the monstrous figure against whom one had struggled for so many years, dwindled to this pitiful wretch, whose obvious need was not for punishment, but for some kind of psychological treatment.

'Hatred', Orwell had concluded earlier, 'is an impossible basis for policy, and curiously enough it can lead to over-softness as well as to over-toughness.'

Allied policy towards postwar Germany – including the Nuremberg trial – was accused of both. There had been disagreement about it from the start. Henry Morgenthau, US Secretary of the Treasury, had favoured a draconian regime, including the tracking down of all war criminals, the establishment of group detention and labour battalions, and if necessary summary executions without full trial. An enthusiastic agronomist and owner of a model farm outside New York, Morgenthau also proposed to 'pastoralize' Germany, with all but the lightest industries closed down or placed under international control.

His colleague at the War Department, Henry Stimson, quickly retorted that 'such methods do not prevent war: they tend to breed war.' President Roosevelt was undecided. He liked to try out ideas on other people; and he put the Morgenthau Plan to Churchill at the second Quebec Conference in September 1944. Churchill's first reaction was negative: 'Europe would be chained to a dead body,' he said. But he had always personally favoured a draconian policy. A year earlier, at a private party, he had asked for three encores of Noël Coward's heavily ironical song 'Don't let's be beastly to the Germans'; and in a paper for the War Cabinet he had proposed that an agreed list of fifty to a hundred 'major criminals' be shot out of hand. Sensing that he could be influenced, Morgenthau's assistant Harry Dexter White suggested to Churchill's friend 'the Prof.', Lord Cherwell, formerly F.A. Lindemann, that if Britain accepted the Plan she might find it easier to obtain American aid after the war. Within forty-eight hours, Churchill had changed his mind: and on 15 September 1944, he and Roosevelt initialled a memorandum 'looking forward to converting Germany into a country primarily agricultural and pastoral.'

Morgenthau was delighted: but his triumph was brief. The case against his Plan was powerful, and it was forcefully argued in both Washington and London, where there had even been doubts about the need for formal war trials. In the process, Churchill reverted to the motto he later used in his war memoirs: 'In Victory, Magnanimity.' In January 1945 he wrote to the Foreign Secretary, Anthony Eden:

It is a mistake to try to write out on little pieces of paper what the vast emotions of an outraged and quivering world will be either immediately after the struggle is over or when the inevitable cold fit follows the hot.

Soon, in Washington too, Morgenthau's opponents won the day, and his project was tacitly dropped. But its spirit lived on; and it haunted Allied policy in the formative stages, as expressed most notably in the US Joint Chiefs of Staff directive JCS 1067, which imposed restraints on German industry and on contacts with the German people themselves.

For a long time after the war, moreover, the Allies insisted on 'reparations' – despite the fact that after World War I these had been one of the errors condemned by John Maynard Keynes in *The Economic Consequences of the Peace*. In all, after World War II, the Allies removed about 500 million dollars' worth of machinery and equipment – to say nothing of loot unofficially 'liberated' by the troops. One serviceman, it was said, sent home a complete motor-cycle, in three separate shipments. Others sold PX and NAAFI supplies on the local black market: in July 1945 alone, US personnel in Europe remitted to America a million dollars more than their official pay. Perhaps understandably, the Soviet Union was especially eager for 'benefits in kind'. The composer Nicolas Nabokov, Russian-born but anti-Communist, saw one truck leaving Berlin for the East with 'a mountain of brass: tubas, trumpets and trombones, covered by heavy Bokhara rugs', and another carrying 'thousands of naked typewriters'. How many thousands, and how many tons of other material, the Soviet Union never disclosed; but Western intelligence reported that many Eastern sidings were crowded with freight cars full of rusting machinery. Advocating the Morgenthau Plan, Lord Cherwell had argued that it would 'eliminate a dangerous competitor'. Reparations, and the dismantling of German heavy industry, were certainly expected to have the same effect. There were even cases of private firms' seeking to steal both plant and patents. But the policy was doubly self-defeating. In a country crying out for food, housing, clothes, transport, and jobs, and kept alive – only just – by Allied subsidies, the further destruction of industry seemed like madness to occupied and occupier alike. Furthermore, as Morgenthau himself had predicted, the removal of obsolete equipment, followed by modernization, in the long run gave German industry a keen competitive edge.

That was for the future. An immediate question was how the German people should be treated. JCS 1067 was categorical: in the words of General Lucius D. Clay, Eisenhower's Deputy Military Governor, 'Germany was to be occupied as a defeated nation under a just, firm, and aloof administration which would discourage any fraternization.' The other Allies took a similar stand.

'Non-fraternization' was short-lived. As early as 12 June 1945, Field-Marshal Montgomery officially authorized British troops to talk and play with German children. 'They were, of course, doing it already,' he wrote. Soon, fraternization, or 'frat', came to be the slang for Allied soldiers' local love-life – not always mercenary, and sometimes surprisingly innocent. Even so, an immense gulf separated the vanquished from the victors. What emerged was a species of colonial rule.

The officers and staff of Allied Military Government or the Control Commission had clubs and messrooms forbidden to German civilians – unless they were servants or waiters. The families of the occupation forces had German maids to clean their houses or apartments, all of them requisitioned, sometimes at cruelly short notice. Allied rations were in some cases more plentiful than for civilians in Britain; they were princely compared with the Germans' meagre fare. In Bonn in 1945, a British transport officer told Stephen Spender that, simply to maintain efficiency, he was giving some of his own rations to his German workers, three of whom were ill through undernourishment. 'The rations for a week for a German consisted of about a dessert-spoonful of some kind of fat, 4 lb. of bread, two thin slices of meat, the size of a crown piece each, if he was lucky, and, also if he was lucky, once a month, about half a pound of substitute tea or coffee.' A year later, the left-wing British publisher Victor Gollancz, himself Jewish, was horrified by what he saw in the Ruhr. 'Many were living, the day I visited them, on a cup of milkless "coffee" for breakfast, potatoes with cabbage for lunch, and the same in the evening, bread being entirely absent.' In a series of letters and articles in the British press, later collected into a book under the title *In Darkest Germany*, Gollancz campaigned passionately against what he saw as injustice – even reprinting as evidence some five-course menus from a Control Commission officers' mess. Half the book consisted of photographs, a heartbreaking record of ruin, poverty, squalor, hunger, and disease.

Much of the hardship was inescapable. There was a world food shortage; other parts of Europe had equal or greater needs; transport and distribution were a perpetual headache, with roads and railways crippled, and engines, trucks, and cars lying idle for want of spare parts. But material problems, intractable in themselves, were compounded by powerful and complex emotions on both sides.

To many Germans, the ruin of their cities was the fault of Allied bombers; and their own suffering now was intensified by the attitude of their conquerors, at best aloof, at worst vindictive and punishing. To the occupying forces, on the contrary, Germany seemed a land defiled: every German, surely, must bear some share of the general guilt. *Die Mörder sind unter uns* – 'The Murderers are Amongst Us' – was the title of a disturbing, uneasily ambivalent film about a war criminal made in 1946 by Wolfgang Staudte; but it was more than a title: it expressed a fact which thoughtful Germans – like Staudte himself – had to acknowledge. 'Once,' wrote Stephen Spender,

I was roused to explain to a professor and his wife that all their complaints were groundless, because the Germany of Hitler had called down upon itself, not an army of liberating angels, but simply the Occupying Forces, the Red Army, the GIs, the Tommies and the Poilus, with all the defects of the individual soldiers of whom these were composed. The Occupiers of Germany did not wish to be there, I insisted, it was the Germans who had invoked them. Nor did they want to stay; it was the Germans, in effect, who kept them. There was a silence in which I realized that I had definitely convinced my friends, then the professor's wife said: 'What you say is quite true, and we should certainly never complain whatever happens.' A moment later she added: 'All the same, nowadays, sometimes there are moments when one feels extraordinarily depressed.'

The Stuttgart poet Felix Berner was 27 when the war ended: he had been in the German army since 1939. In *'Ich hab' es nicht gewollt'* – 'I didn't want it' – he expressed the feelings of a whole generation:

> When I bit into the earth,
> wet earth, kneaded with blood,
> when the ground split open,
> I expect I prayed.
> I no longer know, no longer clearly,
> except this: the sky was blue.

And if you ask me:
How did it begin?
I didn't want it.
But I went along.

When I was hunted through the wood
with running, fallen, kneeling,
with dead and tattered men,
I expect I screamed.
I no longer know, no longer for certain,
except this: that darkness reigned.

And if you ask me:
How did it begin?
I didn't want it.
But I went along.

When I went through the streets,
from balconies, windows, stairways
hung the bodies of Jews,
and I said nothing.
This I know still, this I am sure of,
no one can take it from me.

And if you ask me:
How did it begin?
I didn't want it
and passed by on the other side.

How many others had done the same? It was a question with no certain answer. As Churchill had said when first rejecting the Morgenthau Plan, 'I agree with Burke. You cannot indict a whole nation.' Nor, as the Allies soon discovered, could a whole nation be effectively screened.

It was hard enough in the case of individuals. How, for instance, were the Allied authorities to judge a world-renowned musician like Wilhelm Furtwängler, conductor of the Berlin Philharmonic? He had certainly worked throughout most of the Nazi period, and had held his last concerts in Berlin, in the Blüthner-Saal near the Potsdamer Platz, as late as April 1945. Yet he had quarrelled with the Nazis in the first year after Hitler came to power. He had been penalized for defending Paul Hindemith; he had also shielded Jewish musicians within the orchestra, and with one exception had refused to perform in Nazi-occupied countries. On these and other grounds he was cleared by a court in Austria in March 1946; but despite an eloquent plea by the Jewish violinist Yehudi Menuhin, he had to wait nine months for final permission to conduct in Germany again. Among the crowd outside the court, there were cries of 'It's stupid, this "De-Nazification"!' and 'Who are they to judge such a man?'

At a far less exalted level, I vividly recall how difficult such judgments were. One night, outside the camp where I was stationed, a British army sergeant was murdered. In the investigation that followed, two German prisoners were witnesses. The first was a young army officer, professedly anti-Nazi, all smiles, civility, and eagerness to be of service. I found him a nauseating toady. The other, a naval captain, was gruff, overbearing, and almost insolent: he loathed captivity, and resented having to deal with a pipsqueak British officer. But he was the one who really helped.

Applied to a whole population, attempts to judge character were like trying to sift the sea. Did working for Nazi organizations in itself constitute guilt? If so, the humblest cleaner at SS headquarters should be on trial. Was a founder-member of the Nazi party, deluded perhaps by its prospectus, worse than someone who joined later, when its real aims and methods had become clear? How guilty were those who joined merely to keep their jobs and feed their families? Who, in ordinary life, had really known about the death camps? How many had remained ignorant, as it were, by choice? What was to be done with the mass of the people, no better but little worse than in happier countries, who had felt unable to change things, and had been carried along by the tide?

Seeking answers to such questions, the Allies distributed thousands of so-called *Fragebogen* or questionnaire forms, each 131 sections long. Those seeking release or office were called upon to complete them, answering queries about their nationality, their religion, any convictions for crime, their education and professional qualifications, their employment and military service, their membership of various organizations or part-time service with them, their writings and speeches, their income and assets, and their travel or residence abroad. The responses were often inconclusive; but, correctly filled in, the *Fragebogen* could become an autobiography. In one instance, it did.

Ernst von Salomon was its author – a proud, embittered, rather sinister blend of old-fashioned patriot, artist, and political adventurer. Born in Kiel of a family originally Huguenot, he had been a cadet at the Karlsruhe and Berlin military academies, but was still only sixteen when the 1918 armistice ended his hopes of an officer's career. Instead, he enlisted in the freebooting volunteer *Freikorps* to fight on the Eastern front. When the *Freikorps* was disbanded in 1920, he joined some of its other members in subversive politics. Two years later, implicated in the assassination of the Foreign Minister, Walther Rathenau, he was sentenced to five years in prison. He then retired from politics to writing. His books were hailed by the Nazis as 'documents of the struggle for the rebirth of the Nation'; but although in some senses a proto-Nazi, Salomon played no directly political role in the Third Reich. He spent the war writing film-scripts. Arrested in 1945, he was released a year later; and in 1951 he published *Der Fragebogen*, using the framework of the Allied questionnaire to recount his career from 1918 to 1946. Cynical, mocking, and defiant, it was as tricky an apologia as Albert Speer's defence at Nuremberg: but it proved what problems there were in disentangling the past.

To do so – to identify the accused, disprove false allegations, attribute responsibilities, reconstruct circumstances, establish guilt, and uncover intentions and motives – was an enormous task. It required, among other things, office machinery, punched cards, paper, and a central filing system. Above all, it needed skilful and experienced German-speaking personnel. All were in very short supply. In London and elsewhere, many officials and politicians shared George Orwell's misgivings about conducting a general witch-hunt. Even those who favoured it had other preoccupations: they were reluctant to divert scarce resources from tasks which seemed more urgent – dealing with 'displaced persons', repatriating prisoners, keeping order, tending the sick, feeding and housing the civil population, and gradually winding down the huge and wasteful machinery of war. In the end, efforts to trace and punish the guilty fizzled out into uneasy bureaucratic oblivion. Many thousands escaped just retribution. Noël Annan, then a British member of the Control Commission, admitted afterwards that 'de-Nazification' was 'a process which failed to achieve its object, lost us friends and credibility, and got us the worst of both worlds.' Handed over to the German courts, it was still dragging on more than thirty years later, amid complaints that the Allies had turned a 'blind eye to murder', to quote the title of an angry exposé by a British reporter, Tom Bower.

No one, in the wake of World War II, could have avoided raking over its human ashes. Some kind of cleansing was a necessary act. But unless the Allies had stooped to the methods of the Nazis, they could not have countenanced either summary 'justice' or guilt-by-association. This ruled out any wholesale purge on the scale some envisaged in retrospect. But if 'de-Nazification' of that type was out of the question, a different variety had much greater success. This was what might be called, more aptly if no more elegantly, 're-democratization'. It involved, rather self-consciously, reintroducing freedom to a country numbed by tyranny and intellectually starved: spreading truthful information, fostering free speech, re-educating teachers, assisting the revival of trade unions and political parties, republishing books and newspapers, rebuilding the cinema industry, re-starting radio stations – and giving astonished broadcasters the right to criticize the Allies.

It was a mammoth enterprise; and like all such ambitious undertakings, it involved mistakes. Some Allied officials were naïve and self-righteous in their crisp attempts to implant Anglo-Saxon attitudes. Others were paternalist or patronizing; a few were autocratic. One of their victims was Dr Konrad Adenauer, later to be Chancellor of the German Federal Republic. In 1945, aged sixty-nine, he was re-appointed Mayor of Cologne – an office from which the Nazis had dismissed him. Stephen Spender was one of his visitors.

It is now with a special personal emotion that he takes up the restoration of that Cologne which was broken like a trayload of crockery when it was taken out of his hands.... He has an energetic, though somewhat insignificant appearance: a long lean oval face, almost no hair, small blue active eyes, a little button nose and a reddish complexion. He looks remarkably young and he has the quietly confident manner of a successful and attentive young man.

To Spender, Adenauer outlined his plans for Cologne:

'There are two aspects of Reconstruction which we consider of equal importance,' he went on. 'One, the material rebuilding of the city. But just as important is the creation of a new spiritual life.... There is a hunger and thirst now for spiritual values in Germany.... Only the best should be our aim. We should have in Cologne the best education, the best books, the best newspapers, the best music.'
He spoke like a man filled with a sense of civic pride for Cologne, some of whose ruins, on the other side of the square, I was looking at through the window behind his head as he spoke.

That was in the summer of 1945. Within a few months, on 6 October, the Regional Commander of the Rhineland, Brigadier John Barraclough, summoned Adenauer to his office – it was a Saturday – and summarily dismissed him for lack of 'proper supervision and energy' in 'the general task of preparing for the coming winter', 'the repair of buildings and the clearance of the streets'. He ordered him to leave Cologne 'as soon as possible, and in any case not later than 14 October', and forbade him 'to indulge either directly or indirectly in any political activity whatever.'

It was an affront that long rankled; and it had an unexpected outcome. Two months later, with the help of Noël Annan, the ban on Adenauer's political activity was lifted, and he was free to throw his energies into the Christian Democratic movement. Had he remained Mayor of Cologne, he might never have become so prominent on the national scene.

By the time he did so, however, the future of Germany had been still more decisively shaped. The old, draconian policy of Allied tutelage was gradually being abandoned. The Western Allies, at least, had learned the lesson that Keynes had drawn from the Versailles Treaty of 1919: to avoid *revanchisme*, the vanquished must be helped back to their feet. The dismantling of German industry was ending; restraints of all kinds were being lifted; the past was being buried. In a few years' time, rightly or wrongly, even a munitions manufacturer like Alfried Krupp was to be freed and reinstated. The Germans, like the Italians before them, were 'working their passage' back to normal life.

In one crucial respect, however, the Allies' initial policy of imposing their own rule on the Germans left a permanent mark. For good or ill, postwar Germany was drastically hobbled by being divided.

This might not have come about if the Allies had not insisted on the Nazis' 'unconditional surrender'. Publicly launched in January 1943 after the Casablanca Conference between Churchill and Roosevelt, and later gladly endorsed by Joseph Stalin, 'unconditional surrender' had two main aims: to prevent the resurgence of Nazism, and to forestall any claim, as after World War I, that Germany had been betrayed, not defeated. But what it meant in practice was that after the Nazi surrender Germany became a power vacuum, with no government of her own. The Allies were left with a free hand to do what they chose. And yet, like so much else in their postwar policy, the division of Germany resulted from discord and indecision as much as from conscious choice.

Already at the end of 1941, Stalin had proposed that Germany be 'dismembered'. East Prussia, he proposed, should be transferred to Poland, and the Sudetenland to Czechoslovakia; Austria, the Rhineland, and possibly Bavaria might become separate independent States. At times, and with variations, Winston Churchill entertained similar ideas. So, too, did Roosevelt: during the Teheran Conference in November 1943 he suggested splitting the former Reich into five self-governing entities. The British Foreign Office, on the contrary, proposed that all ex-enemy countries be administered jointly, with an Allied Commission in each of them. The US State Department agreed: it argued for a centralized Germany under democratic rule. Roosevelt, meanwhile, continued to hedge his bets. On 20 October 1944, he wrote to Secretary of State Cordell Hull: 'In view of the fact that we have not occupied Germany, I cannot agree at this moment as to what kind of a Germany we want in every detail.' Even at the Yalta Conference in February 1945, the question still seemed to be open; and on 9 May 1945, Joseph Stalin actually proclaimed: 'The Soviet Union does not intend to dismember or destroy Germany.'

But if 'dismemberment' were supposedly ruled out, plans for partition were already far advanced. As early as the summer of 1943, a special committee of the British War Cabinet under Deputy Prime Minister Clement Attlee had recommended that postwar Germany be divided into three zones of occupation, with Berlin under joint Allied control. At the end of their Teheran meeting that November, Churchill, Stalin, and Roosevelt agreed to this proposal, and instructed a tripartite group of senior officials, the European Advisory Commission, to draft a detailed plan. After an informal session ten days before Christmas, the Commission began work in earnest on 14 January 1944.

It met in Lancaster House, London, an imposing early-nineteenth-century building tucked away near St James's at the Buckingham Palace end of the Mall. Its tall Corinthian portico, its marble double staircase, and its ornate salons, newly decorated in white and gold, with red and green hangings, seemed unmistakably vice-regal; and the task of the assembled officials was vice-regal too. Their chairman was Sir William Strang, shrewd, bespectacled, and donnish, a dry professional to his finger-tips. His Soviet and United States colleagues were the respective Ambassadors in London: Fedor T. Gusev, whom Strang later called 'a grim and rather wooden person, with, as a saving grace, a touch of sardonic humour and, as a virtue, a somewhat blunt straightforwardness'; and John G. Winant, 'a self-tortured soul, noble and passionate, inarticulate, deceptively simple, the pattern of honour.' The French Ambassador, René Massigli, soon joined them. In nineteen months of discussion and drafting, they played a key role in deciding the shape of postwar Germany.

Astonishingly, the map of the occupation zones was quickly settled: as Strang put it, there was 'little discussion and early agreement'. The only real dispute was between the United States and Britain, each wanting the industrialized north-west area which Britain at length secured. The American zone comprised South Germany as far north as the Weser and as far west as Wiesbaden, together with the port of Bremen from the British zone. The French zone, carved out later, was virtually two areas, joined by an isthmus of land to the west of Karlsruhe: they covered the western fringe of Germany in South-Württemberg-Baden, and the southern Rhineland and the Saar.

The Soviet zone consisted of Mecklenburg-Pomerania, Brandenburg, Saxony-Anhalt, and Thuringia, as well as areas further east to be placed under Polish administration – in all, 40 percent of Germany's 1937 territory, 36 percent of her population, and 33 percent of her productive resources, including the bulk of her food-growing lands. Berlin, under four-power control, was to be deep inside the Soviet zone.

Two abortive suggestions were made for keeping the zones together. One was that each of them should be manned by mixed Allied contingents, on the pattern portrayed in Vienna by the Swiss director Leopold Lindtberg's 1950 film comedy, *Four in a Jeep*. That idea was dropped as 'administratively impracticable'. The second plan seemed more promising: that the zones should be redrawn so as to meet at Berlin.

It was a notion that Roosevelt himself had once mooted. In November 1943, on board USS *Iowa* bound for Cairo and Teheran, he had pencilled on a *National Geographic* map of Germany an East-West boundary running through Berlin. Two weeks later, in Cairo, the US Joint Chiefs of Staff made a similar proposal, but with the border leaving Berlin just inside the Eastern zone. A third suggestion, made by State Department officials, was for three zones converging on Berlin like slices of pie; while a fourth, put forward by Professor Philip E. Mosely, then also with the State Department, envisaged a corridor linking Berlin with the Western zones.

Of all these tentative plans, only the Joint Chiefs of Staff proposal was ever submitted to the European Advisory Commission at Lancaster House, and that with no further explanation. When puzzled officials raised the matter with Roosevelt, he laughed. 'Why, that's just something I once drew on the back of an envelope,' he said: and the matter was dropped. The zonal boundaries remained unaltered: Berlin remained an island in the East.

A soldier made last-minute efforts to change what officials and politicians had decided. This was Field Marshal Bernard Montgomery, the gaunt, austere, and wilful hero of El Alamein, who commanded 21 Army Group in General Eisenhower's expeditionary force. From August 1944 onwards, Montgomery argued for 'one really powerful and full-blooded thrust towards Berlin'. This, he thought, 'would not only have shortened the war; it would also have held out possibilities of bringing it to an end in Europe with a political balance very much more favourable to an early and stable peace' – in effect pre-empting the Lancaster House draft agreement on the shape of the occupation zones. Montgomery was backed by Churchill: but Eisenhower vetoed the idea on both military and political grounds. The veto was confirmed in Washington both by General George C. Marshall, Eisenhower's superior, and by President Roosevelt himself. Some months later, the issue was re-opened. On 11 April 1945, when the armoured vanguard of the US Ninth Army crossed the Elbe near Magdeburg, Eisenhower asked its commander, General Omar Bradley, what it would cost to press on as far as Berlin. Told that it might mean the loss of 100,000 men, Eisenhower hesitated. The question was really political, and called for a decision in Washington; but by now the ailing Roosevelt had less than one day to live. His successor Harry S. Truman, until then Vice-President, passed the buck. 'The question of tactical deployment of American troops,' he said, 'is a military one.' On Sunday 15 April the Ninth Army was ordered to stop at the Elbe. By that time, its forward patrols were only 48 miles from the German capital. Within ten days, when American and Soviet troops finally met across defeated enemy territory, the Red Army had finally encircled Berlin.

So it was that while other Europeans groped their way back to something like normality after the war, the Germans found that life was permanently altered. Through their own homeland ran the new frontier that was to divide them, and Europe, and the world, between East and West. Only to the West of that line could a new generation recover the true spirit of Germany, freed from the tyranny of either Right or Left.

3
Business as Usual

A few hours before dawn on Sunday 29 April 1945, a truck drew up in the Piazzale Loreto near the central railway station in Milan. Out of it were unloaded twenty-three corpses. Fifteen of them were the bodies of Fascists whom Italian partisans had killed in reprisal for the shooting of hostages seven months earlier in this same Milan square, after a bomb attack on a Nazi army lorry. Five of the corpses were never identified. One of the others was that of Achille Starace, formerly Secretary of the Fascist Party. The other two were the bodies of the Italian dictator, Benito Mussolini, and his green-eyed mistress Claretta Petacci. With scrawled placards to show who they were, the bodies were hung head downwards from the roof of a nearby filling-station. They remained there all day – a gruesome *memento mori* in a city which already could hardly count its dead.

So long as the war continued in Italy, Milan had been a key target for Allied bombers, not only as an industrial centre, but also as a vital link in the rail line from Germany which supplied the Nazi armies in the South. In August 1943, while Marshal Badoglio's short-lived Government was still only toying with surrender, the British and Americans resumed their bombing of the Northern industrial towns; and on the night of 12 August a thousand aircraft dropped more than two thousand tons of bombs on Milan. Much of the city centre was destroyed, and with it thousands of homes. The carnage was appalling. One of those who witnessed it was a 42-year-old professor of literature at Milan's Giuseppe Verdi School of Music – the poet Salvatore Quasimodo. He wrote:

> In vain you search in the dust,
> poor hand, the city is dead.
> Is dead: we have heard the last throbbing
> from the heart of the canal. The nightingale
> has fallen from his perch, high up on the convent,
> where once he sang before sunset.

> Don't dig wells in the courtyards:
> the living have lost their thirst.
> Don't touch the dead, so red, so swollen:
> leave them in the earth of their houses:
> the city is dead, is dead.

It certainly seemed so to the survivors. Adding insult to injury, the bombing had reduced to rubble many of Milan's historic buildings. The Galleria, once the heart of local and political life, was a mass of twisted metal and shattered glass. The Brera palace and art gallery was in ruins. Leonardo's fresco of The Last Supper, in the fifteenth-century church of Santa Maria delle Grazie, was laid open to the elements. By a miracle, most of the Cathedral was intact: but bombs had fallen on another monument almost as deeply cherished: the Teatro della Scala. The great opera house was gutted: only its outer walls still stood.

The Milanese are known for their tough resilience. In spite or perhaps because of the bombing, they had organized a number of anti-Fascist strikes. Within weeks of the war's ending, they set about rebuilding their city; and one of their top priorities was to resurrect La Scala. Railway installations, factories, the Galleria, even housing would if necessary have to wait. Nothing must delay the re-opening of the opera house. And for the re-opening, no one would do but the great Arturo Toscanini, exiled in New York since the 1930's.

Toscanini had long been an anti-Fascist symbol. In 1931, he had tartly declined to play the Fascist anthem, *Giovinezza*, at a concert in Bologna, and had been set upon by Mussolini's thugs. Since then, he had refused to conduct in Italy. When Hitler came to power in Germany, Toscanini would no longer go to Bayreuth; after the Nazi annexation of Austria, he had boycotted Salzburg too. Imperious as he was – in better days he had ruled La Scala with a baton of iron, excluding latecomers, silencing chatter, ensuring the curtain rose on time and the house lights were dimmed during performances – Toscanini was sorely missed by Italians in all walks of life. I remember sitting one evening in a small village café when a Toscanini recording was played on the radio. At once, there was silence for the maestro's crisp and delicate art.

So La Scala's orchestra invited him: but to their chagrin he refused to come. Before he would consent to conduct again in Italy, he declared, 'every vestige of the ignominious past and of betrayal must disappear.' But he would be proud, he added, 'to return among you as a citizen of a free Italy and not as a subject of the kings and princes of the House of Savoy.'

Already, in fact, King Victor Emmanuel III had withdrawn from public life when Rome was liberated in June 1944. But his place had been taken, with the title of Lieutenant-General, by his son Crown Prince Umberto; and although some saw Umberto as untainted by his father's Fascist associations, it soon became clear that the House of Savoy was doomed. In May 1946, King Victor Emmanuel abdicated in favour of Umberto: but it was too late. Three weeks later, in a referendum held on 2 June, Italians opted for a Republic by 12½ million to 10½ million votes. Reading the omens, Toscanini had already made up his mind. In late April, while workmen were still putting the finishing touches to La Scala, the 79-year-old maestro returned to Milan and to the opera house which had been a second home to him since 1898.

Rehearsals started at once; and on 11 May 1946, with the smell of fresh paint still in the air, Arturo Toscanini conducted La Scala's concert of re-dedication. Short-sighted as always, he still relied on his memory rather than the score: but what a memory – and what a reception. From floor to ceiling, the house was full of admirers, applauding and cheering as if they wished the evening would never end. Not far away, in the vast Piazza del Duomo outside the Cathedral, the people of Milan in their tens of thousands listened to loudspeakers relaying the sound. It was a national, a world occasion. La Scala was restored. Toscanini was back. Life had begun again.

'Back to normal' is a powerful idea. 'Return to normalcy' was the slogan that helped the Republican Warren Gamaliel Harding win the US Presidency in 1920, against a Governor of Ohio named James M. Cox and his 38-year-old running mate Franklin Delano Roosevelt. And in the aftermath of World War II, the appeal of 'business as usual' was very strong. The story of the professor who resumed his lectures with the words 'As I was saying when I was interrupted...' may have been apocryphal: but it reflected a general mood. Nor was it altogether a matter of choice. In the chaos of postwar Europe, it was often vital to restore law and order.

In Toulouse after the Liberation, as elsewhere in France, the danger of civil war was averted only by the presence of Commissioners of the Republic appointed by General de Gaulle. In this case, the key figure was an incisive 36-year-old university teacher named Pierre Bertaux, who later became Director-General of the Sûreté Nationale. Years afterwards, he described his experience to the American journalist and historian Theodore H. White:

For weeks, all through the summer of 1944, I was alone. Power is a terrible thing. When you have absolute power you are isolated. No one but the police tell you anything. That's why a *corps d'élus* – call it an assembly, a parliament, a congress – is so important.... The insurrection in Toulouse happened on August 20, 1944; it was weeks and months after that day before law came back.

Not until December 1945, in fact, did Bertaux feel once more the power of Paris, 500 miles away. Then, after rioters had stormed a warehouse, he found that 54 policemen were expecting parcels of stolen sugar. He dismissed them on the spot. Two days later, an order came from Paris: reinstate them pending a full judicial inquiry. It was irksome; but it was a welcome return to the normal rules.

Equally pressing, everywhere, was the need to 'bring the boys home' – not only from the armed forces, and not only the boys. But demobilization was less simple than the slogan suggested. The United States had twelve million men and women in the services, more than half of them overseas. Britain had five million people in uniform; France had to repatriate some two-and-a-half million prisoners and deportees. After World War I, the return to mufti and 'civvy street' had been mismanaged: there had even been mutinies among servicemen kept waiting for release. This time, plans had been made long in advance; in the United States, optimistically, they had begun in 1942. There were complex issues to be settled. How many troops would still be needed to look after occupied territory? How many to cope with prisoners of war, not only in Europe, but also in the Middle East? Long after the war was over, I myself was in charge of some unhappy veterans of the German desert armies, still baking under the Egyptian sun, still dreaming – and singing – of *Heimatland*. What transport would be needed to bring everyone home? What arrangements could be made for their reception? What help would they need to find clothing, shelter, retraining, and jobs?

In the event, of course, there were slip-ups and anomalies; but none was as glaring as after World War I. The Pentagon caused a brief outcry when it proposed to ship veterans of European combat to fight in the Pacific. Britain compounded its own problems by continuing conscription, initially at the rate of 25,000 a month. France felt almost daunted by the size of its task. In early April 1945, Henri Frenay, the Resistance leader and former Army officer who was now Commissioner for Prisoners, Deportees, and Refugees, was delighted but alarmed to hear that Allied aircraft were likely to be flying them into Paris at the rate of 15,000 a day. Working round the clock, Frenay requisitioned and prepared as reception centres such diverse places as the Reuilly barracks, the Vélodrome d'Hiver – itself the scene, earlier, of mass deportations – the Hotel Lutétia, the Rex and Gaumont Palace cinemas, and a large Parisian circus. By the end of the month he had repatriated 330,000 former captives, and within a further month, a million. The millionth homecomer, a tall, fair-haired young man from the French Alps, was driven across Paris, alone and rather bewildered, in an open limousine.

In Britain, there were few limousines to greet returning members of the forces: but there was meticulous preparation. With the exception of 'Class B' releases for builders and others needed for postwar reconstruction, everyone was demobilized according to age and length of service. Women were given cash and coupons to buy civilian clothes. Men, both officers and 'other ranks', were given cardboard boxes. Each contained a 'demob suit', a tie, a pair of shoes, two pairs of socks and – sign of unchanging times – a shirt with two detachable collars, a pair of cuff-links, and a hat. My own outfit, I remember, included an abrasive ginger tweed jacket, a pair of grey flannel trousers, and suède 'brothel-creeper' shoes. Amid standardization, little gestures like that seemed worthwhile.

Some ex-officers found the loss of rank disconcerting – no salutes, no batman, no cheap drink and horseplay in the mess. Others found their old jobs kept warm for them by Government decree, and their wives or sweethearts waiting. Soon, Europe would have a 'baby boom', christened 'the bulge' only when it came of school age. Everywhere, not surprisingly, the great demand now was for housing. In Britain, some home-hunters had to wait weeks even to get an advertisement into the 'classified' columns of the shrunken evening newspapers: one result was that *Dalton's Weekly*, a purely advertising medium, became a best-seller. Some resorted to 'squatting' in empty properties and even in former service camps, a few of which were officially turned into temporary dwellings.

The urgency of the task put housing well before town planning. The British and French Governments both put up prefabricated houses – 'prefabs' – on bombed and other vacant sites. Germany, in particular, was a wasteland of temporary shacks. In France, one visionary planner hoped to launch 'a really great programme'. 'But', he confessed later, 'any allusion to the fact that man in society and his habitat were one single problem, and that housing and town planning were indissolubly linked, was dismissed as utopian. It was a nuisance. The first job was to rebuild.' And while distinguished architects like Auguste Perret were able to rebuild Le Havre and other towns, the most 'advanced' example of collective dwellings, Le

Corbusier's '*Unité d'habitation*' in Marseilles, failed to suit the individualist habits of many ordinary Frenchmen, who preferred the more traditional new houses put up by Emile Aillaud at Creutzwald or Paul Nelson at Noisy-le-Sec. Where people had the choice, in fact, what they wanted was something more like what they had known. In Britain's prosperous outer surburbs, some burned-out villas were painstakingly reconstructed – as the city centres of Warsaw and Dresden were – exactly as they had been before the war. In the first postwar years, the physical rebuilding of Europe was in many respects along traditional lines.

The same was true of less tangible matters. Even some deliberate attempts to make a fresh start involved partial reversions to type. Two new postwar newspapers, one French, one German, each intended as a break with the past, revealed in their different ways the tenacity of tradition. Both, essentially, bore the same title. One was *Le Monde*, the other *Die Welt*.

Le Monde was a child of the Liberation. War and Occupation had weakened and tainted much of France's prewar press; and although some newspapers had survived or been resurrected, while others, like *Combat*, had emerged from the Resistance, in the autumn of 1944 there was still one serious gap: France still had no 'newspaper of record' to match either the London or the New York *Times*. Then, on 19 December, came the first issue of *Le Monde* – a brand-new evening paper, closely printed on a single large-format sheet twice the size of its tabloid page today. Under the title-piece, alongside a report of De Gaulle's Franco-Soviet Pact which characteristically included the treaty's full text, the paper carried an announcement 'To our Readers'. *Le Monde*'s aim, it declared, was to provide 'clear, truthful, and as far as possible rapid and concrete information'. It added:

> But this is no time for merely observing and describing. The peoples of the world are being swept along by a flood of tumultuous and tragic events in which everyone, like it or not, is as much an active participant as a spectator, a beneficiary, or a victim. . . .
> Hackneyed as the word may be, what is needed is a revolution – a revolution by due process of law: one which will restore the greatness and liberty of France through the unity and creative effort of all Frenchmen worthy of the name.

The language seemed to echo that of Albert Camus's *Combat*; but in reality it was of a different stamp. *Le Monde*'s founder, and its director for many years, was the protean Hubert Beuve-Méry, a 42-year-old ex-professor of law, with a square, sombre, thoughtful face slightly reminiscent of the actor Sydney Greenstreet, famous for playing suave, pessimistic villains, as in John Huston's film *The Maltese Falcon*. In American eyes, Beuve-Méry's mistrust of United States policy may sometimes have heightened the resemblance. In fact, however, he was very much a product of the French Catholic Church, and particularly of the progressive-minded Dominican teaching order. During the war, before joining the active Resistance, he had helped to run seminars and colloquies at the medieval mountain retreat of Uriage castle near Grenoble.

And if *Le Monde*'s inspiration was partly Christian, its appearance was almost identical with a prewar newspaper which had been France's closest counterpart to *The Times*: *Le Temps*. Sober, traditional, and conservative, *Le Temps* had been widely regarded as the mouthpiece of French heavy industry as represented by the *Comité des Forges*. During the war, despite this backing, and despite its preoccupation with economic and financial news, the paper had never been collaborationist. Like many others, it had ceased publication in November 1942 when the Nazis had invaded the former Unoccupied Zone in South-Eastern France. Nevertheless, in the climate of Liberation it stood no chance of revival. Some even claimed that the government decree of 1944 banning the reappearance of newspapers which had continued after 26 November 1942, had been drafted precisely to incriminate *Le Temps*, which had not closed until 29 November. Now, at all events, *Le Monde* took over the aged presses that had served *Le Temps*: some of the machinery dated from 1911. This was partly why the new paper looked so strikingly like the old one, with its central main title in Gothic script, flanked by a list of subscription prices, and with tightly-packed columns of small grey print under headlines in tall narrow characters – reminding me, for one, of the narrow windows of tall, grey-roofed nineteenth-century buildings in Baron Haussmann's Paris. Many of *Le Monde*'s original staff, too, had worked on *Le Temps* – including, from 1935 to 1939, Beuve-Méry himself. Their style as journalists, certainly, was in the old tradition. Since the headlines on most stories were complete sentences giving the nub of the news, the 'lead' or first sentence of the text was free to break all the rules of modern American or British reporting: long, allusive, seemingly irrelevant, it often read like the start of a literary essay – as indeed it sometimes was. *Le Monde* was and remains one of Europe's most professional and influential publications; but despite its claim to be 'a new newspaper', it bore and still bears many traces of the now quite distant past.

Die Welt, later owned by the Axel Springer chain, was actually founded by the British. In the lean grey days of Allied Military Government, the Foreign Office was anxious to ensure that Germans should be properly informed. To supervise this task, an obvious candidate was the formidable Sefton Delmer, a large man who spoke fluent German and who in the thirties had been one of the most brilliant and obstreperous reporters on Lord Beaverbrook's *Daily Express*. During the war, Delmer had had an extraordinary career helping to run 'black propaganda', largely through broadcasts in German that purported to come from a series of Nazi radio stations, all of them fictitious. Now, in 1945, Delmer was despatched to start up genuine news and information media for occupied Germany and Austria. He set out with high hopes. Hitler, he thought, had traded on the fact that the German people were basically ill-informed; and this in turn, in Delmer's view, was because their newspapers had been 'unreadable' – pompous, abstract, long-winded, and stodgy. There had been no really outspoken large-scale popular press: the local and provincial papers, with their small circulations, had been too poor to be wholly independent.

Delmer wanted to change all that. He planned to start a punchy vernacular newspaper, midway in style and appearance between the *Daily Telegraph* and the *Daily Express*. His enemies accused him of wanting to copy only the latter. And enemies he had – among the military, who resented Foreign Office 'meddling'; among other officials, put off by Delmer's breezy manner; and among politicians who disliked and distrusted the Beaverbrook press. Despite such motley opposition, Delmer succeeded in establishing a good German news agency, which later became the Deutsche Presse Agentur. But his attempt to found a newspaper failed. When he produced the dummy number of what he proposed to call *Die Norddeutsche Zeitung*, in two alternative formats, both were vetoed from on high. In the subsequent storm, Delmer and four of his British colleagues threw up their jobs. In place of Delmer's brain-child, the authorities produced *Die Welt*, a twice-weekly prestige paper under the supervision of another British journalist, Peter de Mendelssohn. Initially, this was not far from Delmer's original concept: it at least had short paragraphs and sharp sentences. But before long, old national habits proved too powerful. The paragraphs grew longer, the sentences more involved. By the time that Springer bought it in 1950, *Die Welt* was as Anthony Sampson described it eighteen years later – 'beautiful to look at, dull to read'.

In every field, tradition died hard – partly because what many Europeans wanted, consciously or not, was to recover a world they had lost. In music, some of the losses were permanent. At least four outstanding figures had long since settled in the United States. The Austrian-born Arnold Schoenberg had been driven out of Germany, as a Jew and a composer of 'decadent music', as early as 1933. In the same year, Paul Hindemith, banned by the Nazis as musically 'degenerate', had left Berlin for Turkey, then gone to America six years later. Igor Stravinsky had left Paris for the United States in 1939. Béla Bartók had settled there in 1940 – and died in poverty in 1945. Other distinguished veterans, however, like Toscanini himself, now re-emerged.

Pau or Pablo Casals, the great Spanish 'cello virtuoso, was 69 when the war came to an end. In 1940, in protest against General Franco's dictatorship, he had left Spain, never to return. During the later years of the war, he had played in England: now, he was back in France at his modest home in Prades, not far from Perpignan at the Eastern end of the Pyrenees. His apartment was reached by the outside staircase of a small house whose other occupant was the Catalan poet with whom Casals composed his Catalan Mass. Humble though it was, this house on the Route de Ria became a place of pilgrimage; and from 1950 onwards, until he moved to Puerto Rico in 1956, Casals helped organize and conduct an annual Prades Festival. For a man in his seventies, it was a remarkable feat.

Meanwhile, from Garmisch in Bavaria, an 81-year-old composer gave the world the unexpected gift of some fine, late works. This was Richard Strauss, best known for *Der Rosenkavalier* over thirty years before. His last completed opera, in 1942, had been the small-scale *Capriccio*. Although his *Four Last Songs* (1948) were mellowly Romantic, other late works, like the *Concerto for oboe and orchestra* (1946) and the posthumously published sonatinas or *Symphonies for wind*, echoed quite strongly the nostalgia for Mozart and the eighteenth century that had haunted some of his earlier scores. Elsewhere in Germany, moreover, two leading composers now in their forties, both with Mozartian names – Kurt Amadeus Hartmann and Wolfgang Fortner – felt free to undertake another kind of revival, returning to Schoenberg's twelve–tone experimentation, which the Nazis had banned. Perhaps it was typical, too, that Carl Orff, the most solidly original German composer of that generation, born in 1895, should seem on the surface at least, the most backward-looking. Best known nowadays for his settings of medieval songs, *Carmina Burana*, first performed in 1937, he spent the early postwar years working on *Antigone*. This strange work startled and disconcerted me and many others at the Salzburg Festival in the summer of 1949. Consisting mainly of recitative and rhythmic choruses with multiple percussion accompaniment, it sounded in some respects like a throwback to the earliest days of opera, or pre-opera. In fact, it was a word-for-word setting of Friedrich Hölderlin's version of Sophocles's tragedy. Its blend of modernism with scholarly revival now seems characteristic of those postwar years.

Paris, that ageless veteran, was re-emerging too. After four years of gloom and oppression, the capital of France was reviving its claim to be also the capital of Bohemia. Suddenly, the old prewar zest was back in the air... or underground. In the Rue Dauphine, running down from the Carrefour Buci to the Left Bank of the Seine and the Pont-Neuf, there was a late-night bar used mainly by lorry-drivers and printing workers. Here, late one night in November 1945, a weird, ancient vehicle drew up: it was a 1926 six-horsepower Renault looking rather like a World War I armoured car – except that it was painted in a checker-board pattern of black and yellow. Out stepped four young people, casually dressed in roll-necked sweaters and narrow pants: two girls and two boys. They were looking for a place to rehearse a play, to hear jazz, and to dance. The café owner offered them his cellar. Within a few days, they had cleaned it up, installed an out-of-tune piano, and opened a makeshift night-club. They called it Le Tabou. On the piano, a young man played boogie-woogie and bebop: he was the son of the Socialist politician Christian Pineau. In the small space left for dancing, the customers precariously jitterbugged. One of them was a long-haired, doe-eyed 'sweater girl' of sixteen named Juliette Greco. As the club became better known, it attracted such older celebrities as Maurice Chevalier, Marlene Dietrich, Orson Welles, and even Greta Garbo. Soon it had its imitators. One was Le Lorientais, in the Rue des Carmes on the far side of the Boulevard St-Germain, beyond the Boulevard St-Michel. There, Claude Luter ran a jazz group whose trumpeter was the novelist Boris Vian. Another, La Rose Rouge in the nearby Rue de la Harpe, featured as comic singers the moustachioed Frères Jacques, wearing top hats and leotards which made them look like nineteenth-century gymnasts. Once again, the past seemed to have a powerful appeal.

The fashionable term for the habitués of such Left Bank dives was 'existentialists'. It had nothing – or very little – to do with the philosophy of Jean-Paul Sartre, although it undoubtedly helped to spread his fame. Soon, tourists would be coming to gape at the Café de Flore in St-Germain-des-

Près, where in wartime Sartre and Simone de Beauvoir had hurried down to work and talk in the only warm place, behind the sawdust stove. Since then, the Flore had become a general haunt of local writers and painters, as had its neighbour and competitor, Les Deux Magots. Among the writers were Camus, the comic novelist Raymond Queneau, some of whose work was performed by both Juliette Greco and the Frères Jacques, and the film-script writer and popular poet Jacques Prévert, whose *Paroles*, published in 1946, attracted innumerable readers to its haunting if rather facile urban nostalgia and sad pity.

But it was the painters, above all, who signalled the renaissance of Paris; and here, too, the keynote was a return to past traditions. As in music, the removal of Nazi censorship made it possible to revive modernism. The co-founder of the Surrealist Movement, André Breton, who had just published the romantically nostalgic *Arcane 17*, now came back to Paris; and left-wing circles, in particular, once more debated the merits of rival schools: abstract versus figurative, surrealist versus socially committed. Fernand Léger, whose surname in no way suggested either his solid physiognomy or his heavily blocked manner of painting, now made what critics called 'a return to subject-matter', in pictures of static, stylized men of the people at work and play. Léger had spent most of the war years in America; and on his return to Paris, in his mid-sixties, he ran an influential teaching studio, many of whose apprentices were themselves from the United States. Also back in Paris in 1946 was Jean Arp, one of the co-founders of Dada during World War I. It seemed like the reunion of old familiar faces.

One of the most notable was 'the Great Stone Face', as Scott Fitzgerald once described her: the writer, patron, connoisseur, and modern art collector, Gertrude Stein. Her wartime exile had been in Culoz, a village in the Rhône valley. Soon after Paris was liberated, she hired a local charcoal-burning taxi to drive her all the way home with her luggage, her maid, and her faithful companion Alice B. Toklas. It was dark, and twenty-four hours later, when they reached their old apartment in the narrow street near the Pont-Neuf,

there at last was the Rue Christine, and out we got and in we came. Yes, it was the same, so much more beautiful, but it was the same.

It was indeed: her astonishing collection of pictures, bought so long ago so comparatively cheaply, was intact. The Cézannes, the Renoirs, the Gauguins, the Matisses, the Picassos, the Daumier, the El Greco, and the

Toulouse-Lautrec – all these and many more were still there, crowded on the walls like a giant album of stamps. She went on:

Picasso has been impatiently waiting our return. He came in the next morning and we were very moved when we embraced, and we kept saying it is a miracle, all the treasures which made our youth, the pictures, the drawings, the objects, all there.

Picasso himself, now sixty-four years old, was living not far away, at No. 7 Rue des Grands-Augustins, a little nearer to Notre-Dame, in an apartment and studio crowded among other things with books, antiques, plants, sculptures, musical instruments, and cage-birds. One of his first visitors, at the Liberation, had been another old-timer, Ernest Hemingway, now a war correspondent: as a present, he left a case of hand grenades. Hemingway's visit was followed by that of countless GIs: for Picasso had now become, as his companion Françoise Gilot put it, 'the man of the hour'. The Autumn Salon of 1944 showed a retrospective exhibition of his work. Next, in June 1945, came a smaller post-Liberation show entitled 'Picasso Libre'. That year's Autumn Salon was a retrospective of the 76-year-old Henri Matisse, who was still producing work almost as fresh as Picasso's. In January 1946, yet another retrospective show was devoted to the short-lived genius of Amedeo Modigliani, who had been dead for twenty-five years. It seemed as if Paris was poring over its souvenirs.

There was more novelty in the theatre. Already, under the Occupation, it had flourished quite unexpectedly, bringing to the fore such younger talents as those of Jean-Louis Barrault, Jean Vilar, and Gérard Philippe, and introducing Sartre's first two plays: *Les mouches*, based on Greek mythology, and the claustrophobic *Huis clos*. After the Liberation, it was the turn of Camus to be tempted by the footlights. As well as various adaptations, including a version of Dostoevsky's *The Possessed*, he now produced the first of four plays of his own, *Le malentendu* in 1944, followed a year later by *Caligula*, with Gérard Philippe in the title role.

Striking and accomplished as Sartre's and Camus's first postwar plays were, they could hardly fail to reflect the grimness of the recent past. In 'existentialist' Paris, I sometimes felt, it was impossible to be both intelligent and optimistic: only folly or forgetfulness could ever make anyone happy. It was no coincidence, perhaps, that one of the biggest theatrical successes at that time was the 1946 production of *La folle de Chaillot*, by the late Jean Giraudoux, whose heroine triumphs by virtue of being 'mad'. As one critic remarked, the play belonged in some respects to the prewar period; and its popularity was partly due to its brilliant director, the sharp-eyed, bleak-faced Louis Jouvet, now 58, and only recently returned from spending the war years in South America.

Before the war, although mainly a stage actor, Jouvet had begun to make his name in the cinema. His glittering performance as the sly priest in Jacques Feyder's *La Kermesse Héroïque*, in 1935, had led to roles in a number of other notable films by Jean Renoir, Julien Duvivier, and Marcel Carné. Now, for the prolific Christian-Jaque, he made his first film in postwar France. Its title, *Un Revenant* – 'A Ghost from the Past' – was apt.

Close observers had certainly seen something ghostly in French films made during the last winter before the Liberation: the studios were so cold that the actors' breath turned to mist unless they were given ice-cubes to suck. But now other ghosts were re-emerging. *Sylvie et le Fantôme* was one of them – a slight and escapist fantasy by Claude Autant-Lara, chiefly memorable now because Jacques Tati played a minor role in it. Tati also had a small part in Autant-Lara's next film, *Le Diable au Corps*, with Gérard Philippe playing the very young lover of an older married woman in a fine, delicate adaptation of Raymond Radiguet's novel, set in 1918. Radiguet, who had died in 1923 aged only twenty, had been a friend of that gaunt, febrile master-of-all-trades Jean Cocteau. During World War II, Cocteau had written some scripts for the cinema, but he had not made a film of his own since his avant-garde début with *Le Sang d'un Poète* in 1930. Some people dismissed him as an *enfant terrible* who had outlived his epoch: but now, all of 57 and looking to one unkind observer 'like an aged cockatoo', he made a sustained and astonishing comeback. In 1946, he wrote and directed *La Belle et la Bête*, a magically lush and dreamlike adaptation of the fairy-tale, with camerawork by Henri Alekan and costumes by the artistic director Christian Bérard. For many, the film's most lasting image was that of Cocteau's companion Jean Marais, in full feline make-up as the lonely and unhappy Beast.

Cocteau's next film was less remarkable: an adaptation of his rather Ruritanian stage play *L'Aigle à Deux Têtes*. Only later, when he placed perennial themes in contemporary settings – in *Les Enfants Terribles*, *Les Parents Terribles*, and *Orphée* – did Cocteau reveal unmistakably his mastery of cinema. But in 1946 and 1947, period and costume drama still had immense nostalgic appeal. During the Occupation, Marcel Carné had made two historical films, both with his script-writer Jacques Prévert. One, made in 1942, was *Les Visiteurs du Soir*, an elegant and beguiling medieval allegory. The other was *Les Enfants du Paradis*, with Arletty, Jean-Louis Barrault, and

Pierre Brasseur: a less 'cinematic' film, but a loving and lavish-looking slice of theatre life in nineteenth-century Paris. When finally released in 1945, it proved that the past was a horn of plenty for audiences starved of passion, turmoil, and spectacle – all provided, in this instance, by ingenious stopgap means. And still more ghosts from the past were called forth when René Clair, now in his late forties, returned from wartime exile in America and began planning his first postwar French film, the rather mannered and careful *Le Silence est d'Or*, set in 1906.

There were, of course, exceptions. Another wartime exile now back in Paris, Julien Duvivier, chose a contemporary subject in 1946 for *Panique*, an absurdly self-parodying melodrama; while in *Falbalas* and *Antoine et Antoinette* Jacques Becker began to explore life in modern Paris with fastidious, penetrating eyes. The Resistance, too, supplied the subject for René Clement's powerful semi-documentary, *La Bataille du Rail*: but Resistance themes were done to death by lesser directors, churning out countless implausible adventure-yarns.

Films in Britain at that time catered for a similar escapist demand. Ghosts, quite literally, dominated *Dead of Night*, an eerie 'episode' film produced in 1945 by Michael Balcon and variously directed by Alberto Cavalcanti, Charles Crichton, Basil Dearden, and Robert Hamer. Any British film at about that time seemed likely to feature either Mervyn Johns looking mystical or Margaret Lockwood in a plumed period hat. Lavish historical spectacle reached its apogee with Gabriel Pascal's £1¼-million *Caesar and Cleopatra*; but minor romance and costume melodramas abounded. Against the soft-focus background of films like *The Wicked Lady*, *The Seventh Veil*, and *Madonna of the Seven Moons*, Noël Coward began to look like a social realist. In 1945, continuing a collaboration with Coward that had begun with *In Which We Serve* three years earlier, David Lean made two Coward adaptations in quick succession. One, *Blithe Spirit*, was a sparkling supernatural comedy. The other was *Brief Encounter*, the tale of a platonic unhappy love affair between two middle-aged people, both separately married, meeting furtively in railway refreshment rooms and the like. After seeing it, the critic Richard Winnington noted that four different people had said to him 'It was more like a French film' – meaning, he thought, that it was 'emotionally grown-up'. In fact, it was restrained, earnest, and perhaps a little dim, with awkward touches of class-conscious humour. Many at the time, however, some of them facing similar agonies after wartime separation, found *Brief Encounter*'s understated pathos very moving.

Far more impressive, then and in retrospect, was the film with which David Lean followed it: *Great Expectations*. This introduced to the screen the young Alec Guinness. It also proved, as David Lean put it, that Charles Dickens was a brilliant script-writer. Nor was it surprising, in the mood of the time, that Lean's best film, and one of the best of that whole period, should be a spirited version of a novel by the nineteenth century's greatest popular entertainer. Writing in 1947 in the second issue of *Sequence*, the Oxford University Film Society's magazine which he had helped to found, Lindsay Anderson scolded middle-brow escapists who 'demand nothing more from the cinema than . . . light entertainment.' Like it or not, they were the vast majority. All over Western Europe, films were enjoying their postwar heyday. There were bad times just around the corner, as Noël Coward's song was to put it: but for the present the queues went on forming outside the cinemas, waiting to see the cartoon, the newsreel, the advertisements, the trailers, the second features, and at last the big picture – a full evening's family worship of those household gods, the stars.

The great names in literature were honoured in others ways. In 1939, the Nobel Prize awards had been interrupted. The Prizes for science were resumed in 1943; but the Peace Prize had to wait another year – it went to the Red Cross. The 1944 Prize for literature was awarded to the 71-year-old Danish novelist, poet, and visionary essayist Johannes Vilhelm Jensen, prophet of what might be called 'the Nordic twilight'. The 1945 Prizewinner was the Chilean poet Gabriela Mistral; but then, in the three following years, the Swedish Academy's choice fell on three key figures in Europe's postwar literary scene.

The first was Hermann Hesse, the German-born author of *Der Steppenwolf*, now 69, who had been a Swiss citizen since 1923. From his mountain retreat at Montagnola near Lake Lugano, too frail to travel, he wrote to express his thanks for 'this last great gift':

In honouring me with the Nobel Prize, you have at the same time honoured the German language and the German contribution to world culture. In this I see a gesture of conciliation and goodwill, a move to restore and enlarge cultural cooperation among peoples.

To friends in Germany he wrote:

I have grown old and tired, and the destruction of my work, begun by Hitler's ministries and completed by American bombs, has given my last years a ground bass of disillusionment and sorrow. My consolation is that an occasional little melody rises above the ground bass, and that there are still hours when I am able to dwell in the timeless. . . .

Among the good things which I am *still* able to enjoy, which still give me pleasure and compensate for the dark side, are the rare but undeniable indications that an authentic spiritual Germany lives on.... I thank you for it. Preserve the seed, keep faith with the light and the spirit. There are very few of you, but you may be the salt of the earth.

Here and there, indeed, German writers were beginning the long task of coming to terms with the nightmare past. Two of them on the far Left, Alfred Andersch and Hans Werner Richter, who had both been prisoners of war in the United States, jointly edited a polemical magazine, *Der Ruf*, which eventually was banned by the Allied authorities. They thereupon founded, partly in protest, partly as a substitute, the *Gruppe '47* or '1947 Group', a loose-knit but at times highly effective left-wing pressure-group of writers, which was later to include such major figures as Heinrich Böll and Günter Grass. But their great works were as yet unpublished; and the immediate postwar years in German writing were marked by a kind of dazed documentary, groping back towards normality after too long a season in hell.

Although sadly infirm, the lean, thin-lipped, round-spectacled Hermann Hesse strikingly resembled the next Nobel Prizewinner, André Gide, diarist, critic, novelist of the '*acte gratuit*', and co-founder of the influential *Nouvelle Revue Française*. Since mid-1942, he had been in North Africa, and after the Liberation he made a leisurely and roundabout return. 'He is boyishly demure, demurely boyish,' remarked one of those who met him shortly after the war, 'and he is almost eighty years of age!' Back in Paris, he renewed old acquaintances. The playwright and novelist Jules Romains was there; so was Georges Duhamel. Colette, author of the 'Claudine' novels, was still living with her second husband Maurice Goudeket in their Palais-Royal apartment, arthritic but still coquettish, claiming to be 73 instead of 76. She telephoned Gide with birthday greetings, and invited him to call. 'No doubt I shall go,' he wrote: 'but knowing only too well that after the first effusiveness we shall have nothing to say.'

But the social round was hard to avoid. At one small luncheon party, Gide met André Maurois, biographer, novelist, and creator of 'Colonel Bramble'. Maurois's real name was Emile Herzog: as a Jew, he had spent the war years in England and America. Now in his sixties, he had returned to Paris in the autumn of 1946. Among the first of the old friends he rediscovered were the Catholic writers Paul Claudel and François Mauriac, both veteran fellow-members of the Academy, official custodian of the French language. The Old Guard of letters was beginning to re-form.

On 1 November 1946, André Gide let himself be driven to the theatre, somewhat against his better judgment. Laurence Olivier and the Old Vic company were visiting Paris in Olivier's New Theatre production of *King Lear*, with Alec Guinness as the Fool. The Franco-British entente, assisted perhaps by De Gaulle's retirement nearly a year before, and soon to be sealed by the Treaty of Dunkirk, seemed to be bearing fruit – an example of Hesse's 'cultural co-operation among peoples', then relatively novel. It was certainly necessary. Gide found *King Lear* utterly alien – 'almost execrable', 'the least good of Shakespeare's great tragedies', 'absurd from beginning to end'. But even he could not resist the performance: when the curtain fell, he joined in the general ovation for Olivier and the company.

In Britain, the production had had its critics; but it was generally taken as further evidence that the British theatre was alive and well. Soon, indeed, the theatre would tempt back the last of our three Nobel Prizewinners, the American-born British poet Thomas Stearns Eliot.

Only recently, Eliot had at last published as a whole the separate sections of his *Four Quartets*: 'Burnt Norton', 'East Coker', 'The Dry Salvages', and 'Little Gidding'. In the last of them he had written

> A people without history
> Is not redeemed from time, for history is a pattern
> Of timeless moments. So, while the light fails
> On a winter's afternoon, in a secluded chapel
> History is now and England.

The elegiac sense of oneness with the past was apt for a poem's ending; but the lines reflected an insight deep in the well of Eliot's spirit, and one which many, less articulately, shared. Tradition was vital, and widely felt to be vital. Men found strength as well as refuge, inspiration as well as escape, in remembrance of the past. This was why Olivier's 1944 film of *Henry V* had meant so much, when British soldiers were once more fighting in the fields of France. Some inkling of that awareness may even have touched the millions who enjoyed historical tushery like *The Wicked Lady*. And it certainly helped account for one wartime and postwar feature of the British theatre, which already owed so much to Shakespeare: the effort to revive 'poetic drama'.

T.S. Eliot himself had already practised it. His first two plays, *The Rock* and *Murder in the Cathedral*, had been written for the church, not the stage. But in 1939, in *The Family Reunion*, he had used a conventional, contemporary, naturalistic setting for a verse drama on the model of the ancient Greeks. Ten years later, at the Edinburgh Festival, he was to do the same in *The Cocktail Party*, followed later still by *The Confidential Clerk* and *The Elder Statesman*. Meanwhile, others had been working in a similar, but far from identical vein – notably Ronald Duncan in *This Way to the Tomb*, Anne Ridler in *The Shadow Factory*, and Christopher Fry in *A Phoenix Too Frequent*, all put on by the Pilgrim Players at the Mercury Theatre in Notting Hill. Duncan, Anne Ridler, and Fry, like Eliot himself, were all religious writers: the style and content of their work was in sharp contrast to the political verse dramas of the nineteen-thirties. Its feeling was romantic and numinous: it sought to cast spells; and in the case of Christopher Fry it was also witty and playfully archaic, crying out for spindly illustrations by Rex Whistler. 'What we have seen', wrote the *New Statesman*'s theatre critic, T.C. Worsley, 'is the development in the theatre-going public of a new hunger for the fantastic and the romantic, for the expanded vision and the stretched imagination, in short for the larger-than-life.'

At its most serious, this was a return to tradition: it accorded with Eliot's Anglo-Catholic strictness, and found visual expression in italic handwriting or the fine austere carved lettering of Reynolds Stone. At the other extreme it reflected a new, would-be elegant frivolity – a reaction to the grimness of wartime and the earnestness of postwar planners. There was a great vogue, now, for Angela Thirkell's novels of 'gracious living', for revivals of Ronald Firbank, and for the mask of crusty defiance assumed by Evelyn Waugh, whose early novels had seemed zestfully destructive, but whose *Brideshead Revisited*, published in 1945, made quite explicit his Catholic and romantic conservatism.

The general mood, as I remember it, was not so much a taste for the archaic as a renewed delight in what had so long been missing. It echoed more mundane rediscoveries: tangerines, bananas, and pineapples in the shops; fresh paint on the buildings; the statue of Eros back in Piccadilly; Covent Garden re-opening with the Sadler's Wells Ballet in – appropriately – *The Sleeping Beauty*; the first Antique Dealers' Fair since 1938; the first MCC cricket team to visit Australia for ten years, captained by Wally Hammond, who had first played for England in 1925. And for some returning servicemen and others, re-discovery included surprise. On 18 December 1946, Duff Cooper re-visited the House of Commons. He had been a Member of Parliament himself before the war.

I suffered no nostalgia. On the contrary, I felt like an older boy who revisits his preparatory school and despises the folly of it. The same foolish questions, the same silly laughter, the same childish anger and quarrels still going on.

Coming out of the army to read for a degree in history, I myself was amused to discover, as I wrote in a magazine at the time,

alongside the new democratic Cambridge an older, more exclusive phantom – a hard, bright unapproachable world of superior young men straight from the pre-Renaissance public schools, polished and elderly at eighteen, regarding their tutors and supervisors with worldly tolerance, and hardly regarding their lesser contemporaries at all.

'They are beginning to dress for dinner again in London,' wrote one glowing reporter. In Paris, the Tour d'Argent and the Véfour restaurants were flourishing while, to the chagrin of purists, the modernist magazine *Art et Décoration* began to discuss antiques. Early in 1947, the former Conservative MP Harold Nicolson went over to the Labour Party. His mother, Lady Carnock, took it as 'a cruel blow'. 'I never thought that I should see the day', she said, 'when one of my own sons betrayed his country.' Nicolson's brother, the second Lord Carnock, added: 'I suppose you will now resign from all your clubs.' Was he, perhaps, joking? A few months later, on 10 July 1947, Nicolson noted in his dairy:

At lunch at the Beefsteak we have an amusing talk about clique accents. There was the intonation of the Devonshire House circle, the nasal drawl of the ultras, the 1890 voice, the Bright People voice, the Bloomsbury voice and now the Bowra voice [after Maurice Bowra, Warden of Wadham College, Oxford].
    Then I go to Buckingham Palace for the garden party. It is raining slightly, but I wear my top-hat.... Everybody is straining to see the bridal pair – irreverently and shamelessly straining.

The 'bridal pair' were Princess Elizabeth and Philip Mountbatten, whose engagement had been announced that morning. It was a great event, and an index of how little had changed. In Eastern Europe, the prewar monarchies had been swept away. Elsewhere, much had depended on the conduct of the monarch. In Italy, Victor Emmanuel's Fascist connexions had led to his downfall; in Belgium, King Leopold was under attack for having surrendered in May 1940 and not having gone into exile during the war. Eventually, he was forced to abdicate in favour of his son Baudouin. But in Britain, Denmark, Norway, Sweden, the Netherlands, and Luxembourg, as well as Monaco and Liechtenstein, royal families were still on the throne – a living embodiment of Europeans' feeling for tradition.

In a number of ways, then, the European victors of World War II seemed to be returning to normal. But there were also signs of strain. One was their slight air of trying too hard, protesting too much that all was well.

'Britain Can Make It' was the title of a big official exhibition staged in London at the Victoria and Albert Museum in the autumn of 1946. Designed by a young Scottish architect, Basil Spence, it put on display 6,000 products from 1,300 firms now released from war work. Huge queues waited to see it; but at that time almost every item was marked 'For export only'.

A few years later saw another, much more spectacular show on a similar patriotic theme: the Festival of Britain. Plans for it had begun when the war had scarcely ended. Already in 1943 the Royal Society of Arts had privately suggested that the Great Exhibition of 1851 be marked by a centenary; and in September 1945 Gerald Barry, editor of the *News Chronicle*, proposed it publicly to the President of the Board of Trade, Sir Stafford Cripps. Although Cripps was commonly regarded as the fanatical father of 'austerity', he fed the idea into the Government machine. After long rumination, and a timely intervention by Cripps's successor Herbert Morrison – himself a patriotic Londoner – the project began to emerge in a series of weird shapes on the South Bank of the Thames. They included a Dome of Discovery, 365 feet across, to keep the rain off the scientific exhibits, and the 'Skylon' – a striking but purely decorative exclamation mark in the sky, held up by thin cables. The designers, headed by Hugh Casson and Mischa Black, filled the site with fountains, walkways, grilles, screens, and every kind of ornament. There were sculptures, murals, and mobiles by such artists as Henry Moore, Barbara Hepworth, Jacob Epstein, Graham Sutherland, and Feliks Topolski. There was a water-mobile imitating waves on the seashore; and there were popular attractions. These included open-air dancing, a tree walk alongside a forty-foot Chinese dragon, and a quaint little railway based on the comic drawings of Rowland Emett in *Punch*.

The Festival was accounted a great success. It certainly left a permanent legacy – the Royal Festival Hall. Eight-and-a-half million people attended it and enjoyed it. I was one of them. But although it was innocent and jolly and novel, with a kind of dainty airport elegance, it had one feature that jarred. It exuded self-congratulation in a way that smacked of the 1949 Ealing comedies *Whisky Galore* and *Passport to Pimlico*. Those films, produced by Michael Balcon and backed and distributed by J. Arthur Rank, were popular, bright, and original – almost as much so as their stable-mates *Kind Hearts and Coronets* and *The Man in the White Suit*. But, to my mind at least, they suffered from one all-pervasive weakness: their portrait of the British was appallingly smug.

Seen through those Ealing lenses, what a race of knobbly paragons we were – this happy breed in our right little, tight little island, getting tighter still on shipwrecked whisky, and even more insular within the frontiers of independent Pimlico. Lovable, eccentric, even daft, but utterly dependable and always successful in the end: it was a self-image all the more addictive for being partly true.

In May 1943, watching the Victory Parade in Tunis, and seeing the tough sunburnt men of the First and Eighth Armies march past to the sound of all the pipers they could muster, Harold Macmillan had cast his mind back to Kitchener's Army and the men who had fought the battle of the Somme:

I had always thought that these were the finest British formations that had ever taken the field. But now I had to admit that the First and Eighth Armies were just as good. These men seemed that day masters of the world and heirs of the future.

It was a far cry from that proud parade in Tunis to Ealing Studios and the Emett railway on the South Bank. If all was now well with a Britain returned to normal, did we really have to pat ourselves so cosily on the back?

The same question, in a different form, might well have been asked of the French. That 'France could make it' would soon be evident in such triumphs as the design and production of the Mystère jet. But in 1947, when Paris startled the world with what came to be called 'the New Look', was there not in that gamble an element of whistling in the dark?

The challenge was flung down at 10.30 on the morning of 12 February 1947, in a sumptuous grey-and-gilt salon at No. 30, Avenue Montaigne. It was an overcast day, and bitterly cold: but no one seemed to mind waiting in the street to be admitted, three at a time so that invitations could be checked, to the first independent fashion show put on by Christian Dior.

A calm, methodical, balding man in his forties with prim lips and gentle eyes, Dior looked less like a couturier than a cultivated banker, diplomat, or composer. In his youth, the child of wealthy parents, he had indeed studied music, and later in life wrote the score for a ballet, for which he also designed the costumes. After a time at the Ecole des Sciences Politiques, he had opened a picture gallery, showing among other things work by Matisse and Picasso. Then had come disaster. The Wall Street crash of 1929 had ruined the Dior family – and Dior himself had contracted tuberculosis. After a long convalescence, he had tried his hand at dress designing. He was just beginning to sell some of his drawings – for 20 francs each – and get them published in the press, when war and the fall of France put an end to his hopes. Still virtually penniless, he went to stay with his father, who had a small house in the country. To support themselves, they grew and sold vegetables. At length, a friend introduced him to the Paris designer and perfumer Lucien Lelong. Dior joined him for the next five years. In Paris, he also made the acquaintance of Marcel Boussac, the textile magnate, who had been planning to revive an ailing fashion house, and proposed to Dior that he should run it. Firmly but courteously, Dior refused: he wanted a house of his own. Eventually Boussac agreed to back it. He never regretted the decision. Within a few months, Dior and his dresses were the talk of Paris, London, and New York.

In Dior's *belle-époque* salon, on that bleak February morning in 1947, all talk stopped when the first model appeared.

For several years, women had dressed like soldiers – in square-shouldered, boxy, utilitarian clothes, with longish straight-cut jackets and short, dumpy-looking skirts. Some even wore military-type hats. One of Dior's Paris rivals, the house of Schiaparelli, had made a virtue of austerity by exaggerating the style. And Paris itself, once the centre of world fashion, was now no longer supreme. Its European markets had shrunk; and outside Europe, American firms and even British designers like Norman Hartnell had begun to compete in what was still a multi-million-dollar business.

Now, in a matter of hours, Dior reversed both trends.

His models no longer looked like soldiers: they looked like women – and women from the opulent past. They wore long, full skirts; their dresses had soft, moulded shoulders, with delicious curves, waists, hips, bosoms; yards of luxurious tissue wrapped them round. Strangest of all in 1947, they wore rustling petticoats. It was a sound from a vanished world.

Soon, all was telegrams and congratulations – and anger. In Britain, the radical *Picture Post* was reproving. 'Paris forgets this is 1947,' it declared.

Straight from the indolent and wealthy years before the 1914 war come this year's much-discussed Paris fashions. They are launched upon a world which has not the material to copy them – and whose women have neither the money to buy, the leisure to enjoy, nor in some designs even the strength to support, these masses of elaborate material.

Sir Stafford Cripps suggested a boycott of 'the New Look' in order to save cloth. The large Mrs Bessie Braddock, MP, called the fashion 'the ridiculous whim of idle people'. 'Ludicrous', 'preposterous', and 'over-sexy' were other terms of would-be abuse. In the United States, there was even pressure to keep out any foreign magazines and newspapers that featured the dread garments. 'Out of one Paris model you can cut two American dresses,' it was claimed.

In the end, of course, Dior won. By 1949, the house of Dior was responsible for 75 percent of France's fashion exports, and 5 percent of French exports as a whole. And within only weeks of his launching 'the New Look', nearly all the Paris houses had adopted something similar. 'Femininity' was back. But, in some places, feelings still ran high. When Dior visited Chicago, he faced placards bearing the legend: 'Mr Dior – we abhor – dresses to the floor.' And in the poorer districts of Paris, some women wearing 'the New Look' were actually set upon, physically, by angry working-class housewives.

Their fury was understandable. In the Europe of 1947, 'the New Look' was like a slap in the face. For despite nearly two years of peace, most Europeans were still hungry, shabby, and cold – some of them even more so than during the war.

Rationing was universal, partly because of the world shortage of food. In 1945, admittedly, North America had had a bumper wheat crop: but world food production had been 12 percent below normal, and European production 25 percent down. In the first half of 1946, wheat supplies had been 7 million tons short of what the importing countries had hoped. In Asia, the rice crop was 15 percent below normal; and to prevent famine, thousands of tons of wheat were diverted from Europe to the Far East. As US President Harry S. Truman wrote later, 'More people faced starvation and even death for want of food during the year following the war than during all the war years combined.'

To save wheat, all sorts of measures were tried. The United States raised its flour extraction rate to 80 percent, and Britain to 85 percent – producing a dun-coloured, roughage-packed loaf which one master baker dismissed as '35 percent cattle food'. This in turn left little residue for feed grains, and so affected the output of pork, poultry, and eggs. In April 1946, Britain ran short of even 'austerity' flour. The bakers advised aerating the dough to make lighter loaves look no smaller; but the Ministry of Food refused. When the smaller loaves appeared, people simply bought more of them: so finally, bread was rationed – a privation never imposed on Britain during the war. In

France, in the following year, with the prospect of a grain harvest half the 1946 total, the Government reduced the bread ration below even its wartime level, to only 200 grams a day.

Nor was bread the only food in short supply. By the end of 1947, weekly rations in Britain were below the wartime average: 13 ounces of meat, 8 of sugar, 6 of butter or margarine, 1½ of cheese, one of cooking fat, two pints of milk, and one solitary egg. Most other foods were rationed on a 'points' system, which allowed for choice, but not abundance. In France, successive governments tried varying combinations of rationing and price control; but for those who could not afford black-market prices, the results were little better. With a weekly meat ration sometimes as low as 150 grams, butchers were allowed to open only three days a week, later reduced to two. Eating out was no solution for the poor in France or the hungry in Great Britain. In France, although produce seemed plentiful, prices were exorbitant. The uncertainty of gas supplies made cooking precarious; electricity cuts were frequent; in Paris, especially, dimmed lights and 'brown-outs' were a matter of course. Coffee was still often *ersatz*, if no longer made from acorns, and even deliveries of wine were erratic. In Britain, inured to a five-shilling maximum charge for lunch and six shillings for dinner, restaurant customers were less demanding. In contrast to some makeshift meat dishes and to the notorious South African tinned fish, snoek, unrationed whale steak seemed succulent, although some gourmets complained that it tasted of oil. But when bread was made one of the standard three courses allowed at any restaurant meal, sweet-toothed Englishmen were furious. If they wanted bread with their soup, they would have to go without their pudding.

Restrictions led to evasion. In France, dealers flouted price controls; and although the Government uncovered major scandals in the wine trade, in sugar, potatoes, vegetables, fruit, meat, and almost every other saleable commodity, the black market and the '*système D*' continued to bend the rules. In Rome, a friendly policeman, of all people, once offered me illegally imported American cigarettes. Even in Britain there were scandals. The most publicized was the subject of the Lynskey Tribunal, a judicial inquiry into the colourful and devious activities of Sidney Stanley, a Polish-born 'business agent' otherwise known, at various times, not only as Solomon Koszycki, Schlomo Rechtand, and Sid Wulkan, but also – at bankruptcy hearings – as Blotts. Stanley, a pale, stocky figure with heavy-lidded eyes and an evasive manner, claimed to have bribed a junior Minister, whose career was duly ruined; but all that could be proved against him was mythomania.

For substantial 'considerations', he had boasted, he could secure import licences, paper quotas, or other illegal favours, from various 'influential friends'. But if Stanley was an exception, 'fiddling' – minor infringement of the regulations – was fairly general. 'Spivs' – usually shifty-looking men in flashy suits, with loud ties, side-whiskers, and two-tone shoes – sold nylon stockings, cigarettes, razor-blades, and even gin from illicit street barrows or quickly-closing suitcases. Scarce luxuries regularly 'fell off lorries'. Back-street cafés did a roaring trade in dubious shish-kebab.

Illegal, unfair, and socially divisive as all this may have been, a 1947 'austerity' meal in France or Britain would have seemed a banquet elsewhere. One Austrian I knew, now a professor, weighed only 110 pounds in 1947. For their midday meal, he and his family had nothing to eat but spinach, flavoured with salt. It cost him a whole month's wages to buy a loaf of black-market bread. In Germany, Italy, and many other countries, especially in Eastern Europe, his story could be multiplied by millions. In Norway in 1947, the daily food ration was reduced from 2,500 to 2,200 calories; and in Germany, conditions were immeasurably worse. There, the meagre rations had already had to be cut in the spring of 1946 – to 1,275 calories a day in the US occupation zone, and to 1,040 in the British. This was about a fifth of the amount needed by a physically active man. It was no wonder that the British Prime Minister Clement Attlee, although under pressure to ease 'austerity' at home, felt obliged to ship 400,000 tons of food to Germany. As he wrote to President Truman,

> The ration there is already very low and substantial further cuts will bring starvation and unrest, which, apart from humanitarian considerations, will increase our military commitments and retard Europe's economic recovery by reducing the export of essential supplies from Germany, particularly the coal which is so urgently needed.

Coal, in 1947, was still Europe's most vital source of energy, supplying ninety percent of her needs. Incredible as it seems over thirty years later, oil played only a minor role in the economy: total consumption in Western Europe was less than 13 million tons. If factories were to produce, cities to be lighted, homes to be warmed, it was coal that would have to fuel them; and in 1947 European production was only three-quarters of what it had been in 1939. This was better than the 1945 figure of less than 60 percent; but the shortfall was still a staggering 114 million tons.

At the best of times, this would have meant costly imports from America, shortages, shivering, power cuts, and gloom. But the winter of 1946–7 was not the best of times: the weather made it nearly the worst. Suddenly, Western Europe felt like Siberia. And when the temperature eased slightly, there followed the biggest blizzard for more than fifty years. Roads and railways were blocked by snowdrifts; villages, farms, and factories were cut off. In places, the drifts were tree-top high. Then came a slight thaw – then a further freeze-up. Canals and locks were covered with thick ice; roads became skating-rinks; much of industry came to a halt. Worst of all, the weather paralysed the coal mines. Even when miners could dig their way in, they found the winding-gear frozen solid; and when at length the thaw came and the snow melted, one final hazard was still awaiting them: floodwater in the pits. Even then, the weather had not finished with Europe. That summer, for the second year in succession, it shrivelled much of the harvest with drought. And as if Nature had not done enough damage, those same ruinous months saw industry further crippled by a long series of strikes.

Some of them were inspired by Communists. In France, in May 1947, the Socialist Prime Minister Paul Ramadier had won a vote of confidence for his policy of price cuts, a wage freeze, and increased productivity, then dismissed the five Communist ministers who opposed it. The Party retaliated with further strikes. But unrest had begun already on account of genuine grievances: hunger, poverty, unemployment, rising prices. And behind it all, in Britain, Italy, and other countries as well as France, was a deep, unexpressed sense of disappointment. Where were the social changes that so many had hoped for? What had become of the 'peaceful revolution'? Social security, the health service, and the rest were advances, certainly: but what essential difference had nationalization made? In many nationalized industries, the same managers still sat in the same offices; not all of them even had different titles. Theoretically, every such state enterprise was now owned by the people; but they felt no pride or power of possession: they had even less influence than shareholders in a firm.

Above all, they were still living in austerity and crisis; and Europe was still living from hand to mouth. This was the heart of the matter. Behind all the brave claims and gestures, behind the revival of art and letters and brittle civilization, lay one stark truth revealed by one harsh winter. The countries of Western Europe were going broke.

Already during the war they had had to live on credit. By October 1945, under the Lend-Lease Act, the United States had advanced what amounted to more than $46,000 million in non-returnable loans – $30,000 million of them to the British Empire. The other main recipients had been Soviet

Russia, France, the Netherlands, Greece, Belgium, Norway, Turkey, and Yugoslavia.

With the end of the war, Lend-Lease had abruptly stopped – and at once there had been panic. Country after country sent its emissaries hurrying to Washington: men like Jean Monnet for France, or Lord Keynes for Britain. One after another, they secured stopgap loans – a huge credit of $3,750 million for Britain, three loans totalling $1,920 million for France, smaller sums for the Soviet Union, the Netherlands, the Netherlands East Indies, and Belgium. Canada, too, loaned $1,250 million to Britain, $240 million to France, $100 million to Belgium, and $140 million to the Netherlands East Indies. For the time being, at the cost of some national pride, the situation was saved.

Of all these debtors, Britain felt her pride the most deeply wounded – the one country in Europe which had not only won the war, but stood alone against the Axis, and kept her territory intact. Now, she had to do the bidding of the Americans. To meet the conditions of her loan agreement, she was obliged to make sterling convertible: from 15 July 1947, those who held pounds were free to change them into dollars. As soon as it happened, speculators fled from the pound. In July, Britain's reserves were drained at the rate of $115 million a week. In August, this increased to $150 million; in the third week of August alone, $237 million were lost. On 20 August, Britain suspended convertibility, five weeks after it had begun. Had she not done so, it was reckoned, the entire American loan would have run out by the end of October.

As it was, one-third of the loan had been effectively wiped out by price rises in the United States; and Britain's own overseas expenditure was still alarmingly high. In addition to buying food, fuel, and raw materials, she had heavy foreign commitments. In 1946, she had spent $60 million trying to feed the German people; in only the first quarter of 1947, it had cost as much again. While her own industries lacked manpower, she was still maintaining a million-and-a-half men in the armed services, guarding outposts of the Empire, and acting as policemen and administrators in troubled areas of India, Egypt, Palestine, and Greece.

Looking back, it may be tempting to condemn the British for over-stretching themselves – just as it is to blame Britain and other European countries for the network of national restrictions with which they hampered their postwar trade and their collective recovery. But few things are harder than shedding ancient habits, including the habit of trying to preserve world peace; and few things are less natural for nations than to see their separate problems as facets of a common plight. Some may smile indulgently at the spectacle of Europe's nation-states still behaving as if they were world powers, and each trying stoically to stand on its own feet, alone. But hindsight is misleading. Future generations, after all, may smile with similar condescension, but perhaps less kindness, on today's nationalistic European reactions to an oil crisis, a slump, or a Common Market squabble.

But Europeans in 1947 had one advantage that their successors may envy. From across the Atlantic, there was still more help at hand. It was a heartening prospect. Winston Churchill, in 1941, had found words to express a feeling that was now general, this time borrowed from one of his favourite poets, Arthur Hugh Clough:

> ... While the tired waves, vainly breaking,
>   Seem here no painful inch to gain,
> Far back through creeks and inlets making,
>   Comes silent, flooding in, the main.
>
> And not by eastern windows only
>   When daylight comes, comes in the light,
> In front the sun climbs slow, how slowly,
>   But westward, look, the land is bright.

4
Westward, Look

It was like the opening scene in a novel by John Buchan or C.P. Snow – an improbable gathering of the miscellaneous great. There was a world-famous poet, a top-flight nuclear physicist, a much-decorated academic, and two outstanding senior generals. The place was Cambridge, Massachusetts; the occasion, the 296th Harvard Commencement. The host was the University's President, 54-year-old James Bryant Conant, a former professor of chemistry who during the war had headed the National Defense Research Committee. Three of his guests had similar connections: Dr J. Robert Oppenheimer, the government adviser on atomic energy who had been director of the Los Alamos Scientific Laboratory; the D-Day commander General Omar Bradley; and General George Catlett Marshall, the US Army's wartime Chief of Staff. The fourth distinguished guest was the odd man out – T.S. Eliot. All were due to receive honorary degrees, amid polite applause and speeches. But if the atmosphere indoors was formal, outside in Harvard Yard there was warm spring sunshine. It was 5 June 1947. What General Marshall was about to say in his ten-minute address to the Harvard alumni would make that date memorable not only for Americans, but also in the history of Europe.

Conferring Marshall's honorary degree, President Conant called him 'an American to whom freedom owes an enduring debt.' Quiet, level-eyed, incisive, and intensely loyal, Marshall had wanted a field command in World War II; but President Roosevelt had convinced him that his duty lay in Washington. There, he had masterminded the immense logistical and human task of liberating Europe and winning the war. Now, in his mid-sixties, he had been recalled to be President Truman's Secretary of State. He had made an immediate impact. In the State Department he was always known as 'General Marshall'. He knew how to delegate, but demanded 'complete and even brutal candour': he had no feelings, he said, 'except those which I reserve for Mrs Marshall.' To one senior official his advice was 'avoid trivia'. And yet, when he stood at the Harvard podium, tall, erect, and commanding, those who knew only his giant reputation were surprised at the gentleness of his voice. As always when obliged to use a written text, he read his speech rather badly. He fiddled with his spectacles, and looked at his papers instead of his audience. But there was no mistaking the considered weight of his words.

In Europe, he reminded his hearers, war had brought about not only death and destruction, but 'the dislocation of the entire fabric of European economy.' Machinery was obsolete or in disrepair; business was disrupted; currencies were discredited. Loans from abroad, which should have gone into investment and reconstruction, were having to be spent on importing raw materials, fuel, and food. The recovery of Europe, it was now clear, was going to take much more time and effort than had once been hoped.

The truth of the matter is that Europe's requirements for the next three or four years of foreign food and other essential products – principally from America – are so much greater than her present ability to pay that she must have substantial additional help or face economic, social, and political deterioration of a very grave character.

Marshall's concern was hard-headed as well as altruistic. If Europe suffered, so would the United States:

Aside from the demoralizing effect on the world at large and the possibilities of disturbances arising as a result of the desperation of the people concerned, the consequences to the economy of the United States should be apparent to all. It is logical that the United States should do whatever it is able to do to assist in the return of normal economic health in the world, without which there can be no political stability and no assured peace.

And so, in a nutshell, Marshall called the New World into action to redress the bank balance of the Old.

For action to be effective, he went on, three conditions would have to be fulfilled. First, American aid would have to be systematic.

Such assistance, I am convinced, must not be on a piecemeal basis as various crises develop. Any assistance that this Government may render in the future should provide a cure rather than a mere palliative.

Secondly, the Europeans must get together to work out their needs and plans.

There must be some agreement among the countries of Europe as to the requirements of the situation and the part those countries themselves will take in order to give proper effect to whatever action might be undertaken by this Government.

Finally, public opinion must endorse the policy.

An essential part of any successful action on the part of the United States is an understanding on the part of the people of America of the character of the problem and the remedies to be applied. Political passion and prejudice should have no part. With foresight, and a willingness on the part of our people to face up to the vast responsibility which history has clearly placed upon our country, the difficulties I have outlined can and will be overcome.

Marshall's peroration, like the rest of his speech, was no masterpiece of oratory; but it won its applause. Did all those who applauded realize the significance of what they had heard? In fact, it was a solemn promise. The United States was willing to help pay for the recovery of Europe. The 'Marshall Plan' was born.

Like most such plans, it was the work of many other people, and the outcome of a lengthy process. Former President Harry S. Truman, reminiscing about his years in the White House, described Marshall's role in typically crackerbarrel terms:

He said to me, 'I've got to make this damn speech, and you know how I hate to make speeches. And I don't know what to talk about.'
I said, 'I want you to spell out the details of this plan that's being worked out over in the State Department to save Europe from going under.' And I said, 'This plan is going down in history as the Marshall Plan, and that's the way I want it.'
He blushed. He was just about the most modest man I ever did know, and he said, 'I can't allow a thing like that to happen, Mr President.'
And I says to him, 'You won't have anything to do with it, but that's what will happen, and that's what I want to happen.' And I was right. It did.

Marshall himself made the story sound more businesslike. He had wondered, it seems, when and where to make just that speech. An address scheduled for May in the mid-West he had dismissed as premature; another, planned for Massachusetts towards the end of June, would have been too late. To forestall isolationist opposition in Congress, he wanted his proposal to break with 'explosive force'. 'It is easy to propose a great plan,' he wrote privately, 'but exceedingly difficult to manage the form and procedure so that it has a fair chance of political survival.'

This may well have been hindsight. Dean Acheson, Marshall's crisp, elegant, and immensely capable Under-Secretary of State, had advised against unveiling the plan at Harvard: commencement speeches, he said, were 'a ritual to be endured without hearing'. He was even more unhappy at how hastily the text had been prepared. Marshall was still amending it as he flew north to Boston, and the original draft had been cobbled together by Charles ('Chip') Bohlen on the basis of memoranda by various of his State

Department colleagues, including George F. Kennan, head of the Policy Planning Staff, and Will Clayton, Under-Secretary for Economic Affairs. All were members of a small select group, under Acheson's leadership, which had focused its attention on Europe for many anxious months.

The alarm bells had begun to ring in Washington on 21 February 1947. It was a Friday afternoon. General Marshall had left on an official trip to Princeton, New Jersey, and Dean Acheson was holding the fort. His office announced an urgent telephone call: it was the private secretary to the British Ambassador, Lord Inverchapel. Could the Ambassador come round and see the Secretary of State? He had to deliver in person 'a blue piece of paper' – professional jargon for a formal and important message. Acheson asked to speak with Inverchapel, who was a personal friend although a perplexing colleague: 'unquestionably eccentric, he liked to appear even more eccentric than he was, producing an ultimate impression odd enough to be puzzling.' But this time there was no aristocratic ambiguity. The British message, said Inverchapel, concerned the future of British aid to Greece. From on-the-spot reports, Acheson already knew of the Greek Government's difficulties – the economy in ruins, the Cabinet in disarray, the Army having to rely on British troops to fight Communist insurgents in the Pindus mountains and the Peloponnese. Guessing what might be afoot, Acheson arranged for Inverchapel to see Marshall on Monday morning; but he asked for a copy of the British note right away. It turned out to be not one message, but two. 'They were shockers,' Acheson recalled. They announced that British economic and military aid to both Greece and Turkey would have to be discontinued in just over five weeks' time. The United States would have to step into the breach.

Facing so abrupt a crisis, the State Department reacted with unbureaucratic speed. Acheson and his colleagues worked that night and through the weekend to prepare their draft proposals. By 10 a.m. on Monday 24 February, when Marshall received the Ambassador, he had already studied the British notes and Acheson's comments. As soon as Inverchapel had gone, Marshall went to see President Truman and the Secretaries of War and the Navy. Meanwhile, Acheson's staff was busy completing its definitive 'Position and Recommendations'. By Wednesday afternoon the President had approved them. Next day, he called congressional leaders into the White House, and Acheson gave an off-the-record briefing to the Washington press. At the congressional meeting, Truman and Marshall made heavy

weather of explaining the emergency, so Acheson chipped in to stress the
strategic importance of the Balkans, and the danger of further Communist
subversion. There was a long silence. Then Arthur H. Vandenberg, the
heavily-built Republican Senator from Michigan, leaned forward on the
sofa. He was known to be touchy, and had long been an isolationist. His
words now came as a surprise. 'Mr President, if you will say that to the
Congress and the country, I will support you and I believe that most of its
members will do the same.' It was a crucial change of heart.

On the following day 28 February, Acheson talked with Inverchapel
again. Really, he said, 'the British should not set such short and arbitrary
deadlines, especially for the withdrawal of their troops.' He quoted the motto
of the Seabees: 'We do the difficult at once; the impossible takes a little
longer.' Next week, the President and the Secretary of State were both going
to be away – Truman on an official visit to Mexico and then Texas, Marshall
at the Foreign Ministers' conference in Moscow. Even so, there was no
delay. On Monday 3 March, the Greek Government put in its formal
request for aid – drafted, incidentally, with American help. Truman
returned to Washington late on Thursday 6 March. Next morning he put his
aid plan to the Cabinet, and announced that he would meet congressional
leaders again on Monday. If all went well, he planned to make his official
request to Congress two days later, on Wednesday 12 March. 'I came back
to the Department,' wrote Acheson, 'somewhat breathless. When President
Truman had made a decision, he moved fast.'

That Wednesday was fine and sunny on Capitol Hill. The House of
Representatives was crowded with Congressmen and Senators, meeting in
joint session. At 1 p.m. Truman rose to make his speech. 'Immediate and
resolute action' was what he urged. He spoke with vigour – as well he might.
Congress was no longer controlled by his own Democratic party; yet he was
asking it to vote $400 million of taxpayers' money for aid to Greece and
Turkey. He was seeking authority to send American civilians and servicemen
5,000 miles away to help and supervise what was done in the Balkans, and to
train Greek and Turkish personnel. Even more, he was giving a solemn, far-
reaching pledge. 'I believe', he declared,

that it must be the policy of the United States to support free peoples who
are resisting attempted subjugation by armed minorities or by outside
pressures.
    I believe that we must assist free peoples to work out their own destinies in
their own way.
    I believe that our help should be primarily through economic and financial

aid which is essential to economic stability and orderly political processes.

The world is not static, and the *status quo* is not sacred. But we cannot allow changes in the *status quo* in violation of the Charter of the United Nations by such methods as coercion, or by such subterfuges as political infiltration....

The free peoples of the world look to us for support in maintaining their freedoms.

If we falter in our leadership, we may endanger the peace of the world – and we shall surely endanger the welfare of our own nation.

That, in essence, was what came to be called 'the Truman Doctrine'. In later years, in the light of the Vietnam war, it had its critics. Even at the time, George F. Kennan regretted its 'sweeping language'. But Truman's declaration of 12 March 1947 was less a personal statement of faith than a political recognition that world power involved world responsibilities. And now, with Europe weak and divided, the United States was the greatest power on earth.

America had already been growing rapidly long before World War II. Between 1900 and 1938, her industrial production had increased by 163 percent – twice as fast as in France and three times as fast as in Britain. War itself had strengthened her position. The Battle of Midway in 1942 gave the United States command of the oceans; the atomic bombs exploded three years later set a grim seal on her military might. Less spectacular, but no less real, was the wartime growth of her economy. From 1940 onwards America had become, in the phrase that Roosevelt borrowed from Jean Monnet, 'the arsenal of democracy'; and California, in particular, had become the arsenal of America. Along the Pacific coast, 'Liberty ships' poured from Henry J. Kaiser's shipyards. San Francisco, Los Angeles, and San Diego became naval bases and embarkation ports. In Santa Monica, Burbank, San Fernando and elsewhere, aircraft factories multiplied. Alfred Hitchcock's 1942 movie *Saboteur* caught something of the war production fever. What it failed to show was that the Lockheed works were soon to dwarf the Hollywood studios – or that the millions who then and later came West to find prosperity and sunshine would soon create a new pollution problem: smog. By 1944, America's defence production accounted for 45 percent of her total output – which itself had doubled from $90,000 million to $180,000 million. At the same time, the United States had begun to play a much bigger part in world trade. By 1946 she was exporting nearly four times as much as before the war.

Much of America's wealth, however, had crossed the Atlantic in the form of aid. 'Lend-Lease' had supplied some $46,000 million. UNRRA, the United Nations Relief and Rehabilitation Administration set up in 1943 by the wartime Allies but funded and manned largely by the United States, had distributed $3,700 million worth of food, clothing, medical supplies, manufactures, raw materials, farm equipment, and machinery – although a 'means test' on recipients had confined most of its work in Western Europe to Italy, Austria, and Greece. The United States had also taken the lead in setting up and financing the International Monetary Fund and the International Bank for Reconstruction and Development, the so-called 'World Bank'. To these, America had subscribed nearly $6,000 million. It had further increased the lending capacity of its own Export-Import Bank, and had already granted several very large loans.

So the Truman Doctrine largely made explicit a policy already embarked upon: using part of America's vast wealth to help needy and vulnerable allies. As in most acts of statesmanship, vision and generosity were spiced with self-interest. At home, the wartime boom was ending; and the world was now more closely knit. America could hardly prosper if her trading partners remained poor; nor could she be safe if Europe's freedom were endangered.

These arguments helped to win the debate in Congress, securing large majorities in both the House and the Senate. It was a slow process: not until 22 May 1947 was Truman at last empowered to sign the Greek–Turkish Aid Act. Fortunately, Acheson had persuaded the British to postpone their original deadline. But, as the weeks went by, it became very clear that Greece and Turkey were not the only countries in Europe desperately needing help.

As early as February, in the first discussions of what became the Truman Doctrine, General Dwight D. Eisenhower had voiced a Pentagon proposal that funds be requested for other countries as well as for Greece and Turkey. Acheson disagreed. Time was too short, he felt, to risk opening a wider debate at this stage. But he was well aware of Europe's problems, and he asked the State Department's Foreign Aid Committee to work out a plan of campaign. The Committee included three determined young men from Will Clayton's economic staff, all experts on Europe: Ben Moore, Harold van Buren Cleveland, and Charles Kindleberger, who had recently returned from army service in Germany dismayed at what he had seen. All three now argued for a new, more radical approach. So far, America had responded to national distress signals by mounting specific and limited rescue operations. But the countries of Western Europe were all in the same boat. Each might think itself alone with its economic headaches: in reality, the basic problems were common to them all. America should encourage them to recognize their mutual dependence; to tackle their difficulties together, and at length to stand on their own feet.

It was the exact opposite of the old imperialist's adage, 'divide and conquer'. It anticipated later calls for European unity and equal partnership with the United States. And even in 1947 it found a ready response. On 20 March, Walter Lippmann argued in his syndicated column that American aid should go to Europe as a whole. Three days later, in a report on conditions in Germany and Austria, former President Herbert Hoover also urged that Europe be treated as a single economic unit, and that Germany be allowed to contribute to its recovery – a point later echoed by George Kennan. This had been one of Marshall's aims at the Moscow conference of Foreign Ministers. By the time he returned, empty-handed, Europe's prospects looked more sombre still. As Marshall put it in a broadcast on 28 April: 'The patient is sinking while the doctors deliberate.'

Meanwhile, not for the first or last time, chance had intervened. President Truman had long ago promised some close family friends in Cleveland, Mississippi, that he would visit them that spring and make a speech at the Delta Council, a well-established forum for discussion of foreign affairs. But the local Democrats were bitterly divided over the succession to their Senator, the corrupt and scurrilously racist Theodore Bilbo, who was dying of cancer of the mouth. If Truman himself were to visit Mississippi, he would risk dragging the Presidency into an ugly party brawl; yet he hated to disappoint his friends. In the absence of General Marshall, who was still in Moscow, Truman asked whether Dean Acheson would take his place.

A town in the deep South was an exotic setting for a major foreign-policy initiative: but Acheson seized the opportunity. He had in mind, he told the President, ' a speech which very much needed to be made, but which must be very carefully considered.' By the end of the fiscal year, the Administration would have no funds for Europe except Greece and Turkey. Acheson's aim, he went on, was not to propose ' a solution or a plan', but to state the facts and 'shock the country into facing a growing crisis.' Would the President agree? He did; but to be on the safe side, Acheson asked him to read the text beforehand. It was a wise precaution, because the nub of the speech made four unpalatable points:

We in the United States must take as large a volume of imports as possible from abroad. . . .

The United States is going to have to undertake further emergency financing of foreign purchases....

We are going to have to concentrate our emergency assistance in areas where it will be most effective....

The fourth thing we must do in the present situation is to push ahead with the reconstruction of those two great workshops of Europe and Asia – Germany and Japan – upon which the ultimate recovery of the two continents so largely depends.... European recovery cannot be complete until the various parts of Europe's economy are working together in a harmonious whole.

Acheson delivered his Delta Council speech on 8 May 1947. On 23 May, George Kennan's policy planning staff submitted thirteen pages of proposals for restoring 'the economic health and vigor of European society.' On 27 May Will Clayton, back from a six-week tour of Europe, urged

the President and the Secretary of State to make a strong spiritual appeal to the American people to sacrifice a little themselves, to draw in their own belts just a little in order to save Europe from starvation and chaos.

It was the final cue for the Marshall Plan, announced just nine days later. Only fifteen weeks had elapsed since Britain had sought help for Greece and Turkey. Within that time, a handful of far-sighted men in Washington had settled the course of America's postwar foreign policy and Europe's postwar recovery. As President Truman characteristically put it, the Truman Doctrine and the Marshall Plan were 'two halves of the same walnut'. The nut had matured rapidly. The question remained: who was to crack it, and how?

Here once more chance took a hand in events. The Washington press corps at that time included René McColl of the London *Daily Express*, Leonard Miall of the BBC, and Malcolm Muggeridge of *The Daily Telegraph*. All three had inside experience of officialdom – McColl with the British Information Service in New York, Miall in the Political Warfare Executive, and Muggeridge in the Intelligence Corps. All three were 'fed up', as Miall put it to me, with the way in which important news seemed often to be 'leaked' to the American press, and they wanted to improve their own contacts with the Administration. Miall, who knew Dean Acheson, invited him to lunch with his two friends. The date was fixed for 2 June – just three days before Marshall's Harvard speech. Muggeridge suggested booking a private room at the United Nations Club: he added that they should offer Acheson sherry and 'some decent wine' instead of pungent American cocktails. On the way to the lunch, as if by prescience, Acheson remarked to the State Department Press Officer, Lincoln White: 'If these Limeys offer me sherry, I shall puke.'

Despite this contretemps, the lunch went well. Acheson took the opportunity to enlarge on his Delta Council speech. In Britain it had had wide coverage, especially in the London *Times*. Only two days before, *The Economist* had written: 'It does not behove the Western Europeans simply to wait in attitudes of passive despair for their salvation to be thrust upon them.' This agreed entirely with Acheson's view. A gesture was needed, he said, from the other side of the Atlantic.

That week, Miall had an unusual assignment. At 10.30 every Thursday evening, soon after the Nine O'Clock News, the BBC broadcast an 'American Commentary'. Normally, this would have been given by the American broadcaster Joseph Harsch; but he was off on a trip to Europe, and Miall had been asked to replace him. On the Wednesday afternoon, before writing his script, he talked on the telephone with a friend in the British Embassy. The friend suggested that he look at the embargoed text of what General Marshall was planning to say at Harvard on the following afternoon – by British time, only shortly before 'American Commentary' was to be broadcast. Miall went round to the State Department to collect the press release. Reading it, he suddenly realized how closely it tallied with what Acheson had said at lunch. One sentence of Marshall's, in particular, stood out: 'The initiative, I think, must come from Europe.' Here was the ready-made theme for the next day's broadcast.

That Thursday evening, as the sound of Big Ben died away, the BBC'S Nine O'Clock News led with a factual report of Marshall's Harvard speech. The newsreader added that it would be discussed in 'American Commentary'. When Miall came on the air, he told his radio audience that the United States was hoping for an immediate European response to Marshall's offer of help.

It came. One of the BBC's listeners that night was Ernest Bevin, the British Foreign Secretary. Having heard the news, he tuned in again for the commentary. He realized at once that America was holding out just the lifeline he needed. He had fought as long as possible to maintain Britain's aid to Greece and Turkey against the cuts demanded by Hugh Dalton at the Treasury: but the facts had been too much for him. Now, with the 1945 American loan fast draining away, the situation was desperate. Even Bevin himself, sturdy as he seemed, was showing signs of strain. He was overweight and short of breath; during the past hard winter, his heart had begun to give trouble. That being so, 'it was astonishing,' as one of his staff remarked, 'the way in which he, with his elephantine frame, sprang into action.' He at once asked the Foreign Office for the text of Marshall's proposal, but it had not yet arrived: allegedly, to save cable expenses, it had been sent in the diplomatic bag. What the Office had received, however, was a helpful dispatch from the Chargé d'Affaires, Sir John Balfour, based on a talk with Acheson on the previous Sunday. With this and with the *Daily Express* and *Daily Telegraph* versions of Marshall's words, Bevin had to be content. His Permanent Under-Secretary, Sir William Strang, suggested asking the Washington Embassy if Marshall's speech really meant what it seemed to have said. 'No,' said Bevin. 'I don't want to ask Marshall that question. I don't want to take any chances that it wasn't meant. I want to go on the assumption that it was fully meant, and give an answer myself.'

The next few days were filled with what was then called 'intense diplomatic activity'. An early priority was informal contact with the French. Bevin's counterpart in Paris, Georges Bidault, was in many respects his opposite – slight, volatile, highly-strung, and sometimes indecisive; a skilled orator; a devout Catholic; a former history teacher, dismissed by Vichy, who had joined the Resistance and at the age of 47, in 1946, had become Prime Minister of France. Now Foreign Minister in Paul Ramadier's left-of-centre Government, he was just as concerned as Bevin with the need for American aid: but French official opinion was mixed. Hervé Alphand, Director-General of Economic Affairs at the Quai d'Orsay, noted at the time that 'such solidarity has few parallels in history, particularly since these gifts or credits have no political strings attached.' But another French Foreign Office official, Jacques Dumaine, confided to his diary a more cynical view:

Secretary of State Marshall has offered all indigent European nations economic and financial aid, which would at the same time enable America to dispose of the enormous excess production which will soon saturate her home market.

Gallic scepticism matched France's preference for acting alone. Like many of his colleagues, René Massigli, the French Ambassador in London, would have liked Paris and Washington to continue bilateral talks on American aid, without involving other European countries. This piecemeal approach, of course, was just what Marshall and Acheson were anxious to avoid. On 6 June 1947, the day after Marshall's Harvard speech, Lewis Douglas, US Ambassador in London and a firm Francophile whose father had been a friend of Clemenceau, warned Massigli that France must join in a swift response to the American offer, or risk facing the *fait accompli* of arrangements between London and Washington which it would be difficult to change.

Next day, the French news agency Agence France Presse put out a semi-official statement welcoming 'an appeal to the peoples of Europe that will be heard with especial sympathy because it corresponds to a concern for international organization and economic recovery that France has always shared.' On 10 June, Duff Cooper, British Ambassador in Paris, proposed on Bevin's behalf a meeting with British officials to study the American plan. As Massigli had to admit, 'it was difficult to say no' – especially when three days later Bevin announced that he was willing to come to Paris himself. That same day, 13 June, in a talk to the London Foreign Press Club, he made the first public announcement of Britain's eagerness to respond.

Bevin arrived in Paris on 17 June, with a retinue of twelve economic and financial experts from the Treasury and the Board of Trade – 'a large staff,' one of his hosts noted, 'for what is merely a preliminary consultation.' In fact Bevin was forcing the pace. As he told the House of Commons just after the Paris meeting, 'When the Marshall proposals were announced, I grabbed them with both hands.' Accordingly, on 18 June, he and Bidault issued a joint statement expressing 'the greatest satisfaction' at Marshall's offer. They also invited their Soviet colleague Vyacheslav Mikhailovich Skryabin, better known as Molotov, to a three-power meeting during the following week. On 22 June the Soviet Union accepted, and the rendezvous was confirmed for 4 p.m. at the Quai d'Orsay on 27 June 1947. There seemed to be a chance that Marshall Aid might bring together the whole of Europe, East as well as West.

This had certainly been Marshall's own hope. In his Harvard speech, he had offered help to Europe, not just Western Europe; and he had urged that the recovery programme be 'a joint one, agreed to by a number of, if not all, European nations.' On 12 June he had made the same point again – echoed next day by Ernest Bevin, who saw the plan as a possible 'bridge to link East and West'. Will Clayton's European advisers had written in very similar terms. At one point, they had even argued that aid ought to be channelled through the pan-European Economic Commission for Europe, set up in March of that year by the United Nations. After the Moscow conference of Foreign Ministers, they had to admit that this was unlikely: the Soviet Union still wanted to delay the revival of Germany, and might well decide to oppose or boycott a European recovery plan in which Germany was involved. So the watchword had to be: 'Solidarity for ever if at all possible, but a well-protected flank if not.' George Kennan was more pessimistic, insisting that 'we cannot wait for Russian agreement'; and Bevin himself warned the House of Commons that if necessary Britain would go ahead without the Soviet Union. Even after Bidault had assured the French National Assembly that the invitation to Molotov was genuine, not merely formal, many were still wondering, like another Quai d'Orsay observer, how the Soviets would react: 'Will they succeed in throwing a spanner into the machinery of the Marshall Plan, or shall we be able to circumvent their delaying tactics?'

There was no delay in Molotov's reaching Paris. His aircraft landed at Le Bourget a quarter of an hour early, and he had to wait five minutes on the hot, dusty tarmac to be met by Bidault, who was on time. If Bevin's entourage of a dozen the previous week had seemed excessive, Molotov's was astonishing: it numbered no fewer than eighty-nine. To some, this seemed encouraging. The conference itself dispelled their hopes.

Bidault opened it with a long and careful statement. He proposed a series of committees to evaluate needs, resources, and production targets, and submit joint proposals to the Economic Commission for Europe. Germany, he added, could not be left out. Bevin agreed. Molotov differed.

Already, on 17 June, the Soviet daily *Pravda* had attacked Marshall's proposal on the grounds that it was part of President Truman's alleged 'plan for political pressures with dollars and a programme for interference in the internal affairs of other states.' This became a monotonous refrain. On the second day of the conference the Paris correspondent of Moscow's Tass agency took it up – and so did Molotov. Instead of 'attempts made from without to intervene in the economic life of various countries,' he proposed that each country, except Germany, submit its own list of requirements to the United States.

Bevin and Bidault both protested that co-operation and co-ordination were not the same thing as interference: but Molotov was unmoved. 'The drawing up of such an economic programme for the whole of Europe, even with the participation of other countries, would inevitably result in the imposition of the will of strong European Powers upon other European countries, and would constitute intervention in the domestic affairs of those States and a violation of their sovereignty.'

For four days, with a break on Sunday, the argument continued. To give Molotov one more chance to examine a compromise proposal, Bidault prolonged the conference for a further day. 'It really must not look', he told a colleague, 'as if we were showing them the door.'

By this time, Molotov was visibly tense. On the last day of the conference, he had a permanent telephone line through to Moscow. Afterwards, Bevin described the scene to Acheson:

It seems that Molotov has a bump on his forehead which swells when he is under emotional strain. The matter was being debated, and Molotov had raised relatively minor questions or objections at various points, when a telegram was handed to him. He turned pale and the bump on his forehead swelled. After that, his attitude suddenly changed and he became much more harsh. I suspect that Molotov must have thought that the instruction sent to him from Moscow was stupid.

Stupid or not, he stuck to it. Once again, he attacked the notion of 'a new organization standing over and above the countries of Europe and interfering in their internal affairs.' If this were the case, 'American credits would serve not to facilitate the economic rehabilitation of Europe, but to make use of some European countries against other European countries in whatever way certain strong Powers seeking to establish their dominion should find it profitable to do so.' Shorn of insinuation and bureaucrats' prose, these were themes that were to grow familiar: Soviet fear of Germany and mistrust of the United States – plus a wild over-estimate of how much the Marshall Plan would 'interfere' with national sovereignty. As Bevin had already said, 'if it were to do such a thing I should not wish to be a party to it.' That too was a theme which later became familiar.

The conference, meanwhile, had become a dialogue of the deaf. Summing up, Bidault declared his disappointment. France had done her best, he said; she was still determined to go ahead on the basis of Marshall's proposals, together with 'all those who would like to co-operate':

I express the hope here and now that no refusal is definitive and that, as a result, the labours ahead of us will not be the work of only a part of Europe.

As Bidault spoke, Molotov and his delegation sat in silence. Then they rose and filed from the room. They flew back to Moscow at 4 o'clock the next morning. It seemed a bleakly appropriate time.

That same day, 3 July, Bevin and Bidault met again and issued a joint invitation to 'all European States, with the provisional exception of Spain,' to help draw up a reconstruction programme in response to Marshall's proposal. 'This invitation', the communiqué carefully stressed, 'will remain open to all European countries.'

In fact, one country from Eastern Europe accepted it. This was Czechoslovakia – which Molotov had actually singled out as a possible victim of 'interference': the Marshall Plan, he alleged, might require her 'to increase her agricultural production and to reduce her engineering industry'. The Czech Cabinet, headed by the Communist Premier Klement Gottwald, was less pessimistic. Jan Masaryk, its plump and affable Foreign Minister, recommended taking part. His colleagues unanimously agreed – whereupon Stalin summoned Masaryk to Moscow. He left on 9 July, expecting to discuss among other things a Soviet loan. 'Russia', he told a reporter, 'is like a big fat cow with its head grazing in Prague and its udders in Moscow. I'm hoping to turn the cow around.' He had no such opportunity. Icily, Stalin told him that the Marshall Plan was 'solely a device to isolate Soviet Russia': to accept it would be seen in Moscow as 'an unfriendly act'. Twice that afternoon, Masaryk telephoned Prague to warn the Cabinet that it must change its mind. It did. Masaryk returned in deep humiliation. 'I went to Moscow a free man,' he said, 'Foreign Minister of a sovereign state. I came back as a servant of Stalin. *Finis Bohemiae.*' It may not have been the end of Masaryk's country. It certainly wrote finis to any hope that Marshall Aid might link East and West.

These few momentous months had marked a decisive turning-point. The countries of Western Europe were now to turn increasingly towards the United States. For both Europe and America, this meant changes. Europeans were to benefit from America's wealth, skill, and generosity. Americans were to become more deeply involved in Europe than ever before. And their views of each other, so long determined by myth and folk-memory, were to grow more acute and more ambivalent as their respective societies converged.

Practical work on the Marshall Plan was as brisk and busy as its preparation had been. On 12 July 1947, representatives of sixteen nations met in Paris: Austria, Belgium, Denmark, France, Greece, Iceland, Ireland, Italy, Luxembourg, the Netherlands, Norway, Portugal, Sweden, Switzerland, Turkey, and the United Kingdom. Four days later, they set up a temporary Committee of European Economic Co-operation, under the firm and resourceful chairmanship of the British delegate, Sir Oliver Franks. By the third week in September, it had produced a first four-year recovery programme – later, rather painfully, to be amended and pruned. At first, the European governments had not wanted to establish any permanent body; but at length, under powerful and repeated American pressure, they agreed to form the Organization for European Economic Co-operation, OEEC, officially inaugurated on 16 April 1948. They chose for its headquarters a discreet grey building in the well-to-do Passy district of Paris, on the site of the sixteenth-century Château de la Muette – the scene of many orgies under the Regency.

Meanwhile, there had been much to-ing and fro-ing across the Atlantic, much wooing and lobbying of Congressmen, much speech-making, many press articles, half-a-dozen special reports on Europe's needs and America's capabilities, and 3,735 pages of testimony from some 350 congressional witnesses. At the very beginning, the President had had to overrule his own Secretary of the Treasury, John W. Snyder, characteristically nervous about what the Marshall Plan might mean. During the months that followed, the Administration had deployed all its talents to cajole Congress into endorsing a foreign policy that was now firmly bipartisan. In the process it had become evident, in both America and Europe, how much depended on congressional consent. At last, on 3 April 1948, the European Recovery Program, ERP was approved. To run it, Truman appointed the 56-year-old Paul Hoffman, until then President of the Studebaker Corporation. He was a reluctant recruit: but he learned fast. As a hard-headed Republican businessman, he at first saw no need for large food shipments. Faced with the effects of chronic under-nourishment, he soon changed his mind. Within two weeks of Hoffman's appointment, the freighter *John H. Quick* sailed for Europe from Galveston, Texas, with 9,000 tons of wheat.

It was the first of many such argosies from the West. They carried all kinds of commodity, from Spam and dried egg to John Deere tractors, from animal feedstuffs to semi-finished products, from textiles to timber, from raw materials to machine tools. They made possible some spectacular European projects: a 'dam above the clouds' in Austria to harness power from melting glaciers; hybrid maize transplanted from the Deep South to the Pyrenees; the farming of land reclaimed from sea and swamp, not only in the Netherlands but also in Austria and Italy; new liners and tankers in Trieste and on the Clyde; irrigation schemes in Greece; automobile plant in the bombed-out cities; oil installations in the Po Valley; electric steel-refining in Norway; synthetic yarn in Britain's textile towns. In all, Marshall Aid brought grants and credits totalling 13,150 million dollars – some five percent of America's national income. The biggest single sums went to Britain, France, Italy, and West Germany: but this still left 4,405 million dollars for Europe's smaller countries to share. American citizens, moreover, made their own private contributions. The newspaper columnist Drew

Pearson organized a 'Freedom Train' which collected 12,120 tons of food for Europe on a coast-to-coast trip. In Massachusetts, the 'American Silent Guest Committee' arranged for families to donate the cost of one Thanksgiving meal each. College students in New York spent their vacations collecting food for distribution via alumni abroad. Altogether, with the help of a 22-million-dollar mail subsidy, private relief parcels amounted to more than 500 million dollars – an average of over three dollars from every American man, woman, and child.

In 1948, the British Board of Trade estimated that, without Marshall Aid, the weekly rations of bacon, butter, cheese, and sugar would have had to be cut by a third. Supplies of cotton goods in the shops would have dwindled to almost nothing; the shortage of timber would have reduced house building from 200,000 to 50,000 a year; the scarcity of other raw materials would have caused widespread unemployment. In other countries, matters would have been still worse.

As it was, Europe began to revive. The autumn of 1948 saw the first good harvest since the end of the war. Within three years, with the help of new machinery and artificial fertilizers, West European farm production was ten percent above its prewar level. In the first year of the Marshall Plan, half of Europe's aid shipments had had to consist of food; by 1951, the proportion had dropped to a quarter. Early in 1949, inflation slowed down in Italy, and almost stopped in France. In Britain, austerity was relaxed to allow the replanting of London squares. By 1950, trade within Western Europe had resumed prewar dimensions, two years earlier than anyone had expected. By 1951, industrial output was 43 percent greater than before the war.

No less crucial was the psychological impact of Marshall Aid. West Europeans no longer needed to feel that they faced their plight in isolation. The Americans were very much with them, in more senses than one.

The Marshall Plan's Special Representative in Europe was William Averell Harriman, a tall, commanding man then in his late fifties, who had worked on Lend-Lease and been United States Ambassador in Moscow before becoming President Truman's Secretary of Commerce. He left Washington on what he thought would be a roving commission. By the time he reached Europe, it had been decided that his headquarters should be in Paris. At first, they consisted of just two rooms on an upper floor of the US Embassy. A visiting reporter described the scene: 'Crammed into alcoves and under and over each other were dignitaries with hundreds of millions of dollars at their fingertips, whose immediate battle was to win a telephone, a wastebasket, a desk for one's private secretary.' Eventually, Harriman's staff was housed in an eighteenth-century mansion in the nearby Rue Saint-Florentin, just off the Place de la Concorde – 'a labyrinthine maze of cubicles, pens, partitions, and squeaking old corridors.' Like the OEEC's establishment in Passy, this building also had a past. The wily Bishop Talleyrand, Napoleon's Foreign Minister – and ultimately his betrayer – had lived there with the last of his mistresses.

Upstairs in Harriman's green and gold office there was a bust of Benjamin Franklin, author of the maxim, 'Time is money', and also of the lament that 'Our geniuses all go to Europe.' Hustle was certainly the watchword of most Marshall Plan officials, cutting red tape, pressing for quick decisions, hardly pausing to snatch fast food at the canteen, and continuing their discussions after office hours over dry Martinis in the Crillon bar. In Paris, at least, it was no accident that so many of them seemed clean-cut: for reasons of 'face validity', the personnel officer refused to hire any American who wore a beard. And on every plane, it seemed, American experts were descending on Europe – bankers, businessmen, engineers, professors, lawyers, economists, advisers on labour relations, specialists in plant biology, animal husbandry, oil, chemicals, or transportation. There was even, it was said, an osteopath to straighten deskbound backs. By 1952, the US Embassy in Paris was responsible for 2,500 American officials and employees, who with their families formed an expatriate community of some 7,500 people. Within a decade, 40,000 Americans were to settle in Western Europe as dependants of 3,000 US companies, whose investments there had grown from 2,000 million dollars to nearly four times as much. 'The Americans are everywhere,' said a German businessman; 'they swooped down here like birds on a field.' Nor were all of them executives in grey flannel suits. They also included drop-outs, folk-singers, Fulbright students, faculty members on sabbatical, jazz musicians like Sidney Bechet, novelists like James Baldwin or Mary McCarthy, painters like the Californian tachiste Sam Francis, and actors like Eddie Constantine, perennial American tough guy of French gangster films.

It was a peaceful invasion: but it aroused mixed feelings. Europeans had already felt ambivalent about American servicemen – the three-and-a-half million GIs whom war had brought to Europe. The Normandy beaches and the war graves were permanent memorials of a human debt too deep to be repayable. Nevertheless, in Britain as elsewhere, there had been envious gibes at plump, soft-faced, affluent American soldiers – 'over-fed, over-paid, over-sexed, and over here.'

In 1947, the year of the Marshall proposals, the Italian director Roberto Rossellini made a film about the liberation of Italy, with the dialect title *Paisà*. Its six separate episodes recorded a variety of reactions to Americans in Europe, seeing in the GIs a puzzling mixture of naïvety, compassion, clumsiness, warmth of feeling, ecumenical benevolence, courage and comradeship. In the first episode, an Italian peasant girl gives her life to save some American soldiers: they mistakenly believe that she betrayed them. As the British director and critic Basil Wright remarked, 'What one remembers most from this is the horrifying but innocent expressions on the faces of some of the GIs. Strangers in a strange land, their incomprehension makes it seem like a Zoo.' In the second episode, a small boy steals the boots off a drunken black GI, who follows the thief home intending to punish him, but relents when he sees the squalor in which the family lives. In the third episode, a young US officer meets a prostitute in peacetime Rome – and fails to recognize in her the unsullied young girl who had welcomed him at the Liberation. The fourth episode in *Paisà* introduces an American woman, determined, energetic, full of desperate bravery: she leaves her nursing post to pursue her Resistance lover through street fighting in Florence, only to learn, casually, that he has been killed. The fifth episode brings three US Army chaplains to a Franciscan friary. The friars look forward to sharing a good meal of American provisions – but feel unable to enjoy it when only one of the chaplains turns out to be Catholic: the others are a Protestant and a Jew. In the last episode, set in the Po marshes, the theme is shared sacrifice: Italian partisans, American special service agents, and a British aircrew are all indiscriminately killed.

Even Simone de Beauvoir, later so unfailingly critical of the United States, was pleased as well as perplexed to see her first GIs in Paris:

Huge khaki soldiers, chewing gum, were the proof that we could once more cross the ocean. They lounged along casually, often lurching; they sang and whistled as they lurched down the streets and the subway platforms; they lurched as they danced at night in the bars, and their frank laughter showed their childlike teeth. . . .
For me, the casualness of these young Americans was the incarnation of freedom.

To many Europeans, America had long seemed glamorous. Tales of the Wild West – many of them written in Europe – had thrilled young readers since before the turn of the century. Their most colourful exponent was the German Karl May, a convicted swindler and mythomaniac whose 35 or so stories of 'Old Shatterhand' and 'Winnetou the Warrior', complete with phrases like '*Howgh, ich habe gesprochen*' and '*Uff, Uff*', sold more than 26 million copies. Adapted later for German television, they were among the ancestors of Italian 'spaghetti Western' films; but, for decades before these, Hollywood had flooded Europe with visions of America as a land of adventure, plenty, wide open spaces, skyscrapers, gadgets, wisecracks, syncopated music, and organized crime. To British children growing up in the nineteen-thirties, an American accent had multiple appeal – it was classless, modern, tough, exciting, and slick. Less superficially, some European writers saw in America a wealth and range of demotic vigour which their own culture seemed to lack. Between 1931 and 1942, the Italian novelist and poet Cesare Pavese translated books by Sinclair Lewis, Herman Melville, Sherwood Anderson, John Dos Passos, John Steinbeck, Gertrude Stein, and William Faulkner. He discovered in them, as he wrote in 1947, 'a thoughtful and barbaric America, happy and quarrelsome, dissolute and fruitful, heavy with all the world's past, but also young and innocent.' All the same, he added, 'We realized during those years of study that America was not *another* country, a *new* departure in history, but simply the gigantic theatre in which was played out with greater frankness a drama common to us all.'

A rather similar attraction led a sensitive, elderly French *savant* like André Gide to follow the advice of the novelist André Malraux and read the detective stories of Dashiell Hammett. He did so 'with considerable astonishment very close to admiration.' In *Red Harvest*, Gide found 'the whole story told with implacable skill and cynicism'. 'The dialogue', he noted in his wartime journal, 'could be a lesson to Hemingway or even Faulkner.'

Faulkner undoubtedly struck a chord in France. In 1951, Albert Camus wrote to the *Harvard Advocate* that 'he is, in my opinion, your greatest writer.' Already in 1933 André Malraux had likened his work to Greek tragedy. 'We have the impression', said the philosopher and critic Jean Pouillon in 1946, 'of characters irretrievably choked by fate.' Two years later another French critic, Claude-Edmonde Magny, described Faulkner's universe as 'more than a slice carved out of the flow of time.'

It is the memory of a race, of a country whose secret disease is the amnestic lack of roots and traditions.... And, as in all memoirs which appear true, there is a kind of natural 'afflux', the irresistible flow of the artesian well which sweeps away anything the author might have contrived or purposely intended.... It is not the murky depths of an individual self, but a collective subconscious which is flushed to the surface. Its emergence into broad daylight is felt with the same irresistible giddiness which accompanies the exploration, by dreams or analysis, of our own past.

Lacking 'roots' or not, it was a profusion that seemed to match the sheer bulk of many less distinguished American works. The apocalyptic Southern mood was familiar too. Jean-Paul Sartre, in his 1938 novel *La nausée*, had consoled the lonely Roquentin with the sad sound of a black jazz artist singing 'Some of These Days'. Now, he saw Faulkner as equally 'lost'. 'It is because he feels lost that he takes risks and pursues his thought to its uttermost consequences.'

All these, in their various ways, were tributes to the scale and daring of so much American writing. To Germans, isolated and starved by years of Nazi censorship, the shock was greater still. The novelist Martin Walser, a sharply perceptive critic of postwar Germany, told me that the power and freedom of American novels seemed breath-taking when at last he was able to obtain them. They revealed a whole new sweaty world of real, energetic people – working, fighting, drinking, travelling, chasing power, money, sex, and dreams.

American movies opened similar vistas. Looking back in 1975, the 'new wave' director François Truffaut, who had been 13 years old when the war ended, recalled 'the fanaticism all of us French movie lovers displayed when the first American films reached us after the Liberation.' During the first year of the Marshall Plan, European cinemas were still partly substitutes for transatlantic travel – picture windows looking out on fascinating scenes. There were embellishments of the Western legend like King Vidor's lurid *Duel in the Sun*, John Ford's leisurely 'epic' *My Darling Clementine*, Howard Hawks's fine, spectacular *Red River*, or John Huston's sourly ironic *The Treasure of Sierra Madre* – itself from a story by an exiled European, the enigmatic 'B. Traven', in some respects a latter-day Karl May. The countless crime films of the period included not only Hawks's mannered adaptation from Raymond Chandler, *The Big Sleep*, but also such grainy, realistic works as Henry Hathaway's *Kiss of Death* and *Call Northside 777*, Jules Dassin's *Naked City*, or Nicholas Ray's *They Live By Night*, and a dazzling, fantasticated melodrama by Orson Welles, *The Lady from Shanghai*. A cosier, small-town 'middle America' was revealed in William Wyler's *The Best Years of Our Lives*, about returning veterans; while current concern at corruption and anti-semitism was voiced in Elia Kazan's 1947 'problem pictures', *Boomerang* and *Gentleman's Agreement*.

To many Europeans, some of these films seemed overblown – sensational, sententious, or sentimental, their simplifications disguised by surface gloss. But a younger generation of *cinéastes* was thrilled by Hollywood's energy, as well as by its sturdy neglect of 'good taste'. Cinema, wrote Truffaut in the grip of that early euphoria, 'was born American and remains so.'

It was not quite true. The year 1947, in fact, saw a small but significant European riposte. This was *L'Ecole des Facteurs*, an 18-minute comedy written by Jacques Tati, now 39, and hitherto known only as an actor and music-hall performer. The film should have been directed by René Clément, who had made his name the previous year with the Resistance semi-documentary *La Bataille du Rail*: but Clément fell ill, and Tati directed it himself. It won a prize, and the producer persuaded him to turn it into a 90-minute feature, *Jour de Fête* – his first full-length celebration of the gentle, shabby, friendly, old-fashioned and eccentric world he was to make his own. The 'fête' of the title is held in a small French village. Its attractions include a documentary film on high-speed mail delivery in the United States. Tati, the village postman, who brings round the mail on an ancient bicycle, stopping to chat with everyone and lend a hand at odd jobs, is egged on to copy the Americans. The results are chaotic. At length, in the words of the original scenario,

It has to be admitted that the village postman has advantages which the Americans, for all their worship of speed, could not replace.

On reflection, the villagers decide to calm down their frantic functionary: it's better he should take his time, as before. After all, this is France.

Begun in 1947, *Jour de Fête* was released in 1949 – just when American Marshall Plan officials were most assiduously urging Europeans to improve their productivity.

In this respect, undoubtedly, Europeans lagged far behind. The United States, with a population of 150 million, was producing some 300,000 million dollars' worth of goods every year – twice as much as the recipients of Marshall Aid with a combined population of 260 million. One American producer of heavy equipment estimated that what took 100 man-hours to make in America needed 180–200 in Britain, 240 in Germany, 250 in Belgium, and 250–260 in France. Other American manufacturers reported that productivity in Europe was between 60 and 80 percent of its level in the United States.

As head of the Marshall Plan, Paul Hoffman had long believed that 'the adoption of American labour and management practices would be a great boon to European labour, European management, and European consumers.' His chance to do something about it, he wrote later, came on a warm summer day in Paris – 26 July 1948.

Sir Stafford Cripps, Britain's ascetic Chancellor of the Exchequer, and I were talking over the economic recovery obstacles that lay ahead.

'If we are to raise the standard of living in Great Britain,' he said, 'we must have greater productivity.' My heart quickened; this was the kind of talk I wanted to hear from a European. Then he continued: 'Great Britain has much to learn about that from the United States and' – he paused – 'I think we have a few manufacturing secrets we've been concealing for a generation or so that you might like to learn. Why don't we interchange this information?'

Naturally, I jumped at the idea. 'Let's set up a system of transatlantic visits,' I replied. 'We can take British management and labour on tours of American factories and send Americans to Britain for a look at your shops.'

Sir Stafford made the deal right there, and within weeks he had thrown his amazing vegetarian energy into the creation of an Anglo-American Council on Productivity.

This, in fact, had already been prepared by informal discussion between Cripps and representatives of British management and labour, as well as in talks with less senior United States officials. Nor was the process of comparison and consultation confined to Britain. Soon, all Europe was involved in the quest for productivity; and Americans were on hand with diagnosis and advice.

To such impartial observers, there seemed a variety of reasons for Europe's backwardness: tradition, hierarchy, cartellization, lack of mobility, the class system, unequal education and – partly in consequence – politicized labour unions. None of these, clearly, would change overnight: nor would Europe quickly remedy the results of under-investment. But in the meantime, two facets of the productivity problem seemed to stand out. One was chronic over-manning. The other was inadequate management.

'If I wasted labour the way these people waste labour,' said one visiting American, 'I'd be bankrupt in a week. They don't know how to use men at all, they pay them dog's wages, and to tell the truth they aren't worth more than that for the kind of work they put out. They've got three men doing every job I use one man for back home.' The complaint was not novel. As early as 1903, in *The People of the Abyss*, a study of London poverty, Jack London had compared conditions in the merchant fleets. 'In an English ship, they say, it is poor grub, poor pay, and easy work; in an American ship, good grub, good pay, and hard work. And this is applicable to the working populations of both countries.'

'The Americans work their men, but they are fair,' was the verdict of a British trade union official. They were certainly fairer than some Europeans. One Marshall Plan representative, himself a staunch Republican, had repeatedly to badger a left-wing French government to spend more money on housing. And such concern for welfare was only part of what Americans expected from responsible management. As a Paris banker put it,

American managers listen, and they ask questions. If company figures are not precise, they force their associates to dig up new, precise figures. If statements are based on opinion, they ask for testing and proof. They force decisions out of people – and they set deadlines.

Some visiting Americans, undoubtedly, preached American practice like a creed. Not for nothing were the Marshall Plan's national outposts known as 'Country Missions'. 'There is a touch of the missionary in most Americans,' confessed an economic reporter, perhaps unconsciously echoing the British popular philosopher Olaf Stapledon, who before the war had noted 'that strange blend of the commercial traveller, the missionary, and the barbarian conqueror which is the American abroad.' 'Americans need to have less the spirit of missionaries,' said Robert Buron, a junior minister for economic affairs in Georges Bidault's 1949 Government. In Britain, Sir Stafford Cripps had to assure the House of Commons that there would be no 'broad investigation of British industry by American specialists'. Both France and Britain resisted United States pressure to form a European customs union on the model of the vast American home market, free of internal barriers to trade. On instructions from London, Sir Oliver Franks objected that the United Kingdom's links with the Commonwealth and other countries made her 'an extra-European as well as an intra-European power'.

In reality, Britain's world power was waning; and many British people, including Harold Nicolson, put the blame on the United States. 'Gradually,' he wrote in his diary,

they are ousting us out of all world authority. I mind this, as I feel it is humiliating and insidious. But I also mind it because it gives grounds for anti-American feeling, which is, I am sure, a dangerous and quite useless state of mind. They are decent folk in every way, but they tread on traditions in a way that hurts.

As long ago as 1920, the poet Paul Valéry had said that it was the ambition of Europeans to be governed by a committee of Americans. If this had ever been more than a jest, it was certainly not true now. In France, in November 1947, the Communist-led Confédération Générale du Travail helped foment a series of disorders: marches, riots, looting, and strikes by miners, dockers, automobile workers, railwaymen, teachers, postmen, and garbage collectors. All had specific grievances; but the Communists' main target was

American aid: the stoppages were known as 'the Marshall Aid strikes'. Even some non-Communists in France resented having to take charity and advice from a country they·regarded as prodigal. A British resident in Paris testified:

Every French person who had ever been in the vicinity of a US Army camp or supply depot during the war had seen the trash-cans piled with half-loaves, rejected vegetables, half-sucked oranges, half-worn garments and all the stuff discarded by the most pampered army in the world, and had come to the conclusion that the Americans, besides being unbelievably wasteful, were all egregiously rich.

It was a widespread belief, eagerly exploited by guides, waiters, barmen, pimps, and even dental surgeons. In Milan, an English-speaking dentist used to keep two price-lists in his drawer – one for Italian clients, the other for rich and gullible Americans.

Some of those who came to Europe with the Marshall Plan confirmed these unfortunate impressions. Reminiscing with a US visitor, an American-trained Swiss engineer remarked, 'I could understand why the technicians your Government sent over often did not know as much as our own: your best men were busy in industry.' The Marshall Plan representative in Rome, a former vice-president of the National Association of Manufacturers, publicly opposed the Italian Government's policy of land reform – redistributing huge inherited estates – because he feared that it might reduce farm efficiency. And if some Americans were guilty of extravagance, naïvety, ignorance, or political tactlessness, others could be painfully insensitive and brash. One well-established French firm, using bankers as intermediaries, delicately approached the head of an American machinery company to start cautious soundings about a possible *rapprochement*. 'Sure,' was the instant, disconcerting reply. 'What kind of *rapprochement* do they want?'

Directly transposing American ways to Europe caused problems for US companies themselves. Maxwell House discovered that its boast of being 'America's Favorite Breakfast Coffee' cut no ice with Europeans, who preferred their own strong national brews. Salem, the makers of menthol cigarettes, found that their green-tinted boy-and-girl advertisements were counter-productive in Germany, because they suggested mock cigarettes for callow youth. Gleem stopped calling itself 'the toothpaste for people who can't brush after every meal' when its researchers learned how few Europeans brushed even twice a day. Kleenex tissues proved too flimsy to sell in Germany as men's paper handkerchiefs. And German husbands and fathers, who chose and paid for the family consumer durables, were upset by advertisements for vacuum cleaners which depicted their wives lounging about in easy chairs. Instead, the typical *Hausfrau* had to be shown wielding the cleaner – although she was allowed to smile.

In a handful of cases, European resistance was intractable. In Geneva, some American businessmen tried to start cut-price dry cleaning. They got the necessary permits from the city, the canton, and the state – but only on condition that they joined a professional guild and charged its standardized prices. On Clydeside in Scotland, a US firm set out to double its productivity, with the chance of double wages as a reward; but beyond a certain point the employees showed no interest in earning more. Another US company in Scotland, instead of cutting its prices in line with lower wage costs, at length decided to improve the surface finish of its products, to please British instead of American tastes.

Europeans were quick to seize upon such instances. A German marketing expert argued: 'In America you have consumers. Here in Germany we have them also, but in Europe you should also try to understand the concept of the burgher. He is a man who wants to possess things, not to consume them.' A British entrepreneur complained: 'We are rapidly becoming managers, and ceasing to be businessmen or traders.' When one American company required systematic reports from its European salesmen – 'at first the sales people screamed about our field-reporting system, claimed they were salesmen, not book-keepers.'

'At first' was the operative phrase. Time after time, Americans were assured that this or that 'would never go down in Europe': teabags, barbecues, electric shavers, blister packs, fast food, frozen vegetables, *franglais* expressions like '*un deal*' or '*le quick-lunch*', meticulous cost accounting, systems analysis, business consultants, public relations advisers, executive recruitment bureaux, the habit of arguing with the boss. Time after time, the innovations gained ground. The most obvious were American products. Coca-cola was the prime example, giving rise to jokes about 'Coca-colonization'; but other visible imports included hamburgers, Uncle Ben's rice, Aunt Jemima pancake mix, Camay soap, Campbell soup, comic books, crew-cut hairstyles, baseball caps, jeans, T-shirts, US Army clothing and outfits made to resemble it, bubble-gum, sneakers, intellectual paper-backs, disposable diapers, dental floss, and countless other things now so familiar in Europe as to be taken for granted.

It was hardly surprising, as time went on, that Europeans complained of 'Americanization'. The English poet Stephen Spender put it in a nutshell:

'Americans fear the European past; Europeans fear the American future' – of 'hardware and glittering junk'. Like most such fears, it was familiar. In the 1850's, as Spender noted, Charles Baudelaire had predicted the end of 'our civilization':

We shall perish as a consequence of the means by which we have sought to live. Mechanization will have Americanized us to such a degree, progress will have so atrophied the spiritual side of our natures, that nothing among all the sanguinary dreams, anti-natural and sacrilegious, of the Utopians, will compare with the result.

'Materialism' was a charge often levelled at the Americans by some beneficiaries of Marshall Aid. It was left to an English-born US citizen, the novelist Christopher Isherwood, to retort from California:

What's our way of life? A building code which demands certain measurements, certain utilities and the use of certain apt materials; no more and no less. Everything else you've got to supply for yourself. But just try telling that to the Europeans! It scares them to death. The truth is, our way of life is far too austere for them. We've reduced the things of the material plane to mere symbolic conveniences. And why? Because that's the essential first step. Until the material plane has been defined and relegated to its proper place, the mind can't ever be truly free. One would think that was obvious. The stupidest American seems to understand it intuitively. But the Europeans call us inhuman – or they prefer to say immature, which sounds ruder....

Isherwood might have been answering such gibes as that of the Spanish writer Salvador de Madariaga, who had called America 'a land of boys who refuse to grow up'. Both had some justification; but in the years after World War II such European reproaches seemed out of place. The scholarly achievements at American universities; the bold experiments of the New York school of painting; the unrivalled brilliance of the Chicago Symphony Orchestra; the continued vigour of American novels and poetry – all these remained beacons for Europe, conclusive proof that great wealth and high civilization could go hand in hand.

One country in Western Europe never seemed to doubt it. This was Germany. To an Englishman it was very striking, a few years after the war, to see how Germans and Americans took to each other: they even began to look and sound alike. It was partly a matter of temperament. To many Americans, Germans seemed blunt and straightforward: 'It's uncomplicated; they get right down to the point,' said a US marketing man. To many Germans, America represented wealth, modernity, success, and strong protection; but to the most thoughtful among them, the appeal was deeper than that. Britons and Frenchmen might voice misgivings about American influence, or the mass consumer society that had first evolved in the United States. They might shrug off American talk of 'democracy' and 'liberty'; they might argue that violence, injustice, inequality, or racial discrimination belied the American ideal. Germans felt differently. They saw the blemishes on US civilization; but they saw also the public spirit and energy with which Americans set about reform. Above all, they saw in a free and open society the only real guarantee against a recurrence of the nightmare that had ended in the *Götterdämmerung* of 1945, and the main bulwark against the newer tyranny developing in the East.

5

Lost Horizons

Jan Masaryk enlivened any gathering. Well over six feet tall, he was burly and ebullient: he had a boisterous laugh and dark, brooding, humorous brown eyes. Despite his bulk he was small-boned, with a pianist's supple hands and a light step. He moved quickly, like his mercurial moods. English and American acquaintances marvelled at his command of their language; but his warmth and gusto were exotic. 'At luncheon,' one lifelong friend remarked of their first meeting, 'he had been gay, ribald, and in language and manner ultra-American. At the piano he was a Slav of Slavs.' His face, with his domed bald head, could look grave and reflective – then crumple into self-mockery, the left eyelid drooping, a rueful smile merging with the frank, comfortable double chin.

He had begun life as the scapegrace son of a great man: Tómaš Masaryk, the austere, white-bearded professor of philosophy who from the 1890's onwards fought to free the Czechs and Slovaks and other subject races from the grip of the Austro-Hungarian Empire. After World War I, Tómaš Masaryk was to become founder-President of the new Republic of Czechoslovakia; but his own father had been a Slovak coachman on an estate in Moravia, and for many years a Habsburg serf. Jan Masaryk liked to picture his grandfather as a roistering rough diamond, fond of a dram of plum vodka: he himself, his friends noted, served 'dreadful slivovice and vermouth cocktails'. As a child, he was regularly beaten for rebellious escapades; but he worshipped his father, and perhaps despaired of living up to him. In his presence, he would fall silent, listening attentively, full of admiration and affection. He never finished his university studies, in Prague and Vienna, but begged to be allowed to travel: he wanted to see his mother's native country, the United States. At length he set sail, aged eighteen, with as much money in his pocket as the family could then afford: it was less than a hundred dollars.

He spent nearly ten years away, in New York, Bridgeport, Chicago, and elsewhere; but he refused to batten on his mother's relatives, and worked at a variety of jobs – as a messenger, a clerk, a factory hand, and even a pianist in cinemas and dance-halls. Afterwards, characteristically, he made light of his adventures. He had liked gambling and girls, he said: but he had also taught English to illiterate immigrant workmates. Finally, on the eve of World War I, he returned to Prague. The Austro-Hungarian Empire was soon to crumble, but for the time being it was still intact; and Masaryk was conscripted into the Imperial Army – perhaps as surety for his father, who had now become an active dissident, siding with Britain, France, and the other Allies against Austro-Hungary and Kaiser Wilhelm's Germany. In December 1914, old Tómaš Masaryk slipped out of the country and made his way to unhappy exile in London. 'There was a report in the American papers', he wrote later, 'that our Jan, serving in the Austrian army, had been, or was to be, hanged on my account.' In fact, Jan had been posted to the Polish front. He claimed afterwards that he had never had to fire a shot. All he had done, he said, was acquire some colourful army language and a fund of stories worthy of his compatriot and contemporary Jaroslav Hašek, creator of that arch-scrimshanker, *The Good Soldier Švejk*.

Not until the end of World War I was the Masaryk family at last reunited – this time no longer in their dark, cramped, unfashionable Prague apartment, but in the new President's quarters in Hradčany Castle, the fortified palace of the Bohemian kings.

Jan Masaryk was now past thirty – long overdue for an orthodox career. There was no shortage of openings: he was even offered a princely salary to head the Škoda works. But, as he said afterwards, 'I felt, you know, that Masaryk's son ought not to make instruments of war but instruments of peace, and that is why I became a diplomatist.' In 1919, he joined the Czechoslovak delegation to the Paris Peace Conference, serving as assistant to the 35-year-old Foreign Minister Edvard Beneš. He spent a further year as Chargé d'Affaires in Washington, then returned for two years to the Foreign Ministry in Prague. His next post was London. While Counsellor to the Czechoslovak Legation there, he contracted a short-lived, childless marriage to the daughter of one of his father's American friends.

In 1925, at the age of 39, Jan Masaryk became his country's Minister in London, and for thirteen years made the Legation in Grosvenor Square a focal point of social and diplomatic life. Envious colleagues complained of nepotism: borrowing a title from the dramatist J.M. Synge, they nicknamed

Masaryk 'The Playboy of the Western World'. But part of his job was precisely to bring his nation to the notice of Westminster, Whitehall, and Number Ten, Downing Street. 'I spend most of my official time in there,' he said, 'explaining to the gentlemen inside that Czechoslovakia is a country and not a contagious disease.'

It was a necessary task. Britain seemed dangerously inattentive to the trouble that was brewing for Czechoslovakia and Europe. For several years, there had been unrest among the German-speaking inhabitants of Northern Bohemia, the Sudetenland. This region, highly industrialized, was also the site of Czechoslovakia's main military defences. It lay on the Czech side of the mountains which formed the natural, strategic, and legal frontier with Germany. Its people had never been Germans, but citizens of Austro-Hungary. To Austrian-born Adolf Hitler, of course, this was a distinction without a difference. From 1935 onwards, to exploit and foster discontent, the Foreign Ministry in Berlin secretly paid 15,000 marks a month to Konrad Henlein, leader of the Nazi Sudeten German Party. When Henlein visited Jan Masaryk at the Czechoslovak Legation in London, he came with an SS man. 'My friend here accompanies me wherever I go,' he explained. Masaryk opened the door into his drawing-room and whistled for his Aberdeen terrier. 'My friend here,' he said, 'accompanies *me* wherever I go.'

Henlein seemed amused. The SS man was not – perhaps because he, in fact, was Henlein's master. For Hitler, Henlein was a puppet, and troubles in the Sudetenland were merely a pretext for annexing it. During the summer of 1938, Hitler's demands brought the quarrel to a crisis and a threat of war. In September, after agitated solo missions to Berchtesgaden and Bad Godesberg, the British Prime Minister Neville Chamberlain agreed with his French counterpart Edouard Daladier to meet both Hitler and Mussolini in Munich. There, on 29–30 September, with no representatives of Czechoslovakia present, Chamberlain and Daladier gave in to Hitler's threats. They handed over 10,000 square miles of the Czech Sudetenland to Nazi Germany, 5,000 square miles of Southern Slovakia to Hungary, and a smaller area in Silesia to Poland. Later apologists argued that they had thereby gained time to improve their military defences: but so had Hitler. What really swung the decision was insularity and a panic fear of war. 'How horrible, fantastic, incredible it is,' said Chamberlain in a broadcast before going to Munich, 'that we should be digging trenches and trying on gas-masks here because of a quarrel in a far-away country between people of whom we know nothing!'

When Chamberlain returned from Munich proclaiming 'peace for our time... peace with honour', Jan Masaryk was present to hear the House of Commons go wild with joy. Perhaps fortunately, Tómaš Masaryk had died a year earlier, on 14 September, his son's fifty-first birthday. Long before, in ailing health, he had passed the Presidency to Edvard Beneš – small, dapper, and rather didactic, a man sharply but not unfairly described by David Lloyd George as 'impulsive, clever, but much less sagacious and more short-sighted than Tómaš Masaryk.' The old President had the measure of Beneš. On his deathbed he had told his son: 'Very bad times are coming for the nation ... and for Europe. Beneš will have to bear the brunt of it. He is not equal to it alone. He is not big enough. You must help Beneš. You know much of the world better than he does. Stand by Beneš always. Promise me that you will never leave him alone.' Jan Masaryk had given his word. Now, with the frenzied, shameful cheers of the House of Commons still ringing in his head, he went to see Chamberlain and the Foreign Secretary, Lord Halifax. His words to them might have been his father's. 'If you have sacrificed my nation to preserve the peace of the world, I will be the first to applaud you. But if not, gentlemen, God help your souls.'

The Munich agreement merely postponed World War II. On 1 October 1938, Hitler's troops marched into the Sudetenland. President Beneš mobilized the Czechoslavak army, but stood it down again under pressure from Britain and France. He then went into exile, and Jan Masaryk resigned. But this was only the beginning. Later, Hitler told his generals: 'It was clear to me from the first moment that I could not be satisfied with the Sudeten territory. That was only a partial solution.' Within six months, he had occupied Prague itself, and the Nazis' swastika flag was flying from Hradčany Castle, where Hitler spent the night of 15 March 1939, in the apartment that had once been Tómaš Masaryk's. He turned the Czech half of the country into a Nazi 'protectorate', effectively swallowed up in the Third Reich; the Slovak half became his first 'satellite' state. A further six months later, all Europe was at war.

That war, a Czechoslovak poet wrote, was like 'broken glass in our arteries and our blood.' The country itself was drained by the Nazis: loot and other losses amounted to some 14,000 million dollars in six years. Between March 1939 and May 1945, 350,000 Czechs and Slovaks were deported to concentration camps: only 100,000 of them came back. The Czechoslovak underground movement *Obrana Naroda*, 'Defence of the Nation', was probably the biggest resistance network of the whole war – although in clandestine operations size and security seldom go together: some 38,000 partisans were killed by the Gestapo. The best-known instance of Nazi brutality was the destruction of Lidice, one of two villages razed to the ground, with the murder of 2,000 hostages, in revenge for the death of Reinhard Heydrich, the ruthless *Reichsprotektor*, mortally wounded on 27 May 1942, by three Czechoslovak patriots parachuted in from the Special Operations Executive (SOE) in London. These three – who were betrayed, and who killed themselves after a losing gun-battle with the SS – were not the only Czechoslovak exiles who fought a heroic war. General Ludvík Svoboda, a regular soldier who escaped through Poland to the Soviet Union, became commander of a Czechoslovak Army Corps attached to the Red Army. In the West, Czechoslovak pilots and aircrew flew in special squadrons of the British Royal Air Force. And a few hours before Hitler had entered Prague, the effective head of the Czechoslovak military intelligence service, with help from MI6, had flown through a blizzard to London with ten of his staff and all his essential files.

After the débâcle of Munich, both Beneš and Jan Masaryk had gone to the United States – Masaryk on a lecture tour, Beneš to teach at the University of Chicago. Now, they both returned to Britain. Beneš took a country house at Ashton Abbots in Buckinghamshire. Masaryk, who preferred to be nearer the centre, rented a small apartment in Westminster. On 8 September 1939, he began a series of radio talks to Czechoslovakia. One commentator thought that these made him, 'with the single exception of Winston Churchill, the most effective Allied broadcaster of the war.' To his listeners, who risked death when tuning to the BBC, he became known as '*naš Honza*' – 'our Johnny'. Despite the Munich agreement, he was still a firm Anglophile: he wanted nothing better for the world, he said, 'than that all countries should have the same qualities as these islands of Britain.' Describing the calm of Londoners under nightly air attack, he declared: 'The British people know anxiety; they do not know what fear is.' Asked what his war aims were, he answered: 'The right of Jew and Gentile to read *Das Kapital* and *Mein Kampf* in Prague streetcars – every citizen must have the right to shout in the streets "I don't like my Prime Minister."' Or, simply: 'I want to go home.'

Home, for Masaryk, was still six hundred miles away; but in preparation for their eventual return to Prague, he and Beneš and other exiled members of the former Government and Parliament set up in London a Czechoslovak National Committee, and lobbied hard to secure its recognition by the Allies.

They had no luck while Lord Halifax remained Foreign Secretary; but at the end of 1940 he was replaced by Anthony Eden, and on 18 July 1941, Britain officially recognized the Czechoslovak Provisional Government-in-exile, with Beneš as its President and Masaryk as Foreign Minister. It took a further year to persuade the British Government formally to repudiate the Munich agreement.

Meanwhile, Beneš and Masaryk had to reckon with potential rivals. At and around the time of Munich, a number of leading Czechoslovak Communists had also fled the country. Two of them had come to London: Dr Vladimír Clementis, a smooth, clever, podgy, rather amiable lawyer, and Václav Nosek, a tall, bony former miner and steelworker. Most of the others had sought refuge in Moscow, where they had set up their own shadow Cabinet under Klement Gottwald, a Catholic of Austrian origin who had become General Secretary of the Czechoslovak Communist Party long before the war. One American visitor, the writer and journalist John Gunther, described Gottwald as 'a short man, pleasant-looking, taciturn, and conventional in exterior, even to the item that he smokes a pipe.' In fact, he was a hard-liner as well as a hard drinker. 'He has "a stubborn untrained mind",' Gunther added, 'and so is hard to argue with.'

Difficult as agreement might prove, Beneš believed that it was possible and essential to bring together both groups of Czechoslovak exiles. In late 1943, he went to Moscow to negotiate a Treaty of Friendship with the USSR. Welcomed with full honours as a Head of State, he professed himself delighted. The Treaty of Friendship promised 'mutual respect of sovereignty and non-interference in internal affairs.' Beneš cabled to Masaryk: 'I did not expect such prospects of cordial and harmonious co-operation.... I regard it as certain that all treaties not only with us but also with the British and Americans will be kept.'

Jan Masaryk was less sanguine. In the words of his friend Sir Robert Bruce Lockhart,

He recognized the necessity of an understanding with the Soviet Union. On more than one occasion he said to me – in rather coarse language – that he would rather go to bed with Stalin than kiss Hitler's behind. On the other hand he was instinctively suspicious.... As a defender of small nations he could not find any sign of liberty, equality and fraternity in the Communist dictionary. 'For me Russia after the revolution remains the same imperialistic Great Power that it was before.'

For this reason alone, Masaryk would have paid any price to see Czechoslovakia liberated by the British and Americans. 'Send us your troops,' he told President Roosevelt, 'and you can have a blank cheque to do as you like.' It was a forlorn hope. As the Allied forces closed in on Nazi Germany, Czechoslovakia lay in the path of the armies from the East.

The Czechoslovaks did their best to liberate themselves. In late August 1944, Slovakia rose against its puppet regime. The Nazis soon occupied the Western regions; but those in the centre proclaimed a 'Free Slovakia', defended by part of the Slovak army, with the aid of partisan bands and some escaped French prisoners of war. Both Britain and America tried to help. SOE flew a mission in from Bari, but its commander was captured and shot; and although a Czech airborne brigade came in from Moscow, the Soviet Union refused airport facilities for SOE or its American counterpart, the Office of Strategic Services, OSS. A large OSS detachment, dropped into the Tatra mountains on 25 September, failed to make contact with the Slovak army, and was later captured. In October, after a coup had prevented Hungary from breaking off its alliance with Hitler, Nazi forces were able to move in from across the Hungarian border, and the Slovak rebellion was crushed.

Six months later came one final upheaval. By now, the war was nearly over, and in Czechoslovakia the Soviet Red Army was the dominant force, sweeping across Slovakia and then Moravia – the armoured divisions, the marching columns, the staff cars and supply trucks followed by the Agitprop Brigade and Political Commissariat, with small light carts drawn by Cossack ponies bringing up the rear. Rape, pillage, and drunken riots were commonplace: soon after Brno was liberated, more than 2,000 women sought hospital treatment for the effects of sexual assault. Knowing the Red Army's reputation, the inhabitants of Prague decided to forestall their liberators. On Saturday 5 May 1945, they came out on the streets, built anti-tank barricades, and began attacking the Nazi occupation forces. They also appealed to the Americans for military help. This was perfectly possible: the US Third Army under General George S. Patton was only 56 miles away, and the impetuous Patton was straining at the leash. Holding him back was General Eisenhower, the Supreme Commander. Through General Omar Bradley, commander of the Twelfth Army Group, Eisenhower ordered Patton to advance no further than a NW/SE line running through Plzeň, or Pilsen. Passing the message on, Bradley added that Patton 'could and should reconnoitre as far as Prague.' That same day, an OSS team headed by an American captain of Slovak origin actually drove from Pilsen to Prague in a jeep flying the Stars and Stripes. On the way, they passed through weary columns of German soldiers heading West to surrender to the Americans rather than the Russians. After contacting the Czech partisans, the jeep raced back to Patton, intending to guide him and the Third Army into Prague. Patton called Bradley. He was sympathetic, but felt obliged to check with Eisenhower. When he did, the order came to stop. Eisenhower, it seemed, had put the idea to the Soviet Chief of Staff, General Alexei Antonov; and he had turned it down categorically. Bradley broke the news to Patton. At this late date, he explained, Eisenhower was anxious to avoid 'international complications'. 'For God's sake, Brad,' said Patton, 'it seems to me that a great nation like America should let others worry about complications.' But he obeyed orders. The Third Army stayed put, and even Czechoslovak pilots of British aircraft were forbidden to fly to Prague. Partly as a result, more than 2,000 of its resistance fighters were killed by the time the Red Army arrived on Wednesday, 9 May 1945 – the day after the end of the war in the West.

In the wake of the Red Army came the new Czechoslovak Provisional Government, an amalgam of the London and Moscow groups. In March, Beneš and Masaryk had flown to Moscow to discuss its composition. For Masaryk, the experience was dispiriting. 'I've been moving mountains', he told a diplomatic colleague, 'to convince Stalin that I'm on his side; but he refuses to believe me.' Ignoring the pledge of non-interference made in the Friendship Treaty two years earlier, Stalin and Molotov insisted that the new Czechoslovak Government must reflect the Russian and Communist role in the country's liberation. Beneš could still be President, and Jan Masaryk Foreign Minister; the Government could also include three 'National Socialists', or Left-wing Liberals. But the Agrarian and other right-wing parties which had figured in the London Provisional Government were excluded; and the Communists were to be the biggest single group, with a total of seven seats. The Deputy Prime Minister was to be their leader Klement Gottwald. Masaryk disliked him on sight. There were three Slovak Democrats, three Populists, and three Left-wing Socialists – including the Prime Minister, Zdeněk Fierlinger, whom Beneš had sent as his wartime Ambassador to Moscow, but who while there had become a Communist pawn. 'He is worse than Gottwald,' said Masaryk: 'I'd rather deal with the devil face to face than with something crawling in the woodwork.' Masaryk's friend Marcia Davenport, the American novelist, described Fierlinger as having 'a terrible face, narrow and pointed, with slitted eyes that never looked straight at you. Rat, I thought.'

More telling than their physical appearance were the key posts the Moscow group held. The Minister of Defence was General Svoboda. The Ministers of the Interior, of Information, of Education, and of Agriculture were all Communists; so were junior ministers in the Foreign Office and the Departments of Industry and Social Welfare.

None of this should have surprised Edvard Beneš. From his first visit to Moscow in 1943 he had brought back – in an open envelope – a letter from Gottwald to his Party colleague in London, Václav Nosek. The Czecho-slovak Communist Party, Gottwald had written, would

in all probability be the strongest party after the war. So we consider it obvious that Communists must be able to play a truly effective role in the new Government. This means, among other things, that the portfolios of the Interior and of Defence must be held by the Communists. The new Prime Minister, of course, must be a man of the bloc.

At the time, Beneš had privately noted: 'The Communists' participation in the Government has one aim: to get hold of positions and have decisive influence in preparation for seizing all power in the State.' To his democratic colleagues, Beneš had said nothing of his fears.

The Provisional Government ruled Czechoslovakia for just over a year. As was to be expected, it made some sweeping reforms – expelling German-speaking minorities, redistributing farmland, nationalizing a number of industries. Then, on 26 May 1946, the country went to the polls to elect a Constituent Assembly. The Communist Party, which before the war had represented about 10 percent of the electorate, now won 38 percent of the votes. The Left-wing Socialists had 13 percent. This gave both together 153 of the 300 seats – a narrow majority. Klement Gottwald became Prime Minister. His Government included two more Communists, making nine in all, and two fewer Slovaks. Otherwise, little seemed to have changed. Beneš remained President, and Jan Masaryk was still Foreign Minister. Mean-while, like other countries in Europe, Czechoslovakia was beginning to recover from the worst effects of the war. Output increased, and so did foreign trade – notably with the West. Prague bookshops were full of translations from English and American authors; street kiosks sold Western magazines and newspapers; people flocked to American films; many students, offered the choice, preferred to learn English rather than Russian. Pro-Western euphoria culminated at the beginning of July 1947, when in a tense all-night session Masaryk persuaded the Cabinet to accept the American offer of Marshall Aid. That evening, there was dancing in the streets of Prague.

The mood changed abruptly when Stalin forced Czechoslovakia to reject the Marshall Plan. A few days earlier, President Beneš had suffered a stroke. Even the weather turned hostile. That summer, all Europe was parched by drought: in Czechoslovakia, it caused forest and field fires which destroyed essential crops. Grain production reached only 63 percent of the target level, and the potato crop only 48 percent. Food soon became scarce, and had to be imported; to pay for it, consumer goods intended for use at home had to be sold abroad. Discontent mounted, and tension within the Cabinet became acute. On 11 September, a crude, botched attempt was made to assassinate Jan Masaryk and two of his democratic colleagues – the Minister of Justice, Prokop Drtina, and the leader of Beneš's Socialist Party, Peter Zenkl. Each was sent a wooden box, labelled 'Perfume' but containing high explosives. When the bombs were safely defused, the Communist Party accused their recipients of staging a fake plot; but, despite obstruction from Nosek's Ministry of the Interior, Drtina managed to trace the maker of the boxes, the maker of the bombs, and their sender. All were Communist officials – and their instigator proved to be Gottwald's son-in-law.

The non-Communists were further alienated, that October, by the setting-up of the Cominform, the international propaganda bureau dominated by the Soviet Union. A few weeks later, even the Left-wing Socialists were sufficiently stirred to depose their leader Fierlinger, who had signed a joint-action pact with Gottwald, but without even consulting his own Party. His colleagues now found the courage to denounce Communist bullying, especially in the factories. Their daily paper, *Pravo Lidu*, pointed out that 'Meetings are usually called after working hours, when the majority of workers have left, and methods of voting are controlled by direct intimidation.' 'Don't trifle with the Communists,' said Fierlinger. 'They won't tolerate it: nor will the Russians.'

Jan Masaryk, meanwhile, had gone to America, representing Czechoslovakia at the United Nations. To his chagrin, the Prague Government sometimes compelled him to vote with the Soviet Union against the United States. 'It is too true', he wrote to an American friend,

that I am standing (not yet squatting) between two not too static and not too savoury stools. . . . I have been toying with the idea . . . to let myself go at one of the closing sessions. . . . I am certainly not going down the drain without making a considerable squawk. . . . Somewhere, sometime, somehow, I am going to stand on my hind legs and shout to the Great Powers, 'Gentlemen, your fly is open!'

But the timing – that's the problem.

He was still hoping, in fact, for help from the United States. Food at home was desperately short, and Czechoslovakia had appealed for 200,000 to 300,000 tons of American wheat. But in November, when Masaryk went to Washington, he found that US officials were reluctant to recommend it. The Ambassador in Prague, Laurence Steinhardt, was certainly in favour of 'strengthening anti-communist forces in the government' there; yet in the previous June – at the time of the Marshall proposals – he had written in one of his dispatches:

It is my experience over the last 25 years that the hope of obtaining credits accomplished much more for us than once the credits had been extended.

Now, the State Department still seemed to feel that it could best invigorate the Czechoslovak democrats by withholding rather than granting aid.

It was a tragic miscalculation. 'At this point,' said the Czechoslovak Foreign Trade Minister Hubert Ripka, 'Gottwald got in touch with Stalin, who promised us the required wheat.... And now these idiots in Washington have driven us straight into the Stalinist camp.... The fact that not America but Russia had saved us from starvation will have a tremendous effect inside Czechoslovakia – even among the people whose sympathies are with the West rather than Moscow.'

Masaryk did his best to explain his compatriots' plight. They were separated, he said, 'by a great distance from the western nations which could give them help directly and they were forced to make the best of a difficult situation caused by their contiguity to the Soviet sphere.' He himself, he added, was 'not always free to adopt the kind of position he would like to take.' Sometimes, 'Czechoslovakian policy had to cut across that of the US.'

But the head of the State Department's Central European Division, James Riddleberger, distrusted what he called Masaryk's 'smiling persuasions'. 'This man', he had written earlier, 'might well have utilized his background and name to stand up to the Communist extremists.... I judge that he has been weak or blind.'

Masaryk asked to see either President Truman or his Secretary of State, General George C. Marshall. The Truman Doctrine, after all, had condemned 'coercion' and 'political infiltration' everywhere, not just in the West; Marshall Aid had been offered to the whole of Europe; and Stalin had broken many promises since the war. But in 1947, as before and since, *Realpolitik* and *force majeure* won the day. On 6 November, in a top-secret briefing, Marshall told the US Cabinet: 'The halt in the Communist advance is forcing Moscow to consolidate its hold on Eastern Europe. It will probably have to clamp down completely on Czechoslovakia, for a relatively free Czechoslovakia could become a threatening salient in Moscow's political position.' As in 1938, Czechoslovakia was still 'a far-away country', and the United States seemed to have written it off. Neither Truman nor Marshall had time to see Masaryk – even to explain themselves. He left Washington deeply depressed, but determined: he and his compatriots would have to fend for themselves.

Several American friends urged him to stay in the United States. His answer was always the same: he had promised his father that he would stand by Beneš. Nor was he wholly pessimistic. An election was due in May 1948. The Communists feared that they might lose it: the democrats were certainly planning to fight a vigorous campaign. Passing through London on the way back to Prague, Masaryk saw Sir Robert Bruce Lockhart, who recalled later:

As we said goodbye, he made a great effort to be cheerful, clapped his hand on my shoulder, and smiled. 'Never mind, old boy, we'll beat the b . . . . . s yet.'

That opportunity never came. In early February 1948, to forestall the danger of a free election, the Czechoslovak Communists prepared a coup. Their Minister of the Interior, Václav Nosek, had already organized a network of secret-police units, and set up an illegal Workers' Militia. He had also systematically packed the regular police with members of the Communist Party. Now, on 13 February, he dismissed Prague's last eight non-Communist divisional commissioners – the only police rank entitled to issue arms and ammunition – and replaced them with his own men.

Prokop Drtina, the Minister of Justice, was furious – and alarmed. At his prompting, a majority of the Cabinet called upon Gottwald to rescind the order. He refused. Thinking to outflank him, the Government's twelve non-Marxist Ministers made what looked like a clever move: on 20 February they resigned. They hoped thereby to overthrow the Govenment – but the manoeuvre misfired. The Left-wing Socialist Ministers, who had backed the original protest, stayed on in office, giving Gottwald a quorum of thirteen. 'Believe me,' he told Masaryk afterwards, 'we have spent months thinking how to carry out the *putsch*, what excuse to use, how to do it, then those ex-Ministers handed it to us on a plate. They gave us a perfect excuse, and all that was needed was to stand there and kick them in the behind, and this is what we did.'

Masaryk had not been told of the resignation plan: he might well have opposed it. He heard about it afterwards, by telephone, when the resignations had already been handed in. As the only independent Minister, the bearer of his father's name and a symbol of his country's unity, Masaryk refused to take a party position; but to deny Gottwald his quorum he staged a diplomatic sore throat.

The next move was up to Beneš. As President, he was empowered to reject the resignations; he could also call an early election. The twelve Ministers claimed that their plan had had his approval: some even alleged that he had actively encouraged it. Beneš, on the contrary, said later that it had taken him by surprise. Whatever the truth of the matter, he was dangerously out of touch. As late as 12 January, he had pooh-poohed the notion of a coup by the Communists. 'I enjoy a certain authority in the nation,' he had told a colleague. 'A *putsch* would be directed against me as well, and they could not afford it.'

But Gottwald had additional resources. On Sunday, 15 February, Soviet secret police had been flown in from Moscow. Twenty-three NKVD agents were in place at the Hotel Flora, and sixteen at the Grand Hotel Steiner. On 19 February, the day before the fatal resignations, Valerian Zorin, the former Soviet Ambassador, now a Vice-Minister for Foreign Affairs, had arrived in Prague unexpectedly, and 18,000 Red Army reinforcements had entered the Soviet zone of Austria, just across the Czechoslovak border.

Assured of this ominous backing, Gottwald went to see Beneš in Hradčany Castle, together with Nosek and General Svoboda. Curtly, he demanded that Beneš accept the resignation of the twelve democratic Ministers, and replace them with Communist sympathizers. He had conclusive proof, he claimed, that the twelve were plotting 'a vast criminal conspiracy' against the Communist Party and the State – an allegation repeated by the State-owned radio. It was the exact reverse of the truth.

Beneš hesitated. Next day, a delegation of fifty-five workers invaded his office to repeat Gottwald's demand. Beneš answered that he would not 'let the streets decide'; but when he proposed to broadcast to the nation that evening, the Communist Minister of Information declared: 'We will not allow Beneš to appear before the microphone again.' The twelve democratic Ministers faced a similar ban.

In the end, the streets decided. On the evening of the resignations, the radio had announced a mass meeting of workers in Prague. Through snow and bitter frost, busloads of Communist sympathizers were brought into the capital, to be addressed by Gottwald and his colleagues, shouting slogans, waving red flags, and singing the *Internationale*. While the regular army was confined to barracks, trucks escorted by Nosek's National Security Corps arrived with 10,000 brand-new rifles and 2,000 sub-machine-guns to arm the Workers' Militia. During the weekend, 15,000 militiamen paraded through the streets. For Monday 23 February a general strike was called. Those who refused to join it were beaten up, thrown out of the factories, and sacked from their jobs.

By now, the police had sealed off the frontiers. When the twelve democratic Ministers returned to their offices on Monday morning, they found them controlled by Communist 'Action Committees', and their own desks occupied by their political opponents; if they protested, they were manhandled from the premises. Non-Communists were likewise expelled from the broadcasting studios and the Ministry of Information. The radio faithfully relayed Gottwald's rabble-rousing speeches. Hundreds of journalists were arrested; several newspapers were taken over by the Communists; those that resisted found their newsprint supplies cut off. In the streets of Prague, police armed with sub-machine-guns patrolled the bridges and crossroads. They cordoned off all public buildings, and raided those of the democratic parties, arresting their staff and impounding their documents. Five truckloads of Fierlinger's supporters, armed to the teeth, moved in on the headquarters of the Left-wing Socialists, threatening to kill his opponents and forcibly securing his return to power.

For two days, some ten to twelve thousand students from Prague University led a counter-demonstration, marching up to Hradčany Castle to show their loyalty to the Republic and to Beneš, calling on him to address them. Masaryk's friend Marcia Davenport saw for herself what happened next:

Eight abreast, they were carrying the national tricolour and they were singing the national anthem, whose tragic refrain is 'Where is my home?' They were fine and beautiful young people and they were the last honest open faces I saw in that country. I seized a coat and ran out of the house to go along near them on the pavement.... Then I heard another noise, a heavy roar, and another kind of tramping; it seemed to come from many directions. The students were nearing the gates of the Hrad. I stood still for a moment as I saw their ranks break and flailing violence falling on them. Then I heard shots. I knew I should not be in the street so I went back to the house. I stood at the window again and saw platoon after platoon of marching men, in ordinary clothes with red rags tied round their left arms, carrying rifles. Workers' Militia is what their Red bosses called them, but I did not know that or care. I clutched the sill and screamed, 'Armed civilians! Shame! Shame!'

By Wednesday afternoon, 25 February, it was all over. Shortly after 4 p.m., a vast throng of Gottwald's supporters cheered and applauded him as he drove back from the Castle to Vaclavske Namesti – Wenceslas Square – in the heart of Prague. He was wearing a Russian sheepskin cap, and he was drunk. He had just had his last audience with the President: Beneš had finally given in. Half the new Cabinet were Communists: the rest, with one exception, were puppets.

The exception was Jan Masaryk, who stayed on as Foreign Minister. 'With this government, I shall enjoy governing,' he told the press. Some of his friends, scandalized, took him literally. Others, who knew him better, feared that the Communists might see through his Švejk-like irony. Privately, he put inverted commas round the word 'government'. Why did he stay? Because Beneš had stayed – to avert a civil war and invasion by the Red Army. 'In 1938,' Beneš told him, 'I had to bear the brunt of Munich alone when you were abroad. Now you must stay and help me and the country.' Masaryk remembered his promise to his father, and stayed.

The Government, meanwhile, was conducting a purge. Friends and former colleagues were arrested. Masaryk himself lost his regular body-guard, and was now accompanied everywhere by two leather-jacketed thugs. On the morning of 27 February, the former Minister of Justice, Prokop Drtina, was found lying seriously injured on the pavement below his third-floor window: he had tried to kill himself, it seemed, the night before. 'It's a stupid way to go about it,' Masaryk commented, 'and besides, there's no guarantee of success. Furthermore, suicide doesn't absolve anybody of his responsibilities. It's a very poor escape.'

Masaryk was talking at luncheon in Beneš's country house on Saturday, 6 March. By all accounts, the discussion was stormy. The atmosphere in Prague was certainly tense. A week earlier, Beneš had left Hradčany Castle, he said, for the last time; and on 2 March, against Masaryk's advice, the Ambassador in Washington had resigned and denounced the new Government. Inevitably, Masaryk was blamed. On Sunday, 7 March, he packed Marcia Davenport off to London. 'If I know you are there waiting for me,' he told her, 'it gives me something to live for.' He himself, she wrote, 'looked and acted like a haunted man.'

That same Sunday was his father's birthday. In the morning, he attended a commemorative rally in the pink-and-ochre Renaissance setting of the Old Town Square, to hear the Communist orators claim that Tómaš Masaryk would have approved of his country's 'new course' and his son's presence in the Cabinet. 'How dare they?' Masaryk growled. That afternoon, he went with his sister and niece to the quiet cemetery of Lany, to pay the regular family visit to Tómaš Masaryk's grave.

Next day, Monday 8 March, Masaryk spent some time going through his papers: according to one of his staff, he burned several basketsful. In the evening, he attended a further commemorative ceremony, this time at the Theatre of the Fifth of May.

On Tuesday morning, 9 March, just after 9 a.m., the family doctor, Oskar Klinger, paid his usual visit. He was a close friend, and had long been advising Masaryk to take a rest, suggesting a trip to the spa of Gräfenberg near the Polish frontier. But now, according to Dr Klinger, Masaryk unveiled other plans. 'He reproached himself for having joined the new Government': the Communists' misuse of his father's name had 'proved in the crassest manner that he, too, had been used as a puppet.' He was making final plans to leave the country.

'We must leave together, Oskarku,' he said. 'I'll ring you tomorrow morning at seven o'clock and ask you for an injection. You understand? But you won't come here. This will be the signal that all is in good order. You jump into your car and drive straight to Brezany' – a country house outside Prague with a meadow big enough to be used as an airstrip. 'We will be flown to England,' Masaryk added. 'Take only the barest necessities with you.'

After Klinger had left, Masaryk again went out to Beneš's country residence, this time to attend the audience for the new Polish Ambassador. Twice on that occasion, he and Beneš talked together alone. Afterwards, Masaryk seemed cheerful, but Beneš rather depressed. All three of Masaryk's secretaries said later that the two men had agreed in principle to break with the Communist régime. Any such discussion in the President's house would undoubtedly have been picked up by the microphones of the secret police.

In the early afternoon, Masaryk returned to the Foreign Ministry at the Černinský Palace – a vast, imposing, coldly formal building with high vaulted ceilings, echoing reception rooms, and marble, glass-clad corridors. Near the north-east corner, on the second floor, was Masaryk's official apartment, reached by a small private lift. Except on formal occasions, he preferred to work here, in the long narrow sitting-room and library in which he also slept. After a few words with his secretaries, he dismissed them for a moment and changed into pyjamas: he was feeling tired, he said; his sore throat had developed into a cold, and he was going to work in bed. He went through some routine papers, then resumed a meeting, interrupted that morning, with a visitor from the Czechoslovak Embassy in London, whom he asked to come back tomorrow for a letter he planned to compose overnight. With his senior secretary, he began to draft the speech he was going to make – on Czechoslovak-Polish co-operation – when the new Cabinet was presented to Parliament on the following day. Finally, they discussed the next day's schedule. After the official ceremony, Masaryk planned to leave Prague – for a 14-day rest cure, he said.

Soon after 8 p.m., he had his dinner brought in on a tray: cold roast chicken, potatoes, and salad. He ate heartily, saying how much he had enjoyed it. He settled comfortably in bed with a large writing pad, and a bottle of beer and two bottles of mineral water on the night table. The window was open as usual, and he asked to be called at 8.30 a.m. Some time later, he took his two nightly Seconal pills – normally enough to rest him until 5 or 6 in the morning – and went to sleep.

It was the last night of his life.

They found the body in the early hours next morning – a blur of blue silk in the grey of the palace courtyard. It lay huddled, half on its back, the head a few yards from the wall, the legs slightly bent, the left arm folded, the right flung straight out. The fingertips were scratched; under the nails, there were traces of paint or plaster. The ankles were broken, with small splintered bones protruding. The blue pyjamas were soiled, the face contorted. On the belly was a narrow vertical scratch; like the hands, it was dirty with dust.

One of the palace stokers ran for some blankets. A sergeant from the National Security Corps telephoned for an ambulance, while another guard called headquarters. A police doctor confirmed that the body was lifeless, and it was carried on a stretcher up to the apartment. Soon, the palace was buzzing with guards, police, officials, and Ministers. A little later, the body was taken to the mortuary, and an autopsy was performed. Soon afterwards, the authorities announced that Jan Masaryk had committed suicide by jumping from the window of his bathroom.

Even at the time, there were those who doubted that story. Witnesses contradicted each other. When precisely had the body been found? Who exactly was on duty at the Černinský Palace that night? Who had access to Masaryk's apartment? Had there, or had there not, been visitors during the night? If Masaryk had wanted to kill himself, why risk failure – like Drtina – by throwing himself from a window, when he had access to sleeping pills?

Why draft a speech for the next day's ceremony? Why use the bathroom window, which was obstructed, stiff to open, and smaller than the window of his bedroom, already left open the night before? Why had the body fallen three or four feet to the side of the bathroom window, not directly underneath?

And what about the state of the apartment? The bedroom was in total disorder – the bed awry, the pillows missing, the under-sheet torn from the mattress, the night table tilted, with books jutting over the edge, the ashtray full of varied cigarette-ends, the chairs overturned, doors and drawers open, broken bottles, glasses, and a cup lying on the floor. The bathroom was in a worse state still. The medicine chest was empty, the floor littered with crushed glass, the bathmat tossed across the room, the towels in crumpled heaps. In the bath was one of the missing pillows; the other was under the basin. The window-seat was overturned, with fingermarks on the wall around it. The lavatory bowl was filthy, and there was a smear of excrement on the window-sill. Razor-blades had been scattered all over the room, and from a hook on the door hung a knotted cord made of drawstrings from several pairs of pyjamas – a hasty attempt, some thought, to mimic wild efforts at suicide.

Twenty years later, during the brief liberal lull of Alexander Dubček's 'Prague Spring' in 1968, the American reporter Claire Sterling did her best to piece together what must have happened to Masaryk. By then, sundry witnesses had died, many of them far from peacefully. Those dead from natural causes included two of the palace guards, and the doctor who had done the autopsy on Masaryk's body. He had failed to sign the burial certificate: some of his friends alleged that he had suspected murder, and had signed the post-mortem report only under duress. The police physician who had first pronounced Masaryk dead had himself died suddenly not long afterwards – at police headquarters: he was said to have injected petrol into his veins. A confidant of his, the editor of a Catholic newspaper, had been arrested on the same day, and had died in prison. A police superintendent who had seen Masaryk's body and declared that there was evidence of murder had also died, under interrogation. A security officer who had tried to investigate the case had been tortured and then shot. A few weeks earlier, on 27 May 1948, an alleged NKVD officer, Major Augustin Schramm, whom some believed to have been responsible for Masaryk's death, had been assassinated. Two supposed 'hit men' had been tried and executed for the assassination, but both had protested their innocence: they had gone to

Schramm's home, they said, but found another team there already. The security man who had investigated Schramm's death had shortly afterwards been dismissed from the service; so had the Prague CID officer who had briefly looked into Masaryk's death before the security police took over. The Chief of State Security had himself been dismissed two months after Masaryk's death; and Vladimír Clementis, Masaryk's deputy and successor as Foreign Minister, had been one of those hanged after the Slánský trial in 1952, when fourteen Jewish Communist officials had been arraigned on trumped-up charges of treason.

Examining evidence from the survivors, Mrs Sterling had to pick her way through thickets of evasion, innuendo, and fear. One of Masaryk's secretaries, who insisted that his master had killed himself, proved both shifty and misleading. Even the State Prosecutor assigned to reopen the case in 1968 was caught out in several lies. It was impossible to determine, so many years later, just how Jan Masaryk had met his death; but Claire Sterling's conclusion, after exhaustive inquiries, was that he had indeed been murdered. Intruders, she believed, had broken into his quarters during the night: there were eleven ways in, and twenty-five keys to his private lift. They had awakened him quietly, and sat at his bedside, smoking and haranguing him. They knew all about his escape plan: that way out was stopped. Instead, he must jump to his death. When he refused, they had hauled him from the bed and tried to force him through the bedroom window; but he had fought back. Even at sixty-two, he was still big and powerful. Perhaps he had made a dash for the bathroom – the door was close to the bed. The struggle had left the bedroom in chaos. In the bathroom, someone's shoulder or elbow had hit the medicine chest, spilling its contents. One of the intruders had grabbed the pillows, to stifle him, perhaps in the bath. Suffocation can cause loss of sphincter control. As his strength ebbed, they had heaved him up on to the window-sill, then with a final struggling effort pitched him out into the night.

However it happened, Jan Masaryk – brave, funny, sad, scrupulous, loyal – had become a carcass. Almost to the end, he had seemed to hope that he could side-step, parry, and mitigate oppression like Jaroslav Hašek's *Good Soldier Švejk*. Now, it was as if that book had been cruelly rewritten by another author, born like Hašek in Prague and in the same year, 1883 – the true prophet of nightmare, Franz Kafka. Two months after Masaryk's death, the Communists held a fresh election: but this time there was only one list of candidates. In June, Edvard Beneš resigned the Presidency; in September, he died. Czechoslovak democracy had already died that spring.

It was the last, textbook example of Soviet-backed Communist usurpation in Eastern Europe. Before long, indeed, the Czechoslovak Communist Party produced just such a textbook: *How Parliament Can Play a Revolutionary Part in the Transition to Socialism and the Role of the Popular Masses*. The methods it described were classic: later theorists would call them 'salami tactics'. First, impose Communist Ministers on a coalition Government, if possible in key posts like the Ministry of the Interior. Then gradually establish or infiltrate centres of power outside Parliament, for example by 'arming the proletariat', forming Action Committees, and expanding your own secret police. This creates 'a pincer movement operating from above and below'. The end product is anti-democratic revolution, as in Prague in 1948:

While, prior to the elections in 1946, the bourgeoisie had a relatively strong mass basis, a short time of under two years of people's democratic government [sic] was sufficient for the disintegration of the political army upon which the bourgeoisie could formerly count.

By the time this happened in Czechoslovakia, the process had become so repetitive as to seem like a ritual. Five countries of Eastern Europe – Albania, Poland, Bulgaria, Rumania, and Hungary – had all suffered a similar fate. The only partial exceptions were those with geography on their side, and powerful patriotic armies: Finland and Yugoslavia. Each was just able to maintain a degree of independence under a basically Marxist regime.

In Finland, no government could afford to ignore Soviet wishes: but Stalin himself respected the toughness that Finns had shown during the 1939–40 'Winter War'. The result was an uneasy stand-off. In March 1945, a Left-wing coalition won the election, and the Communists secured the Ministry of the Interior. War trials and purges followed; but the country never quite became a Soviet puppet, and remained formally neutral as between East and West.

Muscle, distance, and Marxism did the same for Yugoslavia. Here, a coalition Government was established in March 1945; but at the general election that November there was no opposition list of candidates, only a separate ballot-box in which to express dissent. Opposition leaders had meanwhile been arrested or harassed in other ways, and within a short time the Communist partisan leader Marshal Tito – Josip Broz – was in undisputed command. He had always chafed at Soviet pretensions, even making fun of 'socialist realism' in official Moscow art; in May 1945 he had declared: 'We demand that everyone be master in his own house.' His quarrel with Stalin came to a head in June 1948, when Yugoslavia was expelled from the Cominform and became the conscious champion of 'positive neutrality' and 'active co-existence'.

For the other countries of Eastern Europe, no such alternative existed. All were soon turned into Soviet colonies – 'satellites' was the common euphemistic term.

In Albania, there was no intermediate, coalition stage. At the first postwar elections in December 1945, voters were offered a single list of candidates; 86 percent of the electorate endorsed the Communists, led by Enver Hoxha, who in the following year deposed King Zog and ruled as a military dictator. An American journalist aptly described Hoxha's Albania as 'a kind of Communist outhouse – the real end of the line.'

In Poland, the London Government-in-exile under Stanisław Mikołajczyk had had to accept not only a re-drawing of the frontiers but also, as in Czechoslovakia, a minority role in a coalition with its Soviet-backed rival, the so-called 'Lublin Committee'. Again, the Lublin Poles held the key positions, including the Ministry of Public Security; and they used censorship, threats, and even murder against the 'bourgeois' parties and press. By May 1947, a Western correspondent could write with some accuracy: 'Russia operates a sort of absentee Government in Poland.'

In Bulgaria's coalition Government, set up at the Liberation in September 1944, the Minister of the Interior and the Minister of Justice were both Communists. Purges, intimidation, and the imprisonment of opposition leaders made a travesty of the eventual elections. 'By January 1948,' wrote another Western reporter, 'Bulgaria was not simply in Communist hands; it was directly in Soviet hands.'

In Rumania, King Michael himself had broken with the Nazis in 1944, and set up a coalition Government in which the Communists were represented. They, according to their Moscow-trained leader Ana Pauker, had numbered only a thousand before the Red Army arrived; but with other left-wing parties they formed a 'National Democratic Front' and organized a series of demonstrations and strikes. The Red Army helped them to disarm the few Rumanian troops still left in the capital; and in February 1945 the Soviet Union insisted that the King accept Communist Ministers of the Interior and of Justice. In preparation for the election eventually held in November 1946, the Government broke up rival parties' meetings, per-suaded printers to black their literature, imprisoned and killed their leaders, and obstructed the registration of their supporters. Needless to say, the Communists 'won' the election. 'In no time,' wrote Tina Cosmin, the wife of an escaping dissident, 'the whole structure of Rumania had become an instrument of terror based upon the NKVD system.'

In Hungary, the 1944 coalition Government included only two Communist Ministers; but Party members were active elsewhere, especially in the Ministry of the Interior. In the general election of 1945, the moderate liberal Smallholders' Party came top of the poll; but the Communists threatened to quit the Government, leaving it in the minority, unless they were given the Ministry of the Interior. They also formed a Left-wing block, organized mass demonstrations, and insisted on the dismissal of twenty-two Smallholders' representatives. In December 1946, the Communist Ministers of the Interior and of Defence began making widespread arrests: they claimed to have unmasked a Right-wing conspiracy. In August 1947, in a highly suspect election, 35 percent of Hungarians still voted for the opposition, which by now was closely identified with the Roman Catholic Church. At length, in 1949, the militant Cardinal József Mindszenty was arrested and sentenced to life imprisonment. Soon afterwards, the Assembly was dissolved, and in a single-list election the Government claimed 90 percent of the votes. Looking back from exile on what had happened, the Smallholders' leader Ferenc Nagy declared: 'One could truthfully say that the Communist party conquered the country with the Red Army.'

Such was the story throughout Eastern Europe, prompting Winston Churchill's resounding words at Fulton, Missouri, on 5 March 1946: 'From Stettin in the Baltic to Trieste in the Adriatic, an iron curtain has descended across the continent.' The cruel irony was that eighteen months earlier Churchill himself had connived at the division of Europe. In Moscow, on 9 October 1944, in a late-night meeting at the Kremlin, he had suggested to Stalin: 'Let us settle about our affairs in the Balkans. Your armies are in Rumania and Bulgaria. We have interests, missions and agents there. Don't let us get at cross-purposes in small ways. So far as Britain and Russia are concerned, how would it do for you to have ninety per cent predominance in Rumania, for us to have ninety per cent of the say in Greece, and go fifty-fifty about Yugoslavia?' While the interpreter was translating this, Churchill took a half-sheet of paper and wrote down the percentages, adding '50–50 per cent' for Hungary and, for Bulgaria, 'Russia 75 per cent, the others 25 per cent'. Stalin looked at it, then made a large blue-pencil tick on it and handed it back. For a moment, there was silence; then Churchill said: 'Might it not be thought rather cynical if it seemed we had disposed of these issues, so fateful to millions of people, in such an offhand manner? Let us burn the paper.' 'No,' Stalin answered. 'You keep it.'

At the time, of course, Churchill could not foresee just how the Russians would behave. 'The disadvantage of them,' he told a political friend, 'is that one is not sure of their reactions. One strokes the nose of the alligator and the ensuing gurgle may be a purr of affection, a grunt of stimulated appetite, or a snarl of enraged animosity. One cannot tell.' At the Yalta Conference in February 1945, Stalin accepted the 'Declaration on Liberated Europe' requiring among other things free elections in countries formerly under Nazi control; and the Western powers recalled this as the 'iron curtain' gradually came down. In Poland, Bulgaria, and Rumania, they actually secured some minor changes in the early coalition governments: but that was all.

Could the West have done more? For four years, from 1945 to 1949, it had a monopoly of the atomic bomb; and at least one experienced Moscow correspondent, Paul Winterton, writing in the aftermath of Hiroshima, claimed to detect 'a marked strengthening of Anglo-American diplomacy in Europe.' 'It is now less certain', he wrote, 'that we shall be obliged to fall in with the Russian plan to divide the world into spheres of influence.'

In fact, any nuclear threat might have led Stalin simply to call the West's bluff. The only real option was conventional war; and the West was no better placed to fight in Eastern Europe now than it had been to defend Czechoslovakia in 1938 or Poland in 1939. Most Western countries, moreover, were exhausted – physically, economically, psychologically. Their troops were being demobilized; relief and reconstruction in Western Europe were absorbing those that remained. And even if military action had still been possible, public opinion would surely have rebelled. To most people in the West now, the place to solve postwar problems was the United Nations; the Soviet Union was still a gallant ally against Fascism and Nazism; Communism still seemed a kind of impatient Socialism; Stalin was still 'Uncle Joe'; and the soldiers of the Red Army were still the heroes of Stalingrad, not the plunderers of Berlin.

Western attitudes to the Soviet Union had long been ambivalent. One strand in the skein was deep feeling for the land of Russia itself. Tómaš Masaryk had written two heartfelt volumes on *The Spirit of Russia* before World War I. 'Russia was and is', he said, 'the most interesting country known to me' – partly because it had 'preserved the childhood of Europe', partly because of the same spell that it cast on Russian writers themselves. In 1906, when

Masaryk was starting his *magnum opus*, Aleksandr Blok apostrophized:

> Russia, girdled with rivers
> and your forests' intricate maze,
> your cranes and your marshy acres,
> and the sorcerer's cloudy gaze;
>
> where peoples with differing features
> from region to region, high and low,
> at nightfall dance their choral dances
> by their burning villages' glow;
>
> where fortune-tellers and wizards
> cast spells on the standing wheat,
> and witches revel through blizzards
> with demons in the whirling street;
>
> where boisterous snowstorms cover
> the poor hut to its pointed roof
> and waiting for her faithless lover
> a girl inside sharpens a knife;
>
> where sapling shoots and branches flail
> the crossroads and the country ways
> and, whistling through bare twigs, the gale
> sings legends of departed days...

Half a century later, the English novelist John Wain evoked a similar landscape of the mind:

I love the Russia I see when I close my eyes, that great ocean of land, where wolves run through the endless forests, where the cart-ruts fill with gleaming water in the spring rain, where people talk hour after hour, with inexhaustible passion, about what is going on in their minds, and drink glasses of tea and talk again, till dawn comes up outside the windows and head-shawled women hurry to obey the church bells; where a gentleman with a long gun, and a game-bag over his shoulder, knocks at a peasant's hut and asks for a night's shelter; where the railway engines are fuelled with birch-logs; where the human spirit, in spite of the malice of unbreakable tyranny, guards its freedom in some inner fastness, so that at any unexpected moment it can happen that we hear a Russian voice saying something swift and leaping and unanswerable. 'Who gave you a place among the poets?' 'Who gave me a place among the human race?'

Turgenev, Tolstoy, Chekhov, Gogol', Dostoevsky, Gor'ky: each, for Western readers, had opened new vistas of feeling – courage, guilt, rage, passion, despair, defiance. In the Don trilogy of Mikhail Aleksandrovich Sholokhov or the broad, spacious films of Eisenstein and Donskoi, those vistas of the human spirit had seemed at one with Russia's vast distances – the harsh unending frozen landscape that had helped defeat Hitler's armies like those of Napoleon before him. And the Red Army's savage, stoical resistance to the Nazis had earned both admiration for a great people and fearsome respect for a great power.

The touch of fear had always been present – especially among Russia's neighbours. The Polish poet Adam Mickiewicz, writing in the 1830's, had felt it when looking at Russian faces:

> I meet the people: broad-shouldered
> Broad-chested, and thick-skulled
> Like the animals and trees of the north,
> Full-blooded, hearty and strong.
> But each face is like their country
> An empty, open and wild plain:
> And from their hearts, as from underground volcanoes,
> No fire has yet risen to light their faces,
> Nor glows from ignited lips,
> Nor goes out in dark lines on foreheads
> As with the faces of people in the east and west,
> Over which so much of life's troubles has passed
> Of legends and events, sorrows and hopes,
> That every face is a memorial to the nation.
> Here, people's eyes, like the cities of this country
> Are large and clear; never does the soul's tumult
> Move the pupil with an extraordinary glance,
> Never does desolation cloud them over long.
> Seen from a distance they are splendid, marvellous;
> Once inside, they are empty and deserted.
> The body of this people is like a fat cocoon,
> Inside which sleeps a caterpillar-soul,
> While shaping its breast for flight
> Unfolding its wings, flexing and adorning –
> But when the sun of freedom shall rise,
> What kind of insect will fly out from that shroud?

The Communist Revolution of 1917 provided no clear answer. For an acute Polish observer like Czesław Miłosz,

the Russian Revolution was personified not by Lenin but by Vladimir Mayakovsky. And quite rightly, I think, because his work welded revolutionary theory with the old dream Russians had of themselves as a chosen nation, and the two messianisms nourished each other: class as redeemer and nation as redeemer.... Mayakovsky symbolized for me the Russians' revolution and – who knows? – perhaps their whole eternally ambiguous civilization, so powerful, human, hungry for justice in literature, and so miserable and cruel in human affairs.

Tómaš Masaryk, writing four years after the Revolution, pointed out that

the Bolsheviks have accepted Marxism and pride themselves on being its only orthodox adherents. They do not realize how much they owe to Bakunin, the adversary of Marx. From him they took over the mystic faith in the revolution, in the Russian people, in its unique socialist and communist capacity.... All the shortcomings which characterized the Russian state, the Russian school and the Russian church, characterize also the Bolshevik state and regime, because they come from the same people and have been formed in the same way.

Initially, some Western observers were less disabused. To them, the Revolution was an embodiment of hope – a proof that utopian aspirations need not remain mere theory, that human beings could throw off their shackles and build a new society founded on reason, equality, and justice. 'In the nineteen-thirties,' wrote the Hungarian-born novelist Arthur Koestler, himself briefly a Communist, 'conversion to the Communist faith was not a fashion or craze – it was a sincere and spontaneous expression of an optimism born of despair: an abortive revolution of the spirit, a misfired Renaissance, a false dawn of history.'

Motives, of course, were mixed. The French novelist Henri Barbusse found in Communism a fulfilment that his claustrophobic writing denied him. He had volunteered to serve in World War I, but had lost his fervour after the slaughter he chronicled in *Le feu*. The Russian Revolution was a substitute crusade. Born in a Paris suburb, he died in Moscow in 1935. For his older colleague Romain Rolland, veteran internationalist and author of the ten-volume *Jean-Christophe*, the Revolution was no crusade, but a safeguard against aggression: in the year that Barbusse died, Rolland produced a collection of essays entitled *Par la révolution, la paix*. Pacifism likewise inspired the German poet Johannes Becher, who went into exile in the Soviet Union in the same year. Across the Channel, also in 1935, the British Socialists Sidney and Beatrice Webb published *Soviet Communism: A New Civilization?* When they reissued it two years later, they left out the question-mark.

By then, the Spanish Civil War had broken out. With Fascist and Nazi aid going to General Franco, many saw the Civil War as a first round in the wider conflict that was coming. Yet the democratic governments did little to help the Spanish Republic: the only effective action seemed to come from volunteers, from Russia, and from the far Left. Long after World War II, the Paris Cinémathèque's copy of *L'Espoir*, André Malraux's film of the Spanish Civil War, was still prefaced by a Ministerial tribute to the Communists' role. In this political atmosphere, marked also by world-wide slump and unemployment, sympathy with the Soviet Union was common among young people, from idealistic left-wing workers to intellectual admirers of Pudovkin's propaganda films. The most celebrated expression of the general mood came from the 'New Writing' movement associated with W.H. Auden, Stephen Spender, Louis MacNeice, and C. Day-Lewis, whose continental counterparts included the French poet Louis Aragon and the Italian novelist Secondo Tranquilli, better known as 'Ignazio Silone'. Far less prominent, at that time, were the Communist sympathizers whose ideals were harnessed to Soviet espionage; they included Donald Maclean, Guy Burgess, Kim Philby, and Anthony Blunt.

Before long, however, doubts had begun to arise. André Gide, the quintessential French man-of-letters, had startled some of his friends in the early 1930's when he announced his 'sympathy for the USSR'. In 1936, he was persuaded to travel there on a widely-publicized semi-official tour. He was fascinated, he said, 'by the strangeness of that most admirable country, and won over by the warm likeability of its inhabitants'. But he felt restricted by 'perpetual surveillance', and was extremely annoyed when his speeches were censored and embellished. A telegram to Stalin, he found, could not address him simply as 'you': it had to say 'you, leader of the workers', 'you, master of the peoples', or some similar phrase. Back in Paris a few weeks later, Gide wrote an account of his visit, *Retour de l'URSS*. In it he expressed both his admiration and his misgivings – including disillusion about the achievement of communism and dismay at the absence of liberty. 'I doubt', he wrote, 'whether in any other country in the world, even Hitler's Germany, thought is less free, more bowed down, more fearful (terrorized), more vassalized.'

Gide's observations provoked a storm on the French Left. An icy silence, two years later, greeted *Homage to Catalonia*, George Orwell's first-hand account of how the Communists had treated their anarchist and Trotskyite allies in the Spanish Civil War. Meanwhile, misgivings had grown as further disclosures leaked out of the Soviet Union: the liquidation of the kulaks, or peasant proprietors, under the first Five-Year Plan; the persecution of non-conformist poets like Osip Mandel'shtam; above all, the so-called 'Yezhov-shchina', the Stalinist purge conducted in 1936–38 by Nikolai Ivanovich Yezhov, head of the NKVD and predecessor of the still more sinister Lavrenti Pavlovich Beria. Many observers of the ensuing Moscow Trials were puzzled by the confessions extorted from accused men who seemed to be innocent: little was known of 'brainwashing' in the West until 1940, when Arthur Koestler published *Darkness at Noon*, a fictional account of the Trials which described convincingly how one of the defendants, 'Rubashov', was broken down.

The Nazi-Soviet non-aggression pact of August 1939 had led to further disillusion. Only in June 1941, when Hitler broke the pact and invaded the USSR, did the tide begin to turn again. The feats of the Red Army and the sufferings of the Russian people, notably in the long siege of Leningrad,

aroused widespread fellow-feeling. The popular song-writers of Tin Pan
Alley caught the mood in a sentimental ballad like 'Russian Rose', with a
Yiddish-Tziganer-Slavonic six-note melody. Hollywood, not yet a prey to
McCarthyite anti-Communist purges, turned out several similar tributes to
the Soviet Union: *Song of Russia*, with Robert Taylor as an American
orchestral conductor who marries a Russian partisan fighter; *North Star*,
from a screenplay by Lillian Hellman, about a Russian village overrun by the
Nazis; *Days of Glory* – guerrilla warfare with Gregory Peck and Tamara
Toumanova; and, notoriously, *Mission to Moscow*. Based on the reminisc-
ences of Joseph E. Davies, US Ambassador to the Soviet Union in 1936–38,
this film actually whitewashed the Moscow Trials, which Davies himself had
condemned as 'horrible', adding that 'the terror here is a horrifying fact.'

In Britain, Winston Churchill had done his best to distinguish between
admiration for the Russian people and detestation of the Soviet regime. For
some time, he had even prevented the BBC from broadcasting the
'Internationale' alongside other Allied national anthems. With the coming of
peace, returning Western correspondents, who had spent the war in
Moscow, were able to correct the bias of their previously censored
dispatches: Paul Winterton, in particular, published *Report on Russia* in the
firm belief that 'international understanding and final world peace can be
built securely only on truth and knowledge.' His words could not stave off
the subsequent outcry: wartime sentiment was still strong. How strong, had
been shown in an unexpected quarter towards the end of the war, when
George Orwell had offered the London publishers Faber and Faber the
manuscript of *Animal Farm*, his parable of how the Russian Revolution had
turned sour. Writing on behalf of the firm, T.S. Eliot of all people felt
obliged to reject it. This, he said, was not 'the right point of view from which
to criticize the political situation at the present time'.

Only gradually, therefore, did many people in Western Europe wake up to
the fact of what came to be called 'the Cold War'. As the USSR clamped
down more and more on the countries of Eastern Europe, there was anxious
debate as to whether its ambitions pointed further west. Was Soviet policy
merely paranoiac? 'We must remember,' wrote Stalin in 1947, in *Problems of
Leninism*, 'that we are surrounded by people, classes and governments who
openly express their intense hatred for us. We must remember that we are at
all times but a hair's breadth from every manner of invasion.' 'Defensive
expansionism' was one Western commentator's term for Russia's urge to

insulate herself with a ring of compliant colonies; but if this was traditional statecraft, Stalin's rhetoric was often more ambitious and alarming. His aim, he declared, was the 'consolidation of the dictatorship of the proletariat in one country, using it as a point of support for the overthrow of imperialism [sic] in all countries.'

France and Italy, in particular, might seem to lend themselves to a possible coup. In each, the postwar coalition Government included Communist Ministers, and the Communists had fomented political strikes. 'Unfortunately,' as the Soviet Communist Party admitted in May 1948, 'the Soviet Army could not render ... assistance to the French and Italian Communist Parties.' What was more, the coalition governments in Western Europe soon lost their Communist Ministers. In Belgium, the Communists resigned in May 1947, in a dispute over coal prices and subsidies. In France they were dismissed in May, after a quarrel about the Government's wage freeze. In Italy, they were dropped a few weeks later; and at the subsequent election in April 1948, despite fears engendered by the recent coup in Prague, the Christian Democrats won a reassuring victory, heralding the series of Centre coalitions that was to last for more than thirty years.

Internal subversion now seemed unlikely: but the military threat remained. Lenin had predicted 'a series of frightful collisions between the Soviet Republic and the bourgeois states', whom Stalin now accused of sending 'spies, assassins and wreckers into our country and ... waiting for a favourable opportunity to attack it by armed force.' To defend itself, he argued, the Soviet Union must forestall attack. On 5 March 1948, nine days after the Prague coup, the US Military Governor in Germany, General Lucius D. Clay, reported confidentially to Washington his fear that 'war could break out with dramatic suddenness.' To make matters worse, the military balance was dangerously asymmetrical. The West might have a monopoly of nuclear weapons, but it was short-lived: in September 1949, the Soviet Union was to explode a device of its own. And Soviet conventional forces were formidable. In mid-1948, the Red Army numbered 2½ million, well equipped with tanks and self-propelled guns, plus 400,000 in the Soviet security forces and 700,000 in the armies of the 'satellite' States – a combined strength of 3,600,000 against an Anglo-American total of about 2,700,000 servicemen, many of them conscripts and most of them heartily sick of war.

It was time for the West, reluctantly, to look to its defences. In Europe, Ernest Bevin made the first move early in 1948, proposing to France, the

Netherlands, Belgium, and Luxembourg a series of bilateral security agreements. The Belgian Foreign Minister, Paul-Henri Spaak, suggested instead a collective arrangement, social, cultural, and economic as well as military. On 4 March 1948, eight days after the Prague coup, negotiations began in Brussels; on 17 March, eight days after Jan Masaryk's death, the Treaty was signed. It pledged its signatories to aid each other against armed aggression – automatically if in Europe, after consultation if elsewhere. Unlike the Dunkirk Treaty signed by Britain and France a year earlier, the Brussels Treaty was not confined to defence against Germany. The new threat appeared to come from further East; and Germany, it seemed, was in some danger of being both a battleground and a prize.

The Potsdam Agreement of 1945 had laid down that 'during the occupation period Germany shall be treated as a single economic entity.' The American, British, French, and Soviet Commanders-in-Chief who made up the Allied Control Council in Berlin were to rule 'jointly, in matters affecting Germany as a whole'. But their decisions were to be unanimous, and each was to have 'supreme authority' in his own zone. In this way, the scene was set for the Soviet Union to treat the Eastern zone of Germany and the Eastern sector of Berlin as yet another Soviet 'satellite'.

The process had begun as soon as hostilities had ended. When the Americans reached Berlin on 1 July 1945, they found an administration already in place, with non-Communists in some of the posts, but Party members in control of education and the police. Even the clocks were set to Moscow time: it was still dark at 7 a.m. on a summer morning, and still light at midnight. In the Western zones of Germany, the Allies were contributing some 700 million dollars a year; from the East, the Soviet Union was taking 500 million in reparations. It also amalgamated two hundred firms into *Sowjetische Aktiengesellschaften,* in which it held a majority of the shares. It carried out a drastic land reform programme; it organized so-called 'anti-Fascist democratic mass organizations'; it set up trade unions whose officials were appointed, not elected. Politically, it forced the East German Socialist Party to merge with the Communists in a 'Socialist Unity Party' – the *Sozialistische Einheitspartei Deutschlands* or SED. The party's appeal was catholic, to say the least: one of its militants coined the slogan 'The SED – the great friend of the little Nazi.'

In the local elections held in the Eastern zone in September 1946, the Soviet authorities used familiar tactics. The SED was allowed to put up candidates in all 11,632 electoral districts; the Christian Democrats were allowed to stand in only 2,082, and the Liberals in only 1,121. Non-Marxist leaders were harassed and in three cases forced out of office; in several areas, their meetings were broken up. In the provincial or *Land* elections that October, the SED was allotted 900 tons of newsprint for its manifestos, while the Christian Democrats and Liberals had only nine. For the SED, the result was disappointing: it won absolute majorities in only two of the five Eastern *Länder*. But it still secured half or more of the Cabinet posts in each of the *Land* Governments; and in four of the five it took over the Ministry of the Interior, thereby controlling the police.

The British and Americans, meanwhile, had been growing more and more restive. Not only was the Soviet Union hindering recovery by refusing to treat Germany as an economic whole: her reparations policy was actually draining scarce resources away from the West. In May 1946, after further argument, General Clay finally halted reparations payments to the East, and proposed to Washington that Britain be officially invited to merge the British and American zones. Agreement was reached in December, and the 'Bizone' came into being on 1 January 1947. The Soviet Union protested; but after inconclusive talks at the four-power Moscow Conference in March and April, the Bizone authorities set up an Economic Council of delegates from the *Land* Assemblies and an Executive Committee representing the *Land* Governments. The Soviet Union riposted with an East German Permanent Economic Commission, a majority of which was Soviet-appointed, and the first of a series of People's Congresses.

In February 1948, the British and Americans enlarged the Economic Council, and added both an upper house or *Länderrat* and a High Court – creating what Clay called 'a realistic political structure of a federal type'. He added: 'We had the machinery for government, if not a government.' The structure was soon completed by a central bank, the *Bank Deutscher Länder*. Meanwhile, representatives of the United States, Britain, and the other four Brussels Treaty powers – France, the Netherlands, Belgium, and Luxembourg – began a conference in London at which they agreed among other things to establish international control over the industries of the Ruhr.

Again the Soviet Union riposted – this time by increasing the powers of the East German Economic Commission and holding a second People's Congress, 'elected' on the familiar basis of a single list. The Congress appointed a People's Council, which in turn set up a committee to draft a supposedly 'all-German' Constitution. Finally, on 20 March 1948, the

Soviet delegation walked out of the four-power Control Council in Berlin.

On 7 June 1948, the London Conference recommended that the Western *Länder* elect a Constituent Assembly to draft a federal Constitution, with a view – formally, at least – to 'putting an end to the present division of Germany.'

In reality, of course, division had been virtually inevitable from the moment the Soviet Union had imposed its own system on the Eastern zone. The moves and counter-moves by East and West were in this sense merely the working-out of a foregone conclusion. But now, in midsummer 1948, events in Germany suddenly came to a crisis. While the world held its breath, the West stood up to a direct Soviet challenge. This time the prize was the beleaguered city of Berlin.

On Sunday 20 June 1948, the Western Allies issued a new West German currency, the Deutsche Mark. The Soviet Union retaliated by announcing its own currency reform – and by trying to impose it on the whole of Berlin. At the same time, it staged a further walkout from the four-power Kommandatura; and at 6 a.m. on Thursday, it halted all rail traffic between Berlin and the West. Soon, the ban was extended to canal and road transport; and by 4 August 1948, the city was in a state of siege.

The Western authorities had realized that their currency reform involved a risk. On 10 April 1948, in a private telex conversation with General Omar Bradley, the Army Chief of Staff, Clay had warned:

You will understand, of course, that our separate currency reform in near future followed by partial German government in Frankfurt will develop the real crisis.... Why are we in Europe? We have lost Czechoslovakia. We have lost Finland. Norway is threatened. We retreat from Berlin,... After Berlin will come Western Germany and our strength there relatively is no greater and our position no more tenable than Berlin. If we mean that we are to hold Europe against communism, we must not budge.... I believe the future of democracy requires us to stay here until forced out. God knows this is not a heroic pose because there will be nothing heroic in having to take humiliation without retaliation.

Ernest Bevin agreed. 'The abandonment of Berlin', he said, 'would mean the loss of western Europe.' 'We were going to stay, period,' added Harry S. Truman.

When the Soviet blockade began, the 2½ million civilians in the Western sectors of Berlin had food for 36 days and coal for 45 days. Any further supplies would have to come in by air. On the first day of the rail ban, Clay asked Air Force General Curtis LeMay to make available his entire fleet of C-47's. Next day, the great airlift began. By 22 July, eighty C-47's and fifty-two C-54's were each making two round trips a day, carrying a total of 2,400–2,500 tons. But even this was only just over half what was needed. The US Air Force was reluctant to commit more aircraft for fear of weakening its fighting strength. Truman and Clay discussed the possibility of breaking the road blockade by means of armed convoys; but although Clay argued for it, Truman decided against. Instead, he intensified talks with the Soviet authorities, and ordered a rapid expansion of the airlift. In Berlin, to accommodate further flights, tens of thousands of people, working in shifts round the clock, built new runways at Tempelhof and Gatow, and laid the foundations for a third airport at Tegel. British Sunderland flying-boats even landed on the waters of the Havel. By 20 August 1948, the airlift was carrying an average of 3,300 tons a day; by September, the average was 4,000; by December, 4,500; by February 1949, 5,500; and by spring, 8,000 tons – as much as had previously come in by rail and water. Day after day, the air throbbed to the sound of engines as machines followed each other in: in one record day, they delivered nearly 13,000 tons of food, fuel, goods, and raw materials. In all, there were 200,000 flights, carrying 1½ million tons of cargo, including 950,000 tons of coal and 438,000 tons of food. Inevitably, there were accidents: they cost fifty lives. Nevertheless, the airlift was a triumph. It was also a spectacular demonstration of Western solidarity.

Another, no less important, accompanied it. Already, in March 1948, welcoming the Brussels Treaty, President Truman had declared: 'I am sure that the determination of the free countries of Europe to protect themselves will be matched by an equal determination on our part to help them to protect themselves.' So saying, he urged Congress to provide for universal military training and to restore selective service. In April, Ernest Bevin proposed a North Atlantic security system; and in June, backed by Arthur H. Vandenberg's Senate resolution calling for regional arrangements and 'mutual aid', US officials began talks with representatives of Canada and the Brussels Treaty powers. In February 1949 the talks became negotiations; and on 4 April 1949, twelve countries signed the North Atlantic Treaty – the original seven participants in the talks, together with Denmark, Iceland, Italy, Norway, and Portugal. Essentially, they agreed 'that an armed attack against one or more of them shall be considered an attack against them all.'

Almost immediately, the Soviet Union agreed to call off the blockade of Berlin. On 4 May 1949, the four occupying powers announced that normal land and water traffic would resume on 12 May. Moderation, strength, and solidarity had won the day.

The division of Germany, however, was now almost complete. On 8 May 1949, the Western Constituent Assembly, renamed the 'Parliamentary Council', adopted the new constitution, the *Grundgesetz* or 'Basic Law'. A week later, the East German People's Congress approved a rival constitution of its own. On Sunday 14 August 1949, the West Germans went to the polls to elect both houses of their new federal Parliament. On 12 September, the Parliament elected as Federal President the Liberal statesman Theodor Heuss. He in turn proposed as Chancellor Konrad Adenauer, now 73 years old. Adenauer squeaked in by a one-vote majority. He admitted afterwards, smiling, that he had voted for himself.

One month afterwards, on 7 October 1949, with no pretence of elections, the East German People's Council declared itself the 'Provisional People's Chamber' and published the new Constitution. Three days later, the Eastern *Land* Assemblies selected delegates to a second legislative chamber; and on 11 October, the two chambers elected as President of the East German Republic the veteran Moscow-trained Communist Wilhelm Pieck – in some ways the mirror-image of Adenauer, even to the point of age.

With that, the division of Germany was complete. Churchill's 'iron curtain' had advanced from Stettin almost to Lübeck, and it divided Berlin. But West Berlin was still free, and so was West Germany. One half of Europe at least could enjoy the fruits of peace.

6
Miracles and Corporation Men

'New Marks for old!'

Unlike the cry that robbed Aladdin of his wonderful lamp, this offer – the German currency reform of 1948 – came from no crafty oriental sorcerer or wicked 'uncle', but from a 51-year-old Bavarian Protestant and professor of economics, Ludwig Erhard. The sequel seemed no less magic than if he had rubbed Aladdin's lamp: an 'economic miracle' that took Germany from penury to affluence in less than a decade. And, to many of his fellow-countrymen, Erhard seemed to incarnate that 'miracle' – a big man in a well-cut, well-filled suit, plump-faced, pink-cheeked, double-chinned, with thinning pale hair, sharp blue eyes, and a small mouth, chain-smoking fat cigars in paper holders.

In private, there was something soft, boyish, even schoolboyish in Erhard's enjoyment of what life had to offer – cheerful company, good food, hi-fi music, Alpine views and sunlight in the glass-walled modern house he had built for him by Sep Ruf, on the shore of the Tegernsee. The impression was well caught in his portrait by Oskar Kokoschka, sitting like Humpty Dumpty in an upright chair with legs uncrossed and chubby hands relaxed, but head erect and eyes beaming fixedly as if for a time-exposure in some school photograph.

He certainly lacked Konrad Adenauer's force and decisiveness. Jean Monnet told me a revealing story about them both. He had been chatting alone with Adenauer – about longevity, as old men will. 'Would you like to live to a hundred?' asked Monnet. 'It's a deal,' said Adenauer. Then Erhard came in. Asked the same question, he philosophized: 'There are cycles in human life . . .' he began. In *Who's Who*, that family vault of vanity, Adenauer gave as his recreation 'Gardening'. Erhard listed: 'Music (classical), discussions (serious themes, especially Economic Science)'.

Yet, at times, Erhard could look greyer, harder, and more formidable. Wounded in World War I, he had taken his doctorate at Frankfurt-am-

Main, joined his father's firm at Fürth in Bavaria, and worked as a research economist in nearby Nuremberg. He had stayed there throughout World War II. Then, one May morning in 1945, an American officer in a jeep had driven to his apartment and said 'Come on.' Erhard thought that for some reason he was being arrested. On the contrary: the US authorities had heard that he was an economist untainted by Nazism, and they wanted him as a member of the Bavarian *Land* Government they were setting up. He served as its Minister for Economic Affairs until the end of 1945. The following year saw him installed as an honorary professor at Munich, and as chairman of the Special Bureau for Currency and Credit at Bad Homburg, near Frankfurt. Early in 1948, in Frankfurt itself, he became Economic Director of the Anglo-American Bizone – the nearest approach, under Allied tutelage, to a West German Minister for Economic Affairs.

He owed his appointment to a minor scandal. His predecessor, offered a supply of American sweet corn, which Germans had never yet eaten, had scorned it as 'chickenfeed' – and been dismissed. Erhard, by contrast, got on well with the US authorities. 'I like the Americans' style,' he said; and they liked his – easygoing, informal, and blunt.

'It would be pious self-deception,' he told the Economic Council, 'to regard the slight improvement in production since 1945 as marking the beginning of a genuine recovery.' Ninety percent of the 1936 labour force was still producing only forty percent of 1936 industrial output. Marshall Aid was vital: but no real progress was possible without a currency which people could trust. At present, the market was flooded with worthless paper money, some of it printed in the Soviet zone. Trade was still based on barter, and the true banknote was still the cigarette. Since money earnings meant so little, workers at all levels lacked incentive. In some industries, half the employees regularly stayed away to scrounge for food.

At last, on Sunday 20 June 1948, came the long-awaited announcement of new Marks for old. In the Western zones of Germany, the old Reichsmark was no longer legal tender. From the next day onwards, ten Reichsmarks would be exchanged for one new Deutsche Mark; later, the rate was reduced to 6.5 Deutsche Marks for 100 Reichsmarks. As a concession, everyone was allowed to exchange 40 Reichsmarks each for 40 Deutsche Marks, with the promise of a similar rate, two months later, for a further 20 Reichsmarks each.

The results were dramatic. Savings were wiped out – but so were illusions. Hoards of paper money and unproductive bank balances were suddenly truncated: but their dazed owners found that smaller amounts of the new

Deutsche Mark could actually buy goods. With everyone thus called back to about the same starting-line, a new race for prosperity began. Many a German businessman who ten years later owned plush offices in Hamburg or Frankfurt was spurred on his career by the currency reform, starting on credit in a half-derelict warehouse or a back room in a shored-up building surrounded by rubble.

But success, as Erhard knew, could not have been achieved by a currency reform alone. Postwar Germany had inherited from the Nazis not only soaring inflation, but also a cat's-cradle of economic controls – rationing, price-fixing, tight restrictions on trade. These had produced a black market and a black economy run by professional 'fixers'. The Allied occupation had added further curbs and complications. To survive without Germany's Eastern food-growing lands, now under Soviet control, the Western zones would have to export their manufactures: but this was less easy than it sounds. Many able-bodied Germans, who might have been working productively, were now employed as clerks or servants in the Military Government. The output of chemicals, metals, and engineering products was squeezed to a trickle by Allied efforts to fragment German industry and impose restrictive 'levels of production'. Exports to the rest of Europe were hampered by American insistence that they be paid for in dollars, which most European countries lacked.

Even for humble domestic supplies, Allied forecasts were bleak. 'It was a time', said Erhard later, 'when it was calculated that for every German there would be one plate every five years; a pair of shoes every twelve years; a suit every fifty years; that only every fifth infant would lie in its own napkins; and that only every third German would have a chance of being buried in his own coffin.' Price-controls, meanwhile, were proving counter-productive. Rather than produce for a pittance, workshops were turning out items whose price was unrestricted: 'ashtrays, fancy lamps, dolls, and chandeliers,' noted one eye-witness, 'instead of the cups, pails, pots, and plates really needed.' The German economy was choking on a diet of decrees.

To Erhard, memories of Nazism made it especially distasteful. He had seen 'the extremes of nationalism, autarky, and government control'; now, he complained of 'too many laws'. He added later: 'We were well on the way to regimenting democracy to death.' Just before the currency reform, he suggested loosening some of the controls; but the US Military Governor, General Lucius Clay, felt obliged to refuse. 'We can unfortunately not negotiate with you,' he explained, 'before we have negotiated with a third power' – Britain? France? The Soviet Union? When Erhard asked whether some German exports might be paid for in European currencies instead of dollars, Clay spoke more sharply: 'I cannot on the one hand request dollar credits from my government and at the same time permit the export of German goods to the dollar-weak countries. The Marshall Plan will end these difficulties. If you think that the dollar clause damages you, then conduct your own foreign trade without dollar help.'

The threat was unmistakable: but on one crucial point Erhard defied it. On Sunday 20 June 1948, the day of the currency reform, he began to dismantle price controls without even warning the Allied authorities. It was the boldest act of his life.

When Monday dawned, there was uproar. Early in the morning, Erhard was summoned to the headquarters of the Military Government, there to be upbraided by its economic advisers. Reading out extracts from earlier decrees, they reminded him sharply that he was not empowered to alter Military Government regulations.

But Erhard stood his ground; and his retort was breath-taking. As he admitted, 'It was strictly laid down by the British and American control authorities that permission had to be obtained before any definite price changes could be made. The Allies never seem to have thought it possible that someone could have the idea, not to alter price controls, but simply to remove them.' Faced with this argument, the officials were furious – and adamant; so Erhard asked to see the US Military Governor. 'I was in good with him,' he said afterwards. Once alone with Clay, he explained why he had acted without warning. 'If I had told your officials, they would have stopped me. You have to help me; the entire horde is against me.' They had a long discussion. Finally, according to Erhard, Clay said: 'I have the impression that you are right, and I will help.' When Erhard told the officials that he had Clay's backing, they were astonished; but they had to acquiesce. Within the week, most prices had been freed from control.

What followed was Germany's 'economic miracle'. Ten years later, Erhard proudly quoted two liberal economists from France, Jacques Rueff and André Piettre, on the effect of his currency reform and liberalization:

The black market suddenly disappeared. Shop windows were full of goods; factory chimneys were smoking; and the streets swarmed with lorries. Everywhere the noise of new buildings going up replaced the deathly silence of the ruins. If the state of recovery was a surprise, its swiftness was even more so. In all sectors of economic life it began as the clocks struck on the day of the currency reform. Only an eye-witness can give an account of the sudden effect which currency reform had on the size of stocks and the wealth of goods on display. Shops filled up with goods from one day to the next; the factories began to work. On the eve of the currency reform the Germans were aimlessly wandering about their towns in search of a few additional items of food. A day later they thought of nothing but producing them. One day apathy was mirrored on their faces while on the next a whole nation looked hopefully into the future.

Whether the change was as rapid as that, it was certainly real. By 1950, West Germany's gross national product had caught up with the 1936 figure. Between 1950 and 1955 the national income rose by 12 percent a year, while exports grew even faster. From a small deficit in 1950, gold and foreign currency reserves reached nearly 13,000 million Deutsche Marks by 1955; unemployment fell from 2½ million to 900,000. Income per head almost doubled. New homes were built at the rate of half a million per year. By 1955, Germany had more than 100,000 television sets, and every other German family seemed to possess a Volkswagen car.

Like Erhard, Volkswagen seemed to typify the German 'miracle'. The original 'People's Car' – a gawkier version of the later 'beetle' – had been launched under Hitler in 1938. A large factory had been built for it at Wolfsburg, in the flat country east of Hanover, now near the East German border; but the plant had been switched to war production, and few 'People's Cars' had been made. In 1945, the workshops had been used to repair and service Allied jeeps and lorries. 'Might even build a few cars,' the British major in charge is said to have remarked. A proposal to move the plant to Britain in the form of 'reparations' was turned down when UK manufacturers dismissed the Volkswagen as too noisy and ugly; instead, it was entrusted to a 48-year-old engineer, Heinz Nordhoff, who was banned from returning to his job with Opel because he had gone on working there during the war. Nordhoff defied the proverb by putting all his eggs in one basket: he staked everything on a single model, the much modified 'beetle'. Cheap, robust, and simple, with an air-cooled engine that needed no water and so never froze, the new Volkswagen was an instant success. By 1955, it dominated the German market, and the Wolfsburg works were producing 1,500 cars a day.

The 'beetle' was only one outward sign of how Germany was being transformed. 'People in the streets', wrote the American reporter Theodore H. White, 'filled out visibly. Their clothes changed from rumpled rags to decent garments, to neat business suits, to silk stockings. Cigarettes disappeared as currency, then became available everywhere, then, finally, were sold from slot machines on every corner. Food returned, food as Germans love it, with whipped cream beaten thick in the coffee, on cake, with fruit. The streets changed face as buildings rose, as neon signs festooned them, as their windows shone with goods.'

Some of the ruined cities were rebuilt almost stone for stone. In Nuremberg, the old town within the ramparts, straddling the River Pegnitz, had been gutted; now, its layout preserved with the help of memories and records, it was carefully reconstructed. Soon, a little too clean perhaps, a touch municipal, it was nevertheless a near-facsimile of the old city. Dürer's house was restored; so was the vaulted choir of St Sebaldus; so was the baroque St Giles's church; so was the fourteenth-century Hospice of the Holy Ghost. The Gothic Frauenkirche was rebuilt, with its ancient clock on which the seven Electors pace round at noon. The seventeenth-century arcades of the vanished Peller house, lost in the rubble of 1945, were rescued and incorporated in the new Municipal Library.

Matching old and new was a major problem for postwar German architects. They solved it, with varying success, in Bamberg, Regensburg, Hamburg, Lübeck, and the Kreuzberg district of Berlin. Also in Berlin, the broken spire of the Kaiser-Wilhelm-Gedächtniskirche was quite deliberately left unrepaired, sticking up like the stump of a tree struck by lightning, to be joined very much later by the bluish transparent glass walls of Egon Eiermann's new octagonal church.

More typical, however, were cities like Hanover, almost wholly rebuilt after the war, with a modern traffic system, a sunken shopping street, and garden-city developments on the outskirts. Not all such innovations were inspiring: they included 'Mediterranean' or 'Alpine' suburban villas, crass office blocks, and ephemeral 'contemporary' façades. But the majority were solid and efficient; and some were very much more. Of all the German cities, Düsseldorf had perhaps the biggest share of them: three immensely elegant straight-cable bridges across the Rhine; the bustling Königsallee; the tall, slim triple slabs of the 22-storey Phönix-Rheinrohr building, and the bullet-like domed nave of St Roch's church, built in 1955 to offset its surviving pseudo-Romanesque tower.

So the German 'miracle' took physical shape. Its workings were more mysterious then Erhard tended to suggest. In speech after speech and several books, he identified its secret as 'prosperity through competition', or 'the social market economy' – 'the free market' with a welfare safety-net. But could this be the sole explanation for Germany's dizzy postwar growth? Some, like the German-born philosopher Hannah Arendt, believed quite simply that it was a rebound after so crushing a defeat. 'Under modern conditions,' she wrote, 'the expropriation of people, the destruction of objects, and the devastation of cities will turn out to be a radical stimulant for a process, not of mere recovery, but of quicker and more efficient accumulation of wealth.' A variant of this thesis was that, with old plant destroyed and dismantled, German industry gained by having to re-start from scratch. American aid, some said, was the vital stimulant – although less flourishing economies had enjoyed it too. Others argued that West Germany's 13 million immigrants and refugees, mostly from the Eastern zone, were the main factor in her postwar revival; some added that her home-building programme had encouraged mobility of labour. Others again claimed that German trade unions were more united, 'responsible', or 'docile' – appeased by 'co-determination' and 'worker participation' in two-tier company boards. Many laymen outside Germany simply concluded that Germans were very hard workers – a double-edged compliment later paid to the Japanese. Some envious taxpayers, finally, pointed out that until the mid-1950's West Germany had no defence budget – although in other countries military spending had boosted the economy as a whole.

Economists, historians, and politicians continued to debate these theories: but two facts stood out. The first was how much Germany's 'economic miracle' owed to the banks, in several senses. The second was that Ludwig Erhard, for all his 'liberal' protestations, was no pure disciple of *laisser faire*.

German banks had long had a large and lasting stake in German business. In 1919, the British economist Alfred Marshall had even criticized them for 'carrying to excess the locking up of their capital in loans' – although he had conceded that 'representatives of banks have exercised, for two generations at least, a strong control on industrial businesses which they support.' Working through the firms' Supervisory Boards or *Aufsichtsräte*, the banks played a very active role. They brought with them broad experience and knowledge: with so many irons in so many different fires, they were equipped to oversee the whole economy more comprehensively than a board of specialized industrialists. They also tended to take a longer view; and, as paymaster-supervisors, they ensured that their views carried weight. Elsewhere in Europe, 'indicative planning' might be carried out by governments. In Germany, where planning was now suspect, it was quietly done by the banks.

The German Government, too, belied its *laisser faire* reputation. German public authorities – central, *Land*, and local – had inherited from prewar days a large share in industry: 96 percent in electricity distribution, 91 percent in gas, 75 percent in lignite, 70 percent in aluminium, 62 percent in electricity generating, 55 percent in iron ore, with further substantial stakes in lead and zinc, crude petroleum, iron and steel, coal, and coke. This gave officials powerful leverage; and it was increased by further government investment. Under the Marshall Plan, every government receiving aid in the form of goods from the United States was supposed to set aside their cost in its own currency – the so-called 'counterpart funds', to be spent on projects approved by the US authorities. In Britain, the counterpart funds were swallowed up, in a paper transaction, to pay off part of the public debt: but in Germany they were used constructively. Through a special Reconstruction Loan Corporation, the *Kreditanstalt für Wiederaufbau*, first headed by the veteran banker Herman Abs, the funds helped prime the pump of investment in priority industries.

In other ways also the Government actively intervened. In 1952, for instance, to finance large investments in coal, steel, gas, water, and the railways, it raised a forced loan from the whole of industry, to the tune of 1,000 million Deutsche Marks, which it allocated as it saw fit. Instead of offering Government bonds to the creditors, however, it issued stock in the individual concerns. As part of the same general strategy, it offered tax concessions to steel, coal and iron ore mines, and electrical power plants – on condition that the money was ploughed back into investment. Exporters, likewise, enjoyed tax rebates between 1951 and 1955. So, until 1954, did the shipyards and, for much longer, the home-building industry.

This last was only one aspect of the Government's concern for welfare – the 'social' element in Erhard's 'social market economy'. Even at the time of the currency reform, if those on fixed incomes suffered, they were helped by a social security system already unusually advanced. By 1949, Germany was spending 18.5 percent of the national income on welfare, compared with 11.2 percent in the United Kingdom. And while at that time the Germans were less heavily taxed than the British, that ratio was rapidly reversed. By 1955, taxes in Britain were 29 percent of the gross national product: in Germany, they had risen to 32.2 percent, and were still going up – partly to provide in advance for German defence spending. The paradoxical result was a pile of unused money which the Germans nicknamed the *Juliusturm*, or 'Tower of Julius', after the 16th-century Prussian prince whose tower at

Spandau had been both a fortress and a treasury.

From 1956 onwards, the tax hoard was eaten into: a so-called *Kuchenaus-schuss* or 'Cake Committee' of Parliament debated ways of slicing it up. In the end, some of it went to agriculture, and some to improve old-age pensions; but much of it was spent on investment – partly through State unemployment and pension funds, which in Germany, almost uniquely in Western Europe, were encouraged to invest in private industry.

In all these ways, then, Erhard's Ministry of Economic Affairs, with Treasury help, was surprisingly *dirigiste*. As the British economic historian Andrew Shonfield put it: 'Rarely can a ministry so vociferously devoted to the virtues of economic liberalism and market forces have taken so vigorous a part in setting the direction and selecting targets of economic development.' Ludwig Erhard, in other words, was virtually a planner in disguise.

If Erhard's reassuring bulk seemed to incarnate the German 'miracle', Louis Armand was equally typical of postwar France. Black-haired, fizzing with energy, he looked like a tougher Charlie Chaplin; there was a touch of the gipsy in his dark eyes and moustache. He came of mountain stock, from a town in Haute-Savoie near the Swiss frontier: Cruseilles, overlooking a fast-flowing river, on the southernmost slopes of the Salève. As a young man he was sent to Paris, to the Ecole Polytechnique. Founded in 1794 to train engineers for the French revolutionary armies, the Polytechnique was still a military school, whose students – known as the 'X' – wore khaki uniforms; but already in Armand's day it was providing France's close-knit administrative and technocratic élite: sharp, articulate, self-assured proconsuls, rigorously schooled in mathematics and engineering, but versed in many disciplines and prepared, like all-round athletes, to meet almost any challenge they chose.

Armand's first choice was mining. In 1926, aged twenty-one, he went as an engineer to Clermont-Ferrand in the Auvergne. He stayed there eight years; then, in 1934, he joined the old Paris-Lyon-Marseille railway company, the PLM. During World War II, the railways played a key role in the Resistance, carrying out in particular the '*Plan Vert*' of systematic sabotage commemorated in René Clément's 1946 film *La Bataille du Rail*. In 1944, in recognition of his Resistance work, Armand was made a *Compagnon de la Libération*. In the same year, he was appointed Director of Works for the State railways, the *Société Nationale des Chemins de Fer Français* or SNCF, becoming its Director-General two years later.

Set up shortly before the war as a 'mixed company' with a minority of private shareholders, the SNCF was now in a bad way. Its wartime losses, partly due to the *Plan Vert*, included 4,000 kilometres of track, 14,000 locomotives, and 360,000 wagons. But, as in Germany, there were advantages in re-starting from scratch. Within a few years, Armand had overhauled the entire French railway system. He wrote off 9,000 kilometres of uneconomic branch line; he ordered new designs for diesel and electric locomotives; and he replaced steam by electrification on nearly all major routes. By the mid-1950's the consensus was general: the French railways were the best, fastest, most punctual, and most enterprising in Europe.

Armand's achievement was matched in other spheres. *Electricité de France*, under Pierre Massé, launched ambitious hydroelectric and thermoelectric projects. The nationalized Renault automobile works raced ahead, first under the wilful Pierre Lefaucheux, then under Pierre Dreyfus – perky, Jewish, Left-of-centre, and a polymath, a reader of Latin in his spare time. At the *Commissariat à l'Energie Atomique*, men like Frédéric Joliot and the bearded, intent-looking Francis Perrin – almost a layman's stereotype of the monomaniac scientist – had built France's first nuclear reactor, Zoë, by 1948. In 1951, French prospectors found a first, plentiful supply of natural gas near Pau in the Pyrenees – the much-talked-of *'gaz de Lacq'*. A hundred miles away, at *Sud-Est* (later *Sud*) *Aviation* near Toulouse, Georges Héreil boldly pioneered what was to become the Caravelle, France's first jet aircraft. Meanwhile, *Charbonnages de France*, the nationalized coalmines, were being modernized as rapidly as the railways. By 1955, their productivity was 23 percent above the prewar level, compared with 6 percent in Britain. There was similar progress, finally, in the economy as a whole. While in 1948 France's total output had been only just above the 1936 level, by 1955 it was half as high again. And from 1955 to 1958, French productivity rose by 8 percent per year – faster than anywhere else in Europe.

Much of this modernizing ferment astonished outside observers, who heard and read mainly about Cabinet crises in postwar France. But, as CBS reporter David Schoenbrun wrote in 1957, 'To judge French affairs from an examination of the agitated surface of government is as incomplete and thereby as inaccurate as a study of ocean life based only upon a description of the waves.' The much maligned Fourth Republic may have faced a choppy sea politically: economically it made impressive headway. Financially, indeed, it sailed close to the wind: the mines and railways, in particular, had to have large government subsidies for their long-term investment plans.

Their managers' expertise ensured that the money was well spent; and it also gave them some guarantee of independence from arbitrary political control.

The '*grands cõmmis de l'Etat*' or State tycoons formed a powerful mafia – partly an old boy network of *polytechniciens*, *normaliens* (from the Ecole Normale Supérieure), or *énarques* (from the Ecole Nationale d'Administration, founded in 1946 as a post-graduate college for future civil servants). They and their counterparts in private industry wore no old school tie or fraternity pin; but their grapevine was remarkably effective, making for continuity amid political changes, and for some degree of consensus in different fields. As in Germany, long-term investment and concerted action were the two main keys to success.

The focus of both, of course, was Jean Monnet's *Commissariat au Plan*. Each of its 'modernization committees' brought together thirty, forty, or fifty people from business, industry, the trade unions, and the administration, to discuss production targets, supplies, shortages, productivity bottlenecks, and future investment plans – not just as representatives of this interest or that, but as members of a team. In a typical year, 3,000 people from all over France might gather in the Plan's headquarters at 18 rue de Martignac, while a single official there might handle the files of 500 separate firms.

But the key meetings took place in Monnet's own office, around his desk – a trestle table fifteen feet long, covered with piles of papers. To begin with, his chief lieutenant was the young economist Robert Marjolin, a former student at the Sorbonne and at Yale who had worked with Monnet in wartime Washington and married an American wife. Tall, dark, and highly intelligent, he looked very much like a college instructor, with his sharp pale face and glasses and a warm, shy, lop-sided smile. In 1948, when the Organization for European Economic Co-operation was established, initially to handle the Marshall Plan, Marjolin left to become its first Secretary-General.

The second leading member of Monnet's brains trust was Etienne Hirsch, an engineer from the Ecole des Mines, who during the war had worked for the Free French in London as 'Commandant Bernard'. Friendly, freckled, pipe-smoking and seemingly placid, Hirsch was as short as Monnet; as they grew older, they began to look like cousins. At the end of 1947, a newcomer completed the circle: Pierre Uri, a *normalien* who had trained to teach philosophy but become absorbed by economics. 'Prodigiously brilliant, ditto vain' was how one colleague fondly described him. Uri, always good-natured, might well have agreed: his only speciality, as he put it, was 'general ideas'. Ruffling his curly hair, puffing at a huge curved pipe, snorting with laughter and sometimes catarrh, he would dictate ingenious solutions to problems not everyone recognized. 'If you ask him how many people there are round the table,' Monnet once remarked, 'he'll dive under it, count their feet, and divide by two.' '*Non, non, non,*' Monnet would say in his small, dry, arresting voice. '*Mon cher ami,* you're too intelligent. Do me a simple note.' At length, after many rewritings, the note would be as clear as water – but as powerful as gin. 'Uri for invention, Hirsch for expertise, Monnet for salesmanship,' said a French commentator. 'No,' replied one of Monnet's colleagues: 'Monnet for action.'

He certainly believed in picking other people's brains. Gravitating round No. 18 rue de Martignac were many influential outsiders – men like the steelmaker Pierre Ricard, a leading figure in the French employers' guild, the *Patronat*; the lively and aptly-named Léon Gingembre, of the small and medium-sized firms' confederation; the Communist Member of Parliament Pierre Waldeck-Rochet; or Pierre Le Brun, economic adviser to the Confédération Générale du Travail, the CGT. And the actual staff of the Planning Commissariat, permanent or temporary, included Paul Delouvrier, a financial expert with a fine Resistance record, later to head Electricité de France; Félix Gaillard, Monnet's personal assistant, a future French Prime Minister; and the quiet but formidable statistician Jean Vergeot, whom everyone from Monnet downwards called 'Monsieur Vergeot'.

In the early days of the Plan, much had to be done by flair and inspired guesswork: the professionals from each industry made their guesses, and Monnet inspired them to do a little better. This was natural enough when shortages, gaps, and bottlenecks were so obvious: planners were obliged to concentrate investment in key industries – a practice that persisted, although priorities might change from one Plan to the next. Reliance on flair and feel also became a habit. In the late 1950's, an official at 18 rue de Martignac amused Andrew Shonfield by revealing how he had detected some suspect production figures:

He picked up a piece of paper which was lying on the table in front of us and ... sniffed at it energetically. 'One relies on one's sense of smell,' he said. 'There is nothing else to do!'

There was certainly little alternative when the Planning Commissariat began. At that time, in the wake of the war, France's economic statistics were scanty and crude compared with those of her neighbours. But as soon as they improved, French planners used them far more rigorously than elsewhere.

By 1952, they were able to predict in detail the national income for at least a year ahead. Far from remaining an academic or civil-service exercise, locked away in the Treasury or the central Bank, each annual forecast was published and debated: it became a means of scrutinizing, contesting, and modifying the Government's economic policy. Soon, the larger private firms were following suit with plans and predictions of their own.

'Indicative planning', of course, was not the only secret of France's postwar modernization. Some successes were due to simple, old-fashioned entrepreneurial verve – like that of Marcel Bich, the ballpoint-pen manufacturer whose inexpensive 'Bic' became a household word and whose private company bought up not only Biro-Swan in 1957 but also, two years later, control of Waterman in the United States. No less important was the tradition of State tutelage, several centuries old, which put men like Louis Armand in positions of such power, often in 'mixed companies' – State concerns with some private shareholders – some of which, in the oil industry, were among the most profitable in France. French higher education, too, with its cult of the polymath and its consequent respect for technology, undoubtedly helped. Yet, behind, all the graphs and indices and technical explanations, Monnet may have been right to see in the French 'economic miracle' something simpler and more fundamental. 'Modernization,' declared the First Report of his *Commissariat au Plan*, 'is not a state of affairs: it is a state of mind.'

To many Italians, the man who most typified their 'economic miracle' was the oil *'condottiere'* Enrico Mattei. He was certainly impressive. 'His personality', wrote the British journalist Anthony Sampson, 'was electric.'

He was small and shy, with the look of an artist – a sensitive mouth, a mobile chin and a penetrating eye – but he visibly dominated his officials with an intimidating aloofness.... He talked with a flood of fast rhetoric: he carried on a separate conversation while his words to me were being translated.

This was the man who struck oil in Italy, and challenged the big international companies with what one Shell employee called 'a one-man band operating on a shoestring'.

Mattei was no professor like Ludwig Erhard, nor like Louis Armand the product of a *grande école*. Born in 1906, he was a self-made man, the son of a policeman, brought up in the small Umbrian hill town of Matelica, where his parents moved when he was four. At sixteen, he was an errand-boy; at twenty, a varnisher in a bed factory; at twenty-four, the representative of a German chemical firm. By 1938, he had two small chemical works of his own, and was employing eighty people. A Catholic, but with little general education, he was much influenced by Professor Marcello Boldrini, an eminent statistician who also came from Mattei's home town, as did many of his lifelong associates – so many that SNAM, the acronym for one of his later companies, was said to denote '*Siamo nati a Matelica*', 'We were born in Matelica'. Boldrini helped to shield Mattei from the blandishments of Fascism. Like all Italians, he had to deal with Fascists; but he never became involved. Some of the raw materials for his factories' war production, it was rumoured, found their way on to the black market.

Before the war was over, Mattei joined the Resistance, handling among other things some of its financial problems. It was no mere desk job. In 1944–45, using two different pseudonyms – 'Monti' and 'Marconi' – he commanded two partisan groups totalling 100,000 people. As 'Monti', he was arrested at Como by the Germans and Fascists, who tried to get him to betray 'Marconi'. Rescued by his own men, he made for Milan, took over yet another group, and became a member of the Military Committee for Northern Italy. Resistance life suited him. In later years, it was only at partisan reunions that he ever seemed really at ease in a crowd.

He entered the oil industry almost by chance. In 1945, as a Christian-Democrat member of the Constituent Assembly, he toyed with the thought of a parliamentary career; but he had also been appointed Commissioner in Milan with the task of winding up one of Mussolini's national enterprises, the *Azienda Generale Italiana Petroli*, AGIP. Unlike Germany, France, or Britain, Italy had virtually no coal. She had developed hydro-electric power but Mussolini – who was not always wrong – had thought it worth while to prospect for oil and gas. So far, the search had been unrewarding; and on 15 May 1945, the Italian Treasury proposed that it be called off.

Mattei thought otherwise. For weeks, he argued with officials; finally, on 1 September 1945, he wrote to the Prime Minister, Ferruccio Parri, to protest against the prevailing 'defeatism'. His letter concluded: 'AGIP must be saved.'

His faith was justified. In 1946, AGIP prospectors found natural gas at Caviaga, near Milan. Then, in the Spring of 1949, came still more dramatic news, which Mattei's skill at publicity made sensational. At Cortemaggiore in the Po valley, twenty miles south of Cremona, and not far from where Giuseppe Verdi had been born in 1813, Mattei's men struck oil.

That natural gas was there had been known for many years. With part of the profits from his operas, Verdi had bought farmland near his birthplace. In some of the fields, he had had to forbid his peasants to smoke, for fear that the gas seeping through cracks in the ground would blow them sky-high.

The prospect of home-produced oil was intoxicating. When the find was announced, the Finance Minister Ezio Vanoni came up from Rome, to be photographed dabbling his hands in it. 'Italy,' he exclaimed, 'has won the battle of oil.' The Milan daily *Corriere della Sera* exulted: 'It will be Milan, used as a refinery centre, that will exploit this enormous economic wealth which God has been good enough to reveal to Italy so that she may have the strength to rebuild after her tragic days of sacrifice.'

Mattei's next thought was to keep the multinationals out. In Sicily, in 1950, a mining law was passed permitting foreign prospecting; and in 1953 the American company Gulf Oil located a field near Ragusa. But the next Sicilian find, near Gela, was made by AGIP; and on the mainland Mattei lobbied for very stringent laws which kept prospecting mainly in Italian hands.

He need hardly have worried. The Gela crude oil proved to be very heavy – a semi-solid bitumen, suitable at first only for making asphalt: large and costly refineries were needed to make it of more general use. And, irony of ironies, the Cortemaggiore field turned out to be meagre, with little crude oil, and the rest mainly liquids derived from wet gas.

None of this stopped Mattei: Cortemaggiore was his trademark. Soon, every tourist on Italy's highways was familiar with the black-and-yellow sign of the six-legged dog, AGIP's emblem, adorning bright new filling-stations with bars and restaurants, together with the proud slogan SUPERCORTEMAGGIORE LA POTENTE BENZINA ITALIANA – although most of this 'Italian petrol' came from imported crude oil, processed by refineries in which AGIP had only a half-share.

Further discoveries boosted Italy's annual production of crude oil to over 200,000 tons in 1955 and over a million-and-a-half by 1958: but even this was less than a tenth of her needs. Despite Mattei's reputation as an oil tycoon, his real breakthrough was in natural gas. By 1955, Italy was producing more than three-and-a-half million cubic metres a year, and by 1958 more than five million – or nearly seventy percent of all the natural gas then produced in Europe.

Mattei, meanwhile, diversified his empire. In 1953, AGIP was incorporated in a new, broader grouping, ENI – the *Ente Nazionale Idrocarburi*, dealing with every aspect of hydrocarbons: prospecting, drilling, refining, transport, tankers, pipelines, and sales. Mattei became its President, resigning his seat in Parliament. In Italy, he invested also in electronics, engineering, automation equipment, housing, hotels, fertilizers, and even a daily newspaper, *Il Giorno*. Abroad, he ran pipelines over half of Europe, and began to compete with the international companies by negotiating for oil concessions in Iran and Morocco. Eventually, he was to undercut the market by importing cheap oil from the Soviet Union. But by then his days were numbered. On 27 October 1962, his aircraft took off from Sicily to fly to Milan – and crashed. There were no survivors.

Persistent left-wing rumour, aired most recently in Francesco Rosi's 1972 film *Il Caso Mattei*, with Gian Maria Volonté in the main role, has alleged that Mattei was murdered. No proof has been offered, and the theory seems unlikely: Mattei was making peace with his rivals just before he died. What remains certain is that his cheap oil policy and his rapid exploitation of natural gas helped to fuel the Italian 'economic miracle'.

If the origins of Mattei's fief dated back to Mussolini, so did Italy's other great public corporation, IRI, the *Istituto di Ricostruzione Industriale*. Founded in 1933 to rescue a number of ailing companies and banks, it had ended up with a payroll of 250,000 people and a portfolio of immense variety: 85 percent of Italy's pig-iron output, 80 percent of her shipbuilding capacity, 65 percent of her mercury production, 62 percent of her passenger shipping, 55 percent of her steel. Even in other industries like cement, where IRI's stake was small, it often included the most efficient and competitive plant. IRI also controlled Alitalia, the national airline, State radio and television, the urban telephone service, most of the toll highways, and a number of banks. Under dynamic management, it gave thrust to the whole economy; and the banks, as in Germany, fostered long-term investment – although in this case under tight central supervision.

Again like Germany, Italy had other advantages. One was plentiful labour, initially on low wages. Another was the amount of leeway to be made up: at an early stage of modernization, growth could be exceptionally rapid. Between 1950 and 1954, Italy's gross national product increased by 32.9 percent – more than anywhere in Europe except Germany, Austria, and Greece; and in the next few years it rose even faster. Between 1950 and 1958, the growth rate in Italian industry was no less than 9 percent a year.

Visitors to Italy could see the transformation: better clothes; smarter shop-fronts; more meat on the menu; bicycles replaced by Vespa or Lambretta motor-scooters, by tiny '*Topolino*' ('Mickey Mouse') cars, and then by family Fiats. They could savour the speed and elegance of the new express highways, sweeping in great curves across the landscape like the *Autostrada del Sole*, the southwards motorway to the sun. They could admire such monuments to modernity as Rome's new Stazione Termini, flanking the ancient Servian Wall; Gio Ponti's swordlike Pirelli skyscraper near the Central Station in Milan; or the functional Olivetti building in Via Clerici near La Scala.

Like Pirelli tyres, Olivetti typewriters travelled far beyond Italy . This book was typed on one of them. Adriano Olivetti, the son of the firm's founder, not only expanded the business – buying Underwood in America to help enlarge his market: he also made the company's headquarters at Ivrea, near Turin, into a model community. He believed, he said, in 'a new kind of enterprise going beyond socialism and capitalism', and he formed a political party to promote it. Above all, he believed in good design. 'The Olivetti products', declared Le Corbusier, 'seem to be illuminated by the exact proportions of the love with which every object should be made.'

He could have said the same of many postwar Italian artefacts. Names like Luigi Nervi, Emilio Pucci, Pinin Farina, or Gucci, came to symbolize the way in which Italians applied a Renaissance instinct for shape and colour to twentieth-century objects and materials. And, ignoring the big names, the bright lights, and the lofty buildings, hundreds of artists in small, dark, primitive workshops were busy fashioning no less elegant shoes, purses, ties, scarves, tapestries, enamels, painted porcelain, carved ivory or alabaster, jewels, medallions, and rings. Italians' perennial vitality and craftsmanship gave their 'miracle' unique verve and style.

There was no British 'miracle'; and no individual wholly typified Britain's postwar economic growth. Sir Stafford Cripps, the apostle of 'planning', symbolized for many people postwar 'austerity'. With his pinched smile and rimless spectacles, he appeared ascetic – as indeed he was. 'The British people', wrote Harold Macmillan, 'became deeply incensed when rations were continued and even reduced some years after the war by a Minister who appeared almost to enjoy their privations with all the emotions of an anchorite. Cripps drank no alcohol and was believed to live on nuts and watercress, and as the terrible strain of his dedication to work began to tell upon his health, he seemed more and more to resemble an Indian fakir.'

Born in 1889, a nephew of Beatrice Webb, and educated at Winchester and University College, London, Cripps had been a brilliant barrister, then a Left-wing Labour MP. A Christian Socialist, he was expelled from the Party in 1939 for advocating a Popular Front. From 1940 to 1942 he served as Ambassador in Moscow, and from November 1942 onwards as Minister of Aircraft Production. In Attlee's 1945 Labour Government he was President of the Board of Trade. Two years later, he was appointed to the newly-formed Ministry of Economic Affairs; then, in November 1947, after Hugh Dalton had resigned over a Budget 'leak', Cripps became Chancellor of the Exchequer and effective overlord of the whole British economy.

The 'austerity' he championed – and which his opponents derided – was not, of course, Cripps's fault. Nor was it unsuccessful. By strict taxation, short rations, and a voluntary wage freeze, the Labour Government certainly curbed inflation. Its great failure, paradoxically, was in neglecting to 'plan'.

'Planning' had long been promised – although some of its advocates seemed to confuse it with 'controls'. In 1944, Cripps had written privately to Sir Richard Acland: 'We have learned in the war that we CAN control industry.' In 1946 Herbert Morrison, who was then responsible for co-ordinating economic policy, had announced: 'Planning, as it is now taking shape in this country under our eyes, is something new and constructively revolutionary which will be regarded in times to come as a contribution to civilization as vital and distinctly British as parliamentary democracy and the rule of law.' And the Government's first annual Economic Survey in 1947 suggested that 'Certain peacetime problems, such as the control of balance of payments, can be handled by much the same techniques as were used for allocating our resources of manpower, materials and shipping during the war.'

The machinery for planning was certainly available: part of it had actually been copied by the French. 'Industrial Working Parties' already existed to bring together officials, unions, and businessmen: they were the model for the French Plan's *commissions de modernisation*. In 1947, Attlee's Industrial Organization and Development Act empowered Ministers to confirm and codify the system by setting up Development Councils on similar lines. Coal had been nationalized: so had the Bank of England; electricity, gas, and the railways were soon to follow. If the Government seriously intended to plan ahead, it had the chance.

Yet Cripps and his colleagues muffed it. Between 1947 and 1950 – partly owing to objections from industry – they set up only four Development Councils: for cotton, clothing, furniture, and silverware. And instead of taking a long-term view of the economy's needs and prospects, they found themselves struggling with day-to-day problems – the shortage of food and raw materials, and the deficit in Britain's balance of payments.

To tackle the shortages, they imposed stringent and irksome regulations – only to get rid of them as soon as supplies eased. On 5 November 1948 – Guy Fawkes Day – the new President of the Board of Trade, Harold Wilson, announced what he called 'a bonfire of controls'. From then on, instead of physical controls, Cripps chiefly used Keynesian budgetary methods to iron out the ups-and-downs of the business cycle and try to avoid crises in the balance of payments due to the 'dollar gap'.

The Conservatives did likewise. They returned to power in 1951 – with fewer votes than Labour – on a promise to end 'austerity'. Partly owing to the effects of Marshall Aid, they succeeded: in 1954, most notably, they at last abolished food rationing. But, despite their libertarian rhetoric, they acted in many respects like their predecessors, maintaining full employment, improving welfare benefits, and scotching a tentative Treasury plan to abolish all remaining controls. Towards the end of the 1950's, some of their theorists began to toy with the notion of 'indicative planning' on the French model; but the Government remained content with Cripps's Keynesian policy of short-term economic management, alternatively applying the accelerator and the brake.

The nickname for this practice, not unnaturally, was 'stop-go'. Its fatal flaw was to discourage long-term investment. In the 'go' phase of a cycle, the Government did all it could to boost economic activity, in particular keeping interest rates down. Firms could raise money cheaply, and sell easily as demand became brisk; meanwhile, wages would rise, largely because the Trades Union Congress was no longer trying to restrain them as it had under Labour. After a while, prices would creep up, and imports would be sucked in: fearing inflation and a balance-of-payments crisis, the Government would call 'Stop' and apply the brake. But instead of damping down consumer demand by increasing taxes – always unpopular, and now a reminder of 'austerity' – the Government usually took the easier course of curbing credit and raising interest rates.

The net result was chronic under-investment. While other countries welcomed new plant and new methods, Britain all too often seemed to make do with the old. In each of the years from 1950 to 1958, Britain invested a smaller proportion of her national wealth than France, Italy, or Germany. The only countries in Europe with lower *pro rata* investment were Denmark (in 1954), Ireland (from 1955 onwards), and Portugal (until 1957). Increasingly put at a disadvantage by ageing machines and archaic practices, both output and productivity grew more slowly in Britain than in her main competitors – at half France's and Italy's rate, and a quarter that of Germany. British exports grew more slowly still. Only costs and prices seemed to rise more rapidly in Britain – faster than in Italy, twice as fast as in Germany, although more slowly than in France. Already in the 1950's, in other words, the British economy was beginning to lag behind. By neglecting to plan for the future, and handicapping investment by those firms that did, both Labour and Conservative governments unwittingly connived at Britain's relative decline.

The picture was not all gloomy. If parts of British industry were sluggish, fragmented, short-sighted, ill-managed, over-manned or under-capitalized, others were far more dynamic – notably some of the giants. In many cases, their size alone obliged them to plan well ahead. At Imperial Chemical Industries, ICI, capital investments before the war had normally been allowed twenty years to depreciate before being replaced; by 1950, the standard depreciation time had been cut to ten years, and was soon to be shortened still more. ICI, like British Petroleum, was among Europe's ten biggest companies. Heading the list were Royal Dutch/Shell and Unilever – both Anglo-Dutch and long familiar, so in a sense domestic, but both also examples of a trend that was not always welcome: the concentration of much advanced industry into large conglomerates, many of them multinational companies based in the United States.

The headquarters of such giant corporations often looked like government offices. Some actually became civil-service buildings when the firms moved on. In the lobby, visitors would face a uniformed guard; they might need a pass to go any further; and in the corridors upstairs they would see rows of identical doors marked with names and titles – the perches on a vast organigram. During the 1950's, the organigram expanded: in Britain, the proportion of salaried staff in industrial firms grew from 17 to 22 percent. And the senior staff of a large company, as the American writer James Burnham had predicted in 1941 in *The Managerial Revolution*, were no longer entrepreneurs in the old, adventurous, risk-taking tradition, but managers – bureaucrats who differed from civil servants only in their high salaries and less well-protected jobs.

Even the giant corporations, of course, still included some family firms. In

Italy, individual families still controlled not only Pirelli and Olivetti, but also the textile giant Marzotto, the Pesenti cement combine, and such makers of refrigerators as Borghi or Zanussi. In France, the Bercot family still ran Michelin and Citroën; in Britain, well-known examples included Marks and Spencer and Pilkington's glass. But even in Germany the old-style barons of industry had begun to share their role with professional managers, like Berthold Beitz at Krupp; and even the most stubbornly private and once piratical of family businesses now had a settled, reformed, institutionalized look: they too had organigrams and neatly clad corporate executives.

The best-selling American novelist Sloan Wilson had found a name for this new breed of middle manager: *The Man in the Gray Flannel Suit*. In 1950, a team of Yale sociologists headed by David Riesman had examined him more closely, in a study of *The Lonely Crowd*. 'Other-directed' was their term for his conformist conscience, taking its values from his colleagues and its consolation from his work. In 1956, William H. Whyte re-labelled him *The Organization Man* – a term amended to *Corporation Man* fifteen years later by the British commentator Antony Jay. The common strand in all these diagnoses was recognition that the new corporate employee sought his status, fought his battles, and fulfilled most of his social needs through and within the company instead of the community – yet again like a national or, still more, an international civil servant.

The company, in fact, had become a world on its own. Giant corporations, national or multinational, no longer fitted the nineteenth-century image of a swarm of competitors, buzzing round the market, fighting for business, triumphing or dying, making the customer king. Often, now, they were monopolies or oligopolies; and while they were seldom as rich as governments, and never formally so powerful, they were sometimes big enough – and international enough – to escape normal restraints.

Executives at the National Cash Register Company of Dayton, Ohio, used to tell a piquant story. In the summer of 1940, when the Nazi armies were entering Paris, the French staff of the firm, watching from their offices at the foot of the Champs-Elysées, were amazed to see a tank leave the column and roar into their driveway. A German major climbed out and rapped on their front door. When the French manager opened it, the officer clicked his heels, bowed, and presented his business card. In civilian life, he was manager of the company's office in Berlin. If, during the Occupation, his French colleague needed help, he had only to get in touch. Giving his unit and location, the officer saluted and returned to his tank.

In peacetime, transnational corporate planning was less rare; and it posed problems for democratic governments. A multinational firm could deeply affect a national economy. Should decisions which might endanger thousands of jobs, impoverish a town or region, and threaten a nation's balance of payments, be taken by accountants or managers in another city, another country, or even another continent? Should the elected parliament and government not have some guaranteed say? And if they did, how could politicians be equipped to match the technical experts?

The questions were real enough in the case of private enterprise. In the nationalized industries, they were still more pressing. How should governments deal with public-sector corporations? How should parliaments monitor them? For the sake of business efficiency, most State tycoons sought independence. Some simply asserted it. In France in 1946, the first head of the nationalized Régie Renault, Pierre Lefaucheux, defied directives from Monnet's Planning Commissariat, and produced the successful Renault 4 CV. Others played politics. In Italy, Enrico Mattei, incorruptible himself, was alleged to have bribed politicians of all parties. Elsewhere, as in Britain, there was a permanent tug-of-war.

All this was to be expected. The industries in question had to be run effectively: but most of them had been nationalized for social or political reasons – to supply a costly public service, or to impose on an economic and technological giant some degree of democratic control. It was an issue big with future conflict – especially after 1956, when the British Atomic Energy Authority opened Europe's first nuclear power station at Calder Hall. The outcome at any given moment would depend on a number of variables: the government's political colour and courage, the state of public opinion, the importance of the nationalized industry, the personality of its leader, and in particular the power of the trade unions.

They too had become part of 'the Establishment' – the term now popularized by the British journalist Henry Fairlie, writing in *The Spectator* in 1955. A typical union's headquarters was now no longer some smoky red-brick nonconformist chapel hall, but an office block much like any other, complete with salaried staff. In Düsseldorf, for instance, a stranger seeing the DGB building, with its initials high on the skyline, might take it for a bank or steel firm before discovering that DGB stood for *Deutscher Gewerkschaftsbund*, or German Trade Union Confederation.

Numerically, the unions were strongest in Britain, with 9 million members by the late 1950's: but the impressive total was offset by fragmentation, which led to obstructive inter-union demarcation disputes and quarrels over differential rates of pay. In France and Italy, union dissensions were political. France had some 3 million members, half of them in the quasi-Communist Confédération Générale du Travail, or CGT, the remainder split between Catholics and Socialists. Just under half of Italy's 8 million unionists belonged to the Communist-Socialist Confederazione Generale Italiana del Lavoro, or CGIL; the next biggest group was the Catholic confederation, followed by a small independent union and a smaller neo-Fascist guild. Only Germany, with the DGB, had a truly unified labour confederation: its membership had risen from nearly 5 million in 1949 to more than 6½ million by 1954.

With a low strike record and a policy of welcoming modernization if workers reaped the benefit, the DGB helped to sustain the German 'economic miracle'. Elsewhere, the unions' role was often more controversial. In France and Italy, notably in 1947, they were responsible for largely political strikes. In Britain, with bitter memories of 1930's unemployment, they seemed to many people unduly suspicious of technological progress. But what was evident throughout Europe was that trade unions had changed their nature. Once the pioneering champions of a downtrodden proletariat, they were now – like the giant corporations – an estate of the realm. And while within industry they were a counterweight to the power of capital, in society their own power was not always democratically controlled. Public concern at this was most widespread in Britain. Presidents and secretaries-general of unions appointed virtually for life; voting by a show of hands at a mass meeting instead of by secret ballot; decisions by local activists leading to a 'block vote' of several millions, cast by a single person or a handful of delegates: these and other practices seemed to cry out for reform; but attempts to change them met entrenched resistance. A recurring dilemma for governments in the postwar era was how to ensure that the will of the electorate prevailed against 'over-mighty subjects', whether giant corporations or mass trade unions which could bring industry to a halt.

But these were problems for the future. For the present, Europe was enjoying unparalleled economic growth; and it masked even Britain's relative decline. In absolute terms, indeed, Britain was richer than at any time in her history: she was caught up, if more slowly, in Europe's general boom. More women went out to work, offsetting poor productivity. There was more demand for services like banking and insurance, in which Britain excelled.

British farmers, already highly efficient, used machines and artificial fertilizers to become the most productive in Europe. Throughout industry, working hours were steadily reduced.

Britain's new prosperity might not be so palpable as in Germany, so purposeful as in France, so proudly paraded as in Italy: but it was none the less real, and far more evenly spread throughout the population. When Prime Minister Harold Macmillan, in a much-misquoted phrase, told an open-air rally at Bedford on 20 July 1957, 'Most of our people have never had it so good,' he was speaking no more – if also rather less – than the truth.

7

Easy Street

Quand il me prend dans ses bras
Quand il me parle tout bas
Je vois la vie en rose . . .

That melody, with its rolling repetitive undertow, redolent of Gauloises, accordion music, and late-night onion soup in Les Halles, will probably always recall the harsh, vibrant, Parisian voice of Edith Piaf – although she originally wrote '*Je vois* les choses *en rose*', gave the rights to a colleague, Marianne Michel, in 1945, and waited two years before singing it herself. I first heard it on a late summer afternoon in 1948 – not in France but in Florence, sitting with two friends at an open-air café in the Piazzale Michelangiolo, looking out on the friendly red Duomo, Giotto's chill green-and-white campanile, and the crenellated tower of the Palazzo Vecchio, amid the terracotta roofs on the far side of the Arno. It was hot and hazy, and the song seemed to encompass all we felt.

We were enjoying our first long vacation from Cambridge. Two of us had seen war service in the British Army; the third, now a successful playwright, had been a 'Bevin boy', conscripted by Ernest Bevin to work in the mines. As a result, we all had 'FET' grants, for 'Further Education and Training'. Between us, we were reading History, English, and Music; and we had come to Italy for a course on Art at the British Institute of Florence.

It had taken a day-and-a-half to cross a continent still scarred by bombs and bullets, and still divided by frontier controls. At Basle, the train had stopped three hours for customs checks; at Chiasso, an hour-and-a-half. Before the inspectors arrived, an Italian in our compartment had opened a large suitcase and taken out four black Homburg hats. One he put on: the other three he handed to us, asking us to wear one each. Feeling and looking ridiculous, we obliged, and his hats entered Italy duty-free.

Currency, rather than customs, hampered the British tourist: our travel allowance at that time was £35 each. We made it last a month by staying in modest *pensioni* – in one case over a cinema noisily showing *Capitano Blood*. But we had no cause to complain. Italy was warm and welcoming. Food and wine were abundant. The war was long over. We were alive; we were free; we were young; we were privileged. And there were thousands like us – released from duty, building our future with government grants and training schemes, taking the chance to travel again as civilians, meeting our fellow-Europeans, learning languages, visiting museums, galleries, and monuments, filling our shelves with art books and our walls with posters or Alinari prints.

Within a few years, Western Europe had a million students in higher education, about a quarter of them women, and the majority getting direct or indirect government aid. There were still only half as many students per head of population as in the Soviet Union, and a fifth of the proportion in the United States: but in most European countries student numbers had doubled since before the war. By 1955, the universities alone were producing more than 100,000 graduates a year – and the number of enrolments was soon to grow more rapidly still.

Being 'students', of course, meant different things in different places. In France, Italy, and Germany, they were packed into ancient buidings originally intended to house a small élite: already in 1950, I remember, some of the Sorbonne lecture-theatres were as overcrowded and stuffy as rush-hour trains. In Italy, there was a shortage of full-time professors – partly because many took outside jobs to make ends meet. In Britain, despite 'austerity' and rationing and hard work, Oxford and Cambridge – 'Oxbridge' – undergraduates kept up sybaritic appearances, aping the 1920's existence evoked in 1945 by Evelyn Waugh's novel *Brideshead Revisited*, complete with 'scouts' or 'bedmakers' and other College servants, wild parties, practical jokes, languid affectation, gowns, 'proctors' enforcing the curfew, parliamentary ceremonial at Union debates, and long, elaborate 'feasts' in Hall.

Much of this was possible because Oxbridge, although expanded, was still catering for a minority. Many of the new intake found their way to 'Redbrick' universities – the term widely popularized in 1943 by the pseudonymous 'Bruce Truscot' (Edgar Peers). In *Redbrick University*, reprinted with revisions in 1951, 'Truscot' had complained that Oxbridge 'half-strangled' Britain's other universities. The eventual response was a huge expansion programme, with five new universities formed from what had been out-of-town Colleges of the University of London, while others like Sussex, York, and

East Anglia were planned and built from nothing, often in imaginative ways.

A similar ferment enlivened Europe's secondary schools. Everywhere they were taking on more pupils – in most countries half as many again as before the war, and in several more than twice as many. Between 1950 and 1958, expenditure per head on education rose by 60 percent or more in Italy, France and the Netherlands, and by more than 100 percent in Germany.

In Britain, the local authorities put up fine new school buildings, and successive governments strove for greater equality of opportunity. The 1944 Education Act had already abolished fee-paying places in 'grammar schools' – the State schools taking the academically able, selected by an examination at the age of 'eleven-plus'. One unexpected result was an expansion of 'public' – actually private – schools: in the 1950's, more than half their intake were 'first-generation' pupils, whose parents had been educated elsewhere. Before long, even the principle of selection came under attack: pupils of whatever ability, it was felt, should share the same school and even the same classroom. In 1954, London opened its first such 'comprehensive' school, at Kidbrooke, south-east of Greenwich. It had 1,700 girl pupils, 90 teachers, 5 gymnasia, and . . . a radio control room.

Technology, in fact, was a general postwar concern. In the Europe of the 1930's, far fewer than a quarter of all graduates had studied scientific subjects. By 1955, the proportion was still modest, but in almost all countries it had risen sharply, reflecting the new importance of science-based industries, many of them spurred on by war.

Atomic energy was the prime example. Wartime technology had turned nuclear physics into the Hiroshima and Nagasaki bombs. The reactor process which had produced their plutonium was soon able to generate energy in exploitable form; and while the engineers were solving the practical problems of handling controlled nuclear fission, the scientists were already proposing not to split atoms but to conflate them by nuclear fusion. At the first International Conference on the Peaceful Uses of Atomic Energy, held in Geneva in 1955, its Indian chairman, Professor Homi J. Bhabha, was able to claim that when man had mastered fusion there would be as much energy as there was heavy hydrogen in the sea – i.e. one to every 6,000 atoms of the ordinary hydrogen in the world's total of H_2O. His boundless optimism was typical of the time. It was echoed more widely in the following year, when Britain's Calder Hall reactor became the first in Europe to feed electricity into the national power supply.

In retrospect, Britain's technological lead may seem surprising. For years after World War II, her governments grappled with nerve-racking economic problems: an overvalued pound, the dollar gap, shortages of raw materials, the price of food imports, the cost of servicing the national debt. Partly for this reason, they found it difficult to look far ahead; and by failing to invest in the future, they set in train the British economy's long, slow, relative decline. Meanwhile, too many ex-service students – like my friends and me – were reading arts subjects, privately disdaining disciplines like engineering in which others were dirtying their hands. Yet, paradoxically, British technology at that time belied the twin clichés of 'austerity' and 'crisis': it was thrusting, efficient, and self-confident.

Nowhere was this more evident than in aviation. In 1940, in the Battle of Britain, the Royal Air Force had, as a Canadian friend put it, 'held up the skies' against the Nazis who had overrun the rest of Western Europe. Pride in that splendid isolation was still fresh; and it stirred anew at every postwar achievement. To many British people, the air now seemed as much their natural element as the sea had been to their forebears. When British European Airways, BEA, was formed on 1 August 1946, it carried 9,300 passengers in its first month – a total exceeded, ten years later, on any single summer's day. Beginning with twenty ex-RAF Dakotas, the BEA fleet soon expanded to include De Havilland Rapides, Avro 19's, Vickers Vikings, and even Junkers JU 52's; later, it took on De Havilland Ambassadors, soon renamed 'Elizabethans'. In 1950, BEA flew the world's first turbo-prop airliner, the Vickers Viscount, on two experimental passenger trips; in 1951 it began a scheduled helicopter service. In 1952, its sister-organization, the British Overseas Airways Corporation, BOAC, inaugurated the world's first purely jet airliner service, using the De Havilland Comet. By the end of the decade, BEA was the biggest airline in Western Europe. Many of its passengers used the brand-new London Airport at Heathrow, developed in the early 1950's in a style recalling the Festival of Britain, and surprisingly compact for the world's busiest international airport.

Britain was not alone in patriotic pride. A national airline soon became a symbol of statehood, in Europe as elsewhere; and continental long-haul carriers like Air France, the Dutch KLM, and the Belgian Sabena were soon covering distances comparable with those of BOAC. By the mid-1950's, London, Paris, Frankfurt, Rome, Copenhagen, and Berlin were among the world's most crowded airports, each handling about a million passengers a year, while European airlines carried more than half of those who flew the

Atlantic. In 1958, for the first time, more travellers crossed by air than by ship.

Air travel, and especially jet travel, transformed everyday experience. The British literary critic A. Alvarez called it

the easiest and most forceful way of feeling what it's like to belong to the twentieth century. You are carried miles up at a ludicrous speed in a cocoon of bottled air and bottled music, while shiny, mass-produced hostesses ply you with the food and the pilot intones his soothing creed: 'Sit back, relax and enjoy your flight.' When it's over, you are decanted into airports of smooth glass and aluminium and swept whisperingly along super highways into the cities. It's marvellous, imposing – even, in a way, rather touching. But it's also unreal, a bit impossible.

It was certainly a way of fulfilling dreams. The eighteenth-century 'Grand Tour' had been a prerogative of aristocrats: the twentieth-century package tour opened foreign vistas to millions, rather as unit trusts or mutual funds introduced them to the stock market. In both cases, there was safety – and economy – in numbers. Guaranteed a regular clientèle, developers built new ferro-concrete hotels in the beauty-spots of soft-currency countries: the white cliffs of Dover were replaced in popular affection by the white cliffs of Benidorm or the Lido di Jesolo. Films and songs began to reflect the fashion: *Roman Holiday* in 1953, *Three Coins in the Fountain* and 'Cara Mia' in 1954, 'By the Fountains of Rome' two years later. A British manufacturer in Poole, Dorset, even found it worth while to produce Paris 'rock' – cylindrical sugar candy, traditionally sold in British seaside resorts, with the name of the town in the middle, legible all the way through.

By 1957, thanks to jet travel, Western Europe had a sizeable new nation of 35 million people – its international tourists, 90 percent of them European. Their favourite destinations were Italy, Germany, France, Sweden, Spain, and Austria. Most were in search of snow or sun, some of them in the 'South Seas' holiday villages of the Club Méditerranée, founded in 1950 by a Belgian and a Frenchman. Surprisingly many, like me and my friends in Florence, travelled with guidebook or score in hand, seeking out art or music.

We had a slightly comical air, assiduously following recommended routes, and hungrier for culture abroad than ever we seemed at home. But the riches before us were a revelation. In 1947, the French novelist and critic André Malraux had first published *Le musée imaginaire*, discussing the effect of museums and galleries on the appreciation of art. Colour reproductions, he had pointed out, now gave everyone access to 'the imaginary museum'; and this, like the great collections themselves, removed works of art from their private or sacred context, making us all, as it were, cool connoisseurs. It was a tempting theory, buttressed by such characteristic enterprises as Skira art books or near-replicas of paintings on canvas-like surfaces, often in 'antique' frames. Yet to examine any original, however familiar from reproductions, was to doubt the thesis that Malraux argued so persuasively. There was no substitute for the real thing. Now, more and more people were able to travel and see for themselves. And for those who stayed at home, art itself went on tour: huge international exhibitions were soon a familiar feature of postwar Europe.

They included not only such art-fairs as the Venice Biennale, the Biennale des Jeunes in Paris, or the 'Documenta' shows in Kassel, but also retrospective celebrations of particular movements or individual artists: Matisse in 1945; Van Gogh in 1947; Braque in 1948; Léger in 1949; Graham Sutherland in 1952; Picasso in 1953; Matisse again in 1955 and 1956; Dada in 1957. Immense crowds flocked to see them: at the Van Gogh exhibition in London, the long lines of people waiting for admission had to be marshalled by the police. And some of the giants thus honoured were still vigorously active. Matisse, for instance, was 82 in 1951 when he completed his last major work, endowing the Chapelle du Rosaire, the Dominican nuns' chapel at Vence near Nice, with its yellow, green, and gold stained-glass windows, its magnificent carved door, and its austere black-and-white line drawings, fired in tiles on the walls.

Other religious buildings married modernity and tradition in similar ways. Also in 1951, a handsome design by the British architect Basil Spence won the competition for a new Coventry Cathedral; and in 1955 Le Corbusier completed his spectacular Church of Notre Dame du Haut, at Ronchamp in the Vosges. Its tall tubular chapel was offset by wide white walls, studded with tiny windows and curving to meet like the prow of a liner, under a tapering winged roof which from some angles looked like a bullock's horn. In boldness and control of fine detail, this was matched only by some of the dazzling structures put up by Pier Luigi Nervi – the Palazzo delle Esposizioni in Turin, completed in 1950, or the casino at Chianciano Terme, built two years later, with its astonishing lattice-work ceiling like a giant lace sunflower petrified in concrete. All these were modern monuments which, in the guide-books' terminology, 'deserved a detour' and were often 'worth the journey'.

Music, too, now attracted innumerable pilgrims. Even in 1949, when Europeans were still busy repairing the ruins, it took all kinds of artifice to secure tickets for the Salzburg Festival – long advance booking, endless waiting in line, polyglot argument, shameless string-pulling, patience, persistence, and bluff. Opera, above all, drew enormous audiences. In 1951, the Bayreuth Festival reopened – with the Germanic chauvinism of Richard

Wagner's music-dramas, so long exploited by the Nazis, tactfully purged by the composer's grandson Wieland Wagner. The same year, in Venice, saw the world première of Igor Stravinsky's new opera *The Rake's Progress*, with a libretto by W.H. Auden and Chester Kallman. It was a glittering occasion: the Teatro La Fenice was crammed with celebrities, including Stravinsky's great French admirer, the 64-year-old teacher and composer Nadia Boulanger, observed at one point carrying the maestro's valises. Save for Elisabeth Schwarzkopf's singing, the performance was unremarkable. Auden found the sets garish and grandiose; despite his coaching, the chorus's English was hard to understand. The work itself was a far cry from its original inspiration in William Hogarth's paintings. The American composer Virgil Thomson – once a pupil of Nadia Boulanger's – dismissed the plot as 'an incredible mélange of *Little Red Riding Hood*, *Dr Faustus*, and *Oedipus Rex*'. Benjamin Britten allegedly said that he liked everything about the score except the music. While composing it, Stravinsky had listened repeatedly to *Così fan tutte*; and in an interview before the first performance Auden and Kallman declared that they too had reverted for inspiration to Mozart and the eighteenth century. Verdi, Puccini and others, they claimed, had carried the Italian tradition in opera to the point of exhaustion.

It was a rash remark. That very year, an American-born Greek soprano made a striking debut at La Scala, specializing in Italian opera. Her name was Maria Meneghini Callas; and her performances in *Norma*, *I Puritani*, *Anna Bolena*, and *Lucia di Lammermoor* helped to endorse a renewed admiration for Bellini and Donizetti. The revival of traditional opera was further confirmed four years later. In May 1955, Austria regained her independence; in November, she reopened the Vienna State Opera, heavily subsidized and sumptuously rebuilt. Its chorus and orchestra were later to record outstanding performances of Donizetti's *Anna Bolena* and *Don Pasquale*. At the end of the 1950's, the Australian soprano Joan Sutherland was to win international fame in *Lucia*, at Covent Garden. By that time London, so long unfairly neglected, had emerged as one of Europe's music capitals – an ambition announced in 1951 by the opening of the 3,000-seat auditorium in the Royal Festival Hall. Even before the Festival Hall was built, in fact, London was selling more than four million tickets a year for concerts, opera, and ballet.

Music-lovers listening at home were also coming to be far better served. Magnetic tape had been perfected in Germany during World War II, making possible what one record company called 'ffrr' – 'full frequency range recording'; but until the end of the 1940's European gramophone records were still rigid discs, played at 78 revolutions per minute (r.p.m.). Thorn or fibre had largely replaced metal gramophone needles, but sound reproduction was still marred by surface hiss. Then came a major change: the introduction of microgroove records, played at 45 or 33 r.p.m. with a stylus on a light counterweighted pickup. Some of the new 'long-playing' or 'extended play' discs were advertised as unbreakable. To prove it, a friend of mine threw Act II of *Don Giovanni* into his tiled fireplace. The result was fatal, but the company made it good. Towards the end of the decade, stereophonic recording began to open new vistas of 'high fidelity' or 'hi-fi'.

What made all this possible was interlinked progress in technology. War, once again, had been partly responsible for accelerating research and development; but no less crucial now was the way in which discoveries in one field prompted advances in others: metals technology and nuclear physics, biochemistry and electronics, polymer science – plastics – and engineering. In workshops as well as laboratories, disciplines interacted. The results were cumulative, a geometric progression of change.

Its symbol, to many laymen, was the computer, born of a marriage between servomotors and electronic instruments, and using magnetic plastic tape. With it came two new words: 'cybernetics' – control and communication in animals and machines – and 'automation' – automatic control of manufacturing. Both were of American origin; but by 1957 a hundred thousand people in at least thirty-seven countries were engaged in the 'computer revolution' that was already transforming the ways in which Europeans thought, worked, and lived.

Even more phenomenal, and at first more widely influential, was the development of plastics. In the 1930's, their only familiar forms had been celluloid, 'bakelite', 'artificial silk' or 'rayon', and polymethyl methacrylate or 'unbreakable glass'. In 1941, two British scientific writers, V.E. Yarsley and E.G. Couzens, produced a popular handbook on *Plastics*. At the time I remember thinking it a work of science fiction. It predicted, among other things, plastic shoes, clothes, flooring, water-pipes, cars, and sailing boats. Fifteen years later, none of them was notably unusual. By 1958, the world was producing four million tons of plastics every year – half of them in the United States, but with Germany and Britain as the next biggest manufacturers, partly owing to Germany's use of '*ersatz*' replacements for other materials during the war. Only France remained a major importer of plastics:

one expert attributed this to her prewar distaste for 'artificial silk'. Even after the war, that reaction was not uncommon. Many people understandably objected when plastic replaced wood or wickerwork, in clothes-pegs, cotton-reels, or bread-baskets – and especially when feeble attempts were made to imitate the original. But the new materials were cheap, durable, and useful. Even French customers soon welcomed nylon stockings, drip-dry shirts, and lightweight polyester suits.

A third great change was in medicine and surgery, largely owing to new drugs. Here, too, war had been a stimulus: the best-known examples – DDT, the sulfa drugs, and penicillin – had all originated earlier, but been developed to meet wartime needs. Penicillin, terramycin, and other antibiotics made a dramatic impact on bacterial infection. They were largely ineffective against viruses – sub-microscopic infective particles which, instead of growing like bacteria, are duplicated by the host cell at its own expense; but in the mid-1950's even viruses began to be overcome. In 1954, the US virologist Jonas Salk prepared an injectable vaccine against poliomyelitis; a year later, two other American scientists produced a strain that could be taken orally.

By that time, even in Europe, what had once seemed 'miracles' were becoming more familiar: high-speed dentists' drills; steel and plastic hip joints; new sections for diseased arteries; artificial aortic valves for defective hearts; hole-in-heart operations; brain surgery; kidney machines; heart-lung machines.

Equally spectacular, if at that time more academic, were the advances being made in genetics. The best publicized was the discovery, by James Watson and Francis Crick, working in Cambridge, England, that deoxyribonucleic acid, DNA, had a 'double helix' structure – a further step towards understanding how genetic information is passed on.

For thousands of Europeans, however, the most important steps forward at this time were in the struggle against pneumonia and tuberculosis. These two, like cancer, were among the last of the old, dreaded killer diseases – like the plague, smallpox, typhus – of which people still often spoke in whispers. In the 1920's, one person in five in Western Europe had been likely to die of one or the other. By 1948, thanks to new vaccines, chemotherapy, mass radiography, and tuberculin-tested or pasteurized milk, the number of tuberculosis victims had been cut by half; by 1956, the death-rate from pneumonia had been halved, and the tuberculosis death-rate reduced to less than a fifth. Nor, for me, were these mere statistics. In 1945, in the British army, I was cured of double pneumonia. Twenty years later, at the age of eighty, my father was cured of tuberculosis; he lived on well into his nineties.

He was not alone. Everywhere in Western Europe, people were healthier and longer-lived. In 1939, the average death-rate per thousand inhabitants had been nearly 14; by 1958 it had dropped to just over 10. Infant mortality had halved; the number of mothers dying in childbirth was less than a quarter of the prewar figure. The birthrate itself had gone up sharply just after the war, as servicemen returned home. Now, it was falling again, partly as a result of more widespread birth control – although the phosphorylated hesperidin contraceptive pill, first tested in the United States in 1952, was not yet generally available.

Western Europe's birthrate had more than offset her wartime casualties. Since the war, too, the population had been swelled by about 12 million refugees from the East. By the mid-1950's, it had reached nearly 300 million, compared with 250 million in the late 1930's. More than a third of them were under 25, and very much fitter than their elders had been at that age. Rickets, once so common in the poorer parts of Europe's large cities, had almost disappeared; so had many skin diseases; dental caries was also on the decline. Young people were taller and heavier; and some of them seemed more athletic. On 6 May 1954, an Oxford medical student, the 25-year-old Roger Bannister, ran the world's first four-minute mile. Within a few years, his record had been broken more than fifty times. And at the other end of life there were many more people, like my father, who were surviving into an active old age. By 1955, nearly 10 percent of Western Europe's total population were 65 or older, compared with 7.5 percent in 1930.

With more elderly people to be cared for, pensions were becoming a bigger item in West European budgets. By 1954, they were absorbing an average 4 percent of the national wealth – in Germany and Luxembourg, more than 6 percent. Medical care and health insurance cost a further 3 percent, family allowances 1½ percent, and unemployment benefit 0.4 percent. In all the richer countries, in fact, social security was now far more comprehensive than before the war. In some cases, it was wholly govern-mental; in others, public and private care were combined. The level of expenditure varied widely: the poorest countries, not surprisingly, spent least. But society in general was becoming more compassionate to the poor, the sick, the elderly, and the defenceless. Its concern was effective because of its growing wealth.

By 1955, all countries in Western Europe were producing more than in the 1930's. In 1949–50, their average growth rate had been 8.3 percent; in 1951–2 it had dropped to 2.7 percent; but in 1954–5 it rose again, to 6.7 percent. Abroad, from 1952 onwards, Western Europe was earning more than it spent: between 1938 and 1955, imports tripled but exports quadrupled. Investments increased, and so did productivity: from 1950 to 1955, employment rose by 7 percent and man-hours by 8.2 percent – but the output of roughly the same human effort went up by 26 percent.

Individuals reaped the benefit. People who before the war had struggled to live on unemployment pay or low wages now began to feel secure, and even comfortable, with money in their pockets, savings accounts, or mattresses, and an apartment or a house, usually rented but often being bought on a mortgage. Some central apartments, as in Paris or Rome, were in former private mansions – old and cramped, but picturesque and cheap, with low State-controlled rentals. Others, on the outskirts of cities, were in new, raw, purpose-built blocks. Houses also varied. They were most popular in the Netherlands and Britain: by 1954, British 'building societies' or mortgage companies had nearly quadrupled their assets since before the war, and were still expanding by more than 10 percent a year. But even in Britain, fewer than a third of all homes were owner-occupied. An increasing number were rented, like apartments, from local authorities, many of which had ambitious housing projects – some in 'new towns' – to clear inner-city slums. Only in Greece, Finland, and Ireland was owner-occupancy more common than not. Everywhere, however, more and more people were buying apartments.

Outside the house or apartment, there would often now be a family Fiat, Renault, Citroën, Volkswagen, Austin, Morris, or Ford. By the mid-1950's, one in 25 of all West Europeans had a car, and two million more cars were being driven on to the roads every year. Congestion was becoming a problem: by the end of the decade, there were still only just over 2,000 miles of express highways in Western Europe, although twice as many again were planned for the next ten years. Fuel, at least, was now more plentiful. In Britain, petrol rationing had been abolished in 1950, and branded varieties reintroduced in 1953. Between 1950 and 1958, Western Europe trebled its imports of crude and refined oil.

The increase in road transport, like the boom in air travel, was beginning to worry the railways. Traffic on Western Europe's rail networks was still growing, but more slowly than before; and many were having to concentrate investment on key routes and trains. Only in Switzerland and the

Netherlands were the railways still making a sizeable profit. Perhaps it was no coincidence that in 1954 it was a Dutch railway official, Dr Den Hollander, who had the idea which led to the Trans-Europ-Express – a luxury 100 m.p.h. train which sped across frontiers without stopping and, with its air-conditioning, reclining seats, and public-address system, rather resembled an aircraft flying on rails – but serving first-class food.

While the railways were having to adapt to new challenges, most of Europe's waterways were flourishing. Between 1949 and 1957, water traffic more than doubled; and along the Seine and the Rhine and many lesser arteries, the sight of fast power barges carrying coal or cement or heavy metals, with a family living aboard and washing fluttering dry like strange pennants, became as familiar again as it had been before the war. The major exception was Britain, whose canals were now carrying less and less freight. But they too soon responded to the challenge, by offering something novel: inland waterway holidays for people who chose to leave the car behind and enjoy the peace of a floating home from home.

Home itself, in the mid-1950's, was growing more attractive. In the richer countries of Western Europe, nearly all dwellings were equipped with electricity, most had inside running water, and a large proportion had fixed baths. In France, Germany, Sweden, the Netherlands, and Britain, national building research institutes were testing new technology – hollow lightweight bricks, under-floor heating systems, ready-made wall sections with built-in insulation. More conventional new dwellings might now have 'open-plan' features, or 'picture windows' made possible by float glass. More and more householders were installing central heating: and almost everyone, except for the incompetent, the overworked, or the very wealthy, seemed now to be busy on some form of *bricolage* or do-it-yourself home improvement, from simple painting or decorating to electrical re-wiring, converting a loft into an attic, or assembling furniture from a kit.

The furnishings made or bought were often of the style then known as 'contemporary': light, doll's-house-type chairs of wood or metal with removable cushions; low tables that looked aerodynamic; plain wood shelving partitions to divide 'open-plan' areas; indoor rubber plants; chunky ash-trays; rugs with bright geometric patterns; standard lamps on stalks of burnished steel. Some designers seemed to want domestic interiors to look like airport 'lounges'.

Perhaps it was appropriate. In default of domestic servants, many homes now contained a multiplicity of machines, from vacuum cleaners and floor polishers to food mixers, electric coffee-grinders, and automatic roasting spits under eye-level grills. In the mid-1950's one West European in five owned a radio set, and one in twelve a telephone. One in every ten families had a refrigerator, one in seven a washing machine, and one in six a television set.

Television was beginning to replace the cinema as popular entertainment. During the war and immediately after it, films had flourished at all levels – and in Europe, especially, had begun to match the depth and maturity of the other arts. At first, France had seemed in the vanguard, with the moody, mannered, rather modish pessimism that pervaded the work of Marcel Carné, Claude Autant-Lara, Henri-Georges Clouzot, Jean Cocteau, or Yves Allégret. All were products of an assured, stylish, literary culture; their films were peopled by doomed lovers, poets, clowns, outcasts, vagabonds, and other victims of ineluctable destiny. It was a closed, elegant, beguiling world of low-key lighting, 'haunting' theme tunes, and slow, elegiac fades. But it soon seemed effete when the new films from Italy burst on to the screen – blowing away the careful studio mists and exposing real, knobbly people to the harsh light of day.

'Neo-realism' was the literal translation of what Italian critics called the new movement: 'new realism' would have suited it better. Coming from Italy, it was doubly surprising. Mussolini had built Cinecittà, 'Cinema City', outside Rome in the hope of rivalling Hollywood; but many of its prewar productions had been 'white telephone' films – stagey dramas about cardboard characters in settings of chromium luxury. At the end of the war, Cinema City had become a refugee camp. Working outside the studio, Roberto Rossellini had turned his back on Cinecittà values and given his war films *Roma, Città Aperta* (1945) and *Paisà* (1946) an urgent, rough-edged authenticity. Vittorio De Sica and his screenwriter Cesare Zavattini, also filming on location, used non-professional actors to tackle immediate social concerns: slum life in *Sciuscia* (1946), unemployment in *Ladri di Biciclette* (1948), shanty-town poverty in *Miracolo a Milano* (1951), and lonely old age in *Umberto D* (1952). At the time, such films seemed tough, rigorous, unadulterated 'slices of life'. Only in retrospect was their artifice apparent; but their quality and integrity endure.

British cinema at that time was still relying on its traditional strengths. Laurence Olivier had followed his stirring *Henry V* (1944) with a restless *Hamlet* in 1948 and a fine, flashing, theatrical *Richard III* in 1955 – the last of his major Shakespeare films. Carol Reed had turned from war pictures like

The Way Ahead (1944) and *The True Glory* (1945) to scrupulous adaptations from literature – *Odd Man Out* (1947) and *The Fallen Idol* (1948) – before working with Graham Greene and Orson Welles on *The Third Man* (1949). But his next film, *An Outcast of the Islands* (1951), was not fully worthy of either Carol Reed or Joseph Conrad; and his later work lacked his earlier brilliance. David Lean, after the achievements of *Great Expectations* (1946) and *Oliver Twist* (1948), moved more and more towards big budgets and spectacular productions; and the team that had made the Ealing comedies – men like Charles Crichton, Robert Hamer, Alexander Mackendrick, and T.E.B. Clarke – dispersed in the later 1950's as public tastes, film-going habits, and financial opportunities all changed.

Throughout Europe, indeed, the film-makers of the immediate postwar period were soon to be in eclipse. In France, Marcel Carné made no film of any great consequence after *Thérèse Raquin* in 1953: his effort to portray (and woo) a younger generation, *Les Tricheurs*, five years later, was sadly inept. In Italy in 1953, Vittorio De Sica disappointed everyone – including his backers – with *Stazione Termini*, a glossy love-story partly financed by David O. Selznick as a vehicle for his wife Jennifer Jones. After that, De Sica made only one more, rather minor 'neo-realist' film, *Il Tetto* (1956).

Several critics at the time noted what one of them termed a 'rising tide of sensationalism'. The reason was not hard to find. Everywhere, film producers were looking for ways of outbidding television: stereoscopic or '3-D' pictures, characteristically publicized with *Bwana Devil* in 1952; the three-screen, three-projector expanse of Cinerama, launched in the same year; or its smaller, wide-screen, single-lens counterpart CinemaScope, first used commercially for *The Robe*, a Biblical epic, in 1953. This, some said, was like watching a film through a letter box. Where expedients of that sort failed, the industry tended to fall back on tried and true attractions like sex and violence, at that time less explicit on the television screen.

It was a losing battle. Already in the mid-1950's some of the larger 'picture palace' cinemas were having to be closed down or subdivided. The changes were first seen in Britain, where television in Europe had begun before the war. Shut down in 1939, broadcasts had resumed on 7 June 1946: transmitted from the old Crystal Palace in London, they could theoretically reach 12 million people, almost a quarter of the British population. In December 1949, a high-power relay station was opened at Sutton Coldfield in Warwickshire; with an antenna 75 feet high, it was the most powerful transmitter in the world. Within two-and-a-half years, three more were completed. With reception thus assured, the public bought television sets. By 1953, Britain had more than two million – 95 percent of the total throughout Western Europe. On Tuesday 2 June that year, twenty million loyal citizens gathered round them to see the coronation of Queen Elizabeth II – the first event which more people watched on television than listened to on sound radio. By 1956, the number of sets in Britain had risen from two to nine million, and there were nearly fifteen million in Western Europe as a whole.

Colour television, video recording, and 'stereovision' were still some years off; but other developments came rapidly. In 1954, the 'Eurovision' network was formed, to link members of the European Broadcasting Union. That same year, in Britain, the police used television for the first time to show the face of a man wanted for murder. And in September 1955, after much controversy, Britain broke the television monopoly hitherto enjoyed by the British Broadcasting Corporation, the BBC, and inaugurated the first purely commercial channel – an operation partly master-minded by the popular novelist Norman Collins, at one time Controller of BBC Television, and author of *London Belongs to Me*. Within two years, commercial television in Britain was taking more advertising revenue than the whole of the London press. This was a considerable sum: since 1950, on average, advertising expenditure had been growing by 13 percent a year. To counter it, consumer movements emerged. Their beginnings went back to the early years of the century; but the new organizations were professional, determined, and longer-lived. An early example was the Consumers' Association, founded in Britain in 1937. Within a short time, its monthly magazine *Which?* had a circulation of 300,000.

The advertising boom reflected and helped to foster new habits of mass consumption, made possible by additional earning power. With 40 million women going out to work, and the number increasing almost everywhere, many West European families in the mid-1950's had more than one breadwinner – in Britain, one family in every five. The result, in the richer countries, was something of a spending spree. Many people were now buying cars and household 'consumer durables' on 'hire purchase' or other consumer credit plans; but they were also enjoying more expensive food, drink, clothes, and so on. In Britain, the volume of consumption per head in the 1950's increased by more than a fifth – as much as in the 26 years between 1913 and 1939. Everywhere, too, the pattern of consumption had altered. West Europeans were eating less bread and fewer potatoes, more fruit and meat. They were spending a smaller proportion of their bigger family budgets on food, and more on pet-food; more on clothing, and very much more on 'foundation garments'; much the same on razor-blades, but more on electric shavers and more on cosmetics – including perfumes for men in the virile guise of 'after-shave lotion'.

Shopping habits were also changing. With more than 4 million retail stores, Western Europe in the mid-1950's was still a continent of shopkeepers: it had one store for every 72 people, compared with one for every 152 in the United States. It now employed 13 million salespeople, compared with 10 million before the war. But something new was on the way: self-service. It began modestly, often in shops of conventional size, sometimes in the food sections of department stores. It developed rapidly. In 1950, there were 1,200 self-service establishments in the whole of Western Europe. By the end of the decade, there were 45,000 – including 600 big enough to be classed as 'supermarkets'. They sold, among other things, packaged, ready-cut meat and, increasingly, frozen food. In these ways, as in others, Western Europe was copying North America.

Alongside the new stores, and sometimes in them, there were new types of eating-place. All were designed to cater for a new, apparently classless clientèle. Previously, shops, restaurants, and cafés in Western Europe had reflected social differences quite sharply, much as the trains had been divided into first, second, and third class. The new supermarkets, coffee bars, 'steak houses' and dispensers of fast food quite deliberately side-stepped the European class system. They opted neither for comforting plebeian 'togetherness' nor for chill aristocratic chic. Instead, with the shining aluminium, plate glass, and bright, toy-coloured plastic of their 'contemporary' decor, they embodied the vision of a new society – smart but not exclusive, well-to-do but unpretentious, offering everyone democratic quality and style. In Britain, it was not only inflation that led the 'Fifty Shilling Tailors', a long familiar chain of stores offering men's suits at bargain prices, to change its name, first to 'FST' and then to 'John Collier' – 'up-market', in the advertising jargon then increasingly fashionable, but still appealing to the plain man. Marks and Spencer, the clothing and food chain, underwent a similar transformation without a change of trade-mark, although it now stressed its brand name, 'St Michael'. By the mid-1950's, its customers spanned the social spectrum – and they looked more and more alike. Off duty, plumbers as well as lawyers might wear narrowed trousers, suède 'chukka boots', and coloured waistcoats; secretaries, factory girls, and public-relations account executives might copy Brigitte Bardot's pout, coiffure, and sweater, or adopt the 'gamine' look made popular earlier by Audrey Hepburn. In France, they shopped at the Samaritaine, in Belgium at the Sarma-Lux, in Germany at Edeka, in Switzerland at the Migros, in Italy at the Rinascente. In Britain, they went to Marks and Spencer, and many of their clothes bore the St Michael label.

Some commentators suggested that the whole of Western Europe was heading for a 'St Michael society' in which class differences would disappear. With a larger 'cake' of wealth to share, it was argued, even small slices would be so much more generous that disparities would seem less cruel. In 1958, in his study of *The Affluent Society*, John Kenneth Galbraith pointed out that, for the developed countries of the West,

production has eliminated the more acute tensions associated with inequality.... The oldest and most agitated of social issues, if not resolved, is at least largely in abeyance and the disputants have concentrated their attention, instead, on the goal of increased productivity.

In France, the sociologist Raymond Aron pursued similar themes. With better conditions all round, greater social mobility, and more white-collar workers, especially in the service industries, the old European class system, he argued, was on the way out. '*Embourgeoisement*', recruiting the former rich as well as the once poor into a new, American-style middle class, would soon give every section of society a comparable way of life.

The growth of leisure pursuits seemed to confirm the thesis. More and more people could now afford not only foreign holidays, but weekend cottages – what the French called 'secondary residences'. These were made possible both by urban affluence and by agricultural change. Farmers in Western Europe had greatly increased their output: by the mid-1950's, only rye, oats, pulses, hemp, and flax were less plentiful than before the war. Everything else was burgeoning. With twice the amount of artificial fertilizers, yields per acre had gone up; with four times the number of tractors, so had productivity per man. Less need for farm labour and better prospects in industry led many workers and their children to leave the land for the city – thereby liberating country cottages for rent or sale to townspeople. As the use of the countryside changed, several governments in Europe saw a need to protect it against tourists and factory-farmers, by establishing 'national parks'. By the end of the decade, Britain had no fewer than ten. And as more town-dwellers escaped from the city, even for brief visits, more of them were attracted to open-air pastimes like riding, skiing, golf, and dinghy-sailing, once the preserve of a minority – as well as by such new sports as parachuting, water-skiing, and scuba diving. On any European beach in August, crowded with bronzing bodies in swimsuits and bikinis, it was easy to believe that Galbraith and Aron were right.

Yet in some respects their intimations of a classless society were premature, if not false. Western Europe suffered less than North America from the contrast between what Galbraith called 'private affluence and public squalor'; but there remained a hard core of poverty, concentrated in particular areas, groups, and occupations – outlying regions and inner cities, immigrants and the very old, ill-paid and declining industries. What was more, while some class differences were diminishing, many class distinctions were not.

Britain, especially, seemed now to be paying them closer attention than ever. In 1949, Angus Wilson published his first book of short stories, pointedly entitled *The Wrong Set*, etching with brilliant malice the now uneasy attitudes of the English upper-middle classes. In 1954, two musical divertissements – *Salad Days* by Julian Slade, an Old Etonian, and *The Boy Friend* by Sandy Wilson – captured a vogue for youthful skittishness which was partly a defiance of the worthy egalitarian trend. In 1955, in a similiar reaction, the novelist Nancy Mitford, daughter of the second Baron Redesdale, published an article in the monthly magazine *Encounter*, classifying English modes of speech as 'U', for 'upper-class', and 'non-U' – terminology borrowed from an article in a Finnish learned journal by Alan S. C. Ross, Professor of Linguistics at Birmingham University. Her *jeu d'esprit* launched many a social mishap. A year later, with Professor Ross, she edited a compilation on the subject, *Noblesse Oblige: An Enquiry into the Identifiable Characteristics of the English Aristocracy*. The contributors included John Betjeman, whose delicately detailed poems of place – some of them imbued with nostalgia for prewar life in large houses with tennis-courts and conservatories – were now immensely popular: in 1958, a collected edition of his verse quickly sold out. Meanwhile, more academic authors had been examining the social strata. In 1954, the Professor of Psychology at Manchester University, T.H. Pear, had published *English Social Differences*; in 1955, Professor G.D.H. Cole produced *Studies in Class Structure*; and in 1957 Professor Richard Hoggart paid affectionate and moving tribute to an older working-class culture in *The Uses of Literacy*. Class-consciousness, in Betjeman Britain, was still very much alive.

With it, in certain circles, went a new kind of snobbery about 'gracious living' – a phrase only then being laughed out of use. Writing at that time in *The Cambridge Review* about Professor Pear's book, I did my best to portray – I was probably aping – a devotee of the new cult:

His trouser-legs, still narrow, have widened.... His shoes are ceasing to be suède. Instead of a waistcoat or sweater, he tends to wear a cardigan: he has abandoned the bow tie, and favours the woollen weave..., He holds all the best opinions, however incompatible: he is a post-Leavisite and a logical analyst, a wide-awake contemporary and a student of Europe's origins, a *bon vivant* with leanings towards the Church. Dining with him, you will savour Italian delicacies from Parmigiani Figlio: you will sit on nursery chairs looped with cushions, sipping Orvieto in shapely Swedish glasses. The walls behind you will be pastel-tinted, the chimney adorned in paper richly striped. As your fingers toy with nuts and raisins, as the port and madeira circulate, you will feel your easy kinship with dry eighteenth-century wits. But after the meal you will drink fresh-ground coffee at a smaller table shaped like a Flying Wing. To hand, on the hanging bookshelves, will be *Bonjour tristesse* and *Cards of Identity*: climbing plants will dangle from baskets of white wire. Over the rush mats and the Parker-Knoll upholstery, coolie lampshades will shed their soft effulgence, and LP recordings of Scarlatti will sing out brilliantly into the night.

Amid the heavy irony, the bookshelves and their contents were apt. *Cards of Identity*, published in 1955, was a fantasy and social satire, suggesting that in the new international mass environment, only experts could tell people who they were. Its author, Nigel Dennis, was himself a cosmopolitan: although born in Britain, he had spent his childhood in Rhodesia, been educated partly in Austria, and worked for fifteen years in the United States. But he cunningly set his fable in a traditional English country house, now converted for use by the exclusive Identity Club:

This sort of house was once a heart and centre of the national identity. A whole world lived in relation to it. Millions knew who they were by reference to it. Hundreds of thousands look back to it, and not only grieve for its passing but still depend on it, non-existent though it is, to tell them who they are. Thousands who never knew it are taught every day to cherish its memory and to believe that without it no man will be able to tell his whereabouts again. It hangs on men's necks like a millstone of memory; carrying it, and looking back on its associations, they stumble indignantly backwards into the future, confident that man's self-knowledge is gone forever. How appropriate it is that these forlorn barracks, these harbours of human nostalgia, should now be in use once more solely as meeting places for bodies such as ours!

Clever, elegant, and expertly playful, the book neatly encapsulated a transitional age.

Bonjour tristesse, the novel by Françoise 'Sagan' (Françoise Quoirez), was equally attuned to its time. Published in France in 1954, it owed some of its celebrity to the fact that its author was nineteen years old, a very personable drop-out from her first year at the Sorbonne, and worldly-wise about love and sex and betrayal in sun-drenched Mediterranean settings. Gossip, or publicity, insisted that Françoise Sagan liked to drive fast cars in bare feet. But, like Nigel Dennis, she was a skilful writer . Her mastery of the cool, precise French *conte*, containing and compressing powerful emotions, appealed to readers at the time as directly as Nigel Dennis's dry, sardonic wit.

And there were plenty of readers. Despite the cinema, radio, and now television, the public for books had greatly expanded since before the war. In Britain and Denmark, this was partly owing to the increased use of public libraries. Many had doubled the number of books they issued between 1945 and 1955. Book clubs, especially in Britain and Germany, also played an important rolc. But the major growth was in paperback and pocket editions, which in the mid-1950's came to include not only popular best-sellers, but 'intellectual' or 'egg-head' paperbacks – soft-covered editions of hardback books, printed in the same format as the originals. By 1956, one person in every ten was a regular purchaser of paperbacks – although even in France and Britain half the adult population still claimed that they never bought books.

The books that did achieve mass circulation were a mixed batch. Prominent among them were practical handbooks. Some, like household machines, were substitutes for domestic servants: the cookbook replacing the cook. Back from *Bonjour tristesse* holidays, Northerners learned to cook pasta and make bouillabaisse from evocative instructions under dust-jackets depicting Chianti flasks and long French loaves. Equally useful, for young families no longer living with or near grandparents, were books on bringing up children. In 1946 in the United States, Dr Benjamin Spock produced his *Common Sense Book of Baby and Child Care*. In 1955 it was published in Britain. Translated into many languages, it became as much a best-seller in Europe as in North America. The French edition alone was to sell some 20 million copies.

Few European authors reached so large an audience; but many were selling in millions. War stories and memoirs were still understandably popular. They ranged widely: from the heartbreaking poignancy of *The Diary of Anne Frank*, first published in the Netherlands in 1947, to such stirring tales as Eric Williams's account of escape from a prisoner-of-war camp, *The Wooden Horse* (1949); from the painful realism of Robert Merle's story of Dunkirk, *Week-end à Zuydcoote* (1949), to the imaginative ambivalence of Pierre Boulle's prison-camp novel, *Le pont de la rivière Kwai* (1952); from the power and pessimism of Pierre Gascar's concentration-camp studies, *Les Bêtes* and *Le Temps des morts*, issued together in 1953, to a skilfully organized 'epic' like Nicholas Monsarrat's *The Cruel Sea*, published in the same year – or, from another viewpoint, the German war stories of Hans Hellmut Kirst.

Other readers turned to more solid historical works: Hugh Trevor-Roper's *The Last Days of Hitler* (1947), Chester Wilmot's account of *The Struggle for Europe* (1952), or Winston Churchill's majestic *War Memoirs*, gradually unfolded in six volumes from 1948 to 1954. In Britain, especially, there was also a taste for earlier periods. Many now read with nostalgic pleasure the work of such national chroniclers as Arthur Bryant, A.L. Rowse, G.M. Trevelyan, or C.V. Wedgwood, who had aptly entitled one of her collections of essays *Velvet Studies*. Others bought, and many tackled, Arnold Toynbee's giant *A Study of History*, which purported to elucidate both past and future in cyclical terms, tracing the 'life' and 'death' of 'civilizations' – a possibly hopeful riposte to Oswald Spengler's prewar *Decline of the West*.

Popular entertainers were also selling well. Agatha Christie went on writing comfortable British detective stories; one of her works – the play *The Mousetrap* – began a London stage run in 1952 that was still drawing audiences thirty years later. In Italy, Giovanni Guareschi found a similar public for his tales of 'Don Camillo', the parish priest in perpetual mock-battle with the local Communist. In France, Pierre Daninos's 'Major Thompson' genially pinpointed the foibles of the French; while with 'Commissaire Maigret' the Belgian novelist Georges Simenon continued to paint an appealing but increasingly archaic picture of the Paris *Police Judiciaire*.

Some best-sellers were hard to classify. Simenon, in particular, posed problems for the tidy-minded. Although amazingly prolific – and financially successful – he was more than a writer of mysteries. He also wrote more ambitious tales; and his crime stories themselves were as intensely felt and resonant as dreams. In Britain, critics found Somerset Maugham no less hard to place. His early novels had been dense with feeling; but much of his most popular work seemed superficial and slick. By the 1940's, in *The Razor's Edge* and *Catalina*, he had virtually reached the end of his writing career. The publication of *A Writer's Notebook* in 1949, however, and his *Complete Short Stories*, three years later, reawakened a critical interest to match the public following that had never flagged.

Other older writers were also still popular. Erich Maria Remarque, whose *All Quiet on the Western Front* had been a runaway best-seller at the end of the 1920's, had never quite repeated that early success; but now, with *Arc de Triomphe* (1947), *Zeit zu leben und Zeit zu sterben* (1954), and a play on the last days of Berlin, *Die letzte Station* (1956), he recaptured some of his former celebrity. Another German exile from the Nazis, the dramatist Carl Zuckmayer, best known for his satire on Prussian officialdom, *Der Hauptmann von Köpenick* (1931), had had a similar success in 1946 with his play *Des Teufels General*, about an air force commander who had stood up against Hitler. In Germany especially, there was a sense of relief and rescue in rediscovering traditional virtues.

Equally traditional in manner, and equally popular by the mid-1950's in Britain, was C.P. Snow. His *Strangers and Brothers* sequence of novels had begun to appear in 1940, recounting the growth to manhood and the advance through society of a lawyer from the provinces, the dull but observant 'Lewis Eliot'. The second and third in the series had appeared in the late 1940's; but it made its first major impact in 1951 with *The Masters*, about a struggle for power in a Cambridge college, which some critics likened to Trollope.

The comparison was not unjust. A complaisant Trollopean tranquillity seemed to pervade C.P. Snow's rather mandarin fictional world: nor was it totally absent from the life of the time outside his books. Some sense of security was certainly needed for a writer to embark on a multi-volume *roman-fleuve*; and Snow's enterprise in this respect was not alone. In France in 1948, with *Les grandes familles*, Maurice Druon had begun the 3-volume cycle *La fin des hommes*, completed in 1951. In that year, with *A Question of Upbringing*, Anthony Powell started the series generically entitled *The Music of Time* – as long as Snow's and more stylish, but less comprehensive and seemingly less purposeful and solid: one critic, rather unfairly, dubbed it 'The Music of Tea-time'. In 1957, finally, Lawrence Durrell published *Justine*, the first movement in his knowingly prismatic *Alexandria Quartet*. Durrell's labyrinthine prose suited his exotic subject-matter – passion, intrigue, and decadence in the fleshpots of Egypt. But Snow, Druon, and Powell were workmanlike traditional narrators, very much of their age.

Graham Greene, a master of narrative on another level, had long classified his books as either 'entertainments' – powerful thrillers – or 'novels' – often, theological debates. The mood of the time, hedonistic but nostalgic for religion, seemed to welcome both. In 1948, Greene had carried his Catholic self-questioning to the limit with *The Heart of the Matter*, whose hero 'Scobie' made the ultimate self-sacrifice by giving up, for another, even his hope of salvation. Had Scobie thereby lost his soul? The answer seemed as uncertain as the Church's attitude to the book and to Greene himself. All were keenly debated. Thereafter, Greene reverted for a time to more mundane themes: international politics in *The Quiet American* in 1955, and intelligence-gathering in *Our Man in Havana* in 1958; but the settings he chose – Indo-China and Cuba – seemed uncannily to foreshadow future world crises.

Greene's guilt-edged Catholicism found echoes elsewhere. In France, its nearest equivalent was in the novels of François Mauriac, with their tortured, fevered, sickroom sexuality. Mauriac's major work was now behind him; but much of it was still being translated, and there was more to come: *Galigai* in 1952 and *L'agneau* two years later, as well as several plays and a long, controversial series of *Bloc-notes* or 'Notebooks', first in the daily *Le Figaro*, then – after protests – in the left-wing weekly *L'Express*. In his old age, espousing democratic causes which shocked the older Catholic establishment to which he and his family belonged, Mauriac showed both discernment and courage. It was a further parallel with the public role of Graham Greene.

In Italy, Greene's and Mauriac's closest counterpart was Riccardo Bacchelli, whose work was a palatable and highly popular blend of sensuality and religion. His best-known historical novel, *Il mulino del Po*, had been published in 1938–40; but it was not widely read outside Italy until the 1950's. Meanwhile, Bacchelli had written among other things a religious novel, *Lo sguardo di Gesù*, in 1948, and an elaborate socio-psychological study, *L'incendio di Milano*, in 1952. But, despite its commercial success, Bacchelli's versatile output was mistrusted by the critics, and was better liked in Italy than abroad.

A study of quite a different world – the closed, doomed, but stubbornly deep-rooted society of feudal Sicily in the 1860's – found more immediate response in Europe generally. This was *Il gattopardo*, *The Leopard*, by Giuseppe Tomasi, Duke of Palma and Prince of Lampedusa. Like a tapestry long hidden from the sun, the book was bright with past glories now fading in doubt and regret. Brooding over it, disabused and stoical, was the patriarch 'Fabrizio', probably modelled on Lampedusa's great-grandfather: he resists the forces of change, but marries off his more pliant nephew, to ally the family with the new, democratic regime. Lampedusa had meditated the work for a quarter of a century: he wrote it in the last three years of his life. It was published in 1958, the year after his death.

The typescript of *Il gattopardo* had been 'discovered' by Giorgio Bassani, editor of the literary magazine *Botteghe Oscure* and a reader for Giangiacomo Feltrinelli's publishing house. Bassani himself was the author of a brilliantly perceptive and evocative series of short novels about life – and especially Jewish life – in Ferrara under the Fascists. Beginning in 1953 with *La passeggiata prima di cena*, and continuing in 1955 and 1958 with *Gli ultimi anni di Clelia Trotti*, and *Gli occhiali d'oro*, he was gradually to create a multidimensional portrait of a city and its inhabitants – *Il romanzo di Ferrara*, in the title he ultimately gave the whole immense 800-page rediscovery of past time.

If Bassani revealed a generation's history by focusing on a single northern city, Carlo Levi's *Cristo si è fermato a Eboli*, *Christ Stopped at Eboli* (1945), revealed – to Italians as well as to others – the bleak, peasant world of Lucania in the south, where he had been exiled by Mussolini. It was a harsh, uncompromising picture, seen with a painter's vivid but distancing eye. Just as characteristic of Italy's 'neo-realist' mood, but more deeply involved and appealing, were the left-wing genre novels of Elio Vittorini, who followed his prewar *Conversazioni in Sicilia* most notably with a Resistance story, *Uomini e no*, in 1945, and the Florentine Vasco Pratolini, whose *Cronache di poveri amanti* (1947) might almost have been a De Sica/Zavattini film.

Meanwhile, Alberto Moravia, who had been writing novels since the 1920's, but for a time had evaded Fascist censorship by the use of allegory, now began to tackle social themes again. *La Romana*, *The Woman of Rome*, a sympathetic portrait of a prostitute, published in 1947, made his name with a very wide audience. Less obviously inviting, but more convincing, was his study of the break-up of a marriage, *Il disprezzo*, *A Ghost at Noon*, in 1954. And as socially aware as Moravia, but even more delicately introspective, were the novels now coming from the graceful pen of Natalia Ginzburg. She was the daughter of a Jewish socialist professor of anatomy, and the recent widow of a Russian expatriate and Resistance fighter who had died as a result of Nazi torture; but her books were very far from being political tracts. *È stato così* was the resigned, bitter title she gave to one early short study of marriage and death: it won the Tempo prize in 1947. In 1952, she won the Veillon prize with *Tutti i nostri ieri*; in 1957, the still more distinguished Viareggio prize with *Valentino*.

Literary prizes like these, or the Immermann award in Germany, were becoming an important, perhaps overrated index of an author's worth. In France, there were more than a thousand, great and small; and two important prizes, the Médicis and the Grand Prix National des Lettres, were actually founded in the 1950's. But the most coveted was the Goncourt prize, whose winners now included Maurice Druon, Robert Merle, Pierre Gascar, Simone de Beauvoir, and Romain Gary.

The Nobel Prize for literature, unlike the Goncourt, was less an award for any specific publication than the recognition of a whole career. If it reflected fashion, therefore, it did so at some distance in time. In 1949, following Hermann Hesse, André Gide, and T.S. Eliot, William Faulkner won the prize. Next came Bertrand Russell, the British mathematician and philosopher; then Pär Lagerkvist, the Swedish author best known for his historical novels *Dvärgen, The Dwarf* (1944), and *Barabbas* (1950). The 1952 laureate was François Mauriac, followed by Winston Churchill and, with fine impartiality, Ernest Hemingway. In 1955, the prize went to the Icelandic novelist Halldór Laxness, and in 1956 to the Spanish poet Juan Ramón Jiménez. In 1957, the winner was Albert Camus.

But the most significant and controversial award of the Nobel Prize in these years was made in 1958, to the Russian poet and novelist Boris Leonidovich Pasternak. It was the first such tribute to a Soviet citizen, and only the second to a writer from Russia: the other had been to the expatriate poet and novelist Ivan Alekseyevich Bunin, in 1933. Was Pasternak's Nobel Prize a sign that times were changing? Was *la vie en rose* beginning to be glimpsed in the East?

Born in Moscow in 1890, Boris Pasternak was a child of the cultivated Jewish bourgeoisie. His mother was a concert pianist, and his father a well-known painter: one of his drawings shows Pasternak as a small boy intently writing, perched on a bentwood chair with his bare right foot hooked round the calf of his left leg, utterly unaware of anyone watching. As a young man, he wrote poetry. His first volume of verse appeared in 1914; but his most fruitful period was after the 1917 Russian Revolution, whose spirit he praised in two epic poems, both published in 1927. Much of his work appeared in the monthly 'thick journal' *Novy Mir*, whose editor from 1928 to 1934 was the much respected Vyacheslav Polonsky. In the 1930's, however, Pasternak came under increasing pressure from the Soviet Communist Party. His early autobiography, *Safe Conduct*, published in 1931, was not reprinted on account of its alleged 'idealism'; and in 1934, two years before the 'Yezhovshchina' political purges, the Party theoretician Nikolai Bukharin, while describing Pasternak as 'the greatest poetic master of our times', criticized his imagery as 'too personal'. Four years later, Bukharin himself was to be tried and shot; but from 1934 onwards Pasternak stopped publishing poetry, and turned his attention to translations from Shakespeare. Not until 1943 did he publish any further poems of his own.

Then, in 1946, came another Party onslaught on the arts, the Zhdanovshchina, named after Colonel-General Andrei Zhdanov, secretary of the Central Committee in charge of ideology. Its victims included the composer Dmitri Shostakovich. His music had already been condemned in 1936 as 'tuneless' and 'freakish' after the first production of his opera *Lady Macbeth of Mtsensk*, or *Katerina Ismailova*. In 1948, after his orchestral *Poem of Fatherland*, he was accused like Sergey Prokofiev of 'bourgeois formalism'. In that same year, Zhdanov died. For the time being, however, the 'Zhdanov line' continued.

Shostakovich admitted his 'errors' and revised some of his scores; but his adjustments were minor compared with the contortions performed by several Soviet writers. The most obviously agile of them was Il'ya Erenburg. 'We Soviet writers', he told a French friend, 'are alive today only because we are the greatest acrobats in the world.' Having satirized Soviet institutions in his first novel in 1919, and bowdlerized another, first printed abroad, for its publication in the Soviet Union, Erenburg had soon adapted his output to the exigencies of the first Five-Year Plan. After winning the Stalin Prize with a war novel in 1942, he won it again in 1949 with the first of two anti-Western pot-boilers, the second of which appeared in 1951.

Then, suddenly, everything changed. On Saturday 28 February 1953, after a film show at the Kremlin theatre, the 73-year-old Joseph Stalin invited his closest colleagues back to his *dacha* at Kuntsevo for one of his customary late-night dinners. He was in a good mood. Nikita Khrushchev, the future Prime Minister, then merely a member of the Party Praesidium, recalled afterwards: 'We all went home happy because nothing had gone wrong at dinner. Dinners at Stalin's did not always end on such a pleasant note.' Less than twenty-four hours later, Stalin suffered a cerebral haemorrhage. By 10 p.m. on Thursday 5 March he was dead.

With rolls of drums and solemn martial music, the Soviet Union went into official mourning. The state funeral took place on Monday 9 March: Stalin's embalmed body was laid to rest in the Lenin Mausoleum. Earlier, in the rush to attend the ceremony in Red Square, many of the crowd had been crushed to death. Now, in the bitter cold at the funeral, there was one more victim: Klement Gottwald, the Communist who had succeeded Beneš as President of Czechoslovakia, contracted pneumonia and soon afterwards died.

Behind all the public lamentations there was a great sense of relief. At the Bolshoi Theatre, it was said, the audience clapped especially loudly at the nightly death of Boris Godunov. In the Kremlin, Stalin was scarcely gone before a power struggle began. His immediate successor was his deputy Georgy Malenkov. Within two weeks, Khrushchev had edged him out of his post as First Secretary of the Party; within six months, the dreaded Commissar in charge of the NKVD, Lavrenti Pavlovich Beria, had been dismissed and shot. In February 1955, Malenkov ceded the premiership to Nikolai Bulganin: but it soon became clear that Bulganin was under the control of Khrushchev, who at the Party's Twentieth Congress in January 1956 denounced Stalin's 'cult of personality', and on 27 March 1958 became Prime Minister himself.

For the arts, Stalin's death meant that an icy weight had been removed. Already, at the Nineteenth Party Congress in October 1952, while Stalin was still alive, Malenkov had chided Soviet authors for their 'stereotyped characterization': now, both writers and editors felt free to respond. Only six weeks after Stalin's death, the official *Literaturnaya Gazeta* published what in Soviet terms was a revolutionary plea, by the poet and critic Ol'ga Berggol'ts, for more humanity in lyric poetry:

I don't mean that there are no human beings in any of these poems. Indeed there are: there are operators of bulldozers and steam-shovels; there are horticulturalists: all carefully described, sometimes well and even brilliantly described. But they are described from the outside, and the most important thing is lacking in all these poems – a lyric hero with his own individual relationship to events and to the landscape.

To be fair, the bulldozers and steam-shovels had already been transforming the Soviet Union and most of the Eastern bloc. Its material progress had echoed, if more faintly, that of the West. Land reform laws had transferred millions of acres from Church and other property to State holdings and peasant co-operatives. Old towns had been restored, and new towns constructed. Housing had improved; rents were low; food, clothing, and consumer goods had become more plentiful. Planners, educationists, and social service workers were struggling with the intractable problems of distance, language, and backwardness in the sprawling empire ruled from Moscow.

Now, with Stalin's death, it began to be possible to decentralize and devolve some economic decision-making. But it was in literature that the new spirit was most immediately felt. Most Russians had long been avid readers; and in private they had long complained at the quality of what they were offered. In the June 1953 number of *Novy Mir*, its new editor Aleksandr Tvardovsky published a poem of his own about a lengthy railway journey during which all his fellow-passengers harped on a single theme: the tedium of official literature. Almost at once, Tvardovsky was attacked by some of his fellow-writers; but at the All-Union Congress of Young Critics that autumn he was hotly defended by others, including the poet Vera Inber. In October, at the Plenary Session of the Writers' Union, speaker after speaker criticized the Zhdanov line; and in the October issue of *Znamya*, the adaptable Il'ya Erenburg published a plea for the individual writer:

An author is not a piece of machinery, mechanically registering events. An author writes a book, not because he knows how to write, not because he is a member of the Union of Soviet Writers and may be asked why he has published nothing for so long. An author does not write a book because he has to earn a living. An author writes a book because he finds it necessary to tell people something of himself....

Znamya went on to serialize Erenburg's new novel: it was published in full in May 1954. Its title was *Ottepel', The Thaw*; and although it too was attacked by some orthodox conservatives, it gave its name to the new phase that seemed to have begun since Stalin's death.

The thaw affected all the arts. Musicians like the pianist Emil Gilels or the violinists David Oistrakh and Leonid Kogan were now allowed to travel and perform in the West. The 'bourgeois' treasures of the Hermitage Museum in Leningrad – Cézannes, Renoirs, and Van Goghs that had long been concealed from the Soviet public – began to be removed from their racks and prepared for permanent exhibition. Film-makers, too, began to breathe a fresher air.

In the last years of Stalin's régime, Soviet cinema had been heavily censored and forced to parrot the Party line. Even Mark Donskoi, with *The Village Teacher* in 1947, and Aleksandr Dovzhenko, with his biography of the biologist Michurin in the following year, had seemed to be cramped by the prevailing conformism. Films take time to make, and the thaw took time to reach the screen. But soon its effects were evident. In 1955, Sergei Yutkevich made a magnificent *Othello*, with the title role played by Sergei Bondarchuk, the protagonist of *Michurin*, and the future director of the four-part

War and Peace. In 1956, Dovzhenko died, but Donskoi made *Mother*, continuing his fine series of adaptations from Gor'ky. In the same year, Grigori Chukrai, adapting one of Boris Lavrenyov's tales, made *The Forty-First*, a love-story which was also an implicit attack on the Stalinist hero cult. It was a world away from the mechanical literature lampooned by Ol'ga Berggol'ts. So, in the following year, was Mikhail Kalatozov's *The Cranes are Flying*, a technically dazzling and very tender film about a love-affair destroyed by war. In 1958, *The Cranes are Flying* won the Golden Palm at the Cannes Film Festival – established in 1946 to rival Venice, and to be followed in 1949 by Berlin and later by many more.

Such was the new climate in the Soviet Union that Boris Pasternak's poems now appeared once more in *Novy Mir*. The October 1956 number published 'Bread'. It began:

> You chart a half-century's findings
> But you keep them out of your books. . . .

In fact, since 1946, Pasternak had been putting a half-century's findings into a novel, *Doctor Zhivago*. 'One should write about this world,' he remarked in 1957, 'in a way that makes the reader's heart miss a beat and his hair stand on end.' *Doctor Zhivago* certainly did that. In July 1956 he submitted it to *Novy Mir*.

The editor was now no longer Aleksandr Tvardovsky. In 1954 he had been replaced by Konstantin Simonov after publishing an article by a critic, V. Pomerantsev, attacking 'socialist realism' and calling for greater sincerity in art. If that article caused a storm, it was as nothing compared with the reactions aroused in 1956 by *Novy Mir*'s publication in three parts of Vladimir Dudintsev's novel criticizing bureaucracy, *Not By Bread Alone*. In the press and at literary meetings, Simonov was mercilessly hounded. In the end, only a small edition of the novel was printed in book form, and in 1957 Dudintsev was publicly reprimanded by Khrushchev himself.

Pasternak, meanwhile, was waiting to hear when *Doctor Zhivago* might be published. After some delay, he received a letter: the editorial board had turned it down:

The spirit of your novel is that of non-acceptance of the Socialist Revolution, that it brought the people nothing but suffering, and destroyed the Russian intelligentsia . . . that the Revolution was a mistake and that all that happened afterwards was evil.

Deeply disappointed and disgusted, Pasternak let a copy of the novel be sent to Giangiacomo Feltrinelli in Milan. He published it – and now there was a double outburst: of praise in the West, and execration in the East. When the Nobel Prize committee announced its award to Pasternak in 1958, he was in two minds. He would have liked to accept the honour: but he feared that if he were allowed to go to Stockholm for it, he might be debarred from coming back. For him, he wrote to Khrushchev, exile from Russia would mean death. Too late, Khrushchev seems to have relented a little. *Doctor Zhivago*, he told the Writers' Union, should have been published in a small edition and 'allowed to be forgotten'. As it was, Pasternak's masterpiece reached a worldwide audience, but he had to decline the Nobel Prize. The thaw had its limits. But so, in the West, did *la vie en rose*.

8

Strangers in our Midst

On the grey western outskirts of the Latin Quarter, where the old, narrow, bustling streets around St-Germain-des-Prés give way to the broader, later, duller boulevards of Ministerial Paris, there are still a few more colourful oases: a café or two, a bookshop, a modest brasserie, a cabaret like the Vieux Colombier. Some years ago, there was also a small, rather primitive minority theatre – the Théâtre de Babylone at No. 38 Boulevard Raspail, near the Sèvres-Babylone Métro station. Here, on the chilly evening of Monday 5 January 1953, the actor-director Roger Blin presented the world première of an extraordinary spectacle. Within five years, it was to play to more than a million spectators in more than a score of countries. But the curtain rose that night on a shallow, bare-boarded stage with a plain, slightly wrinkled backcloth.

The scenery represents nothing, or almost nothing. A road? Let's say, more generally, *out of doors*. The only notable detail is a shrivelled tree, scarcely even a sapling, quite devoid of leaves: a skeleton of twigs.

On the stage are two men, of no fixed age, occupation, or family status. Of no fixed address, either: i.e., two tramps. They look able-bodied. One of them takes his boots off; the other talks of the Gospels. They eat a carrot. They have nothing to say. They address each other by two diminutives, Gogo and Didi, which seem to stand for no recognizable names.

They look left and right; they prepare to leave, to go their separate ways; but they always come together again in the middle of the stage. They can't go away: they're waiting for someone called Godot. We know no more about him than about them – except that we know he won't come. That, at least, was clear to everyone from the start.

The play, *En attendant Godot*, was by Samuel Beckett. The description was by the young 'new novelist' Alain Robbe-Grillet, whose first published work, *Les Gommes*, was to appear that year. He went on: 'There's little point in remarking that nothing happens in the play – that there's no development or plot of any kind. That's nothing new. But here, *less than nothing* happens. As

always with Samuel Beckett, the little that was given us at the beginning –
and which seemed to us nothing at the time – soon rots away before our
eyes.... But then man himself, who is there before us also, comes to a
similar end.'

When Simone de Beauvoir went to see *En attendant Godot*, she was
prepared to be unimpressed. 'I distrust plays which use symbols to present
the human condition in general; but I admired the way Beckett succeeded in
gripping us, simply by depicting the tireless patience that keeps our species
and each one of us on earth, against all the odds. I was one of the actors in
the drama, with the author as my partner. While we were waiting – for what?
– he spoke and I listened. Together, my presence and his voice kept alive a
useless and necessary hope.'

Others felt less directly involved. Scholars debated whether 'Godot' was
based on a character in Balzac called 'Godeau', on a racing cyclist of the
same name, or perhaps on God – an allusion, some thought, to *L'attente de
Dieu*, by the religious philosopher Simone Weil, published posthumously
four years earlier. Theatre critics were also divided. In 1955, when Peter
Hall staged Beckett's own translation, *Waiting for Godot*, at the Arts Theatre
in London – a production which Beckett rather disliked – Ivor Brown noted
the reactions of his colleagues:

Some told me it was a wonderful piece of fancy, some, more numerous, that
it was a wilderness of words. Some said it was prose-poetry of the finest,
others that it was pretentious piffle. It was intimated that you were not fit to
dine in elevated company or join in the consumption of cocktails laced with
culture unless you had seen, heard, digested – or failed to digest – Godot. I
waited for Godot, secretly fearing that I was going to be found wanting and
yawning, a boorish objector to the alleged masterpiece. At last I nerved
myself for the occasion, went in leisure, and repented in haste.

Even those with more sympathy for the play, finally, were inclined to smile at
the paradox of plebeians enjoying vicarious opulence on film or television
screens while the rich, at *Godot*, were enthralled by actors playing tramps.

Vagrants, of course, had long had romantic appeal. A hundred years
earlier, in *Hard Times*, Charles Dickens had set the travelling circus – 'Mr
Sleary's horse-riding' – against the harsh rigidity of 'Mr Gradgrind'. Popular
culture had embraced W.J. Locke's novel *The Beloved Vagabond* in 1906, the
operetta *The Vagabond King*, and a later music-hall performer billed as 'The
Vagabond of Song'. Charlie Chaplin's penniless tramp had delighted
millions of settled citizens; and French readers had relished the low-life
characters in Raymond Queneau's novels, from the fun-fair of *Pierrot mon*

ami (1942) to the fleapits of *Loin de Rueil* (1944). The early films of Federico
Fellini celebrated similar scapegrace worlds: seedy vaudeville in *Luci del
varietà* (1950); ne'er-do-wells in a provincial seaside town, Viareggio, in *I
vitelloni* (1953); travelling fairground entertainers in *La strada* (1954).

Left-wing critics in Italy, including Cesare Zavattini, fiercely attacked *La
strada* as 'a betrayal of neo-realism'. Fellini riposted with *Il bidone* (1955),
implying that the 'victims of society' in Zavattini's and De Sica's world were
sentimentalized: in real life, Fellini's fable suggested, they might well prey on
creatures weaker than themselves. His next film, *Le notti di Cabiria* (1957),
portrayed a prostitute – played unforgettably, like 'Gelsomina' in *La strada*,
by Fellini's wife Giulietta Masina. With her huge hopeful eyes and stoical
smile, 'Cabiria' was exploited, betrayed, and cheated: but she always
bounced back. She seemed a living contradiction of Zavattini's theories.
'Neo-realism', Fellini said later, 'was an enormous stimulus'; but it looked at
life passively, and if the camera did the same there would be no need of a
director. 'For me,' he added, 'the cinema is very like the circus.' With Fellini
as ringmaster, as with Beckett, Chaplin, and Queneau, sawdust and clowns
and gypsies were never very far away.

All these were private obsessions; but like neo-realism they reflected facets
of life. In Paris, not far from the Théâtre de Babylone, real tramps slept out
on the Métro gratings, slightly warmed by stale air from below. In Rome, not
far from cinemas showing Fellini's films, real beggars and prostitutes stood
on the corners of side-streets off the fashionable Via Veneto. Even in
Europe's richest countries, 'affluence' had not reached everyone. The
German 'economic miracle' left pockets of poverty, especially in the cities. In
Britain, many of the elderly were both poor and isolated, as Peter Townsend
showed in his 1957 survey, *The Family Life of Old People*. New towns were
partly responsible, siphoning off younger members of what had once been
'extended families'; but life in some of the new houses and apartment blocks
was far from ideal. Clinical records on one such housing estate revealed two-
and-a-half times as many gastric ulcers as the national average, three times
as many headaches, and four times as many complaints of 'tiredness'. In
London, loneliness became so common that in November 1953 the Rev.
Chad Varah, shocked by a case of suicide, set up 'The Samaritans', a body of
volunteers who could be telephoned for conversation and comfort. The idea
quickly spread.

The Church in France seemed especially aware of those whom 'progress' was leaving behind. In 1952, a new novel caused a sensation. Its author was Gilbert Cesbron: its striking title, *Les saints vont en enfer*. Its theme was squalor, physical and spiritual – the squalor of Paris's slum-suburbs, many of them crowded with North Africans living as semi-outcasts. The 'saints' who went into this 'hell' were the worker-priests: ordained churchmen who had discarded clerical dress to take ordinary jobs in factories or as artisans, living alone in cheap lodgings with a small portable altar for their devotions. The order had been founded during the war, largely in response to a book by the abbé Henri Godin, *France, pays de mission*, arguing that the country was no longer Christian, and that missionaries were needed at home as much as abroad. Worker-priests were soon active in Paris and other cities, including Lille, Lyon, and Marseille; but by the time that Cesbron's book appeared they were causing worry to the Church. Like many ambassadors, they seemed to be over-influenced by their environment: some, it was said, had even turned Communist. In 1954, after much discussion, the worker-priests were virtually disbanded; but at least fifty of them persisted in their chosen tasks.

That winter, another French priest, the abbé Grouès – better known as the abbé Pierre – had dramatically publicized the plight of the destitute. He was a striking figure, gaunt, cloaked, and bearded, with what one writer called 'the face of a Spanish Christ'. A hero of the Resistance, then for a time an MRP member of the National Assembly, he had organized a refuge for the homeless in the eastern suburbs of Paris beyond the Bois de Vincennes. There were many more than he could cope with: the city had 64,000 urgent cases on a waiting-list for 900 dwellings. To raise money, the abbé Pierre tried everything – selling the gleanings from dustbins, competing on a radio quiz show, going out begging in the streets. Then, one bitter morning – it was 7 a.m. on Monday 5 January 1954 – there came a knock on his wooden shutter. Outside stood a workman. He was in tears. In the night, his baby had died of cold.

The abbé wasted no time. The Minister of Reconstruction, André Lemaire, had just refused a special credit for emergency housing. The abbé Pierre wrote him an open letter, and sent it to the press. At 2 p.m. that Thursday, he said, the baby was to be buried. Would the Minister come to the funeral?

He did. The resultant publicity produced an avalanche of private gifts, as well as public grants. New reception centres were established for the homeless. Volunteers helped to run them, and toured the freezing streets at night to rescue still more down-and-outs. Factory workers put in free overtime to provide stoves. Shops donated part of their takings. Painters and collectors auctioned some of their pictures. Theatres put on benefit performances; so did a strip club, the Crazy Horse Saloon. Within two years, 2,820 new dwellings had been built, housing more than 10,000 people, and loans had been contracted to build 12,000 more. A law was passed forbidding evictions in winter. Twenty new centres were established, in Dunkirk, Lille, Limoges, Rennes, Toulouse, and elsewhere. As time went by, the abbé Pierre was sometimes criticized for having overreached himself. But he had aroused his countrymen's compassion by showing them the limits of *la vie en rose*.

In Sicily, Danilo Dolci set himself a similar task. A native of Trieste and a student of architecture, he had been involved with the Resistance while still a schoolboy, and had later worked at a Christian settlement for poor families near Modena. In 1952, at the age of 28, he went to Western Sicily, partly to study classical antiquities – and he was appalled.

The scenery was beautiful. To the South-west of Palermo, high up in the hills past Monreale, there comes a point where the road bends to give a sudden view of the landscape below and the sea beyond it, sparkling deep blue in the Bay of Castellammare. The road winds on down through olive-groves and vineyards; then it comes to a crossroads. Off to the right, well away from the main *strada statale*, lies the town of Partinico. When Dolci went there, it was a forbidding place.

In one house, he saw a tuberculosis patient lying with basins on his bed to catch water leaking through the roof. He met a feeble-minded child with her hands bound in rags to stop her biting them, and a labourer of 32 kept locked behind an iron grille in a corner of the family room. Many of the houses had no drains; the lavatory was often a hole in the ground. Outside, in the unpaved streets, rubbish-heaps swarmed with flies. There was no public wash-house, so the women used a stream that came from the slaughter-house. There was one brothel, whose tariff went as low as 50 lire – less than the price of two inland postage stamps. Of the town's 6,000 families, 1,800 were registered for poor relief. Its 350 known criminals had spent a joint total of some 700 years in school and 3,000 years in prison. Infant mortality was 50 percent higher than in Italy as a whole, and three times as high as in Britain.

Nearby, on the coast – now cut off by a motorway – was the equally desolate fishing village of Trappeto, where Dolci settled first. Soon, he was so much a part of the place that he married one of his neighbours, the widow of a murdered fisherman with five children to support; and he set about trying to combat misery and apathy. Fishing was in trouble: poaching trawlers were using fine-mesh nets to catch the young fry. Farming was parched by drought – alongside an undammed stream. Hunger and ignorance led to hopelessness, violence, and waste. Good intentions were mistrusted. Nothing ever happened on time.

Dolci decided to make it happen. With borrowed money, he built a house for poor children. Already, his own family was growing: eventually, he and his wife had five more children, and took in others whose parents were dead or in prison. Meanwhile, with more outside help, the villagers of Trappeto built a pharmacy, a hospital, sewers, and roads; and Dolci began similar projects in Partinico and elsewhere.

In 1954, he published his first general appeal to the Italian public, *Fare presto (e bene) perché si muore – Act quickly (and effectively): people are dying.* More help came, but never enough; so Dolci had a new idea. He had always opposed simple poor relief, because it encouraged passivity. Now, he organized what he called 'strikes in reverse'. Marching out with groups of unemployed men from Partinico, he started on road repairs. Everyone worked for no pay. It was do-it-yourself Keynesianism: but the sight of seven hundred men doing unauthorized public works was too much for official-dom. The police were ordered to move in; and although no violence was offered they made a number of arrests. Dolci himself was tried and sentenced to two months in gaol for 'trespassing on public property'. He appealed. So did the prosecution, affronted at so mild a penalty. In the end, it was commuted to a suspended sentence of eighteen months, later confirmed by the Italian Supreme Court. But by that time, with his trials, his books, and his example, Danilo Dolci had made his point. An increasingly 'affluent' society could no longer ignore the victims of its neglect.

Many artists and writers were moved by similar fellow-feeling. The painter Renato Guttuso, himself a Sicilian and a Socialist, evolved a busy, glancing, crumpled, neo-baroque style to portray peasants and artisans. In a different baroque idiom, harking back to French classicism, Fernand Léger's bulging, muscular building-workers, cyclists, and acrobats gave the word 'solidarity' a new, more substantial meaning. Less idealized than Léger's workmen, but just as firmly thrust on public consciousness, were the slum-dwellers of Eastern Paris depicted in two novels by the North African actor and writer

Marcel Mouloudji, *Enrico* and *En souvenir de Barbarie*, published in 1944 and 1945, and much influenced by American authors, including William Faulkner. A few years later, Hervé Bazin won notoriety as a social rebel with his first novel, *Vipère au poing* (1948), a blistering attack on the provincial, Catholic, conservative family tradition in which he had grown up. His second book, *La tête contre les murs* (1949), was a passionate indictment of French mental hospitals. In 1958, it was turned into a frightening film by Georges Franju, the director of such harrowing documentaries as *Le sang des bêtes* (1949), about a slaughter-house, and *Hôtel des Invalides* (1951), which made vivid the horrors blandly commemorated by war museums.

The cinema, like television later, seemed a natural medium for 'socially committed' art. In France, one of its most influential exponents was Christian François Bouche-Villeneuve, a tall, humorous, thoughtful-looking polymath better known as 'Chris Marker'. Born in 1921, he had plied many trades before turning towards films. When World War II broke out, he had been studying philosophy; under the Occupation, he had joined the Resistance in the *maquis*, then become a paratrooper in the American Air Force. After the Liberation he wrote poems, short stories, political commentaries, and articles on music for the Left-wing Catholic review *Esprit*. Its film-reviewing space he shared with André Bazin, the co-founder of *Cahiers du cinéma*; and he wrote for that too. As an editor at Les Éditions du Seuil, he launched the 'Petite Planète' series of photo-reportage pocket-books on various countries: inexpensive, informative, stylish, and outspoken, they were a great success. In 1950 he published a novel, *Le coeur net*, about aviation; and in the summer of 1952, after many travels with a still camera, he went to Helsinki for the Olympic Games and came back with his first movie, the 16-millimetre documentary *Olympia 52*. In the same year he wrote the commentary for *Les statues meurent aussi*, made with Alain Resnais. But his major films at this time were a study of the new social order in China, *Dimanche à Pekin* (1955), actually shot in two weeks, and *Lettre de Sibérie* (1958). For the Siberian documentary he wrote a brilliant, witty, self-mocking script, including a parodied commercial for reindeer and showing the town of Yakutsk three times in identical images, but each with a different commentary, 'pro-Soviet', 'anti-Soviet', and 'neutral'. The main concern of all his work, including his later, more solemn propaganda films, was summed up in a sentence from *Lettre de Sibérie*: 'There is only one humanity'. It was more provocative than it sounded.

Marker's dislocation of expected responses may have owed something to that veteran scourge of the bourgeoisie, Luis Buñuel. Having left his native Spain before World War II, Buñuel had worked in Hollywood and Mexico, where he made *Los Olvidados* (1950) about the city slums. In 1955 he returned to Paris, where his first new production was *Cela s'appelle l'aurore*, about loyalty in the revolutionary struggle. By now, the old iconoclast was regularly receiving honours at Cannes. In 1951 *Los Olvidados* won first prize for direction; and *Nazarín* (1958) was to be awarded the Special Jury Prize. But his subversive example was being followed by two of his Spanish admirers: the young Luis Garcia Berlanga, who made *Bienvenida Mr Marshall* in 1953, and his friend Juan Antonio Bardem, director of *Muerte de un ciclista* two years later. Berlanga's film showed the efforts of a Spanish village to impress Marshall Aid officials by hiring some fake local colour. It gained point from the fact that American aid to Spain was not included in the Marshall Plan: in the film, the visiting officials drive straight through without stopping to look. In *Muerte de un ciclista* a university professor, driving with his mistress, knocks down and kills a workman on a bicycle. He wants to confess, but his Lady Macbeth runs him down – only to be killed herself when swerving to avoid another cyclist. Both Berlanga and Bardem had trouble with General Franco's censorship: in 1956, while filming *Calle Mayor*, Bardem was arrested, and only released after two weeks' international outcry. Later, he was to work as a producer on Buñuel's *Viridiana* – which in turn was banned in Spain. Berlanga, meanwhile, under the influence of Cesare Zavattini, tried for some time to import into Spanish film-making the methods and subject-matter of Italian neo-realism.

In Italy itself, the neo-realist movement seemed by now to have petered out. The two young directors who were to revive it, Francesco Rosi and Ermanno Olmi, were still at the apprentice stage. Rosi, whose concern was as much with society as with its individual victims, was working as an assistant to older directors, including Luchino Visconti and Luigi Zampa: his first film of his own, *La sfida* (1957), was a gangster story. Olmi, however, was learning his craft on documentaries about men at work, and already revealing the deep humanism with which he was later to explore and enhance people's everyday lives.

'The significance of the everyday' was one of the watchwords of 'Free Cinema', the cognate movement in Britain at that time. It was first officially recognized by a special programme at the National Film Theatre in February 1956 which included two short documentaries: Lindsay Anderson's *O Dreamland* (1953), about a Margate funfair, and *Momma Don't Allow*

(1955), about a North London jazz club, co-directed by Karel Reisz and Tony Richardson. Later, Anderson, Reisz, and Richardson all made their names with feature films; for the present, they were working in loose association on a variety of related projects. As Films Officer for the Ford motor firm, Reisz helped to finance a film by Anderson, *Every Day Except Christmas* (1957), about Covent Garden market; in 1958, he formed a new production company, Woodfall, with Richardson and the playwright John Osborne. Anderson, meanwhile, had begun directing plays for George Devine's English Stage Company at the Royal Court Theatre in Sloane Square. It was here, on Tuesday 8 May 1956, that Richardson made British theatrical history by first staging John Osborne's *Look Back in Anger*.

Its central character was 'Jimmy Porter', a university graduate who keeps a sweets stall in the market of a Midlands town. Osborne's stage directions describe him as 'a tall, thin young man about twenty-five, wearing a very worn tweed jacket and flannels.... He is a disconcerting mixture of sincerity and cheerful malice, of tenderness and freebooting cruelty; restless, importunate, full of pride.' As the play opens, he throws down his 'posh Sunday newspaper':

'Why do I do this every Sunday? Even the book reviews seem to be the same as last week's. Different books – same reviews.... I've just read three whole columns on the English Novel. Half of it's in French. Do the Sunday papers make *you* feel ignorant?'

So began an invigorating evening. Formally, the play was conventional. It had no obvious 'message' – not even in the line, often quoted, 'There aren't any good, brave causes left.' What it did have was immense verbal punch, a heady, ranting, cathartic outburst from the id. Exploding out of it was Osborne's contempt for the thin, stuffy, polite respectability of London's commercial theatre, with its dinner-jacketed, cigar-smoking, chocolate-box-rustling clientèle. Seldom has a play made its audience feel so drunk. I remember having dinner afterwards with a colleague and two women journalists. We were all close friends. High on Osborne's rhetoric, we almost came to blows.

The set of *Look Back in Anger* featured no 'kitchen sink'; but this term – also applied then to the paintings of such social realists as David Bomberg, Jack Smith, Edward Middleditch, and John Bratby – became attached to Osborne and to other dramatists produced at the Royal Court, including John Arden and Arnold Wesker. But the label hardest to shake off, even fifteen years later, was that of 'Angry Young Man'. Osborne later claimed that it was given him, over a drink in a nearby pub, by the Royal Court's publicity officer. 'I know what you are,' he allegedly exclaimed: 'You're an Angry Young Man!' In fact, the expression had first been used in 1951, as the title of an autobiography by the Christian apologist Leslie Paul; but now, taken up by the press, it was plastered indiscriminately on several other writers, notably John Wain and Kingsley Amis.

Both Wain and Amis were first and foremost poets, associated with what the critic J.D. Scott baptized 'The Movement', and included in Robert Conquest's key anthology of plain-speaking verse, *New Lines*, in 1956. Wain's picaresque first novel, *Hurry on Down* (1953), plotted the nose-dive of a young university graduate through the middle and lower strata of British society. Amis's *Lucky Jim* (1954) showed 'Jim Dixon', a Redbrick university lecturer, comically failing to live up to the ideals of pedantry and 'gracious' decorum in his dim professor's entourage.

The anti-hero's rejection of respectability was a familiar motif in English novels just then. It appeared also in William Cooper's *Scenes from Provincial Life* (1950), Peter Forster's *The Primrose Path* (1955), J.P. Donleavy's *The Ginger Man* (Paris, 1955; London, bowdlerized, 1956), Thomas Hinde's *Happy as Larry*, and Hugh Thomas's *The World's Game* (both 1957), as well as in Andrew Sinclair's *The Breaking of Bumbo* two years later. As the literary historian Robert Hewison remarked, 'it would appear that the intellectual children of the Welfare State were rejecting their parents.'

They were also, perhaps, rejecting social hierarchy. The trend of the time was certainly in that direction. Anthony Eden's 1955 Cabinet might contain nineteen Old Etonians - but no one boasted of the fact: whereas Stanley Baldwin in 1924 had prided himself on having recruited six Old Harrovians. In 1957, amid some consternation, Court presentation parties for 'débutantes' were abolished. But only a year later, another first novel, Alan Sillitoe's *Saturday Night and Sunday Morning*, about working-class life in Nottingham, reminded its readers that Britain was still made up of Disraeli's 'two nations'. In the same year, in *The Rise of the Meritocracy*, the sociologist Michael Young produced the disturbing, satirical view of a future in which class and economic differences might all be based on sheer ability and therefore, perhaps, immune to compassion or reform.

Nor was continued inequality all that troubled critics of 'the affluent society'. In the United States in 1954, Fairfield Osborn pointed out that 'We Americans have used more of the world's resources in the past forty years than all the people in the world had used in the four thousand years up to 1914.' For the moment, he was a lone voice in a throw-away culture. But those Europeans who looked at such matters were beginning to be concerned by how much energy Europe was using – and how much it was having to bring from overseas. In 1937, it had produced all but 7 percent of the energy it consumed: by 1955, it was having to import 25 percent, the bulk of it in the form of oil. And if such dependence on outside resources seemed unhealthy, the technology that needed them sometimes came to grief.

By January 1954, the De Havilland Comet had flown twelve million miles since it had inaugurated the world's first scheduled jet service for BOAC in May 1952. Long and slim, with the inlets of its engines agape like the mouths of small fishes, the Comet was a proud marvel, cruising at 500˙miles an hour, faster than a World War II fighter aircraft, and so smoothly that passengers could stand a coin on its edge in full flight. But disaster was coming. On 2 May 1953, one Comet had crashed as it climbed away from Calcutta. The area was notorious for sudden violent storms: this was thought to be the reason. Eight months later, on Sunday 10 January 1954, Rome Airport lost contact with another Comet not long after take-off. Fishermen near the island of Elba reported that they had heard a high-pitched whine followed by three explosions, then seen a streak of black smoke in the sky, plunging into the sea. This second Comet crash took with it 23 passengers, including Chester Wilmot, author of *The Struggle for Europe*. When another aircraft crashed near Rome on the following Thursday, 14 January, it intensified speculation about sabotage: but after fragments of the wreck were salvaged, that theory was scotched. Fifty modifications were made to the Comet fleet: special armour-plating was fitted between the engines and the fuel tanks. Three months later another Comet, flying from Rome to Johannesburg for South African Airways, dived into the sea sixty miles North of Messina.

This time, at great cost, the Comets were grounded for many months, and their airworthiness certificates withdrawn. It took almost a year to discover the fatal flaw: metal fatigue under the stress of pressurization for flying at such high altitudes. The aircraft were duly modified, and in 1958 a Comet IV crossed the Atlantic in little more than six hours. But the early disasters had left their mark. It was all too clear that technological progress, like Dr Faust's triumphs, could exact a terrible price.

Nuclear power was a prime example. As early as 1954, the British Atomic Energy Authority came under attack for proposing to bury radioactive waste in disused mineworkings in the Forest of Dean. Chemicals, likewise, threatened the environment. Selective weedkillers massacred bees and prevented fertilization. Nor were insects the only victims. In 1952, a farmer near Paris, whose crops were being eaten by rabbits, introduced the myxoma virus. Within a few months, nearly all the rabbits had died – but myxomatosis was out of control. It spread through France and other countries in Europe, in some places condemning 99.8 percent of the rabbit population to a slow, painful death. In the same year, in Britain, the Royal Society for the Protection of Birds pointed out that waste oil jettisoned by tankers was incapacitating seabirds by gumming up their wings. A six-months survey showed that fifty-four species had been affected that winter, involving up to 250,000 individual birds. As Europe's oil imports increased, the report noted, the threat to wildlife would grow worse.

Men and women, too, were paying a price for progress. Some of the new 'wonder drugs' – especially such steroids as cortisone – were found to have unpleasant side-effects. Others, including penicillin, were in danger of becoming what the *British Medical Journal* called 'a wasting asset', as resistance to them built up. And as some older diseases were vanquished, others took a new toll. In 1952, the World Health Organization reported that in several countries the number of deaths from cancer had doubled during the past fifty years: lung cancer, in particular, showed an alarming increase. That year, in Copenhagen, there was a severe, unexpected outbreak of poliomyelitis, with three thousand cases in four months. In Northern Europe particularly, rheumatism and bronchitis were still a burden in old age; and as people lived longer, more of them died from circulatory and respiratory diseases, as well as from vascular lesions of the central nervous system, or 'strokes'. To those between the ages of 45 and 64, moreover, coronary thrombosis was now a far more serious threat than before the war.

This may have been due in part to a richer diet: but it also seemed that a major reason was stress. More and more people in Western Europe were now living and working in large conurbations. In Britain, two-fifths of the population was concentrated in six big towns. A million commuters a day were pouring into and out of London. Everywhere there was a drift from the land. In the 1950's, it involved a quarter of Britain's already scarce farmworkers, nearly a fifth of those in France, and more than a third of the mountain-dwellers in Switzerland. In Germany and Italy, the main rural exodus was still to come; but the trend was beginning. It prompted, among other things, a new urban nostalgia for the rural past. The richer city-

dwellers bought rustic retreats for weekends and holidays. Many adopted an
'urban peasant' style in town or suburban houses, with 'country kitchens',
wooden-handled steak knives, and hand-thrown pottery mugs and bowls. In
France and Germany, advertisements for processed cheese and blended
wine began to feature bewhiskered peasants, while in Britain a new
margarine proclaimed its 'country-fresh' flavour and showed on its packets
an open farm gate. In 1951, the BBC began a nightly radio serial, *The
Archers*, billed as 'An everyday story of country folk'. It was phenomenally
popular, and was still running more than thirty years later.

If many West Europeans now sought the equivalent of an imaginary
'Ambridge' – the 'Archer' family's home village – it was largely because the
towns they actually lived in were becoming less human. What war had begun
by way of urban destruction, high-handed planners and greedy 'developers'
now seemed bent on completing. Large chunks of provincial cities began to
be 'cleared' – i.e. demolished. So blithely were old-fashioned buildings
being pulled down that local amenity societies sprang up to defend them. In
Britain in 1953, the Historical Buildings Council was established, with a
Treasury grant, to help the owners of such property to maintain it. In 1957,
the Civic Trust was formed to co-ordinate the efforts of urban conservation
societies; and in 1958 the Victorian Society came into being alongside the
existing Georgian Society – reflecting a new respect for once-despised
nineteenth-century architecture now threatened by the rising tide of grey
concrete.

In good hands, of course, modern building techniques could work
miracles of grace and elegance. Used badly, they gave birth to monstrous,
forbidding eyesores, some of which made people footsore too. Traditional
buildings, especially private houses, had been notable for their scale, their
shape, and their detail. Their scale, constrained by cost and materials, had
seldom been immodest. Their shape, with a recognizable base and apex, had
been determined by the need to shed rain or snow. Their detail had been a
matter of taste. It was sometimes fussy or mass-produced, as in the late
nineteenth century; it was sometimes false, like the planks pinned to mock-
Tudor façades to simulate timber frames. But, however feebly, it spoke for
the particular against the general, the individual against the mass. Many of
the new buildings, by comparison, seemed ruthless. Set in existing towns,
they dominated the skyline, dwarfed older streets and houses, or blocked the
vista like huge piles of crates. Too often starkly rectangular, with endless
rows of identical windows or perfunctorily repetitive 'modules', they reduced

the idea of 'fitness for function', the 1930's slogan, to a factory uniformity. Most of them looked like offices – as many of them were. Nor were they always functional. Tower blocks of apartments, it was soon found, bred loneliness and vandalism; some of them hardly even saved much space.

Better designers tried to vary the monotony: but their efforts were often thwarted by cost or the passage of time. For five years, I lived across the street from the much-praised Foncolin Building in Rue Montoyer, Brussels, completed in 1958. It was a rather daunting neighbour; but the architect André Jacqmain had enlivened its steel-framed glass wall-panels with horizontals – concrete floor slabs and wooden rails, all set forward from the wall. As the years went by, these well-meant features began to look sad: rain streaked the concrete, and the fine new wood grew faded and shabby. Far worse were those new buildings which seemed designed to affront, by 'brutalism' or excessive size. Fortunately for Europeans, few of the 'megastructures' proposed from the early 1950's onwards were ever actually built; but 'brutalism' left virtually bomb-proof blemishes on parts of the countryside and many towns.

Domineering architecture was not the only new blot on city life. Victorian London had been notorious for its 'pea-soupers' – the fogs of Dickens's *Bleak House* or Conan Doyle's 'Sherlock Holmes' stories. In December 1952 it was as if they had suddenly returned. For five days, the capital was enveloped in thick, suffocating smog. It led to more than 4,000 deaths from bronchial and other disorders: but at least it prompted action. Smokeless zones were established; power stations were built with taller chimneys and better 'washing' devices. Gradually, similar measures were adopted in other European cities: since fumes ignored frontiers, it was a common European problem, like the growing pollution of the Rhine.

Noise was another pollutant. It came from all kinds of source, including the apparently empty sky. In 1947, an American aircraft had first flown faster than the speed of sound. In 1953, Europe recaptured the world record, when Squadron-Leader Neville Duke, the chief test pilot for Hawker aircraft, reached 717 miles an hour. Only after landing did he realize that his 'breaking the sound barrier' had produced a 'sonic boom' – really a loud report – which had been heard on earth. For some years afterwards, greenhouse owners and custodians of ancient churches complained of damage from supersonic aircraft, while the general public grumbled about the noise.

Not that the public in general was noticeably silent. One Saturday afternoon I walked into the Bois de la Cambre on the edge of Brussels and heard what sounded like a giant loudspeaker booming out a commentary on a bicycle race. It took a moment to realize that the commentator's voice was being amplified by hundreds of portable radio sets, dotted about the grass where families were picnicking. Such unison was exceptional. In most public places there was competitive cacophony, brilliantly caught in *La voce del silenzio*, a film made in Italy in 1952 by the 65-year-old Austrian director G.W. Pabst. To set the scene for his subject – a religious 'retreat' into the cloister – Pabst began with a deafening montage of noise in the streets of Rome. When I went to live there in the following year, the din seemed even louder: newsvendors shouting '*Paese Se-e-era!*' and '*Ecco Lo Secolo!*'; lottery salesmen countering with '*Premî di consolazio-o-one!*'; workmen in hats made of newspaper calling '*Ao!*' to each other; the flatulent hiss of the brakes on trolley-buses; the discord of car horns and engines; above all, the snarling roar of motor-scooters. At that time there were 700,000 scooters in Italy alone; by 1958, Western Europe had 17,500,000 scooters and motor-cycles, and 21,500,000 trucks, buses, and cars.

Vehicles demanded roads. Accordingly, cities like Brussels or Birmingham were disfigured by urban motorways and underpasses; others were bypassed at the expense of farmland, also under threat from superhighways. Some of the roads, especially in France and Italy, were elaborately 'landscaped'; others, like Rome's Via Appia Nuova, spawned a litter of 'roadside blight'. And more traffic meant more accidents. Between 1948 and 1956, the death-toll doubled in Germany, Ireland, Luxembourg, the Netherlands, and Norway; in Austria, France, Italy, and Spain it was multiplied by three. Nor, despite the arguments of road-building lobbyists, was there any clear correlation between the number of deaths on the roads and the presence or absence of expressways. The real killers were the vehicles and their drivers.

To escape the fumes, the noise, and the danger, more people took to the water. The fashionable sailing resorts round Europe's coasts, from Cannes to Cowes, from Kiel to Monte Carlo, had once been the preserve of luxury yachts; now, they were invaded by racing dinghies and family cruisers. One result was congestion, even at sea. Before long, marinas would be needed to ease the waiting-lists for moorings.

'Affluence' also involved excess. In Britain, the 1952 Rolls-Royce 'Phantom' was advertised as having 'an atmosphere of Regency luxury', with upholstery in hand-woven petit-point and 'the interior roofing ... hand-painted by an artist, believed to be a Royal Academician'. Going one better – or worse – Sir Bernard and Lady Docker enjoyed fleeting notoriety for ostentatious high living in their steam-yacht *Shemara* and their gold-plated Daimler, its seats upholstered in zebra skin. 'Mink', Lady Docker declared, 'is too hot to sit on.' The remark might have pleased 'Joe Lampton', the young-man-on-the-make in John Braine's 1957 novel *Room at the Top*. His aims in life were simple: 'I wanted an Aston Martin, I wanted a three-guinea linen shirt, I wanted a girl with a Riviera suntan – these were my rights.' His creator claimed to pass no judgment on these ambitions; but if *Room at the Top* was a fairy-tale, it was one in which the hero ditches his ageing girlfriend, then wins the hand and fortune of his princess, the daughter of a Yorkshire textile magnate, by dint of a shotgun wedding.

The world of 'Joe Lampton' was clearly the world in which, two years earlier, an Electricity Board showroom had displayed a Nativity scene with the Magi offering a refrigerator, an electric cooker, and a washing-machine. It was the world of brand names, television jingles, and advertisements for competitive greed: the world of expense accounts and scampi. 'In a hundred years' time,' said the restaurateur Charles Forte, 'I can imagine scampi being looked upon as an old English dish.'

Nor was ostentation confined to Britain. In France, in 1958, Jacques Tati's film *Mon oncle* gleefully contrasted the friendly, dingy 'old quarter', where 'M. Hulot' lived, with the spotless tedium of 'M. Arpel's' plastic tube factory, and the 'contemporary' pretensions of his ultra-modern villa, complete with a geometrical front yard, a vertical metal fish for a fountain (turned on only for visitors), and electronically operated up-and-over garage doors. As always, Tati exaggerated: but the smug 'M. Arpel' and his gadget-snob wife were easy to recognize in France at that time.

In Germany in the same year, Kurt Hoffmann's comic film *Wir Wunderkinder* parodied the plump champions of Erhard's 'economic miracle', armoured in black Mercedes and enjoying such festivities as the famous party organized a few years earlier by Berthold Beitz at the Krupp family's Villa Hügel near Essen. On that lavish occasion, three orchestras had played throughout the evening; Pullman cars had shuttled between Bonn and Essen with hostesses in blue uniforms serving cigars, champagne, and caviar; and each of the five hundred guests had received a silver cigarette-lighter.

Almost simultaneous with Hoffmann's *Wir Wunderkinder* was a far more acerbic film, *Das Mädchen Rosemarie*. Directed by Rolf Thiele, and partly scripted by the Munich playwright Erich Kuby, this was based on the true story of Rosemarie Nitribitt, Frankfurt's most celebrated call-girl, whose regular charge to rich businessmen was five hundred dollars or more. After some of her clients had been blackmailed, by her or by a protector, Rosemarie was found murdered. The police interviewed a number of prominent suspects; but in the end they arrested only an obscure pimp, on evidence which some believed to be false. Thiele's film, as the British observer Terence Prittie put it, 'depicted the twentieth-century conquistadors of the German industrial world as gross, unattractive figures, and their wives as hopelessly humdrum, socially self-conscious women who run early to fat.'

It was much the same greed and pretension that Heinrich Böll had indicted in *Und sagte kein einziges Wort* (1953), translated four years later by the poet Robert Graves as *Acquainted With the Night*. Böll's first two novels had dealt directly with war: this one saw the postwar 'economic miracle' through the stony eyes of a repatriated prisoner. *Haus ohne Hüter* (1954), tackled a similar theme. So did Martin Walser's first book of short stories, *Ein Flugzeug über dem Haus* (1955), and his first novel, *Ehen in Philippsburg*, two years later. In 1956, meanwhile, Walser's contemporary Günter Grass, the future author of *Die Blechtrommel, The Tin Drum*, had published a first collection of such disturbing poems as 'Family Matters':

> In our museum – we always go there on Sundays –
> they have opened a new department.
> Our aborted children, pale, serious embryos,
> sit there in plain glass jars
> and worry about their parents' future.

And in 1957 another poet, Hans Magnus Enzensberger, two years younger than Günter Grass, produced his first book, *die verteidigung der wölfe*. The title poem, 'the defence of the wolves against the lambs', sardonically asked:

> Should the vultures devour forget-me-nots?
> Do you expect the jackal
> to change his skin, or the wolf?

Enzensberger's 'lambs' were the public, who he seemed to feel were gullible and childish –

> shying away from the pain of truth,
> refusing to learn, leaving
> thinking to the wolves.

'I saw no reason why childhood should not last for ever,' said the young Welsh dress designer Mary Quant, whose Chelsea boutique 'Bazaar' opened its doors at the end of 1955. 'I wanted everyone', she explained, 'to retain the grace of a child, so I created clothes that allowed people to run, to jump, to hop, to retain this precious freedom' – as against the formal elegance of the fashion houses. But to many older people her words had wider, deeper resonance. Millions in Europe were now released from poverty and postwar 'austerity'. How would they use their new-found ease? The question had moral overtones – as did another, asked at that time by a North-country English neighbour: 'Doesn't central heating make you soft?' 'Softness', fecklessness, irresponsibility: these had been anathema in wartime and earlier. There seemed to be signs of them now.

Instalment credit, for instance, was expanding rapidly in Europe, especially for cars and household machinery; in Germany, and still more in Britain, it was now much used for buying furniture. As in America in the 1920's, the older generations hated and feared indebtedness: they believed in postponing any purchase, except that of a house, until they could 'afford' it: they were horrified by slogans like 'Buy now, pay later'.

There was similar concern at the general increase in gambling. In France it had risen by 29 percent in one year, from 1951 to 1952. In Britain, after the 1949–51 Royal Commission on Betting, Lotteries, and Gaming, the laws on betting shops were relaxed; later, in 1956, the Government itself entered the lottery business when it started to issue Premium Bonds, which earned no interest but offered the chance of large cash prizes. Meanwhile, *der Fussballtoto, il totocalcio*, 'the pools', *le PMU* and *le tiercé* continued to absorb small punters' savings.

More disturbing to older people was the new emphasis on sex. War had torn aside concealment and inhibitions. Women had shared danger and responsibility, more fully than in World War I: they were no longer content to be passive. Bereavement was common, especially in Germany; there, in particular, marriage bureaux flourished. Everywhere, now, there was greater openness about sexual needs, and greater tolerance of 'deviant' behaviour.

In France in 1944, Roger Peyrefitte had won praise as well as notoriety for his first novel, *Les amitiés particulières*, an account of love and jealousy in a Jesuit college for boys. Its sequel, *Les amours singulières* (1949), was crude and far less moving – as were some of Peyrefitte's later, more abrasive books: *Les ambassades* (1951), *La fin des ambassades* (1953), and in particular *Jeunes proies* (1956). In 1950, in *La ronde*, Max Ophüls had delicately brought to the

screen a once scandalous subject – the loveless serial couplings of Arthur
Schnitzler's play *Reigen* – without causing any of the commotion that its
staging had provoked in Berlin thirty years earlier. And in 1956, the 28-year-
old Roger Vadim – who was later to remake *La ronde*, rather badly – had
immense success with *Et Dieu créa la femme*, a sensuously erotic film which
firmly put on the map not only its location, St-Tropez, but also its star
Brigitte Bardot. The first scene showed her lying prone on the sand, wearing
only a smile, with the sea trickling round and under her. The image endured.
'People thought she was naked all through the film,' Vadim said afterwards,

because she displayed a different attitude to sex from the one that prevailed
in films at that time. She was not submissive. Neither was she a whore. She
was not like Deborah Kerr, Grace Kelly, Michèle Morgan. For the
Americans it was the first declaration in a film that love for pleasure is not
sin.

It was not entirely a new idea. In 1948, Dr Alfred Kinsey had produced
his report on *The Sexual Behaviour of the Human Male*, revealing that 86
percent of American men had had (or boasted of) premarital intercourse. A
year later, Norman Mailer's fine first novel *The Naked and the Dead* had
rather strengthened the impression; and in 1953 Dr Kinsey had confirmed
that it takes two to tango by exposing *The Sexual Behaviour of the Human
Female*. All three books were eagerly read on both sides of the Atlantic.

The following year in Britain saw a puritanical counter-offensive. Five
well-known publishers were prosecuted for having issued allegedly obscene
novels; more damagingly, a number of young men were imprisoned on
charges of homosexual behaviour which in Denmark, Finland, France, Italy,
the Netherlands, Norway, Sweden, and Switzerland would have gone
unpunished. So great was the ensuing public disquiet that the Government
appointed the Wolfenden Committee on Homosexuality and Prostitution. In
1957 it recommended a thorough liberalization of existing laws. Already, in
1951, the 'X' certificate had been introduced to cover films thought suitable
only for adults. Nearly ten years later, a jury decided that D.H. Lawrence's
novel *Lady Chatterley's Lover* could at last be published in Britain with its
'four-letter words' intact.

Some at the time suspected that one reason for Britain's hounding of
homosexuals in high places had been the defection three years earlier of the
two 'missing diplomats', Guy Burgess and Donald Maclean. Although
homosexual and bisexual respectively, Burgess and Maclean seem to have
been no more than friends and accomplices. They fled together on 25 May

1951, taking the night boat from Southampton to St-Malo, then going by a roundabout route to Dunkirk, and thence in a Polish cargo ship to Szczecin and on to Moscow. The brilliant, charming, and dissolute Burgess, then working on 'black propaganda', was generally regarded as relatively small fry; but Maclean, at the time of his disappearance, was head of the American department at the Foreign Office. Under suspicion for some time, partly for irresponsible behaviour, he had been about to be interrogated; and there was much speculation as to whether he and Burgess had been tipped off by a 'third man' – an allusion to the Carol Reed/Orson Welles film of that name. While internal investigations were still proceeding, public disquiet was revived on 11 September 1953, by the further disappearance of Donald Maclean's wife and children during a holiday in Switzerland.

In far-off Australia, meanwhile, a Royal Commission had been investigating the Soviet spy ring revealed there by the defection of Vladimir Petrov and his wife. When its report was finally published on 8 September 1955, it contained a statement by Petrov that Burgess and Maclean had been supplying information to the Soviet Union 'over a number of years'. There was instant uproar in London. On 23 September the British Government published a bland and uninformative White Paper on the subject; but public concern and curiosity were not appeased. On 25 October, prompted by newspapermen in touch with intelligence sources, the Labour MP for Brixton, Colonel Marcus Lipton, asked Anthony Eden whether he would appoint a select committee to examine the disappearance of Burgess and Maclean. It was merely the prelude to a deadly supplementary question:

Has the Prime Minister made up his mind to cover up at all costs the dubious 'third man' activities of Mr Harold Philby, who was First Secretary at the Washington Embassy?

A year and three months later, on 11 February 1956, the Moscow correspondents of *The Sunday Times* and Reuter, together with representatives of Tass and *Pravda*, were summoned unexpectedly to Room 101 of the National Hotel. There they were confronted with Maclean and Burgess, and handed a brief statement as unconvincing in its way as the British White Paper. The two 'missing diplomats' said little in answer to questions. Both denied having been Soviet agents. Neither, understandably, made any mention of Philby. He, by this time, had secured public clearance from the Government and an apology from Colonel Lipton. He kept his secret – from the public at least – for another seven years before following Burgess and Maclean to Moscow.

Spies such as these – and others then still undiscovered – were a special breed of 'strangers in our midst'. Traditionally, espionage agents had been permanent or temporary officials of their own countries or paid traitors from the opposing side. Ideological conflict had changed all that. Treason, now, was often perverse loyalty to a 'higher' cause. Some turncoats, of course, were still mercenaries, seduced from patriotism by bribes or blackmail: but others believed themselves 'all, all honourable men' – 'gentlemen' in every sense of the word. In their clubland or academic camouflage, they were disconcerting and very hard to detect. But World War II was barely over when the first of them began to be exposed.

On 5 September 1946, Igor Gouzenko, a 26-year-old cipher clerk at the Soviet Embassy in Ottawa, removed a bundle of documents from the safe in his office. He took them, first, to the headquarters of the Ottawa *Journal*; but the newspaper showed no interest in them. Next day, Gouzenko tried various government offices, still to no avail. But when he came back to his apartment at 511 Somerset Street, he saw two men loitering outside. A little later there was a knock at his door, and someone called his name. He recognized the voice: it was one of the drivers who worked for the Soviet Military Attaché. Frightened, Gouzenko went to the rear balcony and shouted to his next-door neighbour, a Canadian Air Force sergeant. The sergeant went to call the police, while another neighbour agreed to shelter Gouzenko, his wife, and his young son. At about midnight, four burly Russians from the Embassy broke into the Gouzenkos' empty apartment and began to ransack it. The police caught them red-handed. Next day, Gouzenko and his documents went to the Royal Canadian Mounted Police headquarters, and he and his family were taken into protective custody. His evidence, and the investigations that followed, led on to the exposure of much bigger game – Dr Alan Nunn May, the first of the so-called 'atom spies'. As well as a number of Americans, they also included two other European scientists: Dr Klaus Fuchs and Dr Bruno Pontecorvo.

They hardly knew each other, or so they claimed. Nunn May had studied at Cambridge, Fuchs at Kiel, and Pontecorvo in Rome. All three were physicists; all three had worked on nuclear research; all three were idealists who betrayed their trust. Like Burgess, Maclean, Philby, and the others, they had been young when Hitler's tyranny was trampling over Europe. For them, there could be no 'enemies to the Left'.

Nunn May, shy, bespectacled, and balding, with a small, Hitler-style moustache, had passed classified information and samples of uranium 233 and 235 to a contact in Canada, three months after VE-Day and several days after the explosion of the Hiroshima bomb. He was arrested on 4 March 1946, and brought to trial on 1 May: he pleaded guilty to breaches of the Official Secrets Act, and was sentenced to ten years' penal servitude.

Fuchs, a German Jewish refugee, was thin and wiry, with an intellectual's neat face and very thick spectacles. He had got in touch with the Soviet Embassy while still in England, had continued to pass information to couriers in wartime Washington, and had resumed contact with the Russians in London after the war. 'In the postwar period,' he admitted later, 'I began again to have my doubts about Russian policy.... I disapproved of many actions of the Russian Government and of the Communist Party, but I still believed that they would build a new world and that one day I would take part in it and that on that day I would also have to stand up and say to them that there are things which they are doing wrongly.'

On 1 September 1949, President Truman announced that the Soviet Union had exploded its first atomic bomb. It had been helped, undoubtedly, by information leaked secretly from the Anglo-American project; and earlier evidence had shown that Nunn May had not been the only source. In December, Fuchs was questioned for the first time by the quiet and formidable Security Service ('MI5') interrogator William Skardon. In January 1950 he confessed. 'In particular at Los Alamos,' he said, 'I did what I consider to be the worst I have done, namely to give information about the principle of the design of the plutonium bomb.' Arrested on 2 February, he was brought to trial on 1 March 1950, and sentenced to fourteen years' imprisonment. After his release he went to teach in East Germany.

Bruno Pontecorvo, dark, good-looking, married with three children, and full of extrovert charm, seemed very different from his bachelor counterparts. No public proof was ever offered that he had given information to the Soviet Union – or, indeed, that he had possessed any information not already passed. But at the end of August 1950, while on holiday in Rome, he and his family flew to Scandinavia, reaching Helsinki on 2 September. There, a man and a woman met them with a car, and they drove off to an unknown destination. Several years later, it was disclosed that they had gone to the Soviet Union, where Pontecorvo was now working on scientific research. Some suggested that his knowledge of lithium deuteride production had been needed to help develop the Soviet hydrogen bomb, first tested in August 1953.

Alan Moorehead wrote of Fuchs that he 'had committed the crime society

is least able to forgive: he had made society distrust itself.' Wariness was
certainly in the air. In 1945, optimistically if ironically, Jean-Paul Sartre had
given the title *L'âge de raison* to the first novel in his postwar trilogy *Les
chemins de la liberté*. Two years later, in the United States, W.H. Auden had
named his 'baroque eclogue' *The Age of Anxiety*. In 1951, Arthur Koestler
had published a novel about 'the end of Europe', and called it *The Age of
Longing*. But the most telling phrase was that chosen by the 'new novelist'
Nathalie Sarraute as the title of an essay on the novel, first published in 1950
in Sartre's magazine *Les Temps Modernes*. This was 'L'ère de soupçon' – 'The
Age of Suspicion'. By 1956, when the essay was reissued, with others, in a
book of the same name, it seemed still more appropriate to Europe's mood.

A few years earlier, in 1946, Evelyn Waugh had published a gloomy fable,
Scott-King's Modern Europe, about a classics teacher sucked into the
unsavoury politics of 'Neutralia' – 'a typical modern state, governed by a
single party, acclaiming a dominant Marshal, supporting a vast ill-paid
bureaucracy whose work is tempered and humanized by corruption.' Many
readers mis-identified this as Yugoslavia: in fact, it was inspired by a visit to
Spain – bedevilled, it seemed, by such documents as 'embarkation papers,
medical cards, customs clearance slips, currency control vouchers, pass-
ports, tickets, identity dockets, travel orders, emigration certificates, baggage
checks and security sheets'. At the end of his adventures, rescued at last
from a flotsam of international refugees, 'Scott-King' tells his headmaster: 'I
think it would be very wicked indeed to do anything to fit a boy for the
modern world.' But, like it or not, some facets of modern Europe were much
as 'Scott-King' found them: dangerous, unpredictable, potentially violent,
and full of mutual mistrust.

More directly and less subtly, this fact found expression in Ian Fleming's
very popular thrillers, the first of which, *Casino Royale*, appeared in 1953.
When not concerned with dark satanic millionaires plotting to dominate the
world, these luridly explored the 'dirty tricks' of espionage. What distinguished them from many similar fantasies was that their hero, 'James
Bond', was a cad. Although patriotic and supposedly honourable, he seemed
as sybaritic and lecherous as John Braine's 'Joe Lampton', and even more
obsessed with the brand names of his favourite consumer goods.

And yet, sensational as Fleming's stories were, they kept only a few jumps
ahead of reality. In a twilight world, moral ambivalence was inescapable. In
Germany, for example, Chancellor Adenauer's Christian Democrat
Government could not have afforded to reject all the expertise that was

offered it by General Reinhard Gehlen, the sinister former Head of Army Intelligence under Adolf Hitler. 'It is legitimate', wrote Hugh Trevor-Roper, 'to use Beelzebub to oust Satan.' In 1953, thanks partly to Gehlen's 'Organization', the authorities were able to arrest thirty-nine German members of a spy ring run by Soviet diplomats and controlled from the Institute of Economic and Scientific Research in East Berlin. But Gehlen's methods were not always above suspicion, and he disliked potential rivals. In September 1950, a law had been passed establishing a new Internal Security Office – very roughly, 'MI5' to Gehlen's 'MI6'. Gehlen had applied for the job of running it: but, to his ill-concealed annoyance, he was turned down in favour of Dr Otto John, a liberal conservative who after the 1944 bomb plot against Hitler had fled to London and, as Gehlen put it, 'had then worked there for our enemies.' He added: 'I kept John himself at arm's length.' He certainly shed only crocodile tears in July 1954, when John disappeared into East Berlin, drugged or drunk. Some eighteen months later, John returned to the West, and was sentenced to four years' imprisonment by the Karlsruhe High Court. Gehlen commented: 'I consider Dr John deserves our sympathy for suffering a hideous personal tragedy. His eighteen months in Communist hands must be attributed at most to a momentary aberration, an accident on the job.'

It was not the only Western accident. On 19 April 1956, during a visit to London by the Soviet Prime Minister Nikolai Bulganin and the Communist Party Secretary Nikita Khrushchev, a free-lance frogman, the 45-year-old Commander Lionel Crabb, dived under their cruiser *Ordzhonikidze*, perhaps to measure the pitch of its screws. He never reappeared. A headless body was washed up the following year: it may well have been his.

Still more disturbing, and still more reminiscent of a 'James Bond' extravaganza, was the story that broke in East Berlin five days after Commander Crabb's fatal dive. On Tuesday 24 April 1956, a number of Western journalists were invited to assemble in the cinema of the Soviet officers' mess in Karlshorst. From there, a triumphant Soviet military commander, Colonel I.A. Kozyuba, led them out to the East Berlin suburb of Alt-Glienicke. Here, very close to the border of the Western sector, Russian Army searchlights were trained on a large hole in the ground, surrounded by freshly dug earth. Soviet military engineers had uncovered a Western 'dirty trick' – a tunnel five hundred yards long, starting from Rudow in West Berlin, to enable the British and Americans to tap Soviet cables carrying coded signals and scrambled telephone calls. This had been

'Operation Gold', modelled on a smaller 'Operation Silver' which the British had carried out in divided Vienna. It had cost at least 25 million dollars to build, man, and operate for a year. Its discovery and disclosure were embarrassing enough. What made it preposterous was that even before Western engineers had begun their tunnel, the whole plan had been betrayed to the Soviet Union by the double agent George Blake, then at work in Britain's Secret Intelligence Service ('MI6'). A further five years went by before he was unmasked.

Neither Blake nor Philby was the last of the 'strangers' to come to light. The years that followed were to bring many more rumours and a few more revelations. Not the least of them was the much later discovery that Giangiacomo Feltrinelli, the millionaire publisher of Lampedusa and Pasternak, was involved in funding Italian left-wing terrorism. The growth of such violent dissidence, in turn, was only one index of political frustrations which had been growing since early in the 1950's.

In Italy and France, in particular, some such frustration was understandable. In both countries, the party system seemed to produce perpetual coalitions, whose members might shift but whose policies seldom changed. Whereas in Britain or the United States the two main parties alternated in office, in Italy and France there seemed no acceptable alternative. The Communist Party, with its large 'family' of sympathizers, its own magazines and newspapers, and almost its own social life, siphoned off millions of votes which might otherwise have gone to the democratic Left. The political colour of any coalition, if it altered at all, was seldom determined directly and openly by the voters, as in a mainly two-party contest. Instead, it was decided by politicians on the basis of the election results, doing deals in smoke-filled rooms behind closed doors. In many cases, too, the party 'machines' were exclusive and self-perpetuating – even on the Left, and even in Germany. At the Social-Democratic Congress in Hamburg in 1950, it was reckoned, only 8.2 percent of the delegates were of working-class origin, and of the Party's leaders only 4 percent.

Nor was frustration confined to the Left. In France, the Gaullists were chafing at the Fourth Republic's imperfections. In Italy, Monarchists and Neo-Fascists schemed and squabbled, sometimes with the alleged conni- vance of military or security men. In Germany, from time to time, there were rumours of a neo-Nazi revival – in 1949 through the *Bruderschaft*, a clandestine organization of Army officers; in 1951 in the ranting *Sozialist-*

ische Reichspartei, outlawed a year later; in 1953 in a new *Deutscher Freikorps*; and on several occasions in vain attempts to subvert the respectable German Liberals of the *Freie Demokratische Partei*.

But frustration was not due merely to the constraints of domestic politics. It arose also from a sense of being locked into a world system and an East-West confrontation of which spy fever was only one symptom.

In 1947 and 1948, coughing his lungs out with tuberculosis, George Orwell had written a novel about the future which he thought of calling *The Last Man in Europe*. It was published in June 1949, seven months before he died: by now, its title was *Nineteen Eighty-four*. Remembering *Animal Farm*, some took it as a further indictment of Communist dictatorship. In fact, its target was totalitarianism of whatever kind; and its prophecy of a regimented world frozen in permanent non-nuclear conflict was a bleak extrapolation from the international politics of the time.

On 4 April 1949, while *Nineteen Eighty-four* was still with its publishers, the Russian defector Viktor Andreyevich Kravchenko, author of *I Chose Freedom* (1946), won substantial damages in a Paris court against journalists who had called his book a forgery. The evidence he produced was as chilling as any page of Orwell's novel. Nevertheless, despite Kravchenko's and others' revelations, many were still impressed enough by Soviet achievements in war, social policy, and education, to go on giving Communists the benefit of the doubt – especially when they spoke of 'peace'.

Shortly after the Kravchenko court case, the Communist Party offered Paris a rival spectacle: a World Congress of Partisans of Peace, held in the Salle Pleyel. One of its organizers was the poet Louis Aragon: he helped to enlist celebrities ranging from Paul Robeson to Pablo Picasso, who promised a sketch for the posters. Looking through a folder of recent work in Picasso's studio, Aragon came across a very successful lithograph of a Milanese pigeon – a portrait of one of four birds which had been a present from Matisse. Unlike most pigeons, they had feathers like white gaiters covering their claws. Seeing this, Aragon decided that the lithograph looked like a dove. With Picasso's permission, the pigeon with its claws concealed became the famous 'Dove of Peace'.

The claws showed, briefly, later that summer, when the Soviet Union exploded its first atomic bomb. But in November 1952 the United States went a stage further, by testing the first thermonuclear 'device'. Shortly afterwards, General Dwight D. Eisenhower was elected US President, and he appointed John Foster Dulles as his Secretary of State. Dulles, then 64, was a lawyer, an internationalist, and a Christian. Two years before, he had written: 'It is time to think less of fission bombs and more of establishing justice and ending terrorism in the world.' Few in Europe would have disagreed with that; but many more had noted with alarm his previous sentence: 'It is time to think in terms of taking the offensive in the world struggle for freedom, and of rolling back the engulfing tide of despotism.' Might not the policy of 'rollback', if applied in Europe, lead to war?

In June 1953 the danger came very close. Refugees from oppression and hardship in East Germany had long been pouring into the West: on one day in March six thousand had sought asylum in West Berlin, and by May the total for the whole of Germany was 340,000. Then, on 16 June, the patience of workers in East Berlin suddenly snapped. They went on strike. They stoned Soviet troops and tanks. They tore down the Red Flag from the top of the Brandenburger Tor. Crowds surged through the streets and started fires. Some members of the *Volkspolizei*, the 'People's Police', even joined in. Then the shooting began. The Soviet Military Government called a state of emergency. Soon, the tanks and troops were moving in. Within a few days it was all over, sealed by summary trials and executions. Estimates of the number killed varied from 25 to 569. But, throughout it all, the West had not intervened. The balance of terror made 'rollback' merely rhetorical. That August, the Soviet Union exploded its own thermonuclear bomb.

One anxious witness of these developments was Bertrand Russell. 'Throughout the 'forties and the early 'fifties,' he wrote, 'my mind was in a state of confused agitation on the nuclear question. It was obvious to me that a nuclear war would put an end to civilization.' Late in 1948, he suggested that 'the remedy might be the threat of immediate war by the United States on Russia for the purpose of forcing nuclear disarmament upon her.' But if Russell was ever a 'hawk', it was not for long. '1950, beginning with the OM [the British Order of Merit] and ending with the Nobel Prize, seems to have marked the apogee of my respectability.' Then, in 1953, Stalin died; and on 1 March 1954, the United States exploded a large fission-fusion-fission bomb on Bikini atoll. It covered the Japanese fishing-boat *Lucky Dragon* with radioactive ash, and spread fall-out over an area of 7,000 square miles. These events made Russell, as he put it, 'more favourable to Communism'.

I came gradually to attribute, more and more, the danger of nuclear war to the West, to the United States of America, and less to Russia. This change was supported by developments inside the United States, such as McCarthyism and the restriction of civil liberties.

In December 1954, Russell gave a BBC radio talk on the dangers of nuclear war. He called it *Man's Peril*. Its final words were these:

There lies before us, if we choose, continual progress in happiness, knowledge, and wisdom. Shall we, instead, choose death, because we cannot forget our quarrels? I appeal, as a human being to human beings: remember your humanity, and forget the rest. If you can do so, the way lies open to a new Paradise; if you cannot, nothing lies before you but universal death.

The result was a mountain of letters and requests to speak. Very soon, the 82-year-old Russell became a familiar figure at rallies and conferences for world government. The next task he set himself was to collect the signatures of eminent scientists on a joint international manifesto asking: 'Shall we put an end to the human race: or shall mankind renounce war?' One of those he approached was Albert Einstein. In the Spring of 1955, still waiting for a reply, Russell flew from Rome to Paris. During the flight, the pilot announced that Einstein had died; but when Russell reached his Paris hotel, there awaiting him was Einstein's letter of acceptance, written a few days before. At last, in July 1957, largely in response to Russell's efforts, twenty-two scientists from East and West held the first of a series of conferences that took their name from their first venue, Pugwash in Nova Scotia. Among the dangers they emphasized was the risk of genetic damage from radioactive fall-out caused by continuing nuclear tests.

The Soviet Union and the West were meanwhile discussing disarmament – the slowly maturing fruit of a conference in Geneva in July 1955, at which President Eisenhower, the British and French Prime Ministers Anthony Eden and Edgar Faure, and Bulganin and Khrushchev had sought ways of relaxing 'cold war' tensions. But progress was very slow, and Dulles in particular was not always reassuring. In January 1956, he told an interviewer from *Life* magazine: 'The ability to get to the verge without getting into the war is the necessary art. If you are scared to go to the brink you are lost.' This stance was soon labelled 'brinkmanship', in echo of the British humorist Stephen Potter and his series of spoof manuals, begun in 1947 with *The Theory and Practice of Gamesmanship, or the Art of Winning Games without Actually Cheating*. It caused further alarm among Europeans, well aware that they were a prime and vulnerable target for any Soviet nuclear attack. The British Defence White Paper of April 1957, preceding by a month the explosion of the first British hydrogen bomb, confessed that

there is at present no means of providing adequate protection for the people of this country against the consequences of an attack by nuclear weapons.

In Luxembourg at the time, I remember a civil defence leaflet delivered to every household: it advised citizens, in the event of a nuclear air-raid warning, to start by bringing the cattle in.

Nor were Europeans greatly cheered when on 26 August 1957, the Soviet news agency Tass announced that the Americans too were now vulnerable to direct attack, by a new multi-stage intercontinental missile. At first, some experts refused to believe it. Then, on Friday 4 October 1957, the Soviet Union startled everyone by launching the world's first man-made satellite, known as 'Sputnik I'. Twenty centimetres across and weighing 83.6 kilograms, it took just over an-hour-and-a-half for each orbit of the earth, and it disintegrated three months later. It was followed on 3 November by 'Sputnik II', a much bigger satellite, weighing 508 kilograms and carrying Laika, a female husky dog. The new prospect of space exploration – and the fate of poor Laika – attracted enormous interest: but what impressed defence specialists was the Sputniks' confirmation that Soviet rocket technology was indeed capable of launching intercontinental missiles.

Some naïve Europeans had earlier argued that Europe should 'opt out' of any Soviet-American nuclear exchange. How to avoid the fall-out they never made clear; but the Soviet intercontinental missile lent momentary plausibility to their self-interested picture of a war conducted, literally, over their heads. More cogently, by bringing the United States 'into the front line', it reopened the debate about the credibility of the American deterrent for the North Atlantic alliance. Some now questioned whether Americans would risk their lives for Europe. Others answered that they already had, and that the new Soviet missile involved them inescapably. The argument also affected the national nuclear deterrents maintained by Britain and being developed by France. Were they now a dangerous extravagance?

Soon after the news of Sputnik I, the *New Statesman*, the Leftist London weekly then edited by Kingsley Martin, published an article by J.B. Priestley, 'Britain and the Nuclear Bomb', calling on the United Kingdom to renounce nuclear weapons. 'Our bargaining power is slight,' Priestley admitted; but he added, with an unconscious *hubris* often heard later, 'The force of our example might be great.'

Like Bertrand Russell's 1954 broadcast, this triggered off a huge response. Letters flooded into Great Turnstile, the *New Statesman*'s headquarters off High Holborn, in such quantities that Kingsley Martin invited a number of friends and colleagues, including Russell and Priestley, to discuss what should be done.

The upshot was the Campaign for Nuclear Disarmament, CND. It was formally established in early January 1958, with Russell as President and Canon John Collins as Chairman. Its executive committee included Priestley, Kingsley Martin, and Michael Foot, MP; among its sponsors were Benjamin Britten, Michael Tippett, E.M.Forster, Henry Moore, and Barbara Hepworth. On 17 February 1958, they held an inaugural meeting in London, attended by more than five thousand people. One of the speakers was the historian A.J.P. Taylor. After describing the effects of a thermo-nuclear explosion he asked: 'Is there anyone here who would want to do this to another human being?' There was dead silence. 'Then why are we making the damned thing?' There was a thunder of applause. No one at the time answered: 'To deter others from using such a weapon on us.'

On Good Friday, 4 April, that year, CND organized a four-day march from London to the atomic weapons research establishment at Aldermaston, a few miles South-West of Reading in Berkshire. A procession of several thousand people wound their way through the wet streets and lanes. Some carried the CND sign, the white-rimmed black circle intersected by a white 'drooping cross'. It looked a little like an aircraft with swept-back wings: it was actually the semaphore signals for 'N' and 'D'. 'Those who marched', wrote the journalist Peter Lewis,

were a coalition of wildly different elements: pacifists and Christians, Trade Unionists and Little Englanders, anarchists and rationalists, Beats and ravers, the barefoot and the long-haired and also a great many quiet and concerned young parents pushing prams or carrying infants on their shoulders. There were steel bands and folk singers. The large proportion – estimated at forty per cent – of the marchers who were under twenty-one sang 'Ban, ban, ban the bloody H-Bomb' (to the tune of 'John Brown's Body') or 'When the Saints Go Marching In' and welcomed the fact that there was something different to do for Easter.

It was tempting, in retrospect, to smile a little. But, in 1958, nuclear tests were suspended; and five years afterwards the Test-ban Treaty was signed. Later, Peter Lewis discussed CND with both Priestley and Canon Collins. 'I don't think we were ineffectual,' said Priestley. 'We changed the climate of opinion.' And Collins credited CND with two achievements: 'public awareness of what the nuclear threat was in reality and of the danger from the tests. Khrushchev explicitly stated to me that one of his reasons for suspending tests was because he had studied the effect of the CND on the British public. If you believe that, there was a positive result.'

Some of the young people on the Aldermaston march perplexed their parents. In a booming economy, they formed a new band of 'strangers'. They were better fed: in London, they were an inch taller, on average, than the same age-group ten years earlier. They were also better paid; and having as yet no wives or children to support, they could use much of their earnings as newly plentiful pocket-money. Some of it still went on 'comics' – sometimes 'horror-comics' – barely less juvenile than before; some, already, on science-fiction. But the biggest youth and teenage market, as manufacturers soon discovered, was for records and clothes.

The Aldermaston pilgrims marched to 'trad' (for 'traditional') jazz, which the British blues singer George Melly described as 'the suburbs' escape from their lot'. An American connoisseur reported that it 'is just off the driving Dixieland beat by laggard microseconds, but is popular with the young dancehall set, who gyrate to it with a studied jerkiness.' Already, however, something fiercer had arrived – and, like jazz, it came from the New World.

There, the disc jockey Alan Freed had coined a new expression by coupling two verbs recurrent in American rhythm-and-blues and country music lyrics: his coinage was soon folksily shortened to 'rock'n'roll'. 1954 saw the first rock'n'roll 'hit' record, 'Sh-Boom'; it also saw a nineteen-year-old truck driver, Elvis Presley, make his first professional recording, of 'That's All Right Mama' and 'Blue Moon'. But the real impact on Europe came a year later, when Richard Brooks made a film for Metro-Goldwyn-Mayer based on a novel by Evan Hunter about a tough New York high school. It was called *The Blackboard Jungle*. As a film it was effective: but its soundtrack was dynamite – the urgent, deafening, piledriver beat of 'Rock Around the Clock' hammered out by Bill Haley and The Comets. When the film reached Europe, young audiences pulsated, often jumping up to jive in the aisles. Cashing in on the craze, Haley and his group made a second film with the tune as its title. In several cinemas it sparked off riots. Some cities banned it altogether. In Moscow it was shown in secret. Even there, rock'n'roll had arrived.

All over Europe, the new rock audiences had their own distinctive style. Their hair was much longer than the once fashionable 'crew cut' or the wartime 'short back and sides': in Britain, it was often cut in a 'Tony Curtis' or 'DA' fashion – politely said to stand for 'District Attorney', but popularly taken to mean 'duck's arse'. Some British teenagers affected 'Edwardian' elegance – narrow 'drainpipe' trousers and long jackets, often with velvet collars: hence their nickname, 'Teddy boys'. In France and Belgium their nearest counterparts were known as '*blousons noirs*' on account of their black leather jackets, as worn by Marlon Brando in his 1954 film about a motorcycle gang, *The Wild One*. In Sweden, for the same reason, they were called '*skinn-nuttar*'. In Germany, disapproving elders labelled them '*Halbstarken*', or 'half-strong'; and in Moscow their closest cousins were the '*stilyagi*', primly condemned by the official youth newspaper *Komsomolskaya Pravda*. 'They dress in loud clothes,' it complained, 'take pride in their ignorance of classical music, but play vulgar ditties with enthusiasm.' The British reporter Edward Crankshaw described what he called 'their flaunting eccentricities':

the long draped jackets in loud checks of yellow or green, the painted 'American' tie, patch pockets, padded shoulders, turned-back cuffs, peg-top trousers, and, pride of the whole outfit, yellow or light tan shoes, with thick crêpe soles, worn a size too big so that they turn up at the toe.

Still more upsetting to the Soviet authorities was the *stilyagi* use of English and American slang.

Outlandish dress sometimes went with lawless behaviour. The Teddy boys and *blousons noirs* included also 'cosh boys' and flick-knife experts. In many countries in Europe, crime was on the increase, and juvenile crime was growing faster still. In Britain, by 1951, it had doubled since before the war. By the end of the decade, the number of convictions had doubled again; and more than half of those convicted for 'breaking and entering' were under seventeen. But 'juvenile delinquency', as it was called, seemed universal. It engaged the attention of writers and film-makers as well as policemen and social workers: from 'the forgotten ones' of Luis Buñuel's Mexican film *Los Olvidados* (1950) to 'the five boys from Barska Street' in the 1953 film by the Polish director Aleksander Ford, *Piatka z Ulicy Barskiej*; from the 'stray dogs without collars' of Gilbert Cesbron's 1954 novel *Chiens perdus sans collier* to the street arabs of Pier Paolo Pasolini's *Ragazzi di vita* (1955).

Drugs, as yet, were not a serious problem in Europe; but, as in America, their use was growing. At Cambridge in the late 1940's, I well remember, amateur jazz musicians were already smoking 'reefers'. In London in 1951, some stir was caused by the arrest of a young professional trafficker who had stolen large quantities of heroin and cocaine from a hospital pharmacy. During his three months' activities in the West End he had enlisted a clientèle of fifty customers. In 1953, a heroin smuggling ring in Marseille was broken up. In the same year, France and other countries imposed new restrictions on cannabis, and in 1954 it was removed from the British Pharmaceutical Codex. Sweden, that year, grew suddenly scared about the use of amphetamines and other stimulants: two hundred people, it was thought, were injecting them into their veins. By the end of the decade, the number had risen to a thousand. In Britain, by 1954, only 44 new cases of heroin addiction had been reported in the past ten years; but in the next five the rate almost doubled, while the use of Methadone tripled, and known cocaine addiction increased from a mere six cases to nearly fifty. It was far from being comparable with the drug scene in the United States: but in this as in other respects, Europe appeared to be lagging only a few years behind.

Even without a developed 'drug culture', youth culture in Europe was cutting adrift from the past. It had always been fun to be provocative, and tempting to be self-absorbed. Now, for many young people, these seemed to be ends in themselves. When Jean-Pierre Melville, in 1950, made his film of *Les enfants terribles* from Jean Cocteau's claustrophobic novel about self-destructive young people living in a private world, it was savaged by middle-aged critics. But it excited youthful audiences even more than the original novel. That, as Cocteau confessed, had become 'a breviary for mythomaniacs': countless readers had written to him exclaiming 'We *are* your book!'

In 1951, J.D. Salinger's first novel, *The Catcher in the Rye*, had a similar effect in America and Britain. The slangy insolence of its teenage hero, 'Holden Caulfield', offered cunning instant self-identification for sensitive young readers, calling the bluff of the 'phoney' adult world. On a mass level, the 24-year-old actor James Dean played a similar role in the three films he completed before fatally crashing his sports car, in 1955, at 115 miles an hour. The best of them was aptly entitled *Rebel Without a Cause*.

'Alienation' was the term now fashionably applied to such youthful disenchantment with the postwar world. To the distress and bewilderment of many parents in Europe, it was partly a rejection of the shiny prosperity they had striven so hard to build. In 1954, J.B. Priestley invented a new word: 'Admass'. 'This is my name', he wrote,

for the whole system of an increasing productivity, plus inflation, plus a rising standard of material living, plus high-pressure advertising and salesmanship, plus mass communications, plus cultural democracy and the creation of the mass mind, the mass man.... The people firmly fixed in *Admass* are *Admassians*. Most Americans (though not all; they have some fine rebels) have been *Admassians* for the last thirty years; the English, and probably most West Europeans, only since the War. It is better to live in *Admass* than have no job, no prospect of one, and see your wife and children getting hungrier and hungrier. But that is about all that can be said in favour

of it. All the rest is a swindle. You think everything is opening out when in
fact it is narrowing and closing in on you. Finally you have to be half-witted
or half-drunk all the time to endure it.

Many shared Priestley's dissatisfaction. Some, like Richard Hoggart or
Priestley himself, mourned the eclipse by mass entertainment of an older
popular culture – including the values embodied in the British music-hall,
the French *caf'conç*', *varietà* in Italy, or the scabrous cabarets of Berlin.
Others went much further, deploring the 'materialism' of so acquisitive a
society, and reaffirming the primacy of much deeper spiritual needs.

Their concern was timely. All over Western Europe, the churches had
been losing support. The majority still used them for baptism, first
Communion, weddings, and funerals; but regular attendance was declining
– as were the numbers entering the priesthood. In France, between 1953
and 1956, 5,032 priests died, but only 4,150 were ordained to replace them.
In Paris, fewer than twenty percent of the faithful still went to Mass
regularly; in Rome, only some ten percent of men took Communion at
Easter, and only five percent in Madrid. Protestant churches reported a
similar trend. To remedy matters, some attempted compromise. In Britain,
in the 1950's, there was pressure to exclude 'the devil and all his works' from
the third answer in the Catechism, and a few well-meaning clergymen
encouraged mild rock music or even motor-cycles in church. More robust
souls resorted to rousing evangelism. In the Spring of 1954, the American
Baptist preacher Billy Graham, defying a largely hostile press which disliked
his razzmatazz, drew crowds totalling 1,300,000 to the rallies on his 'Greater
London Crusade'. Writing in the *New Statesman*, J.B. Priestley dismissed it
as mass showmanship; but when I heard Graham preach on a later
occasion, I was impressed by his sincerity and power. As he pointed out in
answer to his critics, there was obviously a hunger for more than worldly
satisfactions. It was confirmed by the response to such Catholic novelists as
Graham Greene, François Mauriac, Riccardo Bacchelli, and the young,
quizzical Muriel Spark, as well as to books of theology by Simone Weil or
Pierre Teilhard du Chardin. It also explained the popularity of religious
films: not merely so scrupulous a masterpiece as Robert Bresson's 1951
adaptation of the Georges Bernanos novel *Journal d'un curé de campagne*, but
also relatively pedestrian works like Maurice Cloche's *Monsieur Vincent*
(1947), a life of St Vincent de Paul partly financed by French Catholic film
clubs, or Jean Delannoy's 1950 *Dieu a besoin des hommes* – both redeemed by
outstanding performances from Pierre Fresnay. Equally typical of this 'age of

longing' – to use Koestler's term – was the growing vogue for Vedanta and
Zen Buddhism, some of which now reached Europe via California.

In 1952, the 26-year-old German poet Albert Arnold Scholl published a
volume of verse entitled *Die gläserne Stadt*. It included a poem, 'Etwas
kündigt sich an', 'Something is starting to happen', which sharply expressed
the current sense of metaphysical unease:

> The great changes
> Which newspapers report
> And the rumours on everyone's lips –
> These are not what I mean,
>
> Nor the minor anxieties
> Which we prefer not to mention:
> The constant crumbling of plaster
> Even in new houses,
> The frequent blowing of fuses
> And the children's dangerous games.
>
> But there is something going on,
> Something we don't understand,
> Things have been set in motion,
> Something is starting to happen –
>
> It has begun:
> In the confusion
> When the newsreader
> Keeps making mistakes –
>
> Or in the hand's hesitation
> Before playing the last card,
> When the gamblers' eyes meet –
>
> And on Sundays, after midday,
> While the roofs bake under the sky
> And black or red a rag flutters
> Casting no shadow
> In the arcades
> Of the deserted city.

Scholl might have been describing the petrified cityscapes of a French
'new novel' such as Alain Robbe-Grillet's *Les gommes* (1953). By training a
scientist and agricultural engineer, Robbe-Grillet described the physical
world in hypnotic detail. His intention, in tune in this respect with the
dictates of a 'new critic' like Roland Barthes, was to strip it of the pathetic
fallacy, which in the past had invested inanimate objects with irrelevant,
anthropocentric feelings and associations. In this, both 'new critics' and 'new
novelists' were developing a theme pursued much earlier by Jean-Paul
Sartre and Albert Camus.

Sartre, in particular, had drawn on the German philosopher Edmund

Husserl and his pupil Martin Heidegger to evolve his own literary version of 'existentialism', exploring the frightening contrast between mankind, endowed with consciousness and will-power, and the alien indifference of everything else. Such awareness of 'the absurd' – a bleak conviction that the world was senseless and man impermanent and insecure – was to haunt postwar literature. Sartre had expounded it in 1943 in *L'être et le néant*, and expressed it most cogently two years later in the hermetic hell of his play *Huis clos*. Albert Camus, in 1944, had put it more pithily still in the curtain line of *Le malentendu*, when a final appeal for help or pity is met with the bleak answer: *'Non!'*

The British philosopher A.J. Ayer, writing in Cyril Connolly's magazine *Horizon* in 1946, argued that existentialist complaints of the world's 'irrationality' and 'lack of ultimate purpose' arose from a misunderstanding and were 'a pointless lament'. He quoted his Austrian colleague Ludwig Wittgenstein:

We feel that even if *all possible* scientific questions be answered, the problems of life have still not been touched on at all. Of course there is then no question left, and just this is the answer.

It seemed cold comfort. As Camus had said in a footnote to his philosophical essay *Le mythe de Sisyphe* in 1942,

Even the most rigorous epistemologies imply metaphysics. And to such a degree that the metaphysic of many contemporary thinkers consists in having nothing but an epistemology.

Or, as the nineteenth-century 'idealist' philosopher F.H. Bradley had put it, the metaphysical quest might be 'finding bad reasons for what we believe on instinct', but 'to find those reasons is none the less an instinct.'

Both Sartre and Camus sought to transcend the 'anguish' or 'anxiety' involved in awareness of 'the absurd' – Sartre by an 'existential leap' of arbitrary decision-making, analogous to a religious 'leap of faith', which committed him to left-wing political causes; Camus by insisting that the mythological Sisyphus, eternally pushing his boulder up the mountainside only to see it roll to the bottom, must none the less be regarded as happy. But Europe's experience in the twentieth century made anguish and anxiety all too appropriate; and neither Sartre's nor Camus's 'solution' seemed really to work. Sartre's political 'commitment' sometimes blinded him to reality; and the 'happiness' that Camus conceded to Sisyphus seemed glum and stoical at best.

A similar numbed joylessness pervaded the work of most 'new novelists'. Like 'the new critics' or 'the Angry Young Men', they were far from homogeneous. Despite his professions of 'objectivity', Robbe-Grillet wrote vivid, seductive prose, vibrant with feeling, especially in his second and third novels, *Le voyeur* (1955) and *La jalousie* (1957). His slightly younger colleague Michel Butor explored personal relationships in more traditional fashion in *Passage de Milan* (1954) or *L'emploi du temps* and *La modification*, both published in 1957. For Nathalie Sarraute, in *Portrait d'un inconnu* (1947) and *Martereau* (1954), the penetration of social masks and the dismantling of personality seemed to hold more fascination, perhaps on account of her prewar experience as a barrister. Claude Simon and Marguerite Duras, also often grouped with the 'new novelists', were both essentially pre-occupied with the nature and effects of time.

Different as they were, they nevertheless shared more than a sombre mood. What made them 'new' was a willingness to experiment which implied great confidence in their readership. They rejected the conventions of the novel, much as the traditional 'well-made play' was now spurned – in France by Samuel Beckett, Arthur Adamov, Fernando Arrabal, Jean Genet or Eugène Ionesco, in Germany by the radio dramatist Wolfgang Hildesheimer, in Britain by the early work of Harold Pinter. Nor were the French 'new novelists' alone in bursting the confines of orthodox story-telling. In Switzerland in 1954, the established dramatist Max Frisch produced the remarkable novel *Stiller*, a phantasmagoric quest for, and rejection of, a lost identity; in Italy, after two neo-realist novels, the 29-year-old Italo Calvino had turned in 1952 to the first of several mock-medieval romances, *Il visconte dimezzato*, about the Jekyll-and-Hyde adventures of the separate halves of a knight blown in two by the Saracens. It was as dreamlike – and as subversive – as the BBC's 'Goon Show' comedies or Dylan Thomas's radio fantasy *Under Milk Wood*, first broadcast in 1954, a year after the poet's death.

The cinema, too, had its 'new wave', also mainly in France. Like many products launched with the label 'new', this was partly the result of economic pressure. A slump in the French film industry, due largely to television, made producers willing to risk money on more modest ventures; and this gave an opportunity to several younger cinephiles who had been writing about movies, chiefly in *Cahiers du cinéma*, and longing for a chance to make some.

The youngest of the group, François Truffaut, was at once the most impressive and the least experimental. His first film, *Les mistons* (1957), was a short, lyrical, and straightforward tale of love and death as seen by rather callous small boys; and his first feature film, *Les quatre cents coups* (1958), although it marked the advent of a major artist, was far from being obtrusively *avant-garde*. Equally traditional in style were Louis Malle and Claude Chabrol. Malle's first feature, the thriller *L'ascenseur pour l'échafaud* (1957) foreshadowed his later commercial career: Chabrol's, *Le beau Serge* (1958), was chiefly remarkable for the documentary virtues of its location work. Jacques Rivette's first short film, meanwhile, *Le coup de berger* (1956), was no more than a stylish sexual minuet.

Jean-Luc Godard, Agnès Varda, and the oldest of the 'new wave', Alain Resnais, were in striking contrast. Godard's first film, *Opération béton* (1954), was a simple documentary; but his second, *Une femme coquette* (1955), based on a Maupassant story, was notable for jump cuts, flash shots, disrupted continuity, and the use of a hand-held camera. Agnès Varda's first film, *La pointe courte* (1955), which Resnais edited, counterpointed two themes in a stylized fashion reminiscent of William Faulkner's novel *The Wild Palms*. Resnais, however, was the most original and disconcerting of all. Since 1948, when he was 26, he had been making short documentaries on art. His first major film, in 1955, was *Nuit et brouillard*, a study of Nazi concentration camps made in collaboration with the poet and novelist Jean Cayrol, who had been an inmate of Mauthausen. Four years afterwards, Resnais was to break cinema conventions quite decisively in the disjunctions and dislocations of *Hiroshima mon amour*, from a script by Marguerite Duras. Later, he was to work with Alain Robbe-Grillet. His films might lack the accessibility and humanism of François Truffaut: but they used the resources of the cinema to seize, bewilder, and change the spectator in ways that no other medium could. Outside France, meanwhile, the films of Ingmar Bergman in Sweden and Michelangelo Antonioni cast similar disconcerting spells.

In the cinema and on television, the general public had grown accustomed to hearing modern music, if not always understanding it. Held by the thread of a story, no one had complained at the lack of an obvious melodic line. Now, in books and films, the thread was often broken or missing; and postwar music, heard in isolation, was for many people no less disorientatingly strange.

It drew on a number of sources. Already before World War II, the Vienna school of Arnold Schoenberg and his pupils Alban Berg and Anton Webern had used the twelve-note series – a 'tonal reservoir' for composition that was mathematical rather than sensuous. Other influences were early music and the traditions of the Far East. The French composer and teacher Olivier Messiaen, in particular, echoed not only Gregorian chant but also the asymmetrical rhythms of Hindu music, notably in his symphony with a solo piano part, *Turangalîla*, first performed in 1947. In the following year Messiaen's compatriot Pierre Boulez, in his *Second Piano Sonata*, extended serial treatment from pitch to the actual duration of notes; while another Frenchman, Pierre Schaeffer, used natural sound or noise to produce '*musique concrète*'. In 1951, electronic music had its first major airing, at the Darmstadt Festival; almost simultaneously, Boulez carried his 'integral serial' technique still further in *Polyphonie X* and *Structures for Two Pianos*. The 'new novelist' Michel Butor said of Boulez that 'as his compositions grow more learned, they also grow more direct.' There was some truth in the remark: Boulez's music now had a tingling complexity. Yet, for many, it was a long way from the comparative accessibility of even such postwar German composers as Hans Werner Henze, who was moving away from twelve-note technique. When Boulez, under the influence of the American John Cage, began leaving options open, looking towards 'aleatory music', older listeners felt the foundations rock once more. In 1953 they felt a further tremor, when Karlheinz Stockhausen's *Electronic Study I* became the first electronic music to be issued on a commercial disc. Things were changing so fast that the great event of 1957, the world première at La Scala of *Les dialogues des Carmélites* by the veteran of 'les Six', Francis Poulenc, seemed to many like a comforting return to the classical past.

If postwar music disconcerted some Europeans, so did postwar art. Surprise was still possible. Matisse, in his old age, turned even more radical, producing free and lyrical shapes in cut-out coloured paper. And art could still shock. In London in 1953, Reg Butler's wiry representation of *The Unknown Political Prisoner* was mangled by an outraged visitor; not long afterwards, Graham Sutherland's fine unflattering portrait of Winston Churchill roused its sitter and his family to destroy it.

But the major battles in European art now were no longer between practitioners and the public, or sophisticates and philistines, but between rival representatives of what the British painter and novelist Wyndham Lewis called, in a polemic published in 1954, *The Demon of Progress in the Arts*.

In Paris, Picasso was still a protean force; but while like Matisse, Léger, Braque, Miró, and Max Ernst he went on pursuing his own vigorous concerns, the centre of interest was shifting. Social realism sputtered here and there; individual painters like Francis Bacon in Britain or Balthus in France produced their own compelling nightmares: but the main thrust of artistic fashion among the 'middle generation' of the Ecole de Paris and elsewhere was now towards the abstract, even when dealing with objective, external themes.

Some critics labelled this '*art informel*'; but the term was hardly apt. Painters like Jean Fautrier and Henri Michaux in France, Manolo Millares and Antonio Tapiés in Spain, Wols and Hans Hartung in Germany, or even Alberto Burri in Italy, with his torn sacking and other mutilated surfaces – all seemed to be producing curiously elegant abstract art, unconsciously embodying the classical decorative principles of balance and harmony which they supposedly eschewed. The 'Cobra' group of 1948–50, which derived its name from Copenhagen, Brussels, and Amsterdam, went further towards a free expressionism, all jolly jumbles of colour; and related to it, if only by a shared interest in children's painting, was a stricter, more organizing artist like Jean Dubuffet. More fashionable at the time, but perhaps less impressive in retrospect, were the French-Canadian Jean-Paul Riopelle, with his thick, appetizing impasto, and – in creamy contrast – the bland, beguiling, semi-abstract work of the short-lived Nicolas de Staël.

What all these painters shared, it seemed, was the influence of a gravitational pull which may have tended to sap self-confidence. The magnet was the United States, whose power had first become obvious when the Guggenheim collection had toured Europe as long ago as 1948. It was not just a matter of money – of rich collectors and patrons, a flourishing art market, or a hopeful, expansionist mood. It was also that American artists were pursuing their goals – and at present, abstract expressionism – with unprecedented vigour and attack.

While Wyndham Lewis tried to exorcise 'the demon of progress', the American critic Harold Rosenberg was producing a fusillade of counter-manifestos later collected as *The Tradition of the New*. In an age when art had deserted nature to follow criticism, the title was a manifesto in itself. It alluded, among other things, to Rosenberg's belief that 'The Frenchman has so much tradition he can easily say anything except what he wants to say.' Against the weary rituals of Europe, in other words, it championed the new art of the United States.

Here was a familiar paradox. Rather as most American families had roots in Europe, so America's postwar painters drew inspiration from previous European giants. The 'tradition of the new' which they represented was a

European tradition: what was 'new' was the energy with which they carried it on. As a critic, Rosenberg went as far as any. He invented the term 'action painting', claiming that what mattered was not merely the end-product, the finished painting, but the whole creative process, including the muscular wielding of the knife or brush. It was a further move away from respect for the art-object: later, it would culminate in auto-destructive art. Rosenberg himself was something of an 'action critic', if not auto-destructive, lashing out in all directions. But his challenge was genuine enough.

A painter friend of mine, himself an expatriate American, exemplified in his way and at his level one European response. In Italy in the early 1950's, he had worked conscientiously in a social-realist tradition, painting peasants and workmen in a style reminiscent of a sunnier Guttuso. In the mid-1950's he moved to England, and began a series of pictures of a dead crow. As they developed, they grew freer and harder to recognize, as well as extremely gloomy. Within months, his paintings were formally abstract. Then he moved to New York, where some of his work was accepted by the Guggenheim Museum. Later, he started producing all-black and all-white pictures, some with holes carefully cut in the canvas.

Not all painters in Europe were so easily influenced – although even Victor Pasmore, as early as 1947, had succumbed to the attractions of abstract art. But the American challenge was permanent. It led some Europeans into paths still less accessible to the general public, increasing the feeling that modern artists were yet another breed of 'strangers in our midst'. Above all, it aroused an uneasy suspicion. Was European art becoming parochial? Could Europe, after centuries of dominance, have ceased to be where the action was?

9

The End of Empire

It was almost time to go. Clambering over the wing-spar that divided the Vickers Valetta's cabin, the men numbered off, shouting above the roar of the engines and the rush of wind from the exit door. They watched the red light over the doorway. How much longer? Surely the – then it switched to green. Lurching forward, cumbersome with gear, they jumped.

As the parachutes jerked open, they saw the airfield below, marked with a smoke flare in the dazzle of the rising sun. But while they hung there, helpless, floating down, six hundred of them, they could hear the crackle of guns and see red tracer fire arching up.

Then, in a rush and a roll, they hit the ground, each man's container crashing first on the end of its rope, the parachute dragging and collapsing and finally freed, the container found and unpacked in thirty frenzied seconds. Armed at last, but still staggering with the weight of their equipment, they turned to face the rifle, machine-gun, and mortar fire from trenches and concrete pill-boxes on the edge of the field. Dodging behind the sand-filled oil drums that had been used to block the runway, they made for the control tower to carry out their battle plan.

In was Monday, 5 November 1956. The Third Battalion of the 16th Parachute Brigade had landed at Gamîl, on the narrow strip of land between the sea and Manzala Lake to the West of Port Saîd. Within half-an-hour they had cleared the airfield and were fighting their way westwards towards the Suez Canal, against Soviet-made rocket projectors, popularly known as 'Stalin organs', and four SU-100's – turretless 100-mm cannon mounted on the chassis of Stalin tanks.

Fifteen minutes after this British drop, five hundred tough, crew-cut *paras* of the French Second Colonial Parachute Regiment landed inland, four-and-a-half miles South-West from Gamîl, to secure the two Raswa canal bridges which were the only outlet from Port Saîd to the South. Their dropping zone was so small that they jumped from 450 feet, nearly 200 feet lower than the normal minimum. Unlike the British, they carried their rifles and sub-machine-guns tucked under their harness: but some of their jeeps and anti-tank guns went astray – a few to the North of the two bridges, others in the water, where their parachutes lay on the surface like giant lily-pads. The smaller pontoon bridge to the East was blown up before the French could reach it; but within an hour they had stormed the main bridge, which carried both the railway and the road.

In the town, fighting continued all day. Command of the air had been secured several days before, when British Canberra and Valiant bombers, aided by French F-84F fighters, had attacked the airfields and destroyed 260 aircraft on the ground. Now, Corsair fighters from the French Navy were strafing tanks, guns, and mortars, while Brigadier-General Jean Gilles, circling above the battle in a Nord-Atlas transport plane converted into a map room and communications centre, was able to direct the ground forces and keep in touch with headquarters in the ships stationed offshore. From mid-morning onwards, helicopters flew a regular service of medical and other supplies.

In the early afternoon, airborne reinforcements arrived – 100 men with heavy equipment at Gamîl, and 450 more *paras* to occupy the mainly residential town of Port Fouâd, facing Port Saîd across the mouth of the Suez Canal. In the evening, there was a brief truce, partly to evacuate wounded and partly to renew Port Saîd's water supplies, which had been cut off at Raswa.

Next morning, through the smoke, din, and flames of a huge bombardment – euphemistically called 'support fire' – a seaborne invasion followed: 130 warships carrying 100,000 men with amphibious 'Buffaloes' and other landing craft, in a smaller version of 'Overlord', the Normandy landings of 1944. The 40th and 42nd Royal Marine Commando Brigades landed on the beaches flanking Port Saîd's Casino, with a squadron of waterproofed Centurions from the Sixth Royal Tank Regiment, and the 45th Commando held in reserve, to be flown in by helicopter. Later in the day, the Second Battalion of the Parachute Regiment landed on the northernmost edge of the Suez Canal near the statue of its architect Ferdinand de Lesseps, ready to head South towards El Qantara with the Sixth tanks. The French First Colonial Parachute Regiment, meanwhile, reinforced Port Fouâd.

As the afternoon light began to fade, the first units made their way South. The day before, a patrol of the Guards Independent Company, who with some British engineers had joined in the drop of French *paras* at Raswa, had reconnoitred the road that led towards El Qantara, finding it almost empty.

They waved on the first squadron of tanks, with *paras* on top, and tried to stop them bombarding a deserted pill-box half a mile down the road. Eventually, the tanks came to a halt at El Tina, a little further on, to wait for more infantry support. By the time that British troops caught up with them, they had settled in for the night; but after an argument and an hour's delay, they motored on down the narrow tarmac Treaty Road.

To the right of them were the salt marshes; to the left, the single-track railway and the Sweet Water Canal, home of the snails that carried the liver-fluke parasite, bilharzia; beyond lay the Canal Company's road, and behind it the embankment of the Suez Canal itself. Except for a few bomb-craters and burnt-out vehicles, all seemed peaceful. 'For those who knew this road of old,' wrote one British officer, 'it even conjured up memories of driving home to one of the Canal garrison towns after dining late and well at some Port Saîd restaurant or club.'

But the world had changed since those privileged evenings. At midnight GMT, 0200 hours local time, the advance party halted, in a huddled position almost impossible to defend, at the village of El Cap, six miles short of El Qantara. It had to. The whole expedition had been called off.

Its abrupt cancellation, like the snap of a hypnotist's fingers, dispelled a number of illusions. For years, often reluctantly, European countries had been withdrawing from the imperial past. The Suez adventure of 1956 revealed unmistakably how far their retreat had come.

Like most great transformations, the end of empire was gradual; and there was cause for regret in it as well as much to welcome. It had become inevitable partly on account of changes brought by the colonists themselves: better communications; travel and the growth of towns; a sense of nationhood to compete with village or tribal loyalties; new technology; medical care; the Christian attack on traditional ways, including cannibalism and human sacrifice; education and scope for political activists; more sophisticated weapons; military training and involvement in war.

Before World War II, the countries of Western Europe had ruled vast areas of the world. Almost the only exceptions were Spain, long ago bereft of empire, and Germany, stripped of her colonies after World War I. Of the rest, Portugal, Italy, the Netherlands, Belgium, France, and Britain remained imperial powers, controlling directly or indirectly most of South-East Asia, parts of the West Indies, nearly all of Africa, and much of the Middle East. Within a few years after the war, what had once been colonies had turned into independent sovereign states – more than fifty of them, with a total population of 800 million people. Few were richer or more peaceful: but now, at least, they were responsible for their own affairs.

To Britain, the Suez Canal had been above all the short sea route to India. Yet India, so long the centre-piece of the overseas Empire, had been the first to go after World War II. For many years, the Indian National Congress Party, led by the ascetic, sandal-shod, shaven-headed 'Mahatma' Gandhi and the more worldly Jawaharlal Nehru, had been pressing for independence. On 3 September 1939, when the British Viceroy Lord Linlithgow had declared war against Hitler on India's behalf, many Indians had been incensed. 'There was something rotten,' said Nehru, 'when one man, and he a foreigner and representative of a hated system, could plunge 400 million human beings into war without a slightest reference to them.' During the war, Indian regiments had fought loyally, gallantly, and ferociously: but Indians were no longer content to be rewarded, as after World War I, with vague promises of autonomy. In 1942, when Sir Stafford Cripps had made just such promises, Gandhi had dismissed them as 'a postdated cheque'.

In the following year, Field Marshal Lord Wavell had been appointed to succeed Linlithgow as Viceroy. A scholarly and sympathetic man, he personally favoured Indian independence, and was discouraged by Britain's prevarications. More discouraging still were the tribal, racial, and religious rivalries which now threatened to fragment the sub-continent. While Congress was hoping to build a united independent republic, the Sikhs demanded autonomy for themselves, and many of the 584 princely States wanted to retain the protection of the British Crown. Moreover, Congress now faced a rival in the form of the Muslim League, headed by the tall, gaunt Mohammed Ali Jinnah – a convert to Islam and a former associate of Gandhi. The League represented only 90 million Muslims in a country of 250 million Hindus: but Jinnah argued that 'Muslims are not a minority as the word is commonly understood. Muslims are a nation.'

In 1946, when Clement Attlee's British Government called for elections in India, the country split along religious lines. Congress gained a majority in the central Assembly, and formed eight governments in the provinces. Jinnah's League won all the 'Muslim' seats in the Assembly, and formed two provincial governments, in Bengal and Sind. The Punjab elected a united government, representing a very mixed population. Soon afterwards, Britain sent Sir Stafford Cripps on a further mission to negotiate a settlement. To reassure the Muslim minority, he proposed the so-called 'three-tier plan': a Constituent Assembly, responsible for foreign affairs and defence; a number of Provincial Groups, most of them Hindu, but Muslim in the North-West; and two Independent Provinces – Bengal and Assam.

Provisionally, both Congress and the Muslim League accepted Cripps's plan. For a while it looked as if Indian unity might be shakily preserved. But then Gandhi and Nehru began to argue that the Constituent Assembly should have greater power – and Jinnah scented danger. Rather than risk being swamped by the Hindu majority, he revived the idea of an independent Muslim State of 'Pakistan'.

This term had been invented – by Indian students at Cambridge, England – as long ago as 1932. At the time, it had seemed like a pipe-dream: 'Pak', in Urdu, meant 'religiously pure'. But even then the word had had geographical implications. P stood for the Punjab, A for the Afghan North-West frontier, K for Kashmir, and S for Sind. Now, with Jinnah's backing, the concept of Pakistan acquired political force. At the end of July 1946, he announced what he called a 'Direct Action Day'. It took place on 16 August, which was declared a public holiday in Calcutta by the Provincial Government in Bengal. What began as a demonstration ended in four days of rioting, which cost the lives of four to five thousand people, most of them Hindus. 'We are not yet in the middle of civil war,' said Gandhi, 'but we are nearing it.'

To forestall further violence, Attlee summoned the Indian leaders to a conference in London. Like Cripps's two missions, it made little progress; and the British Government's final communiqué broadly hinted that partition might be on the cards. At last, in February 1947, Attlee announced that India would become independent no later than January 1948 – and that Wavell was to be replaced as Viceroy by Admiral Lord Louis Mountbatten.

, Handsome, dashing, colourful, and royal, the 46-year-old Mountbatten had been wartime Supreme Commander in South-East Asia. Now, in regal fashion, he and Lady Mountbatten were to preside over the abdication of the British Raj. For ten weeks, from 22 March until 3 June 1947, the British conferred ceaselessly with Nehru, Gandhi, Jinnah, and others. Relations were very friendly. Nehru, in particular, responded warmly to the charm of both the Mountbattens, and some members of the British Mission hoped for general agreement on a variant of Cripps's three-tier plan. But Mountbatten's talks convinced him that partition was necessary, along lines proposed by his Reforms Commissioner, Vapal Pangunni Menon; and his temperament urged speed. At the end of May he flew to London to argue that the

Independence Bill be pushed through Parliament unopposed. On 3 June, speaking on All-India Radio with Nehru, Jinnah, and the Sikh leader Sardar Baldar Singh, Mountbatten announced that in future there would be two countries – India and Pakistan. Asked by reporters when independence would be granted, he gave the date as 15 August, the second anniversary of Japan's surrender at the end of World War II. The Indian Independence Bill raced through Parliament in London, and received the Royal Assent on 18 July. Twenty-eight days later, British rule in India came to an end after 250 years.

Those who witnessed the final scenes were full of mixed feelings. One British friend of mine, a Captain in the Royal Garhwal Rifles, wrote on the day after Mountbatten's broadcast:

In October, then, I shall be saying goodbye to the Garhwalis, not without a lump in my throat. This may amaze a British service officer like yourself, but you would doubtless feel the same had you had the good fortune to come to this particular part of the world....
One feels particularly for our chaps now, as their future is far from rosy. The Viceroy's statement yesterday seemed to imply that there is now no hope of a united India. Pakistan is almost a certainty now, and with it the almost complete disruption of the armed forces. As ours is an all-Hindu class regiment it will become part of the Hindustan army, mercenary and officered to a large extent by Sikhs, whom Garhwalis detest; they are actually the most parochial people in the world, and view with suspicion and contempt any Indian who is not actually a Garhwali.

India was a mass of similar antagonisms. When the lines of partition were laid down, they cut across innumerable human boundaries, slicing through loyalties and traditions, dividing communities and separating friends. The proud Sikhs had to accept that they were a sect, not a nation; and in the Punjab in particular there was a wild scramble to find new homes on the right side of the frontier. The roads and railways, always crowded as in Kipling's day, suddenly teemed with eleven million refugees. Many were fleeing for their lives. In all, at least 200,000 people died in what Nehru called 'an orgy of murder and arson'.

Nevertheless, India was free; and the long-feared civil war with Pakistan did not take place. At 8.30 a.m. on Friday 15 August 1947, the British flags were ceremonially lowered, to be replaced by the Indian Wheel of Ashoka and the star and crescent of Pakistan. That night, Delhi was invaded by jubilant crowds so huge that the military parade which was due to mark the occasion had to be cancelled. When the Mountbattens' coach made its way back through the throng to the Governor-General's palace, Nehru was riding on the hood – 'like a school-boy', Mountbatten said. Nehru's school, as it happened, had been Harrow. When I met him myself, years afterwards, he still spoke in rich Old Harrovian tones, and still obviously felt deep affinities with Britain. For all its faults, indeed, British rule had left the new India with an educated middle class and an efficient civil service; for all its weaknesses, Indian democracy was as genuine as any in the post-colonial 'developing world'.

Gandhi hardly survived to see it. He had long opposed partition. Now, he went on preaching reconciliation between Muslims and Hindus. But moderation, as always, aroused the fury of fanatics. On Friday 30 January 1948, less than six months after the independence he had championed so nobly, Gandhi was shot dead by a young Hindu zealot, at a prayer meeting in the garden of Birla House in New Delhi. His followers, his old opponents, and even people who had never known him – all reeled from the blow. 'It is like a defeat for God,' wrote André Gide.

Gandhi had been a prophet. 'If India becomes free,' he had told President Franklin D. Roosevelt in 1942, 'the rest will follow.' They soon did.

On 4 January 1948, a few weeks before Gandhi's death, Britain withdrew from Burma. A month later, Ceylon acquired Dominion status. Much the same might have happened to the States and Sultanates of Malaya, which the British Government had formed into a 'Malayan Union' as a prelude to independence; but the plan was scotched by social and inter-racial strife. The Malay élites not only objected to centralization and continued British rule: they also resented Britain's offer of citizenship to Chinese and Indian minorities. In a series of concerted moves, they formed a network of nationalist political groups, merged their old cultural societies into a 'United Malays National Organization', and boycotted the official launching of the new régime. Before long, Britain replaced it with a looser 'Federation'.

This satisfied the Malays; but to the Chinese and their left-wing leaders it seemed too much like a return to the past. In the Spring of 1948, several thousand revolutionaries – many of whom had been armed by the British during the war against the Japanese – began a campaign of terror. Digging up their caches of weapons, they formed mobile guerrilla groups deep in the twilit jungle, emerging to attack roads, intimidate villages, and murder estate owners, planters, and foremen. Some of their victims they tied to chairs and shot; others they executed in public, with anti-imperialist lectures addressed to the frightened crowd. Britain declared a state of emergency, and fought back; but by March 1950 the so-called 'CTs' – 'Communist Terrorists' –

had killed 863 civilians, 323 police officers, and 154 soldiers. In 1951, they ambushed and assassinated the British High Commissioner, Sir Henry Gurney.

Some British officials, sympathetic to the villagers and critical of settler and Sultanate society, nonetheless found the terrorists baffling. 'Why', wrote a friend of mine in the UK Commissioner General's office in Singapore, 'do the Malayan Communists continue their most dangerous, uncomfortable, and seemingly hopeless struggle?' 'The answer', he concluded, 'lies in the policy – or rather, lack of it – on the Chinese immigrant community pre-war.' But now –

at the expense of the wretched local inhabitants – the 'cold war' is allowed to 'hot up' in a manner which reminds me most vividly of the thesis of the 'no-man's' area in between the two power blocs which George Orwell expounded in *Nineteen Eighty-four....*
 I have yet to be at all convinced that there is any conclusive reason why the Malayan Communist Party should not, if party interests so dictate, continue its present terrorist campaign indefinitely.

In fact, two things brought it to a halt. One was a dogged, ruthless, and highly sophisticated military effort, fighting the enemy with almost clinical precision, on the ground. Much of it was carried out by the Special Air Service (SAS) Regiment, with other units from Britain, Australia, New Zealand, East Africa, and Fiji. For two years, it was master-minded by General Sir Gerald Templer. Asked in June 1952 how many troops he needed, he coined what became a slogan: 'The answer lies not in pouring more soldiers into the jungle, but rests in the hearts and minds of the Malayan people.' This was the second half of the story. While guerrilla warfare continued, the country made steady progress towards self-govern-ment, disarming opponents of 'imperialism' by removing the target they attacked. In 1957, Malaya became independent, under the Cambridge-educated leader of a multi-racial 'Alliance', Tunku Abdul Rahman. Three years later, the emergency came to an end.

While Britain's empire East of Suez was thus being gradually dismantled, the Suez Canal lost some of its strategic significance. It was still an important commercial artery; but by 5 November 1956, when the British and French invasion forces were so suddenly ordered to halt on the Treaty Road running South from Port Saîd, conditions in Egypt had changed no less drastically than those in the Far East.

Nine years earlier, when I had so often driven along that same road, no such invasion would have been called for: more than 60,000 British troops had been stationed in the Canal Zone, and Egypt was still in the soft hands of King Farouk. Nominally, his kingdom had been independent since 1936. In practice, however relucantly, he was under British tutelage – a fact most sharply demonstrated on the evening of 2 February 1942, when the towering British Ambassador, Sir Miles Lampson, had stormed into the Abdin Palace and demanded that Farouk either appoint a government more favourable to Britain's war effort, or abdicate the throne. Farouk had complied; and although Egypt remained neutral until 1945, Cairo had continued to be in effect a British military base. Even when the GHQ of Middle East Land Forces withdrew to Fayid, halfway down the Canal near the shore of the Great Bitter Lake, the British Embassy's radio link continued to be serviced by British Army signalmen in civilian clothes, ferried to and fro in disguised military trucks. One of them, I remember, pretended to be a laundry van.

The need for subterfuge was a sign of the times. Outside Cairo, British and Egyptians still mingled amicably in such oases as the Young Men's Muslim Association; but by the time I left Egypt in the summer of 1947, any UK troops driven through the capital had to travel in trucks protected by steel mesh. As the years went by, Egyptians grew more restive. In October 1951, Prime Minister Nahas Pasha put forward a series of decrees in effect asserting sovereignty over the Sudan – until then a condominium shared with the British – and repudiating the Anglo-Egyptian Treaty of 1936. In the following January, anti-British riots broke out. Europeans were killed in the streets of Cairo, and the Turf Club and the old building of Shepheard's Hotel were burned down.

Then came the decisive change. On the night of 22–23 July 1952, a group of Egyptian Army officers staged a *coup d'état*. Taking over the Palace, they forced King Farouk to abdicate in favour of his infant son, leaving power in the hands of a Council of Regency appointed by themselves. Within a year, the Council had proclaimed a Republic, and General Mohammed Neguib became its first President. A rugged, soldierly figure, half-Sudanese, Neguib was popular with the masses; but before long he was revealed as little more than a figurehead. The real leader of the revolution had been the 34-year-old Colonel Gamal Abdel Nasser. In April 1954 he became Prime Minister and in the following November he succeeded Neguib as President.

A devout Muslim, tall and graceful, with lustrous dark eyes and a huge curved nose, Nasser confessed that all his life he had been a conspirator. As a child, the story went, every time he saw an aircraft in the sky he had shouted:

Ya 'Azîz, Ya 'Azîz,
Dihiya takhud al-Inglîz!
Oh Almighty, Oh Almighty,
Disaster take the English!

Before joining the army he had studied law, and had been arrested in several
student riots. Although an opponent of the monarchy, he had seen Farouk's
humiliation in 1942 as an affront to all Egyptians. One of his friends aptly
described him as 'a man of ice and fire'. Like most of his compatriots, he
could be a master of courtesy and restraint: but he was also a passionate
orator, and his own polished fury was redoubled when turned into demotic
speech by the propagandists of Cairo Radio, 'The Voice of the Arabs'.

As the French Foreign Minister Christian Pineau was to discover,
Nasser's tone grew violent at any mention of Israel. 'One moment cool,
measured, and reasonable, he changed before my eyes. In a voice swollen
with rage, he launched an irrational diatribe against Israel, blaming the Jews
for all Egypt's troubles. Arguing like a demagogue, he accused Britain of
having set up the State of Israel as a last manoeuvre of colonialism.'

Nasser's emotion was understandable. When Israel had been established in
May 1948, Egypt, Iraq, and Jordan had waged war on her for eight months:
but the only result of their efforts had been to enlarge the new State's
frontiers and further discredit King Farouk. However, to see the establishment of Israel as the outcome of British scheming was to misread recent
history. Previously, it was true, Palestine had been a virtual colony,
'mandated' to Britain by the League of Nations after World War I. Even
then it had been an embarrassment, riven by conflict between the Arabs and
the Jewish settlers. World War II and Hitler's death camps had immeasurably deepened the longing of many Jews for the 'National Home' they had
been promised by the Balfour Declaration of 1917: and the Jewish Agency,
with United States support, had applied for 100,000 immigration permits.
This had alarmed the Palestinian Arabs; and Ernest Bevin, Britain's Foreign
Secretary, had delayed and prevaricated, clamping down meanwhile on
'illegal' immigration.

The response had been a wave of Zionist terrorism. On 22 July 1946, a
bomb planted by members of Menachem Begin's organization, Irgun Zvai
Leumi, had killed nearly a hundred people at the King David Hotel in
Jerusalem. Gruesome as this was, it caused less anger in London than the
hanging of two British sergeants a year later in a eucalyptus grove near

Nathanya – perhaps because by that time nerves had become more frayed. In August 1947, a United Nations Special Committee recommended that Britain's mandate in Palestine be ended as soon as possible; and on 14 May 1948, unreluctantly, she formally withdrew. There was no disguising the fact that her rule had been a failure. The proclamation of the State of Israel was less a colonialist manoeuvre than an Imperial retreat. Nasser might have judged it differently if he had known, or chosen to remember, that in the subsequent warfare the Israelis had shot down five RAF aircraft flying under Egyptian command.

Nor was this the only erosion of Britain's position in the Middle East. Hitherto, friendly or compliant rulers in the desert States had promised political stability and security for oil supplies. Now, Arab nationalists were rapidly gaining ground. Governments everywhere, from Amman to Baghdad, from Damascus and Beirut to Teheran, were beginning to be shaken by plots, riots, assassinations, and attempted coups.

In Transjordan, Britain had enjoyed a 'mandate' which expired in 1946. Three years later, the country annexed territory to the West of the Jordan river, and adopted 'Jordan' as its official name. Its ruler was still the 67-year-old Abdullah Ibn Hussein, who had been an ally of T.E. Lawrence – 'Lawrence of Arabia' – in World War I; he was also an Air Commodore in the British Royal Air Force, and the holder of a knighthood conferred by King George V. In 1951, however, he was assassinated; and a year later his grandson Hussein became King. The young Hussein was a product of Harrow and Sandhurst: but this very fact now offended some of his subjects. They also disliked his continued reliance on General Sir John Glubb, the veteran British commander of the Arab Legion. Such an anachronism, they felt, could not be allowed to last much longer.

Elsewhere, admittedly, World War II had seen a sharp assertion of Britain's power. In a few summer months of 1941, British troops had occupied or helped to occupy four countries: Iraq in May; Syria and the Lebanon in July, together with Free French forces; and Iran in August, in uneasy partnership with the Soviet Union. But once the war was over, wartime expedients had to cease.

The British stayed on in Iraq until 1947, and maintained an air base at Habbaniya for several years more. King Feisal II and his Prime Minister Nuri-es-Saîd were close friends of Britain; and their capital gave its name to the Baghdad Pact, signed in February 1955 by Iraq and Turkey, and later joined by Britain and Pakistan. But the Pact was bitterly resented by Egypt and by some other members of the newly-established Arab League; and in Iraq itself there was a powerful nationalist movement headed by Brigadier Abdul Karim Kassem, whose revolutionaries were eventually to murder both Feisal and Nuri in July 1958.

Syria had become independent on 1 January 1944, and the last foreign troops had withdrawn in April 1946. Meanwhile, the Ba'ath ('Resurrection') Party led by Michel Aflaq had been preaching 'Freedom, Unity, and Socialism' in 'one Arab nation with an eternal mission'; and in 1952 it made common cause with the Socialist Party of Akram Hourani. It was also influential across the border in the Lebanon, which had become independent at the same time – although there French troops had remained even longer, until December 1946. For some years, incredible as it might seem later, the Lebanon was one of the more peaceful of the Arab States. It maintained political stability by combining in office a Maronite Uniat Christian President, a Sunni Muslim Prime Minister, and a Shia Muslim President of the Assembly. But the balance was always precarious, and it became more so after the assassination in July 1951 of Prime Minister Riyadh al-Sulh.

In Iran, where the Soviet Union was seeking oil concessions, trouble had come much sooner. As early as 1945, there had been conflict with a Soviet-backed separatist movement in the North-Western province of Azerbaijan. Three years later, when the Iranian Government began to negotiate a new agreement on royalties with the Anglo-Iranian Oil Company at Abadan, it ran into vehement opposition from Dr Mohammed Moussadeq, a rich 70-year-old landowner and militant nationalist who had been Foreign Minister before the war. In March 1951 the Prime Minister, General Razmara, was assassinated. The Assembly then voted to nationalize the oil industry; and two weeks of rioting in Abadan induced the Shah to appoint Moussadeq in Razmara's place. In October, the Anglo-Iranian Oil Company withdrew its technicians. Without them, the Iranians seemed unable to produce and sell more than small quantities of oil. In January 1952, Britain closed down her consulates in Iran; in August, Moussadeq was granted six months' dictatorial powers. In October, he broke off diplomatic relations with Britain. But his quarrelsome regime and querulous nature grew more and more unpopular; and in 1953 the Shah dismissed him. After an attempted coup and a counter-coup, Moussadeq was arrested and imprisoned on charges of treason. For some years, all was calm. Only a prophet could have known that Iran's misfortunes were by no means at an end.

In all these countries, as elsewhere, European dominance was being called in question – partly by the new nationalist pride of once subject peoples, partly by the hard fact that in a world increasingly dominated by the super-powers, European countries lacked the strength, the wealth, and the arrogance to sustain their former role.

In the Middle East, the change was most spectacular, perhaps, in Egypt itself. The palatial Embassies and Residencies were still there; so were many Europeans – diplomats, advisers, agents, technicians, merchants, experts, long-term resident expatriates of every kind. Taking coffee on the sparse lawn under the palm trees at the French Club in Ismailia, or playing cricket on a coconut-matting pitch surrounded by sand, it was still just possible to fancy that nothing had altered – or, if it had, that charm, experience, and influence could still succeed where power was on the wane.

Anthony Eden evidently thought so, at least at first. On 20 February 1955, while he was still Foreign Secretary to Sir Winston Churchill and still six weeks away from succeeding him as Premier, Eden passed through Cairo on his way to the Far East, and invited Nasser to dine with him at the British Embassy. When the President arrived, Eden greeted him in rather literary Arabic, making graceful allusions to poetry and the Qur'ān. It was well-meant. But, with Eden's patrician air and his elegant dinner-jacket, it seemed to Nasser to smack of condescension, as if 'to a junior official who could not be expected to understand politics'.

In fact, Nasser was anxious to discuss the impending Baghdad Pact, which he saw as an alliance between imperialists and reactionaries, and which he feared might split the Cairo-based Arab League. As he explained afterwards to the American journalist and historian Kennett Love:

I began to express our point of view about the Baghdad Pact and the results of the pact – the splits in the Arab country. And Mr Eden was just listening. I was not, of course, pleased with that – just listening without any comments. Then I talked from the military point of view about the defence of this area. I said to Mr Eden that we can have an Arab Defence Organization – united – and this can represent a defence in depth if there is any aggression from the Soviet Union. But we don't want any other country to be a partner because if you participate in this agreement, this would mean to our people that we are working as agents for your interests, not for the interests of the Arabs.

Eden thought Nasser 'a fine man physically', but told his colleague Selwyn Lloyd, soon to be Foreign Secretary, that he had been annoyed when Nasser had seized his hand just as they were being photographed, before their talk. The resultant raised handclasp looked curiously artificial, like the beginning of a round dance. 'Nasser', Eden wrote, 'was not, however, open to conviction on the Turco-Iraqi enterprise [the Baghdad Pact]. I commented on this in my report to London at the time, adding: "No doubt jealousy plays a part in this and a frustrated desire to lead the Arab world."' It was when that desire no longer appeared frustrated that Eden grew alarmed.

He was already easily upset. Tall, handsome, and urbane, but short-tempered in private, he was described by Christian Pineau as 'a sort of British Nehru, and fragile as well. A marvellous diplomat, he was not built like Churchill to be Prime Minister during a grave international crisis.' Renowned for having opposed the 'appeasement' of Hitler in the 1930's, he had for years been Churchill's adjutant. Now that he was at last taking command, his health was giving him trouble. He suffered from jaundice; a gall-bladder operation in 1953 had damaged his bile duct, and had had to be followed by two more. To make matters worse, Eden was mistrusted by fellow-Conservatives. Some had never forgiven him for agreeing, as Foreign Secretary, to evacuate British troops from their base on the Suez Canal.

The Cairo riots of January 1952 had already shown how vulnerable the base had become. Two months later, fearing a coup, the United States Government had advised Britain to begin withdrawing her forces; and the overthrow of King Farouk in July had seemed to prove the point. In December, the Cabinet had decided to transfer its Middle East headquarters to Cyprus, and had set in hand the practical preparations. Early in 1953, Eden had proposed a package deal: gradually to withdraw British troops, but to leave a military base in the Canal Zone for use if needed, and to involve Egypt in a Middle East defence organization, backed by British and American aid. All along, he had hoped to include the United States in his talks with Egypt: but the State Department had seemed lukewarm, and Egypt's new rulers actively objected, demanding first and foremost Britain's agreement to withdraw her troops. Finally, on 19 October 1954, after laborious negotiations, and with careful provisos about future port and air facilities, the Government had formally agreed to evacuate the Canal Zone within twenty months – i.e., by 19 June 1956.

Defending the decision, Eden argued that it had been unavoidable. Even without a new agreement, the 1936 Treaty between Britain and Egypt would have expired in August 1956, leaving no legal pretext for a continued British presence, and no right to maintain a military base. The argument failed to appease his critics – the more so as the deadline approached. Some thought that he should have postponed it; others objected to Britain's withdrawing at all. Egypt, they admitted, might be an unstable base for Middle East headquarters: but Cyprus, the new location, was already in turmoil itself. Greek Cypriots, led by the fiery, bearded Archbishop Makarios, had long been demanding '*enosis*' or union with Greece. Now, on 1 April 1955, terrorists from EOKA, the *Ethniki Organosis Kyprion Agoniston* or National Organization of Cypriot Fighters, headed by Colonel George Grivas, made a series of bomb attacks which initiated four years of guerrilla warfare. To remove British troops from their familiar surroundings in Egypt to the new hazards of Cyprus seemed to Eden's Conservative critics both undignified and unwise.

Their disquiet was increased by the knowledge that Nasser was in touch with the EOKA rebels. He seemed, in fact, to have a finger in every pie. On 9 April 1955, he even went to South-East Asia, to attend the week-long conference of 29 independent Asian and African countries – with Greek Cypriot observers – at Bandung in Indonesia, the former Dutch East Indies.

These had already been the scene of another imperial retreat. In August 1945, the Japanese surrender had left a power vacuum not yet filled by returning Dutch settlers, and Indonesian nationalists had seized their chance, proclaiming independence in the city of Batavia, which they renamed 'Jakarta'. When the Dutch returned, fighting had broken out; and British help had been needed to secure a truce. Both sides agreed to set up a United States of Indonesia, linked with the Netherlands: but before long they quarrelled and clashed. The nationalists mounted guerrilla attacks. The settlers suppressed them with 'police actions' – so brutally that several countries, including Australia and India, appealed to the United Nations. At length, after a conference at The Hague, all the former Dutch East Indies except West New Guinea became independent at the end of 1949, together with ex-Dutch Borneo. In August 1950, the federation which had originally been proposed was transformed into a unitary State, dominated by Java and ruled by the 49-year-old Achmed Sukarno, a founder-member of the Indonesia Nationalist Party. He it was who now played host at Bandung.

Sukarno's aim in calling the Bandung conference was to persuade Asian and African countries to agree on a policy of 'non-alignment' in the 'cold war' between East and West. In large measure, he succeeded. The spirit of solidarity evoked at Bandung was not to last; but it expressed what Nehru called the 'new dynamism' which had been developing over the past fifty years, not only in Asia but also in Africa.

Only two Black African countries were represented. One was Liberia, economically dominated by the Firestone Rubber Plantation Company, but politically independent since its foundation in 1847. The other was the Gold Coast, which in 1957, under Kwame Nkrumah, was to become Ghana, the first Black African State to emerge from colonial rule. There was also, however, an observer from the African National Congress, led by the Zulu Albert Luthuli, a non-violent opponent of South African *apartheid*; and the conference was watched with interest all over Africa, where some more militant nationalists had already taken up arms. The French had faced rebellion in Madagascar as early as 1947. In Kenya, in the three years following 1952, Mau Mau terrorists – disavowed by the nationalist leader Jomo Kenyatta – murdered 68 Europeans and more than 1,800 Africans before their methods discredited them among their fellow-Kikuyu as well as with other tribes. Even where there were no major clashes, many African leaders were now flexing their muscles. They ranged from Left-wing extremists like Sekou Touré in French Guinea or Patrice Lumumba in the Belgian Congo (later Zaïre) to Christians like Julius Nyerere in Tanganyika (Tanzania) or Kenneth Kaunda in Northern Rhodesia (Zambia). Many were Westernized statesmen like Dr Hastings Banda in Nyasaland (Malawi), the American-educated Mnamdi Azikiwe in Nigeria, the French-language poet Léopold Senghor in Senegal, or – in the Ivory Coast – Félix Houphouët-Boigny, for many years an influential member of the French National Assembly. Westernized or not, their common objective was independence; and it was echoed as far away as Guiana (now Guyana) in the West Indies, where British rule had been challenged most notably in 1953 by the Marxist Dr Cheddi Jagan.

None of them was at Bandung; but altogether the conference represented a population of 1,300 million people, and it was a great success for Sukarno. It was also a triumph for Nasser, who persuaded it to endorse his position over Palestine, and emerged as the eloquent spokesman, if not quite the leader, of the Middle-Eastern Arab world.

If Nasser's role at Bandung caused concern in London, there was more anxiety a few weeks later, when he asked the Soviet Union for weapons – and more still in September, when a first deal was clinched. Anthony Eden was especially troubled. 'On no account must we let the Russians into the Nile Valley,' he remarked. Nor was this his only worry. In May, the Conservative Party had won an increased majority in a General Election, partly thanks to an expansionary, give-away Budget produced the month before by the

Chancellor of the Exchequer, R.A. Butler. Five months later, the Government was forced into harsher measures to curb inflation and help the balance of payments – a classic instance of 'stop-go' economic policy. Shortly afterwards, Eden reshuffled his Cabinet, replacing Butler by Harold Macmillan. Amid mounting Tory criticism, he was predictably nettled when Butler called him 'the best Prime Minister we've got'.

He was annoyed still more on 3 January 1956, when an editorial in the Conservative *Daily Telegraph* denounced not only his 'half measures' in domestic policy but also his 'clumsy courtship of unfriendly and fickle Arab statesmen'. Witheringly, it declared:

There is a favourite gesture of the Prime Minister's.... To emphasize a point he will clench one fist to smack the open palm of the other hand – but the smack is seldom heard. Most Conservatives, and almost certainly some of the wiser trade union leaders, are waiting to feel the smack of firm government.

The words hurt. 'I had never seen Eden so stricken,' wrote his friend and colleague Anthony Nutting. 'He was positively writhing in the agony of this barbed shaft which, unlike some of the blunter and cruder assaults of the Opposition, had struck him at his weakest point.'

What most infuriated Eden, however, was the gradual collapse of his plans for the Middle East. In December 1955, he had sent General Sir Gerald Templer to Jordan, in an effort to persuade King Hussein to join the Baghdad Pact. Instantly, Cairo Radio screamed abuse. Savage riots broke out in Amman, killing 41 people and injuring 150 others. After a series of Cabinet crises, Hussein was obliged to refuse.

Within months came an even sharper setback. On 1 March 1956, the new Foreign Secretary, Selwyn Lloyd, dined with Nasser at a banquet in the Tahra Palace, Cairo, given by the Egyptian Foreign Minister Mahmoud Fawzi – 'a smooth and rather slippery customer,' Lloyd noted, 'but well-mannered and personally pleasant to deal with.' As the dinner came to an end, a message was brought to Sir Humphrey Trevelyan, the British Ambassador. On the way back to the Embassy, he told Lloyd the news: General Sir John Glubb – 'Glubb Pasha' of Hussein's Arab Legion – had been dismissed.

For Hussein it had been a painful decision. 'The last thing I desired was to hurt his feelings, nor was it a pleasant task to dismiss a man who had served our country so faithfully for twenty-six years.' But the King had been worried for a year or more by differences over strategy; and unrest among his own Arab officers now threatened to endanger the throne.

For Glubb, the news was heartbreaking. On his way home to tell his wife, he looked at the cemetery where his second son had been buried nine years before. 'I had thought perhaps I should be buried there too,' he wrote.

For the British Government, Glubb's dismissal was a body-blow – and it smarted the more by pure chance. Nasser believed, he said later, that the British themselves had removed Glubb. Meeting Lloyd again next morning, he exclaimed jovially: 'Congratulations! This was a very good move from your side.' Lloyd, who had spent most of the night conferring with London, was outraged by what he thought a mocking 'pretence'. Eden, for his part, believed that Nasser was responsible – 'the arch enemy', as Selwyn Lloyd called him. 'You love Nasser,' Eden exclaimed to Anthony Nutting, 'but I say he is our enemy and he shall be treated as such.'

A few months later, Nasser gave further cause for concern. The Bandung conference had included a hundred-strong delegation from the People's Republic of China, established in Peking on 1 October 1949, but still diplomatically boycotted by most Western nations, including the United States. On Nasser, the ubiquitous Chinese had made a great impression; and both he and Nehru had found much to discuss with Prime Minister Chou En-Lai. Now, in May 1956, Egypt formally recognized Communist China, marking a further distance between herself and the West. And in July, Nasser went on his travels again – this time to spend a week on the Yugoslav island of Brioni, conferring with Nehru and Marshal Tito.

He may merely have wanted to escape Cairo's midsummer heat: but Eden saw it differently. Nasser, once an obscure Arab colonel, had become a provocative actor on the international scene. Egypt, so long a British base, and still the site of a vital seaway, was slipping out of control. At one time, the offer of Western armaments might have held Nasser in check; but now he had committed himself to buying them from the Soviet Union.

Was there no way to influence this unpredictable man? Perhaps there was one inducement that might tempt him. He had long nursed a great ambition: the Saad el Ali or Aswan High Dam.

Four miles up the Nile from the existing Aswan Dam built by British engineers in 1898, the proposed High Dam would hold 26 times as much water, and increase Egypt's arable land by at least a sixth. It would also, Nasser hoped, make the country self-sufficient in hydro-electric power, and remove any fear that her precious water supplies might be cut off from Lake Victoria. If the West would help finance and build the dam, co-operation might lead to friendship – or, at the least, to the healing of ancient wounds.

Egypt had been discussing the project with Britain and America since November 1955. For a time, the talks had seemed promising; but Eugene Black, President of the International Bank for Reconstruction and Development, had lately begun to have doubts. So had the State Department. As Robert Bowie, then Assistant Secretary of State, explained later, there were three main reasons: Nasser's Soviet arms purchases, which had mortgaged resources that could have gone to the dam; the worries expressed by the Sudan and Ethiopia, further upstream; and growing objections in the US Congress.

The Congressional Committees had shown themselves very reluctant to see any of the funds appropriated being devoted to this Dam project.... It would only be used for irrigation of land suitable for cotton – and a good many of the cotton senators were not particularly eager to finance this additional surplus cotton.

There was one last reason which was still more cogent. Early in the talks, President Eisenhower had secretly sent a private envoy to Egypt, to find out whether finance for the dam might persuade Nasser to reach a settlement with Israel. The mission proved disappointing, and American doubts grew. Sensing hesitation, the Egyptian Ambassador in Washington told the State Department that, if the United States would not help, he felt sure that the Soviet Union would. The implied threat backfired. On 19 July 1956, Secretary of State John Foster Dulles announced bluntly that the offer of aid was withdrawn. Nasser admitted afterwards: 'I was surprised by the insulting attitude with which the refusal was declared. Not by the refusal itself.' Eden professed to be surprised, and 'sorry that the matter was carried through so abruptly'; but the British Government had already cooled to the project too.

What no one predicted was Nasser's response. It came just one week later, on Thursday 26 July. Eden was dining at No 10 with King Feisal of Iraq and Nuri-es-Saîd when he heard the news. Nasser had declared martial law in Egypt and seized the Suez Canal.

He had made the announcement that evening from the balcony of the Bourse in Alexandria. His three-hour speech, full of scorn, menace, sarcasm, hatred, fury, and triumph, swayed the vast crowd like wind lashing a wheatfield. He had tossed aside the language of formal oratory, and was using the harsh vernacular of the streets.

The West's and the World Bank's terms for financing the Aswan High Dam, he declared, would have been crippling – 'tyranny without troops'.

I looked at Mr Black sitting in his chair, and I began to think I was looking at ... Ferdinand de Lesseps!

That name, spoken on the dot of 10 p.m., was a pre-arranged signal to Nasser's men up and down the Canal. Hearing it on their radios, they broke into the Canal Company's premises, turned their guns on its employees, and commanded them to obey Egyptian orders. Within the next ten minutes, Nasser repeated 'de Lesseps' fourteen times.

We dug the Canal with our lives, our skulls, our bones, our blood.... But the Canal did not belong to Egypt – Egypt belonged to the Canal.... Today, O citizens, with the income of the Suez Canal – one hundred million dollars a year, in five years five hundred million – we can do without a paltry seventy million of American aid.... And when they whine in Washington, I shall tell them: 'Drop dead with rage!' We are doing this now to avenge the past and to build for the future, in strength and dignity.

Ezza wa karama: it could also mean 'power and glory'. The crowd thundered its amen.

Nasser's speech reminded Eden of earlier tirades, in Nuremberg and Rome. Nor was he alone in thinking of Hitler and Mussolini. 'This is Munich all over again,' exclaimed Harold Macmillan. Paul-Henri Spaak, the Belgian Foreign Minister, wrote to Selwyn Lloyd: 'I do not wish to hide from you that I am haunted by the memory of the mistakes which were committed at the outset of the Hitler period, mistakes which have cost us dear.' Earl Attlee, the former Labour Prime Minister, called Nasser an imperialist dictator. Hugh Gaitskell, leader of the Labour Opposition, said: 'It is all very familiar. It is exactly the same that we encountered from Mussolini and Hitler.' Even Aneurin Bevan, the impassioned Welsh Socialist, who had visited Nasser two years earlier, was scathing about his 'nationalizing' the Canal. 'If the sending of one's police and soldiers into the darkness of the night to seize someone else's property is nationalization,' he declared, 'Ali Baba used the wrong terminology.'

His reaction was typical. It was not simply concern for the Suez Canal Company, in which the British Government held 45 percent of the shares; nor was there widespread fear for the Company's employees. What counted was the safety of the seaway. In 1955, 14,666 ships had passed along it, a third of them British, and three-quarters from member countries of NATO. Every year the Canal carried some 70 million tons of oil, 60 million of which were for Western Europe – two-thirds of her total supplies. To bring this round the Cape of Good Hope would take twice the tonnage of tankers; and Britain at that time had only six weeks' stocks. Ever since May 1948, Egypt had barred Israeli ships from using the Canal. In September 1954, Nasser had actually seized a small freighter, the *Bat Galim*, which had tried to run the blockade. Might something similar now happen to European vessels? 'The Egyptian', said Eden, 'has his thumb on our windpipe.'

On the evening after Nasser's appropriation of the Canal, Eden cabled to Eisenhower:

> We cannot afford to allow Nasser to seize control of the canal in this way, in defiance of international agreements....
> My colleagues and I are convinced that we must be ready, in the last resort, to use force to bring Nasser to his senses. For our part we are prepared to do so. I have this morning instructed our Chiefs of Staff to prepare a military plan accordingly.
> However, the first step must be for you and us and France to exchange views, align our policies and concert together how we can best bring the maximum pressure to bear on the Egyptian Government.

When the telegram reached Washington, John Foster Dulles was away, on a state occasion in Peru. Eisenhower summoned the Deputy Under-Secretary of State, Robert Murphy, asking him to go to London, to 'see what it's all about' and 'hold the fort'. Reaching London, Murphy found that the French Foreign Minister, Christian Pineau, had already arrived. Both the French and the British sought some form of American intervention: but they were full of bluster. 'If the Government did not take up Nasser's challenge,' Harold Macmillan argued, 'Britain would become another Netherlands.' He wanted, he told several colleagues, to 'keep the lawns of England green for his grandchildren.' To the Americans he insisted that 'Britain would go down against Egypt with flags flying rather than submit to the Suez despoliation.' Only in his diary was he less belligerent. 'We must keep the Americans really frightened,' he wrote. 'They *must* not be allowed any illusion. Then they will help us to get what we want without the necessity for force.'

It soon became clear, however, that the US Government, as Pineau said of Murphy, 'did not attach to the situation the interest which was required.' Murphy afterwards denied the slur; but he confessed that:

> the material interest of the United States was not identical with that of either France or the United Kingdom. France and Britain had very substantial holdings in the Canal Company. American holdings were insignificant. France and Britain were directly dependent on the flow of Middle East oil. The United States was not....
> Eisenhower was determined not to have the United States used as a cat's paw to protect British oil interests.

That November, moreover, the President was running for re-election. The last thing he wanted was armed conflict in the Middle East. Yet this was just what was threatened: British and French service chiefs were preparing the first outline of an invasion plan known as Operation Musketeer. Soon after Dulles returned to Washington, therefore, Eisenhower sent him to London with instructions to calm everyone down.

There followed many weeks of anxious, inconclusive diplomacy. Arriving in London on 1 August, Dulles did his best, as he put it, 'to mobilize world opinion' for a conference of those countries most concerned with the Suez Canal. Some people in Britain, including the young Labour back-bencher Anthony Wedgwood Benn, suggested referring the whole matter to the International Court of Justice in The Hague; but Egypt had never accepted its jurisdiction, and it was 'inconceivable', as Selwyn Lloyd said, that Nasser would agree to it now.

Attention therefore focused on the 24-nation conference of Suez Canal users which met in London on 16 August. By-passing an Indian proposal which would have left the Canal under Egyptian control, eighteen members of the conference proposed that it be run by an international board; but when this was put to Nasser by the Australian Prime Minister Robert Menzies, he turned it down. The Suez Canal Company's pilots thereupon withdrew their services. This, it was supposed, would baffle the Egyptians. Put to the test, they proved no less expert than highly paid Europeans.

In late September, a fresh meeting of the eighteen agreed to establish a continuing Suez Canal Users' Association, SCUA. Then at last France and Britain referred the dispute to the United Nations Security Council, while Nasser complained to it against their threats of war.

For a moment, it began to seem that a peaceful solution might be possible. In early October, the Foreign Ministers of Britain, France, and Egypt agreed on six principles for the future management of the Canal. Transit through it would be open, without discrimination; Egyptian sovereignty would be respected; politics would be kept out of the Canal's operation; Egypt and the users would agree on the tolls; a fair proportion of them would go to development; any issues still dividing Egypt from the Suez Canal Company would be submitted to arbitration.

Embodied in a draft Resolution for the Security Council, these principles might have led to a settlement: but Eden wanted more. He added a rider, demanding that Egypt 'promptly' propose just how to apply the principles, co-operate at once with SCUA, and offer unrestricted passage to all shipping. 'We hoped', he wrote later, 'to open a way for a test case on the banning of Israeli ships.'

He may have hoped for more still. In March that year, when Anthony Nutting had sent him a memorandum proposing to isolate Nasser by helping his neighbours, Eden had called him to the telephone in the middle of dinner, as Nutting recalled.

'What's all this poppycock you've sent me?' he shouted. 'I don't agree with a single word of it.'

I replied that it was an attempt to look ahead and to rationalise our position in the Middle East, so as to avoid in the future the kind of blow to our prestige that we had just suffered over Glubb.

'But what's all this nonsense about isolating Nasser or "neutralising" him, as you call it? I want him destroyed, can't you understand? I want him removed, and if you and the Foreign Office don't agree, then you'd better come to the Cabinet and explain why.'

I tried to calm him by saying that, before deciding to destroy Nasser, it might be wise to look for some alternative who would not be still more hostile to us. At the moment there did not appear to be any alternative, hostile or friendly. And the only result of removing Nasser would be anarchy in Egypt.

'But I don't want an alternative,' Eden shouted at me. 'And I don't care if there's anarchy and chaos in Egypt.'

If the Resolution containing the six principles were passed, Nasser would remain astride the Canal. Eden's rider stood no chance of acceptance, and was duly vetoed by the Soviet Union. Eden wrote in his Memoirs: 'No method was left for harnessing the principles. They just flapped in the air.' The way was open, it seemed, for more direct action; and if the USA would not help topple Nasser, two other countries were spoiling for a fight.

The first was France. In his great speech at Alexandria, Nasser had boasted: 'Arab nationalism has been set on fire from the Atlantic Ocean to the Persian Gulf.' 'From the Atlantic Ocean' – that, for France, was the stinging phrase. French rule in the Maghreb countries of North Africa – Morocco, Algeria, and Tunisia – was being challenged; and Frenchmen's resentment was all the greater because, like the Dutch and the British, they had already had to retreat from the Far East.

They had given the name 'Indo-China' to a million square miles in South-East Asia, an area nearly four times the size of France which they had colonized in the late nineteenth century: a union of settlements and dependencies in Tonking, Annam, Laos, Cambodia, and 'Cochin-China' around Saigon. Already in 1925, left-wing exiles in Canton had founded a 'Vietnamese National Party' to fight for the unity and independence of Tonking, Annam, and Cochin-China. One of its young adherents was an Annamite by the name of Nguyen Tat Thanh. After working as a schoolteacher, a ship's steward, and a kitchen-hand at the Carlton Hotel in

London, he had settled in Paris and become a founder-member of the French Communist Party. He spent three years in Moscow, then went to China and Hong Kong. In 1940 he tried to organize a revolt in Hanoi and Saigon, but was forced to flee to China, where with fellow-exiles he formed the 'Viet-Minh' movement. Three years later, he returned in secret to Indo-China, now calling himself 'Ho Chi Minh' – 'Ho' denoting 'Sender of Light'. As soon as Japan was defeated, Ho proclaimed a 'Democratic Republic of Vietnam'; but when the French returned he found himself fighting a war of independence.

It dragged on for eight years. It ended in a resounding victory for Ho and his General Vo Nguyen Giap at the village of Dien Bien Phu in Northern Vietnam, a hundred miles to the West of Hanoi.

French parachutists under General Henri Navarre had seized the village, deep in Viet-Minh-controlled territory, in November 1953. Navarre's aim had been to draw Giap's peasant army into a set-piece battle, and defeat it by superior weaponry, fire-power, and tactical skill. It was a classic instance of *hubris* – and a very costly mistake. General Giap's 50,000 coolies dragged siege guns up into the hills surrounding Dien Bien Phu, and made it almost impossible to fly in supplies. For nearly two months the 16,500 French *paras* put up a desperate resistance. Finally, on 7 May 1954, they had to surrender. Only 3,000 survived the siege and the prison camps that followed. Within a further two months, an armistice was concluded in Geneva, and Vietnam became independent, partitioned between Hanoi and Saigon.

The Geneva agreements also covered neighbouring Laos. Since 1947, it had been independent within the French Union; now it became a fully autonomous neutral monarchy. In Cambodia, to the South, the reigning Prince Sihanouk had secured independence within the French Union in 1949, and full independence four years later. Trouble and tragedy in the peninsula were by no means over: but French rule had come to an end.

France held on longer to the Maghreb countries of North Africa.

In the protectorate of Morocco, the Istiqlal nationalists had begun to demand independence in 1943. After the war, in 1948, the French had agreed to consultative assemblies. They had failed to satisfy the nationalists, and unrest had continued, sometimes exploding in anti-French riots, sometimes involving clashes between Sultan Mohammed Ben Youssef and some of his Berber subjects. The Sultan, his palace set in the vast Méchouar among the avenues and boulevards of Rabat, was in fact a modernist, and enjoyed the support of the Istiqlal. He was ferociously opposed by the old feudal chieftains, including the aged and rascally Pasha of Marrakesh, El Glaoui, the so-called 'Sultan of the South'. Often tempted to exploit these differences, the French administration yielded in 1953 to El Glaoui's threats of a holy war, and actually deposed Sultan Mohammed, replacing him with his compliant right-wing uncle Mohammed Ould Moulay Arafa. The result was renewed violence. On Christmas Eve, a bomb went off in the central market of Casablanca, killing 19 people and wounding 28 others. On 5 March 1954, the Sultan was wounded by a hand grenade while at prayer in the Berima mosque in Marrakesh. The bomb attacks, riots, and assassinations culminated in massacres: in August 1955, tribes from the interior sacked the European quarter of Oued-Zem, between Marrakesh and Fez, killing fifty men, women, and children, while similar if smaller atrocities occurred elsewhere. At length, on 18 November 1955, the authorities relented and Mohammed Ben Youssef was restored to the throne. He had already secured a promise to negotiate Moroccan independence; and the talks were successfully concluded in March 1956.

In Tunisia, which had also been a French protectorate, nationalist agitation had begun in the 1930's. Its main focus was the 'Néo-Destour' party, led by Habib ibn Ali Bourguiba, who was twice imprisoned by the French. During World War II, Bourguiba refused to co-operate with the Axis invaders; but in 1945 he took refuge in Cairo. Returning four years later, he was again imprisoned by the French authorities in 1952. Meanwhile, unrest was growing. As Bourguiba said: 'If the Tunisian people are still fighting, if blood still flows in Tunisia, if centres of armed resistance are springing up here and there in the South, it is because, instead of the internal autonomy which was promised, attempts are being made to impose the co-sovereignty of the French colony – that is, by devious means, to suppress the Tunisian State.' In June 1954, however, following the débâcle of Dien Bien Phu, Pierre Mendès-France had become French Prime Minister. A left-wing Radical, small, incisive, and courageous, with deep, sad, hooded Jewish eyes, he had already decided that Tunisian independence under Bourguiba was preferable to an endless struggle with greater extremists; and on 31 July 1954, speaking near the ruins of Carthage on the coast ten kilometres from Tunis, he announced that France would grant self-government 'without reservations'. It was nearly two years, however, before the process was complete. One reason for the delay was that the desert of Southern Tunisia had become a refuge, if not a base camp, for the rebels who were fighting the French army across the border in Algeria.

Here, the constitutional position was quite different from that in Morocco and Tunisia. In theory at least, Algeria was 'part of France', to which the *départements* of Algiers, Oran, and Constantine had been attached since 1882. Although most of the Arab population remained without a vote, from 1919 onwards certain Arabs had been able to become French citizens. In the closing stages of World War II, General de Gaulle extended this right in the hope of gradually 'assimilating' the Algerians and the French. Local resistance, however, ran deep. One teacher in the coastal town of Bougie (now Bejaia) dictated to his class, as a handwriting exercise: 'I am French, France is my country.' His Arab pupils wrote instead: 'I am Algerian; Algeria is my country.'

Nor were all the protests so peaceful. On 8 May 1945, while millions elsewhere were rejoicing at the end of the war in Europe, a series of co-ordinated riots broke out. At Sétif, 29 Europeans were killed. There were similar attacks at Bône (Annaba), Batna, Biskra, and elsewhere. For three days, there was turmoil. Several hundred people lost their lives; 88 of them were French. The retribution was swift and savage. Two-and-a-half thousand people were arrested; 28 were sentenced to death; between five and six thousand Arabs were killed in battles with French troops. The Muslim writer Kalif Yacine, who was sixteen at the time, declared later: 'I have never forgotten the shock I felt at that pitiless butchery.... It was there that my nationalism took root.'

For some years, the roots of rebellion spread unobserved. In 1947, all Algerians were declared French citizens and all, including Muslim women, were given the vote – not only for the French National Assembly in Paris, but also for a 120-member body in Algiers. Before the first elections, which secured a Francophile majority, the French arrested some members of the nationalist parties, led by Messali Hadj and the moderate Ferhat Abbas. At the Assembly's first session, there were angry scenes. In April 1950, the police seized caches of weapons in Algiers and Constantine, and arrested some 150 people. These included the 34-year-old Mohammed Ahmed Ben Bella, a former sergeant in the French Army, four times decorated in World War II, who had led an armed raid on the Central Post Office in Oran. Such incidents, however, seemed sporadic: prompt police action, it was thought, could keep them in check. While Morocco and Tunisia were rent by violence, Algerian voters regularly elected moderates to the Assembly; and France confidently prepared to develop oil and other resources at Colomb-

Béchar near the Moroccan border or Hassi Messaoud in the East. She claimed to be pouring more money into Algeria than the whole of United States aid to the less developed countries of the world.

Then, on Saturday night, 30 October 1954 – the weekend of the All Saints holiday – came the signal for armed revolt. In Eastern Constantine and the Aurès mountains, Arab terrorists launched no fewer than thirty separate, simultaneous attacks. Some Frenchmen were forewarned – like the young ethnologist Jean Servier, recording folk songs in a mountain village: the chief advised him to disappear for a week 'while we collect taxes'. Others were less fortunate. A French teacher and his wife, going on holiday by bus, were ambushed in the Tighanimine gorges. Forced to get out, they were machine-gunned in cold blood, together with a village chief who tried to defend them. In all, despite many casualties, only a dozen people were killed. It was a modest total compared with the Sétif massacre of 1945: but it was the fruit of long preparation, and the beginning of the eight-year war that was to win Algeria independence. That war cost the lives of 24,614 French servicemen, 5,288 European civilians, and at least 200,000 Arabs. It divided friends and families, and led to bloodshed on the mainland. It destroyed the French Fourth Republic, and brought General de Gaulle back to power for eleven years. More immediately, it helped determine France's reaction when Nasser seized the Suez Canal.

At first, the Algerian rebels were heavily outnumbered; but French reprisals swelled their ranks as surely as terrorist recruiting. What was clear from the start, however, was that the revolution had been orchestrated from outside. Its leader was Ben Bella, who had escaped from French captivity in 1952. Like Bourguiba earlier, he had fled to Cairo, where he had founded the *Front de Libération Nationale*, or FLN. But Egypt, for Ben Bella, was more than a refuge: it also offered moral and material support. Cairo Radio's powerful transmitter broadcast continual appeals to Algerians to join 'the insurrection of freedom against French imperialism in North Africa'; and Nasser, as he afterwards admitted, supplied arms.

My first shipment was with my yacht, the *Intisar*. It had been Farouk's yacht – not the *Mahroussa* but the other, smaller one called *Fakhr al-Bihar*. This shipment helped them to begin the revolution.

Further deliveries followed – as the French authorities were later able to prove. On 16 October 1956, they actually seized an Egyptian motor yacht, the *Athos*, sailing from Alexandria under a British captain with enough weapons for 1,500 men. This merely confirmed what intelligence reports had long suggested. Jacques Soustelle, who served for a year as Governor-General in Algeria, voiced a general French opinion when he described Nasser as 'the head of the octopus whose tentacles have for so many months been strangling French North Africa.'

Soustelle had left Algeria on 2 February 1956. An anthropologist turned politician, he had come to North Africa with liberal views; but his sympathies had soon shifted towards the settlers. On the day of his departure, they carried him shoulder-high, chanting their defiant slogan *'Algérie française!'* His replacement was to be General Georges Catroux, who had just been appointed by Guy Mollet, the new Prime Minister of France. Mollet, a former teacher and member of the wartime Resistance, was a moderate Socialist and a tough political infighter – although some detected a slight softness in his plump, square, bespectacled face and small mouth. Catroux had had the task of restoring to the throne of Morocco the modernist Sultan Mohammed Ben Youssef. Hearing of his appointment by a Socialist Government, the Algerian settlers were first suspicious, then furious. When Mollet himself came to Algiers on 6 February 1956, for a five-day tour to include the installation of the new Governor-General, they howled him down as he laid a wreath at the war memorial, and pelted him with tomatoes, mud, and stones.

Pale and shaken, Mollet was driven back to the Governor's palace, pursued by 5,000 demonstrators, who lowered the flag to half-mast and tried to wreck the garden. That night, Mollet secured Catroux's resignation, and three days later appointed Robert Lacoste, former Resident-General in Morocco, in his place. In a broadcast on 9 February, Mollet told the settlers:

You have been depicted as colonialists. I do not share this view.... Farmers, workers, tradespeople, teachers, doctors, who have their homes, their families, and their dead in Algeria: since my arrival I have heard the voice of all of them.... Even though for me the experience was painful, the unfortunate demonstration on Monday had a wholesome aspect. It provided many with an opportunity to express their attachment to France.... I assure them that they have been heard. France will remain present in Algeria.

From that moment onwards, Mollet was an implacable enemy of the FLN. Eight months later, his Government achieved a startling coup against it, masterminded by the Under-Secretary for War, Max Lejeune.

The operation was carried out on the evening of 22 October 1956. Ben Bella and other FLN leaders had been conferring in Rabat with Sultan Mohammed Ben Youssef, and had taken off in a Moroccan airliner for a conference in Tunis to discuss a possible Maghreb federation. When the aircraft was flying over international waters, after a refuelling stop in Palma de Mallorca, French Government officials radioed its pilot and gave him secret instructions. All the crew on board were employees of Air Atlas, which was owned by the Moroccan Government: but they were French citizens, and they obeyed what they felt was 'their duty to France'. Shortly before 9.30, the air hostess announced: 'In a few moments we shall be landing at Tunis.' But when the aircraft touched down and Ben Bella and his colleagues alighted, they found themselves surrounded by guards carrying machine-guns. Their aircraft had been flying in a circle wide enough to pass unnoticed, and had landed on schedule – not in Tunis, but in Algiers.

The incident was dramatic, and it caused a scandal. 'We are dishonoured!' exclaimed René Coty, the President of France. But at that very moment a greater drama – involving what many believed was greater dishonour – was already unfolding in the South-Western suburbs of Paris, in a villa at Sèvres. It belonged to the family of Fernand Bonnier de la Chapelle, the 18-year-old boy who had been shot in Algiers in 1943 for assassinating the Pétainist Admiral Darlan. Members of the family were friends of the French Defence Minister, Maurice Bourgès-Maunoury, who as the Resistance leader 'Polycarpe' had used the villa as a safe house during World War II. Now, it was once again the scene of secret meetings. This time, the participants were British as well as French. Their enemy now was not Hitler, but Nasser, and their new ally was Israel.

Although the Israelis had fought off the initial attack on them by Egypt, Iraq, and Jordan in 1948–49, border warfare had continued. In July 1951, not content with forbidding the Suez Canal to Israeli ships, Egypt had blockaded the Gulf of Aqaba, Israel's newly acquired outlet to the Red Sea. Between 1951 and 1955, Israel had set up *Nahals*, or defended outposts, in uncultivated areas from the Lebanese frontier to the edge of the Gaza strip, itself crowded with Arab refugees. In 1954, Israeli agents in Egypt had mounted a fire-bomb campaign against the evacuation of Britain's Canal base; and in January 1955 two of them – a 28-year-old surgeon and a 26-year-old professor of engineering – were hanged in a Cairo gaol, while six others faced long terms of imprisonment. In the ensuing political storm, the Israeli Defence Minister Pinhas Lavon was obliged to resign. His place was taken by the white-haired father of Israel, David Ben-Gurion, who from 1948 to 1953 had been the country's first Prime Minister, and who now soon resumed that post too. It was he who insisted on retaliation, by means of a raid on the Arab town of Gaza on Monday 28 February 1955.

That evening, a large platoon of Israeli paratroopers, armed with rifles, hand-grenades, machine-guns, and rocket-firing bazookas, stormed an Egyptian encampment on the town's Northern outskirts, while a smaller group ambushed reinforcements coming from the South. The Israelis suffered eight dead and thirteen wounded. They left behind them, dead or dying, 37 men and a 7-year-old boy.

Nasser later called the Gaza raid 'the turning-point' in Egypt's relations with Israel. It certainly intensified the fighting between Israelis and Arab *fedayîn*; and it hardened Nasser's determination to seek arms from the Soviet Union and Czechoslovakia. Israel, meanwhile, was already secretly buying weapons and *Mystère* jet aircraft from France. 'They came,' said Ben-Gurion, 'not to a port, but somewhere on the sea at night in coloured ships that you could not see from above.' When Guy Mollet took office, collaboration became closer still; and very soon a new idea took shape. After Nasser had seized the Canal, and while Britain and France were contemplating joint military action, the Director-General of the Israeli Defence Ministry, Shimon Peres, went to Paris to discuss further arms shipments with Bourgès-Maunoury, the French Minister of Defence. At a meeting on 7 August 1956, in the Defence Ministry in the rue St-Dominique, Bourgès-Maunoury asked Peres out of the blue: 'How long would it take Israeli forces to reach the Suez Canal across the Sinai peninsula?' Peres hesitated. 'About a week,' he said. A senior officer then put a further question: 'Would Israel be willing to attack Egypt in concert with France?' Peres answered 'Yes.'

That hectic summer, while the diplomats debated, Franco-British military operations were twice postponed: but the idea of joint action with Israel had caught on. In mid-September, Colonel Robert Henriques, a farmer and writer with a distinguished Service career, went out from London to see Ben-Gurion, bearing a message from an unnamed British Minister:

If, when Britain went into Suez, Israel were to attack simultaneously, it would be very convenient for all concerned. Britain would denounce Israel's aggression in the strongest possible terms; but at the peace negotiations afterwards, Britain would help Israel to get the best possible treaty.

For a time, Ben-Gurion was sceptical; but on 23 September he made up his mind. On 14 October, General Maurice Challe, Chief of the French Air Staff, and Albert Gazier, French Minister of Labour and a close friend of Guy Mollet, went to see Eden and Anthony Nutting at the Prime Minister's country retreat of Chequers. The proposal, in Nutting's words, was that

Israel should be invited to attack Egypt across the Sinai Peninsula and that France and Britain, having given the Israeli forces enough time to seize all or most of Sinai, should then order 'both sides' to withdraw their forces from the Suez Canal, in order to permit an Anglo-French force to intervene and occupy the Canal on the pretext of saving it from damage by fighting.

Selwyn Lloyd, the Foreign Secretary, had meanwhile been at the United Nations in New York, seeking a peaceful solution. When he arrived back in London on Tuesday 16 October, Nutting drew him aside to explain what was afoot and to advise against it. 'You are right,' Lloyd answered: but he was overborne by Eden, who whisked him off that afternoon for private talks in Paris with Mollet and Pineau. 'Over lunch and during the flight to Paris,' wrote Lloyd, 'I discussed my worries with Eden'; and he repeated them in Cabinet two days later, stressing in particular the effect of the plan on Arab opinion. In the end, however, a majority agreed 'that we and the French should intervene to protect the Canal, if Israel moved against Egypt.'

The plot had thickened, and it now seemed firm. But Ben-Gurion was still suspicious. He disliked being cast once more in the role of the aggressor; and although well equipped with French *Mystère* jet fighters, he wanted a guarantee that British Canberras and Valiants, the long-range jet bombers which the French lacked, would actually be used to destroy Egypt's air force on the ground. He therefore insisted that Ministers from Britain, France, and Israel hold one last top-secret meeting. It took place on 22–24 October 1956, in the privacy of the safe-house villa at Sèvres.

Ben-Gurion and Peres, together with General Moshe Dayan in his well-known black eye-patch, landed at the Villacoublay military airfield near Sèvres in the early morning of 22 October. They had had an exhausting flight. Thick fog over Paris had forced them to fly to Marseille to refuel; they had landed, on their second attempt, after seventeen hours in the air. Ben-Gurion had hidden his abundant white hair under a broad-brimmed hat. A worker on the airfield recognized him, and told a reporter friend, but the friend refused to believe it. Pineau drove his own car to the rendezvous. Selwyn Lloyd flew in that evening with his private secretary Donald Logan. On the way from the airfield to the villa, in a small car driven by a French officer, they narrowly escaped a crash.

After first talking with the French, Lloyd went in to meet the Israelis. 'His whole demeanour,' thought Dayan, 'expressed distaste – for the place, the company, and the topic.' He was not fully briefed on Anglo-French military preparations, still less on Franco-Israeli plans; and he was unhappy at what he heard. He agreed to consult his Cabinet colleagues, and at around midnight he and Logan flew back to London. Next day, realizing that a Cabinet meeting would take time, he sent Logan back to explain the delay. Pineau thereupon flew to London, where he dined with Lloyd. At 10 p.m., Eden came in, and they talked for two hours more, finally settling on a further meeting at Sèvres the next day. This time, Lloyd stayed behind – he had to take Question Time in the House of Commons – but he sent Logan and Patrick Dean, a Deputy Under-Secretary of State. Early in the morning of Wednesday 24 October, Dean saw Eden for a final briefing; in the afternoon, he and Logan resumed the talks in Sèvres with the Israelis and the French. Then, as Lloyd described it,

quite unexpectedly a document was produced. It had been typed on plain paper in a neighbouring room and recorded the elements of the contingency plan.... Dean and Logan had a word together about this development. There had been no earlier mention of committing anything to paper and no reason to regard the document as anything other than a record of the discussion on which the three delegations would report. As that, Dean signed it.

The plot had taken its final shape.

Five days later, on 29 October, Israel launched its attack. One armoured column made for Rafah, to the south of the Gaza strip; a second struck at El Arîsh, on the coast further westwards; a third raced across the Sinai desert through Abu Ageigila towards Ismailia; and a fourth, driving southwards, headed for Sharm-el-Sheikh near the mouth of the Gulf of Aqaba. To activate the Sèvres agreement, sixteen Dakotas of the Israeli air force flew low over the Sinai desert, avoiding Egyptian radar, and dropped 385 parachutists near the Mitla Pass, 30 miles from Suez. This was the promised threat to the Suez Canal.

Next day, as agreed, Britain and France issued their ultimatum. It called on Egypt and Israel to stop fighting and withdraw ten miles from the Suez Canal; it also required Egypt to accept the temporary occupation of Port Saîd, Ismailia, and Suez, so as to safeguard navigation. Israel, whose forces were well outside the ten-mile limit, quickly agreed. Egypt refused. In the United Nations Security Council, Britain and France then vetoed both a Soviet resolution calling for a cease-fire and the withdrawal of Israeli forces, and a similar United States resolution which further urged all UN members to refrain from using force in the area.

On the evening of the following day, 31 October – twelve hours later than originally planned, to ensure the cover of darkness – British Canberra and

Valiant aircraft from Cyprus began to bomb Egyptian airfields. Nasser called in the American Ambassador, and appealed for help from the United States; but all that Eisenhower could promise was to seek a solution through the United Nations. On 2 November, the UN General Assembly called for a cease-fire and the withdrawal of attacking forces. Egypt, meanwhile, sank ships to block the Suez Canal. On 4 November, the UN Secretary-General Dag Hammarskjöld asked for all military operations to be halted by 0500 hours GMT on the following morning, 5 November. On that very morning, British and French paratroops landed at Port Saîd, and the Suez invasion began. It ended less than 48 hours later, with the advance party called to a halt on the Treaty road at El Cap.

Militarily, the operation had been a resounding success – co-ordinated from five command centres, long prepared but adroitly adapted, executed quickly, economically, and with great dash. Politically, it was a catastrophe, and a boost instead of a blow to Nasser's prestige. When Britain and France gave the order to halt their forces, they were tacitly acknowledging that the world had changed. They had had to yield under pressure from four directions: the United Nations, the British public, the United States, and the USSR.

By invading Egypt, Britain and France had defied the UN General Assembly; but on that same day they had agreed to stop as soon as Egypt accepted an international force in their stead. On 7 November, the Assembly voted to establish one. A week later, Egypt formally assented; and on 15 November the first blue-helmeted UN contingents arrived. The United Nations Organization had not by itself secured peace: but the UN Expeditionary Force supplied the means of keeping it – the broad equivalent of six infantry battalions from more than half-a-dozen member states. It was no coincidence that among them were two countries – India and Indonesia – which a few years before had still been European colonies.

UN pressure had also affected British public opinion. It was already deeply split. Polls during the crisis showed 53 percent supporting the Government; but there was never a majority for the use of force. Of Conservatives, 89 percent backed Eden: of Labour voters, 63 percent opposed him. The strength of feeling among his opponents was very great. Public meetings and marches, letters and telegrams of protest, hostile editorials, and broadcasts by the Labour Opposition – all showed how high the tide was running. Two of Eden's own colleagues resigned: Sir Walter Monckton, the Defence Minister, in mid-October, and Anthony Nutting on

31 October. Others shared their concern; and it was intensified by growing fears for Eden's health – suspicions confirmed in late November, when on his doctors' orders he went for three weeks' rest to Goldeneye, the Jamaican property of Ian Fleming, creator of 'James Bond'. On 9 January, soon after his return, he resigned the premiership, to be succeeded by Harold Macmillan.

At first, Macmillan had backed the invasion plan: but he had soon changed his mind. At a meeting of the Cabinet's 'Egypt Committee' on the eve of the first landings, it was reported that UN members were discussing oil sanctions against Britain and France. Macmillan threw his arms in the air. 'Oil sanctions! That finishes it!' he exclaimed. Already, two days before, the Syrians had blown up three pumping stations on the Iraq Petroleum Company's pipeline to the coast. But what Macmillan feared most was action by the United States. It was this, in the end, that proved decisive.

Spasmodically, the US Administration seemed to show sympathy with French and British plans to use force. In March 1956, Dulles had spoken to Selwyn Lloyd about the possible need to 'ditch' Nasser. At the SCUA conference in September, he pleaded eloquently against the use of force, but left the impression that he regarded it as a necessary last resort. On 17 November, when the whole affair was over, Lloyd went to see him at the Walter Reed Hospital in Washington, where he was being treated for cancer. He was up and dressed, and Lloyd noted 'a kind of twinkle in his eye'. 'Selwyn, why did you stop?' he asked. 'Why didn't you go through with it and get Nasser down?' Christian Pineau, Lloyd's French counterpart, also recorded that Dulles had second thoughts. Many months had gone by. It was summer, and they were sitting together after dinner in the garden of Dulles's house. There was a long reflective silence. Then Dulles said: 'At Suez, we were wrong. You were the ones who were right.'

Throughout the crisis itself, however, the United States had opposed military action; and American financial pressure was what chiefly brought it to a halt. As Chancellor of the Exchequer, Macmillan could see the dangers. Despite Britain's payments surplus that year, sterling still depended on the vast balances kept on deposit in London. As the Suez crisis worsened, both Arabs and Americans began to withdraw their funds. In August, September, and October, 1956, $328 million poured out of London, bringing the remaining balances dangerously close to the so-called 'Plimsoll line' of $2,000 million. To maintain her currency and survive as a banker, Britain needed credit from the International Monetary Fund, the US Import-

Export Bank, or both: but to secure it she required American consent. It was not forthcoming until she promised to accept a cease-fire in Egypt. Then, and only then, the US Secretary of the Treasury, George Humphrey, agreed to dollar credits of some $1,500 million. 'It was not exactly blackmail,' said a British Minister, 'but compliance with the UN was a postulate of American help.'

At the time, too, there was some anxiety about threats from the USSR. Early in the conflict, the Soviet Union had suggested intervention by the Bandung powers. On 5 November, the day of the first Franco-British landings, it proposed joint action with the United States – a notion rejected as unthinkable. That evening, the Soviet Prime Minister Nikolai Bulganin summoned the Ambassadors of Britain, France, and Israel to hand them threatening messages for their Governments. To Eden, Bulganin wrote:

In what situation would Britain find herself if she were attacked by stronger states possessing all types of modern weapons of destruction? Indeed, such countries, instead of sending to the shores of Britain their naval or air forces, could use other means, for instance rocket equipment. . . .

In reality, as Bulganin had already informed Nasser, the Soviet Union was then still handicapped by distance. It had stocks of the T-1 (M 101), a modified version of the wartime V2 rocket, whose range was only 400–450 miles; and although it had developed an IRBM or intermediate range ballistic missile, the T-2 (M 103), with a range of up to 1,000 miles, this had not yet been produced in quantity. There was more bluff than substance, so far, in the implied Soviet threat.

Moreover, while Britain and France were engaged in their two-day 'colonial war', the Soviet Union itself was imposing its will by force on parts of its own empire much nearer home. 'The end of empire', it was clear, would not apply in Eastern Europe.

Signs of unrest there had begun in Poland, where 'destalinization' in April and May 1956 had brought the release of 30,000 political prisoners, and a reduction of the sentences served by 40,000 more. In June and July, anger at rising prices and Soviet 'exploitation' led to strikes and riots in Poznań, in which 53 workers were killed. To forestall worse troubles, Władysław Gomułka, a moderate who had been dismissed eight years earlier, was re-admitted to the Polish Communist Party and allowed to carry out some limited reforms. Among other things, he put a stop to the collectivization of farming, and curbed the power of the secret police. This angered and alarmed his opponents, who called for Soviet help. Russian tanks came as far as Warsaw; but with strong popular support at home, and some backing from Khrushchev in Moscow, Gomułka finally managed to keep the Soviet Union at arm's length.

It was very different in Hungary. There, the thaw after Stalin's death had produced a similar comeback, by the once disgraced Imre Nagy, a fatherly 60-year-old former Minister of Agriculture. In February 1955, however, Nagy had again been ousted by Mátyás Rákosi, a ruthless and overfed Stalinist. This led to widespread protests, partly inspired by patriotic memories of Sándor Petőfi, the young nationalist poet killed fighting Tsarist Russian troops in 1849, during the abortive War of Independence. The Petőfi Circle of Hungarian intellectuals now organized mass public debates, demanding freedom of the press and calling on Rákosi to resign. In July 1956 the Soviet Union dismissed him: but his replacement was his former henchman Ernö Gerö. 'In place of a bald Rákosi we've got a thin one,' was the typical reaction in Budapest.

Cold wet weather, a bad harvest, and a fuel shortage added to the general discontent. On 23 October 1956, after a broadcast in which Gerö had attacked the 'revolution', angry students and workers surged through the capital shouting for Imre Nagy. Outside the radio building, security police fired shots into the crowd. A nightlong battle ensued, leaving many dead and wounded. In the City Park, another crowd pulled down the 50-foot bronze statue of Stalin. Loading the head into a truck, they dumped it by Parliament Square, crowned with a notice from some nearby roadworks: 'Dead End'. Before the night was out Gerö had called in Soviet troops; but Hungarians of all ages fought back, with stones and bullets and Molotov cocktails. The Kremlin was furious – as much with Gerö as with anyone. On Wednesday afternoon, 24 October, Soviet Deputy Premiers Anastas Mikoyan and Mikhail Suslov arrived in Budapest and demanded his resignation. Imre Nagy replaced him, and János Kádár became First Secretary of the Party.

For one heady week, Hungary seemed on the brink of freedom. Nagy abolished the one-party system and formed a new government, including in it the former President Zoltán Tildy, the Social-Democrat Anna Kethly, and the former leader of the Smallholders' Party, Béla Kovács. He released Cardinal József Mindszenty, who in 1948 had been imprisoned for life, charged with currency offences and treason. On 31 October, Mindszenty broadcast to the nation; and on that day Nagy even announced that Hungary would seek neutral status and withdraw from the Warsaw Pact.

It was too much, too soon – but it was also too late. By that time, Soviet tanks had already entered the country; and on the following night, 1 November, János Kádár abruptly disappeared. He re-emerged in Eastern Hungary, where he set up a new, Soviet-backed Government, to 'save the republic from Horthyite Fascist counter-revolutionaries'. Early on Sunday 4 November, 6,000 Soviet tanks began shelling Budapest. At 5.20 p.m., Nagy came to the radio to announce: 'Our troops are fighting' – but by then it was almost over. For nearly three hours, Budapest and a number of new 'freedom radio' stations, using portable transmitters, broadcast desperate appeals for help – to Western Europe, to President Eisenhower, to the United Nations. Then, at seven minutes past eight, the radio went silent. No one had been able to come to Hungary's aid.

In the end, two hundred thousand fugitives escaped. Imre Nagy took refuge in the Yugoslav Embassy. He came out three weeks later, armed with what he thought was a safe-conduct. He was at once arrested, tried, and sentenced to death. Standing up in the courtroom, a quiet, dignified figure with pince-nez and a drooping moustache, Nagy said:

If my life is needed to prove that not all Communists are enemies of the people, I gladly make the sacrifice. I know there will one day be another Nagy trial, which will rehabilitate me. I know also that I shall have a reburial. I only fear that the funeral oration will be delivered by those who betrayed me.

The Suez invasion and Hungary's bid for freedom made cruelly obvious how circumscribed Western Europe now was. Rich and peaceful she might be: she was no match for the super-powers – the military might of Russia, the political influence of America, or even the economic upsurge of Japan. The imperial age had left its traces, overseas as in Europe and in the minds of Europeans; but the 'Commonwealth', like the French *communauté*, was little more than a palliative for the withdrawal symptoms of a former world power.

Yet the end of the empire was also a new beginning – not only of independence for the former colonies, but of an influx of immigrants into the old 'mother countries', reversing the tide of colonists who had gone the other way. To France, to the Netherlands, and increasingly to Britain, new settlers came to seek their fortune, bringing with them much that was as foreign as European customs had seemed when first transplanted overseas. In 1950, Britain had had fewer than 100,000 coloured immigrants. The numbers began to grow two years later, when the McCarran Act limited Caribbean immigration into the United States. By 1957, Britain's coloured population had doubled; and gradually it came to include more people from India and Pakistan. New faces would mean new problems, so long as old attitudes survived.

But many in Europe, now, were acquiring new respect for cultures once alien and unknown. The films of Satyajit Ray from India or Akira Kurosawa from Japan; the novels of Mulk Raj Anand or R.K. Narayan; Nirad Chaudhuri's *Autobiography of an Unknown Indian*; the work of such Africans as Wole Soyinka or Bloke Modisane; the West Indian stories of V.S. Naipaul; the growing school of French North African writing – all these helped open European eyes. Only six years after the Suez invasion, audiences in Europe were admiring, in David Lean's film *Lawrence of Arabia*, a fine young actor who was soon to be a super-star. He came, of all places, from Egypt. His name was Omar Sharif.

Yet for those who remembered service life in Egypt, the end of the Suez affair left scars. James Morris was in Port Saîd to report it for the *Manchester Guardian*. Years later, in his history of the British Empire, he described the shuttered shops, the streets all but deserted, the funnels and masts of sunken ships at odd angles in the Canal:

Port Said had never been beautiful, but it was familiar, and in their rough way the British had been fond of it. Awful though it was, pimps, touts, slums and all, still it was part of their heritage. It is like a nightmare to find them back in these familiar streets as enemies. The hush that hangs over the town is a hush of shock....

The ethos of Empire, as of war, was acceptable to the British when it was backed by convictions of honour – by the belief, false or misguided, that the British were acting rightly, for the good of themselves and the world....

Now, in Port Said, 1956, there was only pretence – a sham virility, a dubious cause, a nation divided, an army with little verve to its campaigning. Port Said, shattered and appalled, stood as a bitter memorial to the last display of imperial *machismo*.

One final irony was to come. On 31 December 1956, the last of Britain's invasion forces arrived back at Southampton – the 19th Infantry Brigade, with two Scottish battalions eager to be home for Hogmanay. But times had changed in Britain too. The troops had to wait until after the holiday for the dockers to unload the ship.

10
The Road to Rome

Less than six months after the Suez débâcle, Europe undertook a far more promising venture. In Rome, on 25 March 1957, six European Governments pledged themselves to 'ever closer union'. It was a vital stage on a journey still unfinished, but begun many years before, in the midst of World War II.

The frontiers of Hitler's Europe had been hard to cross. To reach neutral Spain or Switzerland, escapers or Resistance couriers had had to climb at night through the mountains, footsore and bone-weary, but alert for sentry-posts, armed patrols, police dogs, trip-wires, or minefields. Even their guides were not always to be trusted. In some remote places, they could not be sure when they were safely through.

Four times – in March, April, May, and July of 1944 – delegates from Resistance circuits in nine countries braved these dangers to meet in secret in Geneva. Altogether, there were fifteen of them: three Italians, three Frenchmen, two Germans, two Dutchmen, a Czechoslovak, a Yugoslav, a Pole, a Norwegian, and – for some of the time – a Dane. The point of their meetings was not to plan military strategy, train derailments, factory sabotage, spying, or insurrection. They had come to discuss the long-term future of Europe.

Some members of the Resistance had been simple patriots, defending their families, their friends, and their countries: but many had fought for something more. The physicist Jacques Bergier, of the 'Marco-Polo' circuit which helped disclose the Nazis' V1 and V2 missiles, wrote later that the French resistance had been 'admirably described' in C. Day-Lewis's lines about a Spanish Civil war volunteer:

> Tell them in England, if they ask
> What brought us to these wars,
> To this plateau beneath the night's
> Grave manifold of stars –

> It was not fraud or foolishness,
> Glory, revenge, or pay:
> We came because our open eyes
> Could see no other way.
>
> There was no other way to keep
> Man's flickering truth alight:
> These stars will witness that our course
> Burned briefer, not less bright.

An Italian partisan leader, 'Duccio' – Tancredi Galimberti, a 38-year-old lawyer from Piedmont – put it more succinctly. Captured and tortured by the Fascists, he wrote to his friends on 1 December 1944, the day before he was shot: 'I have fought in a good cause, and for an idea.'

Those who had met in Geneva that Spring could also see no other way; and the idea that inspired them was simple but radical, born of experience shared. 'It mattered little,' wrote a French sympathizer, 'if they were a handful of people or a million, because what they said was true.'

Resistance to Nazi oppression, which united the peoples of Europe in a common struggle, has forged between them a solidarity and a community of aims.

So began the declaration drawn up in Geneva in May 1944. It concluded by proposing 'a federal union among the European peoples'.

The host at the Geneva meeting was a distinguished expatriate Dutchman, Willem A. Visser't Hooft. Despite his scholarly appearance, he served as a contact between the Resistance in Holland and the Government-in-exile in London. In public life, he was General Secretary of the World Council of Churches; and his internationalism had Christian roots. Others had different starting-points, but came to the same conclusions. In Holland's underground press, the Christian monthly *Vrij Nederland* and the Socialist weekly *Het Parool* called jointly for 'the closest possible union with the other states of Western Europe.' In the Social Democratic Labour Party, the SDAP, the tough and outspoken Alfred Mozer argued on similar lines. Born in Munich, the son of a Hungarian immigrant worker, he had taken refuge in the Netherlands when Hitler came to power; but during the war he managed to keep in touch with his Socialist colleagues and other opposition circles in the Third Reich.

Another German exile in Holland, the lawyer Hans-Dieter Salinger, had formed a Dutch underground group in the summer of 1942. Two of its members, arrested in 1944, died in separate concentration camps. Salinger, meanwhile, had gone into hiding, and had written *Die Wiedergeburt von*

Europa – The Rebirth of Europe, urging a 'federal union of all European countries from the Atlantic to and including Poland'. On 19 March 1945, while the Nazis still ruled over 'Fortress Holland', they arrested and identified him; but when the head of the Gestapo in The Hague read the book, he spent several evenings discussing it. At length, defying a sentence of death already passed, he took Salinger into the woods and set him free.

In Germany itself, the anti-Nazi 'Kreisau Circle' had also been discussing postwar Europe. Named after the Silesian estate of Count Helmuth James von Moltke, a great-great-nephew of the famous Field Marshal, it cast its net wide. Its members ranged from Jesuit priests to Lutheran pastors, from Conservatives to Socialists, from landowners to leaders of banned trade unions. Before the war ended, many of them were executed in the orgy of Nazi vengeance which followed the bomb plot against Hitler on 20 July 1944. Some of the Kreisau Circle had been among the plotters, but not all. 'We are to be hanged,' von Moltke wrote to his wife, 'for thinking together.' What they had concluded, among other things, was that Europe after the war should become 'a federal state with one overall sovereignty.'

Von Moltke and his friends had already risked their necks by getting in touch with a number of like-minded groups in occupied Europe. Many had long shared similar views. As early as 1941, the French Resistance leader Henri Frenay, later co-founder of the 'Combat' circuit, had written in his underground news-sheet *Les Petites Ailes*: 'What we want in Europe is a federation of equal States with a Germany cured of her megalomania.' In July 1942, a 'Combat' manifesto prepared jointly by Frenay, Claude Bourdet, and André Hauriou declared: 'The United States of Europe – a stage on the way to world unity – will soon be the living reality for which we fight.'

The same month saw the publication in Toulouse of a new clandestine paper, *Libérer et Fédérer*. Its first number announced: 'The old parties are dead.' The common struggle had united former rivals: 'We saw at once that our divisions were only factions ... and that we shared the same need for liberty and the same aspiration for justice.' The *Libérer et Fédérer* group comprised a number of French Socialists, including Pierre Bertaux, Jean Cassou, Georges Friedmann, and Vincent Auriol, later to be President of France; but it also had links with the Church. What was more, not all its members were French. Its headquarters was a bookshop in the Place Rouaix on the rue de Languedoc, kept by an Italian exile from Fascism, Silvio Trentin, who had formerly taught law at the University of Padua; and he brought into the group a number of other Italian refugees, some of whom had fought against Franco in the Spanish Civil War.

In Italy, Mussolini had interned many of his opponents on the island of Ventotene in the Gulf of Gaetà, some 30 miles offshore and 55 miles due West of Naples. Prominent among them were Altiero Spinelli, a burly former Communist already sentenced to 20 years' imprisonment in 1927; the economist Ernesto Rossi, first imprisoned three years later; and the Socialist Eugenio Colorni, arrested in 1938. Here, as elsewhere, prisoners had time for reflection and discussion; and in the first half of 1941 Spinelli and Rossi produced the so-called 'Ventotene Manifesto', which in July they managed to smuggle out to Rome. Its central objective was a federation to abolish 'the division of Europe into nation states'.

In 1942, Colorni escaped from Ventotene to the mainland, and in May 1943 he launched a clandestine periodical, characteristically called *L'Unità Europea*. In July, Mussolini was ousted, and the new Government under Marshal Badoglio began to release political prisoners – including Spinelli and Rossi. Once back in Italy, they made common cause with Ferruccio Parri's Action Party, which shared their European ideals. At a secret meeting with other anti-Fascist parties in Milan on the night of 27–28 August 1943, they founded the Movimento Federalista Europea, the European Federalist Movement. Eleven days later, when Badoglio signed an armistice with the Allies, the Nazis took over the front line as far South as Naples, and the anti-Fascists went their separate ways. One group stayed in the North and continued to produce *L'Unità Europea*; Spinelli, Colorni, and others made their way to Rome. Here, at the request of the Socialist leader Pietro Nenni, Colorni became editor of the party's underground news-sheet *Avanti*.

It was a dangerous assignment. Although Rome was an 'open city', the description was as bitterly ironical as its use in the title of Roberto Rossellini's film *Roma, Città Aperta*. The Gestapo was everywhere, and arrests were frequent. In February 1944, Natalia Ginzburg's husband Leone died at the hands of the Nazis; and on 28 May, a few days before the city was liberated, Colorni himself was killed. His place at *Avanti* was taken by the novelist Ignazio Silone. Spinelli and Rossi, meanwhile, travelled North again and crossed the frontier into Switzerland, to attend the Resistance meeting in Geneva. By now, they were more determined than ever to redeem their comrades' sacrifice by building Europe anew.

It was an old ambition.

Fire, ice, sediment, and erosion had long ago shaped the land of Europe with its islands and estuaries – a promontory of Asia, small, temperate, changeable, varied, and rich. The mountains and rivers had only partly divided it; roaming tribes had made it a melting-pot of peoples; its dozen or so languages were mostly cousins; and to many of its inhabitants throughout history its cultural kinship seemed very real. From the classical world, Europe had inherited Greek philosophy and Roman law; from the Christian Church and the Empire, a sense of unity transcending frontiers. The Crusades and early explorations had confirmed Europeans' feeling that they were different from the rest of the world; and as the Empire and the Papacy gave way to national rivalry, nostalgia had inspired many projects for restoring unity and achieving 'perpetual peace'.

Pierre Dubois in the fourteenth century; Antoine Marigny in the fifteenth; Emeric Crucé, Grotius, Leibniz, William Penn, and the Duc de Sully in the seventeenth; the Abbé de Saint-Pierre, Jeremy Bentham, Kant, and the German poet 'Novalis' in the eighteenth; and in the nineteenth century Victor Considérant, Saint-Simon, Victor Hugo, Proudhon, Auguste Comte, Mazzini, and Francesco Crispi – all had entertained elaborate plans or shadowy aspirations for some form of European unity. The later models were often based on the example of North America: not only George Washington, Victor Hugo, Proudhon, and Crispi, but also Lenin and Trotsky referred to a possible 'United States of Europe'. World War I, which killed so many of Europe's young men, made unity seem all the more vital. In 1927, an American visitor noted: 'Many of the common people I talked with in Europe see no salvation for the suspicious squabbling continent but a United States of Europe – if only the antiquated statesmen would realize it.'

At least two statesmen tried. One was Gustav Stresemann, in Weimar Germany; the other was Aristide Briand, in France. Their work for Franco-German friendship won them the joint award of the 1926 Nobel Peace Prize. In 1929, the year of Stresemann's death, Briand actually proposed a 'United States of Europe' as part of his Government's programme; and in the following May he circulated a Memorandum to this effect. But Europe's other Governments were unresponsive. In 1932 Briand died, his proposals decently buried in a series of meetings at the League of Nations. Less than a year later, Hitler came to power in Germany; and before the end of the decade Europe was at war again.

The holocaust of World War II, which inspired so many in the Resistance to seek European unity, spurred many statesmen to similar visions. In 1939, even Clement Attlee had declared: 'Europe must federate or perish' – an appeal that was-lost on his postwar Labour Government. In 1943, Winston Churchill proposed a 'Council of Europe' after the war. In the same year, René Mayer suggested to General de Gaulle an economic federation of Europe: it may well have inspired the General's later proposal for 'a strategic and economic federation of France, Belgium, Luxembourg, and the Netherlands, a federation to which Great Britain might adhere.' In 1944, Belgium, the Netherlands, and Luxembourg signed the Benelux Convention for a future customs union. Pope Pius XII, meanwhile, envisaged a 'close union of the European states inspired by Catholicism – Germany, France, Italy, Spain, Belgium, and Portugal.'

Others with similar, if more secular ideas included not only statesmen like Paul-Henri Spaak, Alcide De Gasperi, Robert Schuman, Johan Willem Beyen, Konrad Adenauer, and Joseph Bech, but also writers like Albert Camus, Raymond Aron, George Orwell, Denis de Rougemont, and Ignazio Silone. All urged, and many helped to organize, efforts to establish what Winston Churchill, in a speech at the University of Zurich on 19 September 1946, called 'a kind of United States of Europe'.

That same year, 4,200 members of Europe's national Parliaments were asked for their views on a federal Europe. Four-fifths of their number replied. Of these, only 3 percent were hostile; and in France, Italy, Belgium, and the Netherlands a majority of the lower-house deputies positively favoured European union. Many were already active in its pursuit. On 16 May 1946, the Belgian Prime Minister Paul Van Zeeland had founded the European League for Economic Co-operation; in December, the European Union of Federalists was formed by seven national movements across the continent from Belgium to Greece. In Britain, at the beginning of 1947, Winston Churchill inaugurated the more right-wing United Europe Movement, while in France a broad Council for United Europe brought together representatives from all parts of the political spectrum. In February 1947 in London, delegates from a dozen countries set up the Socialist Movement for the United States of Europe. June saw the birth of the Nouvelles Equipes Internationales, a mainly Catholic, Franco-Belgian organization, as well as the first moves to establish the federalist Europa-Bund in Germany.

In the winter of 1947–48, a number of these separate organizations appointed an International Committee. It was headed by Joseph Retinger, who during the war had been assistant to the late General Władysław Sikorski, leader of the London-based Polish Government in exile; and its purpose was to mobilize the constituent bodies in a full-scale Congress of Europe. After months of preparation, the Congress met in The Hague from 7 to 10 May 1948. It was a heady occasion, attended by 750 statesmen from all over Western Europe. Paul-Henri Spaak was there; so was Alcide De Gasperi; so was Winston Churchill, with his son-in-law Duncan Sandys. From France came Georges Bidault, Léon Blum, François Mitterrand, Paul Ramadier, Paul Reynaud, and Robert Schuman. Konrad Adenauer led the fifty-strong German delegation. Sitting together in the great Hall of the Knights of the Netherlands – the Ridderzaal, where the Dutch Parliament met – they seemed to many the embodiment of an historic dream: the first States-General of Europe, demanding on behalf of peoples so long divided, so recently reconciled, a political and economic union, a European Assembly, and a European Court of Human Rights.

Those who now argued so persistently for a united Europe spoke from bitter experience but undiminished hope. Their reasons were very clear. First and foremost, they were determined to put a stop to Europe's civil wars. They recognized, secondly, that war had been kindled by a decade's economic nationalism. That too must be brought to an end. They realized, thirdly, that the separate nations of Western Europe were now dwarfed by the United States and the USSR. To recover real world influence, Europe must act as one. Finally, they saw unity in Europe as the beginning of international law and order – a first, modest, practical step towards a united world.

'European peace', the Geneva Resistance meeting had declared, 'is the key to world peace.' It had continued:

In the space of one generation Europe has been the epicentre of two world wars.... What is needed is to put an end to this anarchy by creating a federal union among the European peoples. Only a federal union will permit the German people to take part in European life without being a menace to other peoples.

Later, working in the first European institutions, I found it moving to meet not only Resistance veterans like Alfred Mozer or Altiero Spinelli, not only Hitler's former prisoners like Jean Rey, but also people who in World War II had been on the other side. Some bore proud names like von Moltke or even von Stülpnagel, their honour redeemed by their family's martyrs. Others had been brave but unwilling soldiers, like Walter Hallstein, first President of the EEC Commission – a University professor conscripted into the German army, captured, and sent as a prisoner to the

United States. In his prison camp he had helped found a 'university' for the inmates, and had nearly been lynched by hard-line, unrepentant Nazis. One Italian colleague walked with a limp, a legacy from fighting the British in the Western Desert. A German friend had on the wall behind his desk the splintered propeller of his fighter aircraft, smashed by bullets from a British plane. Neither bore hard feelings. With another, a handsome and rather arrogant Prussian, I was ill at ease for many months: I admired his efficiency but disliked his gall. Then one day, after some particularly infuriating remark from him, I lost my temper. 'You've no right to talk like that,' I exclaimed, 'after the Nazi death camps.' It was unforgivable. He bore no personal guilt. But for the first time his pride crumbled, and he blushed. We sat down then and there, and talked for nearly two hours. It was virtually a psychiatric session – and it worked. From that moment on, there was no restraint or hostility left. And if we, despite the past, could now work happily side by side, there was surely hope for a peaceful future.

Nor was it only a matter of feelings, however deep. Cool reasoning reached the same conclusion. Millions had died, and millions had been enslaved, in World War II: but the nationalist dictators who made that war had been brought to power by nationalist policies in the economic field. After World War I, much of Europe had been fragmented, its internal frontiers lengthened by 7,000 miles. Efforts to maintain cross-border trade had foundered in the slump which had begun in 1929. Seeking self-sufficiency, one country after another had expanded its own farm output and reduced its imports of food. The result had been glut, and a fall in world prices and incomes. To prevent cheap imports ruining its own producers, each country in turn had raised its protective barriers still higher. To ease its own unemployment, each had likewise restricted the import of industrial goods – putting up customs tariffs, imposing tight quotas, or devaluing its currency to give its own firms a competitive advantage. Each, in other words, had tried to solve its own problems by dumping them on its neighbours over the tariff wall. The cumulative result had been self-defeating. Trade had shrunk, or withered into bilateral barter deals; confidence had vanished; unemployment had soared. Attempts to replace beggar-my-neighbour policies by international co-operation had been vitiated by nationalist assumptions and defensive mistrust. With no one to speak effectively for the common interest, each country had had to seek its own salvation: none could break out of the vicious spiral by itself. In desperate plights, people turned to desperate remedies and demagogic men. Now, looking back on that experience, those who sought unity in Europe were determined to find ways of making the common interest heard.

By now, moreover, it had become obvious that the countries of Western Europe shared a common plight. All had been overshadowed by the rise of the Soviet Union and the giant power of the United States. However long their experience, however mature their civilization, they now had to accept that the centres of world decision-making had moved from Paris, Berlin, Rome, and London – to Washington and Moscow as well as, potentially, Peking. Part of the reason, again, was economic. Even before World War II, the only European countries to match the growth-rate of the United States had been Germany, Italy, and Sweden. Now, America's standard of living, by any measure, was at least twice as high as that of Western Europe. Looking for the reason, many Europeans singled out the sheer size of the American home market, which simultaneously made possible more economies of scale, greater competition, and better division of labour among specialist firms. Europe, by contrast, was compartmentalized; and Europeans, once the world's élite, had been further weakened by internecine strife. Exhausted by war, gradually losing empire, divided and impoverished, they felt like ruined aristocrats facing belligerent self-made millionaires. Only by banding together, it seemed, could they recover collectively some of the world influence they had individually lost.

Nor, finally, were their motives for seeking unity wholly selfish. The role that many envisaged for Europe was that of a peacemaker – championing freedom and justice, helping to relieve poverty, and restraining extremist aggression in both East and West. Some were quasi-neutralists who saw Europe as a political 'Third Force' between America and Russia. Others were much clearer in their allegiance to Western democracy; and many of those who worked most ardently for a united Europe were internationalists, whose original aim had been a united world. Disappointed by the League of Nations between the wars, they had placed great hopes in the postwar United Nations: but the UN had involved no merger or delegation of sovereignty, and had soon been paralysed by the national veto. Within four years, the Soviet Union was to use its veto no fewer than thirty times. With little prospect of law and order on a world scale, many now sought the same goal in Europe: common rules and democratic institutions, to tame nationalism and settle disputes peacefully. If former enemies like France and Germany could thus be reconciled, others might follow suit. Meanwhile, a united Europe would be strong enough to replace American leadership by

Atlantic partnership; and if the United States and a uniting Europe acted together as equals, they would be better placed for constructive dialogue with the USSR. World unity, in other words, would not be achieved by 'world government', that shibboleth of wartime discussion groups: but it might emerge from the patient, piecemeal construction of a new and better balanced international system; and the unification of Western Europe was the first essential step.

Such were the aspirations voiced at The Hague and at similar if smaller gatherings elsewhere. Some governments listened sympathetically. The postwar constitutions of France, Germany, and Italy all envisaged limiting national sovereignty: the Preamble to the German *Grundgesetz* or 'Basic Law' specifically looked forward to 'a united Europe'. In practice, however, progress was slow. When the Europeans established OEEC, the Organization for European Economic Co-operation, in response to the Marshall Plan, the United States urged them to go further and form a customs union; but Britain, in particular, refused. Together with the Benelux countries, she also resisted French pressure to strengthen OEEC by allowing majority votes to bypass the veto. Far from developing, therefore, into an embryonic economic union, the OEEC remained what one chastened observer called it: 'a conference of sovereign states in permanent session'.

For a time, the Congress at The Hague seemed more promising. After six weeks' hard lobbying, its sponsors persuaded the French Foreign Minister, Georges Bidault, to put some of its proposals to his British and Benelux partners in the Brussels Treaty Organization. On 20 July 1948, he duly suggested a customs and economic union, and a consultative European Assembly. Bidault's British counterpart, Ernest Bevin, was instantly suspicious. He was worried, he said, by the prospect of Communist deputies in the proposed Assembly. Behind this anxiety lay deeper uneasiness. Britain still felt closer to the Commonwealth than to continental Europe, and any limitation of her national sovereignty still seemed out of the question. But the organizers of the Hague Congress kept up their pressure; and on 18 August a new French Government, with Robert Schuman as its Foreign Minister, formally endorsed a further memorandum from them, proposing a conference of governments to implement the plan.

Once again the British were sceptical: on 2 September, the Foreign Office circulated a supercilious questionnaire which seemed to scorn the whole notion. However, when they saw that other governments were bent on pressing ahead, they reluctantly joined in. The talks went on throughout the winter. Finally, on 5 May 1949, the Brussels Treaty powers and five other countries agreed on the Statute of the Council of Europe, composed of a Consultative Assembly and a Committee of Ministers. Within less than a year, the European Congress in The Hague had borne fruit.

The new Assembly held its first meeting in August 1949 in the gabled city of Strasbourg. It was a significant venue. Deep in the heartland of Western Europe, two miles from the Rhine, Strasbourg had been disputed for centuries between France and Germany. Now French, it still looked German, and the majority of its inhabitants spoke the dialect of Alsace. It straddled, in fact, the great linguistic frontier between Romance and Germanic languages, which ran from the North Sea to the Adriatic. From Belgium, Luxembourg, and the Saar, through Lorraine and Alsace, across Switzerland to the South Tyrol or Alto Adige, that cultural dividing-line had long been a danger-zone, the source and the main victim of endless ambivalence and conflict. But it had also bred men like Alcide De Gasperi and Robert Schuman, deeply committed to healing the historic rift. Konrad Adenauer himself came from the Rhineland; and from Belgium came Paul-Henri Spaak, the Socialist deputy and former Prime Minister who was elected first President of the Council of Europe's Assembly.

Burly, forceful, and a brilliant orator, Spaak was pleased by his resemblance to Churchill. Under his bold chairmanship, the Assembly's first session set a lively pace. Delegates proposed, among other things, a link with OEEC, an economic union, and a European Bank. French deputies André Philip and Paul Reynaud called for 'a political authority of a supranational character'; the British Labour MP, R.W.G. MacKay, proposed 'a political authority for Europe with limited functions but real powers'. When the session ended, Spaak declared: 'I came to Strasbourg convinced of the necessity of a United States of Europe. I am leaving it with the certitude that union is possible.'

The Council of Europe was certainly a step in that direction. Unlike the OEEC, it was explicitly political, not economic. Its Assembly of national MPs took their seats in alphabetical order, not in national delegations. Its shapely new building, *la Maison de l'Europe*, opened in 1950, was an inspiring sight, with the flags of its member nations fluttering outside. Its multinational staff brought together men and women of great talent, integrity, and vision. Its achievements included not only the European Convention for the Protection of Human Rights, backed by a European Court, but also innumerable less spectacular measures to promote rapprochement and mutual understanding.

It was something: but, compared with its sponsors' hopes, it was not much. Some had envisaged a constituent assembly, drafting the constitution for a united Europe. The Hague Congress had proposed an Assembly of three or four hundred delegates, with a Council of Ministers in a fairly minor role. France and Belgium had agreed that the Council must be stronger; but Britain had initially opposed having any Assembly at all. The final compromise had been an Assembly virtually deprived of power. At first, it was not even allowed to draw up its own agenda; and the Committee of Ministers, although empowered in some instances to vote by majority, was handicapped in practice by a self-imposed veto. The result was frequent deadlock between an impatient Assembly and an obstructive Committee of Ministers. As Paul Reynaud bitterly exclaimed, 'The Council of Europe consists of two bodies, one of them *for* Europe, and the other *against* it.' In December 1951, Paul-Henri Spaak resigned in disgust. 'If a quarter of the energy expended here in saying No', he told the Assembly, 'were used to say Yes to something, we should not be in the state we are in today.' Looking back nearly twenty years later, he described the Committee of Ministers as the most timorous and impotent international body he had ever known. From a former President of the United Nations Assembly, it was a barbed remark.

But the European movement was not easily stopped. Time and again, it faced setbacks and disappointments. Time and again, it overcame them. For those committed to the task of uniting Europe, the years that followed were full of suspense and effort – acknowledging failure, seizing opportunities, changing tack to avoid obstacles, pressing forward, alert for a fair wind or a squall. And if Strasbourg, as time went by, seemed more and more a city of lost causes, action was in prospect elsewhere. The initiative this time came not from Europe's frontier zone, but from a native of Cognac, close to its Atlantic seaboard: the mercurial Jean Monnet, then head of the French Planning Commissariat.

Monnet had first shown his concern for Europe's future while working for the Allies in Algiers during the later stages of World War II. The United Nations Organization, he told John Davenport of *Fortune* magazine, would 'involve no real giving up of sovereignty. This is not going to happen on a world scale.... Let us not blind ourselves this time, by the picture of the impressive machinery, to the really tough things that need to be done if we are to have peace.'

Davenport continued:

> What are those tough things? For Monnet, as for most Europeans, the toughest questions of all are Germany and European unity. Monnet would like to see ... the great Ruhr coal and iron fields run by a European authority for the benefit of all participating nations.... But this in turn implies a Europe far more unified than before the war. Here he would like to see ... a true yielding of sovereignty by European nations to some kind of central union – a union that could cut down tariffs, create a great internal European market and prevent that race of nationalism 'which is the curse of the modern world'.

In a paper for the French Committee of National Liberation, Monnet went further still. 'To enjoy the prosperity and social progress that are essential,' he wrote, 'the States of Europe must form a federation or a "European entity" which will make them a single economic unit.'

Stressing such practical priorities, and busy with French economic planning, Monnet took no part in the first political efforts to unite Europe after the war. While the Hague Congress was being prepared, he was in the United States, negotiating for emergency wheat supplies. The experience confirmed his belief that Europeans must learn to stand on their own feet. 'In my opinion,' he wrote to Robert Schuman, 'Europe cannot long afford to remain almost exclusively dependent on American credit for her production and American strength for her security.' To Georges Bidault he declared: 'We must rapidly transform this situation into a position of independence and collaboration'; and, to Schuman again, 'The countries of Western Europe must turn their national efforts into a truly European effort. This will be possible only through a *federation* of the West.'

Watching the high hopes of the Hague Congress fade into the mists of the Council of Europe, he concluded that 'national sovereignty would have to be tackled more boldly and on a narrower front.' His first thought was to revive, in the economic field, the idea of Franco-British union which he had proposed in 1940, when France had been on the brink of collapse.

Britain had always seemed to him France's natural partner. In 1904, at the age of sixteen, he had gone to London for two years to work in the City and learn English: he had come away with deep respect for the discipline and probity he found there. In both wars, he had struggled to co-ordinate Anglo-French supply arrangements; in the second, he had served as a British official. In 1944, discussing with Harold Macmillan his plans for European economic unity, he had argued: 'In this England must take the lead and France must support her.'

What looked like his opportunity came in March 1949. The British Chancellor of the Exchequer, Sir Stafford Cripps, was in Paris to debate with his French counterpart Maurice Petsche the economic plans that their respective Governments were putting to OEEC. Petsche invited Monnet to dine with them; and Monnet spoke his mind. 'You won't reach agreement', he said, 'unless you make it your ultimate aim to merge the British and French economies.'

Both Petsche and Cripps thought this far-fetched: but they agreed to Monnet's request for talks with his British opposite number, Sir Edwin Plowden, whose central planning organization had been partly modelled on the French Plan. So, on Wednesday 20 April, 1949, Plowden came to Paris with his deputy Alan Hitchman and the director of the Economic Section of the Cabinet Office, Robert Hall. Next morning, they drove out to Monnet's small country house at Houjarray, some forty miles South-West of Paris, where he was waiting to meet them with Etienne Hirsch and Pierre Uri, his two closest colleagues on the Plan. They spent four days together, including most of the weekend.

A businessman turned civil servant, educated at Cambridge and in Switzerland, Plowden was slightly younger than Monnet; but he resembled him in temperament as well as in breadth of experience. They took to each other very quickly – especially at Houjarray in Spring. Monnet's rural retreat was an L-shaped former farmhouse, with a low, flagged drawing-room full of family keepsakes and Madame Monnet's paintings. Its tall, rather rickety french windows looked out across the garden and the fields towards the forest of Rambouillet: the view combined the gentleness of the English countryside with the stricter charm of the French. Sitting in armchairs, gathered round the meal-table, or strolling outside, it was possible to talk freely instead of negotiating. No more propitious setting could have been found.

Exchanging information about their economic problems, both sides were extremely frank. Plowden and his colleagues even criticized their own Government's excessive restrictions and controls. But when Monnet asked the crucial question – could France and Britain draw up a joint plan and work towards economic union? – all his stage management and persuasive skill were in vain. Plowden, Monnet wrote later, 'was very interested and full of goodwill'; yet he seemed not to realize what was Monnet's ultimate aim, and the talks centred instead on short-term questions such as mutual trade in French meat and British coal.

On these subjects, long after the Houjarray meeting, Monnet and Plowden went on exchanging information: but without co-ordinated planning, mutual trade and payments soon ran into trouble. On 18 September 1949, Britain devalued the pound by 30.5 percent without forewarning Petsche; on 19 November, France devalued the franc by 22.4 percent. Monnet and Plowden remained very friendly; and towards the end of the year Monnet once more broached 'the idea of exchanging UK coal for French foodstuffs in a manner which would make plain to the world the reality of Anglo-French co-operation'. But coal was scarce, and French meat was expensive. In December, Plowden was obliged to conclude: 'There is at present little basis for an arrangement of the kind you suggest.' As Etienne Hirsch sadly commented, 'the British Government was not interested in drawing up a joint plan for France and Britain, but only in a more extensive exchange of goods along traditional lines.'

It was a fateful decision: it helped determine the shape of Europe for more than twenty years. Having failed to make Britain France's first partner in the quest for unity, Monnet turned to Germany instead. This time, his appeal was answered.

He had raised the question of Germany's future during his talks with Plowden. How would Britain and France cope with revived German competition? How would Europe cope with Germany's political resurgence? To deal with German heavy industry, the Allies had set up the International Authority for the Ruhr: but they disagreed about its aims. The United States wanted to see the Ruhr contribute to Western recovery; France was anxious to keep it under control. 'There was still in many people's minds,' Monnet recalled afterwards, 'the notion that peace with Germany should be based on ... domination – which was the peace of 1918. I felt that that would be a castastrophe.' 'Peace', he remarked to Robert Schuman, 'can be founded only on equality.'

In October 1949, the West and the Soviet Union failed once more to agree on a German peace treaty. The Germans were growing restive under foreign tutelage – especially now that France was seeking to annex the Saar. In mid-January 1950, Robert Schuman tried to mend matters by travelling to Mainz, Bonn, and Berlin – his first visit to Germany as French Foreign Minister. He went with the best of intentions. A quiet, shrewd, stooping, rather bookish bachelor, he described himself as 'a Catholic from the Moselle'. Although deeply French, he had been born in Luxembourg, where his father had taken refuge after Germany had annexed Alsace and Lorraine in 1871; he had studied law at German universities, and spoke the language fluently. During World War II, the Nazis had arrested and imprisoned him: but ever since World War I he had been unshakeably convinced that Franco-German reconciliation was vital for peace. He was shocked and hurt, now, by his reception in Germany. Officials and Ministers were frigidly polite: they left the press and the opposition to express their real feelings of bitterness and thwarted pride. No less disconcerting was the way the United States seemed to be backing Germany against France. Sooner or later, it seemed, France must yield to American pressure, and watch Germany grow strong again – a competitor and a rival, an independent, unpredictable power freed from the restraints that had tamed her hitherto.

There was, however, an alternative: to bind France and Germany together in a system of shared restraints on national power. Konrad Adenauer, Germany's new Chancellor, had suggested something like it as early as the 1920's, arguing that 'lasting peace between France and Germany can be attained only through the establishment of a community of economic interests.' In January 1950 he reverted to the idea in a conversation with John J. McCloy, the US High Commissioner; and in March he went even further. In an interview with Kingsbury Smith of the International News Service, INS, he proposed a political union between France and Germany, open also to Britain, Italy, and the Benelux countries.

This suggestion, which echoed Monnet's plan for Franco-British union in 1940, evoked little response. The French Government seemed pained that Adenauer had put it to an American journalist rather than through official channels: France would wait, said a spokesman, to receive concrete proposals. Even Monnet thought Adenauer 'unrealistic' in offering so general a solution to the particular problems of the Saar and the Ruhr. Instead, he declared later, 'we should start with the difficulty itself, using it as a lever to initiate a more general solution.'

Uncertain what to do, Monnet took his worries to the Alps. Walking, he said, had always helped him to reach conclusions. On returning to Paris at the beginning of April 1950, he brought with him the notes he had scribbled every evening. They revealed an idea taking shape.

Whichever way we turn, in the present world situation we see nothing but deadlock. . . .

Men's minds are becoming focused on an object at once simple and dangerous – the cold war....

This prospect creates among leaders that rigidity of mind which is characteristic of the pursuit of a single object. The search for solutions to problems ceases. Such rigidity ... will lead inevitably to a confrontation.

The German situation is rapidly turning into a cancer that will be dangerous to peace....

It cannot be dealt with by unifying Germany. That would require agreement between the USA and the USSR, which for the moment is inconceivable....

We must start a process of change, and give the Germans a sense of direction – not seek a static solution based on things as they are.

On 10 May 1950, Robert Schuman was due in London to discuss the future of Germany with Dean Acheson and Ernest Bevin. The Germans were eager to increase their steel production, still limited by Allied decree. The Americans were certain to support them. The long-term result, Monnet feared, would be German supremacy and French decline.

The decisions that lead to this situation will be initiated, if not taken, at the London conference under American pressure.

The USA do not want things to take this course. They will accept an alternative solution if it is dynamic and constructive, especially if it is proposed by France.

This, thought Monnet, was his opportunity: to solve the Franco-German problem by changing its context – using it as his 'lever' to begin uniting Europe.

Until now, we have been engaged in an effort to organize the West, economically, militarily, and politically: OEEC, the Brussels Pact, Strasbourg.

Two years' experience ... shows that we are making no real progress....

The peoples of Europe hear nothing but words ... empty speeches and futile meetings....

Words are not enough. Only immediate action on an essential point can change the present situation. This action must be radical, real, immediate, and dramatic. It must make a reality of the hopes which people are on the point of giving up.

Reworked into a connected whole, these reflections turned into 'the Schuman Plan' – the starting point for the real uniting of Europe. It proposed:

to place the whole of Franco-German coal and steel production under an international Authority open to the participation of the other countries of Europe....

By the pooling of basic production and the establishment of a new High Authority whose decisions will be binding on France, Germany, and the countries that join them, this proposal will lay the first concrete foundations of the European Federation which is indispensable to the maintenance of peace.

Five years after World War II, with France and Germany still at loggerheads, it was a revolutionary idea. Monnet's problem now was to get it launched.

The Schuman Plan nearly became 'the Bidault Plan'. Like all Monnet's projects, it went through many drafts and much discussion – with Etienne Hirsch and Pierre Uri; with Paul Reuter, Professor of Law at Aix-la-Chapelle; with Monnet's old friends and colleagues René Mayer and René Pleven, both of them Ministers in Georges Bidault's Government. Monnet also talked at length with Robert Schuman's *directeur de cabinet*, Bernard Clappier, a quiet, resourceful, rather saturnine figure looking a little like the actor François Périer: he later became Governor of the Bank of France. 'M. Schuman', said Clappier, 'is looking for an initiative that he can propose in London on 10 May. The deadline's approaching, and no one seems able to advise him on what to do.' 'Well,' said Monnet, 'I have some ideas.'

He expected Clappier to call him back after talking with Schuman; but circumstances delayed the reply. On Friday 28 April, fearing that Schuman was not interested, Monnet had a copy of his draft sent round to Bidault. No sooner had it gone than Clappier re-appeared, full of apologies. He read the paper. 'May I show it to M. Schuman?' he asked. Armed with a copy, he hurried to the Gare de l'Est, to catch Schuman before he left for a weekend in his quiet country house at Scy-Chazelles, near Metz. He found him already in his compartment. 'Could you read this paper of Monnet's?' he said. 'It's important.'

On Monday morning, 1 May, Clappier was back at the Gare de l'Est to meet the incoming train. 'I've read the proposal,' said Schuman. 'I'll use it.'

Two days later, in guarded terms, Schuman broached the subject at the regular Wednesday meeting of the Cabinet. So far, only nine people were in the know. Afterwards, Schuman handed the draft to Bidault – who was furious, and summoned Monnet. 'Schuman's just shown me this paper,' he snapped. 'It appears that you're the author. I should have appreciated your telling me first.' 'I did,' said Monnet: 'I wrote to you on Friday.' Bidault looked for the letter. It had been on his desk all the time.

There was just a week to go before the London meeting. To discuss how to proceed, Schuman lunched with Monnet at the Planning Commissariat's headquarters in the rue de Martignac. It was a hot day. 'Why not take off your jacket, M. le Président?' said Monnet: 'I'll do the same – it's a habit I picked up in America.' For a moment, Schuman demurred. 'We seldom lunch in shirtsleeves at the Foreign Office,' he explained. 'And besides, I wear braces.' Smiling, he took his coat off, and they began work.

To overcome opposition, speed and surprise were essential. Next Wednesday's Cabinet meeting, due on the very day of the London conference, had to be brought forward to Tuesday. The Secretary-General of the French Foreign Office, Alexandre Parodi, had to be told what was happening, but pledged to silence. Above all, Chancellor Adenauer had to be sounded out before the French Government could be asked to decide.

By 3 p.m. on 6 May, the text of the proposal had reached its final form. In the utmost secrecy, Schuman sent it to Bonn with a private envoy – a magistrate from Lorraine by the name of Michlich. On the evening of 8 May, the day before the Cabinet meeting, Monnet asked to hear the text read one last time. At the first words, he interrupted, and asked everyone to stand. That night, his team burned most of the preliminary drafts.

Next morning, Tuesday 9 May 1950, the French Cabinet met in the Elysée Palace. Clappier waited in an adjoining room, in touch by telephone with Monnet and his friends in the rue de Martignac. The hours ticked by. Midday came and went. The Ministers reached the end of their agenda: but Schuman dared not speak until he had heard from Bonn. The Cabinet adjourned. 'The long silence was agony to us,' Monnet confessed: 'Was everything going to hinge on a matter of minutes?' Then, at last, Clappier's telephone rang. Adenauer had received Schuman's message. He agreed, as he put it, 'with all my heart'.

The Ministers resumed their seats, and Schuman spoke. Some of his colleagues found his words hard to follow, technical, and all in a rush. 'You were like a torrent,' he was told afterwards by the French President, Vincent Auriol. But the Cabinet accepted his proposal. Late that afternoon, in a press conference at the French Foreign Office, Schuman announced it to the world.

The response was rapid. Within three weeks, Germany, Italy, Belgium, the Netherlands, and Luxembourg all accepted France's invitation to negotiate the Schuman Plan.

Britain declined.

It was not for want of encouragement. On the morning after the 9 May announcement, reassured by British press reactions, Monnet sent Plowden a copy of the text, adding that he would be in London soon. Schuman had already taken the boat train the night before, in time for the three-power meeting. He hoped that Britain would join in his venture. Instead, he found himself in a hornets' nest. Ernest Bevin, as Dean Acheson put it, 'bristled with hostility to Schuman's whole idea.'

Looking back, Acheson partly blamed himself for what he called Britain's 'great mistake of the postwar period'. Like Adenauer, he had been let into Monnet's and Schuman's secret: but this had happened almost by chance. After 'a long, strenuous, wearying winter and spring', his colleagues in the State Department had persuaded him not to fly direct to the London conference, but to 'get a few days' rest and please Schuman by starting early and going via Paris.' He had arrived on Sunday morning, 7 May. On the way in from Orly airport, the US Ambassador David Bruce had reported an unusual request from the French Foreign Minister. Instead of a routine courtesy call at the Foreign Office on Monday morning, Schuman proposed that they meet privately at the Ambassador's residence that very afternoon. When they did, Schuman and Monnet explained their proposal, and asked Acheson to keep it to himself. On Tuesday morning, 9 May, Acheson left for London, where he lunched with Bevin and Clement Attlee, the Prime Minister. During luncheon, a message arrived from the French Ambassador asking for an appointment with Bevin that afternoon. Acheson realized what it meant; but he kept his promise to Schuman, and said nothing. That afternoon, when Bevin saw him again at the Foreign Office, 'he was in a towering rage, and at once charged that I had known of Schuman's plan and had kept it from him.... He rushed on to accuse me of having conspired with Schuman to create a European combination against British trade with the continent.' Acheson almost wished that he had not stopped off in Paris, or that he had persuaded Schuman to brief Bevin privately in advance.

In fact, as Bevin's junior Minister Kenneth Younger said, 'the pique was slight and faded quickly.' The real reason for Britain's rejection of the Schuman Plan, Younger saw, was 'a nation-wide attitude which could not be doubted'.

As an island, Britain had long been a refuge and a partial outsider, less deeply marked than the continent by the Roman Empire, Roman Law, and the Roman Catholic Church. As islanders, the British had developed sea power, and had early conquered overseas dominions in temperate climates, where they settled their own kith and kin. As leaders in the first Industrial Revolution, they had made their country the workshop of colonies which served as Britain's home farm. In the words of *European Unity*, an incongruously named pamphlet put out in May 1950 by the National Executive Committee of the British Labour Party:

In every respect except distance we in Britain are closer to our kinsmen in Australia and New Zealand on the far side of the world than we are to Europe. We are closer in language and in origins, in social habits and institutions, in political outlook and in economic interest.

In two world wars, the Channel had helped save the British from invasion, and perhaps defeat. Although impoverished and weakened, they still felt that they had a 'special relationship' with the United States. They had not yet recognized that their real position in the world was so like that of their continental neighbours. To Bevin, as Schuman said, 'it seemed impossible, unthinkable, that ... there should be any authority set above the British Parliament.'

When Monnet reached London on Sunday 14 May, he was bombarded with questions about the Schuman Plan – on cartels, on possible steel mill closures, on the implications for French planning, on relations with the USA and the USSR. But the subject that recurred again and again was the proposed merger of sovereignty. How would the High Authority operate *vis-à-vis* the nation-States?

In conversations, letters, and notes, Monnet did his best to reassure his British friends. The High Authority, he explained, would not usurp the place of governments or impose dictatorial decisions. It would work within rules agreed on by the member nations and subject to a means of appeal. But it must be independent. It could not be merely a committee of national representatives, each seeing only his country's segment of the problems common to them all. That old, intergovernmental method had proved itself ineffective. Those negotiating the Schuman Plan must accept the new principle from the start.

This, it turned out, was the sticking-point for the British. Between 25 May and 3 June 1950, Britain and France exchanged eleven diplomatic Notes, totalling no less than four thousand words. The French – partly written by Monnet – were full of patient but stubborn explanation; the British icily spurned what they called a 'prior commitment', and proposed instead to take part in 'discussions' on 'a different basis'. To Monnet, the only prior commitment was that those negotiating should do so as equals, and agree on their objective: to break with the past and initiate a merger of sovereignty, under rules and institutions accepted by them all.

The exchange of Notes petered out in an agreement to disagree. As it did so, the British Ambassador in Paris, Sir Oliver Harvey, drafted or sanctioned a scornful press statement. Ten years earlier, he had privately described Monnet as looking like 'a mixture of gangster and conspirator'. Now the Paris embassy declared:

There are precedents of international organizations set up with fanfares of trumpets which encounter only difficulties and disappointments when the time comes to put them into practice.

Monnet nicknamed this the 'trumpets communiqué'. Time would tell how mistaken it was.

On 20 July 1950, the Schuman Plan Conference met in Paris. As head of the French delegation, Jean Monnet was in the chair; and his approach foreshadowed the European Community he hoped to build. As one Dutch delegate put it:

He never allowed the negotiations to become negotiations in the traditional sense.... The delegates were not confronted with French positions, but were invited to discuss, to contribute.... Some ... at first believed that they were simply being tricked when, during meetings, they saw the little group of Frenchmen around Monnet disagreeing among themselves just as much as with other delegations. How could one negotiate one nation's special interest in orderly fashion against another's, if the inviting delegation seemed to have no clear idea of the national interest it wanted to defend? But Monnet's method was so contagious, the attempt to find solutions for common problems instead of defending simply one's own national interests was so liberating and exhilarating, that none of the chief delegates resisted this new approach for very long.

Difficulties abounded – over sovereignty, over cartels, over voting rights: but at length, on 18 April 1951, less than a year after the original Schuman Declaration, the representatives of Belgium, France, Germany, Italy, the Netherlands, and Luxembourg signed the treaty establishing the first European Community, the European Coal and Steel Community, or ECSC. It provided for a 'common market', to pool its member nations' basic resources of coal, coke, iron ore, steel, and scrap; and to oversee this first move towards economic integration, it set up four political institutions.

The nine-man High Authority was much as Monnet had envisaged it: independent of national governments, directly financed by a levy on coal and steel production, and able in many cases to take its own decisions, immediately binding on all the member States. On other, weightier matters the High Authority's role was to propose solutions to the 'Special Council of

Ministers', each representing one of the member governments. The Council was dubbed 'Special' because its introduction was a concession to inter-governmental habits; but in many instances it was empowered to vote by weighted majority, and so to bypass any national veto. Disputes and appeals would go to a supreme Court of Justice; and an Assembly would exercise democratic control. Initially, its members would be chosen by the national Parliaments from among their own members; later, they would be directly elected. From the start, however, the Assembly could dismiss the High Authority by a two-thirds majority vote.

As befitted this embryo constitution for a united Europe, the copy of the Treaty signed in Paris was printed by the French Stationery Office on Dutch vellum in German ink, and was bound in Belgian parchment with Italian silk ribbons and Luxembourg glue.

It took a further fifteen months for the Treaty to be ratified. Then, on 24 and 25 July 1952, the six countries' Foreign Ministers met to settle the final details. They appointed Jean Monnet to head the High Authority; they chose Dutch, French, German, and Italian as the Community's working languages; and they failed to agree on a site for its headquarters. Should it be Paris? Strasbourg? The Saar? The Hague? Liége? Turin? At three in the morning, they were still arguing. One of them seemed almost asleep. It was Joseph Bech, stout, moustachioed, and a little like Santa Claus: the Prime Minister, Foreign Minister, and Wine Minister of Luxembourg. Suddenly, he stirred. 'I propose that work begin right away,' he said, 'in Luxembourg. That will give us time to reflect.' So, as the sky lightened, the decision was reached. It was Europe's first all-night 'marathon' meeting. It was not the last.

The Grand Duchy of Luxembourg covers barely a thousand square miles. In 1950, it had some 300,000 inhabitants. To visitors, most of them spoke German or French; but their own language was Letzeburgesch, and their national motto was *'Mir woelle bleiwe wat mir sin'* ('We want to stay as we are') – a natural ambition for a people so repeatedly overrun. Their tiny capital city was like a French or German provincial town. It had one small theatre, five cinemas, and seven night clubs – 'the only leg shows in Europe', said one tourist, 'with varicose veins.' A brass band played in the square on Sunday mornings; trams rattled under the windows of the Grand-Ducal Palace; stout ladies in astrakhan coats filled the fashionable café on the Grand'rue. Placid, landlocked, and prosperous – it annually produced a ton of steel per head of population – Luxembourg was a haven of Ruritanian peace. But on

Sunday 10 August 1952, while a blazing sun glittered on the grey slate rooftops, the city was abruptly invaded by foreign cars, diplomats, pressmen, and busy officials. The High Authority had arrived.

Its members held their first, ceremonial meeting that afternoon in the Town Hall, amid flags and 'Peace' roses and 'New Europe' gladioli. The next day, while most of Europe was on holiday, they settled down to work. Their main headquarters, on the edge of the ravine dividing the city, was the former head office of Luxembourg's National Railways, an old rusticated brownstone building with rickety doors, brown linoleum, and cream-painted walls. While the setting was traditional, the working methods were not. Monnet disliked organigrams and large staffs. 'If one day there are more than 250 of us, we shall be lost,' he said. One of the first officials I saw there was a bilingual Englishman whom Monnet had recruited in Paris: he was climbing in through a ground-floor window to save himself a walk. Officially, the working day began at 8.45 a.m. – but it might start at 6 with a telephone call from Monnet's private house outside the city. At the end of the day, the High Authority's lights burned long after midnight. Free weekends were rare. When a colleague complained at the lack of distractions, Monnet smiled. 'Europe will not be made in night-clubs,' he replied.

Within six months, the High Authority had established the first 'common market', removing national barriers to trade in coal, iron ore, and scrap. The frontiers fell for steel in May 1953, and for high-quality special steels in August 1954. By 1958, when the Community's five-year transition period ended, trade among the six member countries had soared: in steel, it had risen by 157 percent. Jobs had multiplied: so had earnings. The fears of industrialists and trade unions had been allayed. Within its technical field, the Community had been a success.

More important, it had proved that the new institutions worked. Under Monnet's leadership, the High Authority had not tried to act like a supranational government. It had identified common problems, and pro-posed imaginative solutions, coaxing the member States into collective action where attempts to coerce them might have failed. It had even signed an Association Agreement with Britain. 'Now that you are a fact, we shall deal with you,' a British diplomat had said.

So the Schuman Plan seemed to have belied the 'trumpets communiqué'. But that was not the whole story. Success in Luxembourg had been overtaken by failure in Paris – the difficult birth-pangs, decline, and death of Monnet's second European brain-child, conceived soon after the first.

The Schuman Plan Conference had been at work for less than a week when Europe was suddenly gripped again by fear. At dawn on Sunday 25 June 1950, troops from the 'People's Democratic Republic' of North Korea crossed the 38th Parallel and invaded Syngman Rhee's Republic in the South. By 28 June, advancing rapidly, they had captured the Southern capital of Seoul.

The West reacted sharply. The United States summoned a meeting of the UN Security Council, which called for an immediate cease-fire. When this was ignored, President Truman promised aid to South Korea, and ordered General Douglas MacArthur to give naval and air support. That same day, 27 June, the Security Council agreed to take not only economic but also military action, and asked other members of the United Nations to help.

Fifteen countries responded, sending troops to serve under MacArthur's unified command. After heavy fighting up and down the peninsula, in which North Korea deployed nearly 400,000 Chinese 'volunteers', MacArthur asked Washington to be allowed to bomb Chinese bases in Manchuria, even at the risk of full-scale war. The President refused; and in April 1951, when MacArthur publicized their disagreement, Truman dismissed him. By that time, the UN forces had managed to stabilize the shifting battlefront. In July, after it had settled slightly North of the 38th Parallel, peace talks were initiated, leading to a formal armistice two years later.

For once, the United Nations had been given teeth, and had used them: but this had only happened because the Soviet delegation had boycotted, instead of vetoing, the crucial vote. As it was, the USSR condemned the UN action as 'illegal'. Would matters go further than that? The North Koreans were known to be using Soviet arms and equipment, and were thought to have acted on Soviet instigation. Suddenly, in that uneasy summer of 1950, the American and Soviet super-powers seemed close to war.

And war seemed close to Europe – especially in divided Germany. In divided Korea, a well-armed, Soviet-backed 'People's Republic' had attacked its defenceless rival. 'What is happening there,' said Konrad Adenauer, 'is a dress-rehearsal for what is in store for us here.' Many others agreed with him. In East Germany, there were 300,000 highly mechanized Soviet troops, backed by 54,000 armed policemen. In West Germany, the Allies had only 200,000 men. In Europe as a whole, Western forces were yet more heavily outnumbered; and since the summer of 1949 the Soviet Union had had its own atomic bomb.

How was Western Europe to redress the balance of conventional forces?

The United States, committed to the Korean War, could not be expected to do so. The French army was fighting in Indo-China; British troops were still scattered throughout the world. Italy – Belgium – the Netherlands – Luxembourg: none of them could make a crucial new contribution to the defence of Western Europe.

Germany could.

It was a thought long familiar to the US Defense Department. In Europe, only five years after the Nazi nightmare, it caused shudders – not least among the Germans themselves. 'My country has lost blood enough,' said Adenauer: 'it does not want to rearm.' But American pressure was mounting. Already in May 1950, two days before the Schuman Declaration, the US Military Governor in Germany, General Clay, had openly urged a German contribution to Europe's defence. On 22 July the US High Commissioner John H. McCloy argued that it was 'very difficult to deny the Germans the right and the means to defend their own soil.' Finally, at a meeting in New York on 12 September, Secretary of State Dean Acheson formally proposed to Bevin and Schuman that German divisions should be raised to serve in NATO.

To the French Defence Minister Jules Moch, who had lost a son in the Resistance, this was a 'bombshell'. To Jean Monnet, it was what he had feared since the outbreak of the Korean War. On 16 September, he wrote to Schuman:

There seem to be three possible courses to take. To do nothing – but is that possible? To treat Germany on a national basis – but that would stop the Schuman Plan and the building of Europe. Or to integrate Germany into Europe by means of a broader Schuman Plan, taking the necessary decisions within a European framework.

What this implied was a European Army, in which German troops would serve under joint command. Something like it had already been proposed by Adenauer, by the French General Pierre Billotte, and at the Council of Europe by André Philip and Winston Churchill. Later, in the *New York Times*, Arthur Koestler was to suggest a European 'foreign legion'. None of these ideas led to action. But Monnet had one great advantage. In early July, his old friend and former assistant René Pleven had succeeded Georges Bidault as Prime Minister of France. For some weeks, Monnet had been discussing the problem with him. Now, he was able to propose a way out.

With the same small team which had helped to draft the Schuman Declaration – joined, on this occasion, by Hervé Alphand from the French

Foreign Office – Monnet began work on what came to be called 'the Pleven Plan'. By Monday 23 October 1950, the final text was ready. On the following day, Pleven announced his plan to the National Assembly:

The French Government thought that the achievement of the Schuman Plan would accustom people to the idea of a European Community before the delicate question of joint defence had to be broached. But world events have given us no respite. Therefore, confident in the peaceful destiny of Europe and convinced of the need to give all European peoples a sense of collective security, the French Government proposes to solve this problem by the same methods and in the same spirit.... It proposes the creation, for common defence, of a European Army under the authority of the political institutions of a united Europe.

The Assembly approved Pleven's statement by 343 votes to 225. For a moment, a United States of Europe seemed at last on the point of being built.

The international reaction was mixed. The Soviet Union predictably attacked the Pleven Plan. Ernest Bevin told the House of Commons: 'His Majesty's Government does not favour this proposal.' In Germany, the Social-Democratic opposition leader Kurt Schumacher, maimed and embittered by twelve years in Nazi captivity, denounced it with savage scorn. 'The German people,' he cried, 'is not made to be a nation of mercenaries.'

Even in Washington, despite official politeness, the Pleven Plan was greeted in private with what Dean Acheson called 'consternation and dismay'. 'To me,' he wrote later, 'the plan was hopeless, a view confirmed by General Marshall and concurred in by the President, and protracted discussion of it dangerous.' The US delegate at the North Atlantic Council, Charles Spofford, put forward a rival plan, also backed by the British, to recruit German 'combat teams' into NATO immediately, without waiting for the European Army to be formed. In December 1950, with great reluctance, the French Government agreed to a modified version of this 'Spofford Plan'.

It took Monnet months of arguing to bring the US Administration round. The key moment came in June 1951, when he called on the new Supreme Commander, Allied Powers, Europe, General Dwight D. Eisenhower, whom he had known in wartime Algiers. Eisenhower, as he later confessed, had 'disliked the whole idea of a European Army' and much preferred the quick solution of recruiting a German contingent to serve in NATO. Monnet met his objections head-on.

'To rush into raising a few German divisions on a national basis, at the cost of reviving enmity between our peoples, would be catastrophic to the very security of Europe that such a step would be intended to ensure. If, on the other hand, you give France, Germany, and their neighbours common resources to exploit and defend, then Europe will recover the will to resist.'

Eisenhower's interest quickened. 'To sum it up,' he said, 'what you're proposing is that the French and the Germans should wear the same uniform. That's more a human problem than a military one.' To his Chief of Staff he added: 'What Monnet's proposing is to organize relations between people, and I'm all for it.'

Eisenhower convinced Acheson, who in turn convinced President Truman. By the end of July 1951, the US Government was solidly behind the Pleven Plan. With the United States backing it, Britain changed her mind. Although still unwilling to join the proposed European Army, she agreed to 'establish the closest association with the continental European Community at every stage of its development'.

By that time, the Pleven Plan was already taking shape. In January 1951, the French Goverment had invited all European members of NATO to a Treaty-making conference, with the US and Canada as observers. Negotiations began at the French Foreign Office on 15 February 1951, with Hervé Alphand in the chair. At first, only five of the six Schuman Plan countries took part in them: the Netherlands sat in as observers before joining their partners in October 1951. Eventually, on 9 May 1952, the second anniversary of the Schuman Declaration, all six countries initialled the Treaty establishing a European Defence Community, EDC. They formally signed it on 27 May 1952.

The institutions proposed for EDC were very like those of the Schuman Plan: a nine-man executive Commissariat, a Council of national Ministers, the same Court of Justice, and an Assembly – that of the ECSC slightly enlarged – which was to prepare further steps towards political unity. In September, the Council of Ministers of the ECSC actually asked its Assembly to co-opt eight extra members into an *'Ad hoc* Assembly', and to draft a Treaty establishing a European Political Community. Six months later, on 10 March 1953, the *Ad hoc* Assembly produced its project. It envisaged a European Executive Council, to be known as 'Ministers of the European Community'; a Council of Ministers representing the member States; a Court of Justice; and a bicameral Parliament – a Senate chosen by the national Parliaments, and a 'People's Chamber' directly elected.

On 19 March 1953, the German Bundestag approved the EDC Treaty, and the long ratification process was under way. By 17 April 1954, only the

French and Italian Parliaments had not yet voted for the Treaty. But by that time, the whole elaborate edifice was already coming to grief.

In both France and Italy, EDC had provoked a tacit coalition of opponents from the extremes of Right and Left. In France the Gaullists, in Italy the Monarchists and Neo-Fascists, detested the thought of merging even part of the nation's armed forces into a nondescript European Army, no doubt clad in comic-opera uniforms. On the Left, some of the Socialists believed that EDC would jeopardize relations with the East, while many Communists quite straightforwardly feared that it would strengthen the West. All, of whatever party, attacked what they called 'German rearmament' – although now the only alternative to EDC was to revive a German Army. Reporting from Rome at the time, I was struck by the diversity of the anti-EDC parties' propaganda: a virulent poster campaign, a series of strikes, the shameless exploitation of a notorious sex scandal, and even a new Left-wing intellectual weekly, *Il Contemporaneo*, closely modelled on the Left-Centre, pro-EDC *Il Mondo*.

Essentially, however, Italy was waiting to see what would happen in France. There, opinion was deeply divided. Even some of Monnet's friends were unhappy with the EDC Treaty. 'It was negotiated', said Pierre Uri, 'by diplomats and military men who were often hostile to the whole project. For want of imagination, EDC was clumsily copied from the ECSC. But although it looked similar, it was riddled with weaknesses.'

More disquieting to many Frenchmen was the absence of Britain. In the ECSC they felt few qualms about partnership with Germany, despite differences over the Saar. In the proposed European Army, they wanted Britain alongside them. When the Conservative party ousted Labour at the British General Election in October 1951, some continental Europeans began to hope that the new Government might actually join EDC. On 28 November 1951, Sir David Maxwell Fyfe, the former Nuremberg prosecutor who was now British Home Secretary, told the Council of Europe: 'I cannot promise that our eventual association with the European Defence Community will amount to full and unconditional participation because this is a matter which must be left for inter-governmental discussion elsewhere.' At a press conference afterwards, he even added: 'It is quite wrong to suggest that what I said was any closing of the door.' But on the same day, speaking in Rome, Foreign Secretary Anthony Eden slammed the door shut, stating flatly that Britain would not join. To take part in a federation on the continent of Europe, he explained later, 'is something which we know, in our bones, we cannot do.' The most that he would offer – and it was a marked advance on past aloofness – was the pledge he gave three months later: 'to maintain armed forces on the continent of Europe for as long as is necessary.' Beyond that, appeals for tighter British political links with EDC continued to fall on deaf ears.

In Paris, meanwhile, time was fast running out. A series of Government crises weakened the pro-Europeans, and in June 1953 a number of Gaullists joined the Cabinet. Their implacable opposition to EDC became even more obvious when De Gaulle himself, in a press conference that November, poured scorn on 'this monstrous treaty', and lampooned Monnet – without naming him – as 'The Inspirer' of 'supernational monstrosities'. In 1940, the General declared, Monnet had wanted to 'integrate King George VI with President Lebrun'; in 1943, to 'integrate De Gaulle with Giraud'. Now he was trying to integrate Germany with France:

Since victorious France has an army and defeated Germany has none, let us suppress the French Army. After that we shall make a stateless army of Frenchmen and Germans, and since there must be a Government above this army, we shall make a stateless Government, a technocracy. Since this may not please everybody, we'll paint a new shop sign and call it a 'Community'; it won't matter anyway, because the 'European Army' will be entirely at the disposal of the American Commander-in-Chief....

Britain, too, although for different reasons, is demanding that we ratify the so-called 'European Army' – although nothing in the world would induce her to join it herself. Abandon your soldiers to others, lose your sovereignty, lose your Dominions – that's fine for Paris, but not for London.... No doubt there will be a few British soldiers in Germany, and a few attentive British observers attached to EDC.... It's very pleasant to be the guest of honour at a banquet given by a society to which you pay no fees.

Hope revived briefly a few months later, when Britain finally promised an agreement to consult with the future EDC. But still the delays continued; and in June 1954, Pierre Mendès-France became Prime Minister at the head of a Gaullist-Radical coalition. His investiture, I wrote from Rome, 'is generally regarded here as fatal to French ratification of EDC.' Passing through Paris shortly afterwards, I could nevertheless sense excitement in the air. For all that he looked like a melancholy Mr Punch, Mendès-France had undoubted magic, especially for the press. Constantly at his desk, ridiculed by some Frenchmen for drinking milk instead of wine, brooding with dark intensity over a full nest of problems, he seemed to many the 'new man' who would give France decisive leadership.

He had urgent tasks abroad: to grant Tunisia internal autonomy, and above all to fulfil his pledge to end the war in Indo-China within four weeks.

He succeeded in both: but on EDC he confirmed his critics' fears. At one time, he told Paul-Henri Spaak, he had opposed the EDC Treaty. Now, he had changed his mind – but he needed additional safeguards. The executive Commissariat must no longer be independent, but subordinate to the Council of national Ministers. For the first eight years, every member State must have a veto. The plans for a European Political Community must be shelved. Only forces stationed in Germany must be integrated ... and so on. As Anthony Nutting put it, Mendès-France wanted 'a European Army for the Germans and a French Army for the French'.

On 19 August 1954, he met his partners in Brussels to discuss these new proposals. Spaak was in the chair, with Adenauer representing Germany, Attilio Piccioni for Italy, Johan Willem Beyen for the Netherlands, and Joseph Bech for Luxembourg. Facing these pioneer 'Europeans', Mendès-France must have felt a little as if he were on trial. The sombre atmosphere deepened a few minutes before the meeting started, when news came from Rome that Alcide De Gasperi had just died.

Expounding his revised version of EDC, Mendès-France undertook to present it to the French National Assembly, and secure a vote on it, before the end of the year. EDC as it stood, he added, had no hope of being approved. It was just as hopeless, his colleagues retorted, to ask them to tear up the Treaty by accepting proposals which nullified its aims.

For a day and a half, the wrangle continued. 'We shan't agree,' Mendès-France told Spaak in private; 'I'm convinced of it.' Nor did they. The meeting broke up, and Mendès-France left for London, to make what one British Minister called 'a final half-hearted attempt to bring Great Britain into the EDC.' Unsurprisingly, both Churchill and Eden refused. From Brussels, Spaak proposed yet another last-minute compromise; but by now Mendès-France seemed to have hardened his heart. On Saturday 28 August 1954, he put the original EDC Treaty to the French National Assembly, making a low-key, non-committal speech. In the debate that followed, its opponents attacked it savagely – none with more passion than the 82-year-old Edouard Herriot, once the champion of a united Europe.

Two days later, on 30 August, the Assembly rejected the Treaty, on a procedural motion, by 319 votes to 264, with 43 abstentions – a smaller majority than that which had approved the original Pleven Plan. Among those abstaining now were Mendès-France and two of his Cabinet colleagues; those voting against included the Communists, the Gaullists, and more than half of the Radicals and Socialists. When the result was announced, there was uproar. The extreme Right-wing deputies rose and sang the *Marseillaise* – and so did the Communists, amid counter-cries of 'Sing *Deutschland über Alles*' and shouts of 'Go to Moscow'.

For a while, Europeans were nonplussed. In December 1953, John Foster Dulles had threatened an 'agonizing reappraisal' of American policy if France failed to ratify EDC. Would the United States withdraw troops from Europe? Would she revive the Spofford Plan? Would a Bonn-Washington axis emerge? Fortunately, such speculation proved needless. Within a few weeks, largely thanks to Anthony Eden, an agreement had been patched up to enable Germany to contribute to Western defence. In October, she and Italy joined Britain, France, and the three Benelux countries to sign an agreement enlarging the Brussels Pact into a seven-nation Western European Union, or WEU.

Under the new agreement, Germany was freed from Allied occupation and made a member of NATO, contributing up to twelve divisions. Britain agreed to keep her own four divisions and her tactical air force on the continent for as long as a majority of the member States so desired.

The military situation was saved – but what had happened to the uniting of Europe? The proposed European Political Community had collapsed with EDC; and Western European Union was little more than inter-govern-mental. It had an Assembly, but with scarcely any power. As for Germany, her land contingent was limited, and she had agreed not to manufacture atomic, biological, or chemical weapons on her own territory. But those who had opposed EDC because it meant 'German rearmament' within a European defence force now faced a German Army in the looser framework of NATO and WEU. For nationalists, it was a pyrrhic victory. For Jean Monnet and his colleagues in Luxembourg, the beleaguered advance-guard of a routed army, it looked like final defeat.

Yet, once again, Europe's momentum proved unstoppable.

It was partly because the facts had not changed. Stalin was dead; but East and West were still divided. Europe was richer; but the United States was still supreme. Within Western Europe, the wounds of war were healing; but mistrust remained. And while Europe's old nation-states were recovering self-confidence, none could ever again be self-sufficient. In a world of super-powers, large-scale technology, and instant communications, sheer self-interest urged Europeans to unite.

To realize this was one thing: to act on it quite another. In France, the

EDC crisis had left enduring traumas: as Raymond Aron said, it had been the biggest ideological dispute since the Dreyfus case. France's partners, and especially Germany, felt bitterly let down. Who would be willing, now, to risk a new initiative? The answer, as so often, was supplied by Jean Monnet.

Misfortune seldom discouraged him. His impulse was always to side-step and fight back. 'The only true defeats', he said, 'are those that one accepts.' When EDC failed, he admitted to a British friend, 'I was annoyed and – I don't like the word, but – I was pretty mad. Mad at myself, because I was the one who had proposed to the French Government the acceptance of this European Army.' His anger soon turned to action.

Two days after the EDC débâcle, Monnet was in Paris consulting his friends – René Pleven, Robert Schuman, Antoine Pinay, Pierre-Henri Teitgen, and Hervé Alphand. It was the beginning of countless discussions – with Frenchmen, Germans, Italians, Belgians, Dutchmen, and Luxembourgers. Many came to see Monnet at the High Authority; but he also travelled, to Bonn, to Brussels, to Strasbourg, and elsewhere. Between September 1954 and May 1955, he made no fewer than 23 trips to Paris. He saw Spaak half-a-dozen times, Schuman and Pinay seven times; he had nearly a score of meetings with Guy Mollet. In Germany he talked with Adenauer, Erhard, and Hallstein; he also met such veteran labour leaders as Walter Freitag and Heinrich Imig, who helped convert the German Social-Democrats to his ideas. When he was not on the telephone, he seemed to be on the train. A small, quiet man in his sixties, sitting alone in a window-seat, wearing an old dark-brown overcoat and a grey English trilby hat, he looked insignificant – a retired chemist, perhaps, or an elderly provincial lawyer. In fact, he was a weaver of webs. He was patiently persuading a network of like-minded statesmen that there was still a future for them to build together.

It was a task increasingly hard to combine with running the High Authority. On his sixty-sixth birthday, 9 November 1954, Monnet announced to his colleagues that he would not seek re-appointment when his term of office expired in a few months' time. He wanted, he said, 'to be able to take part with complete freedom of action and speech in the achievement of European unity.'

What he should do remained uncertain. He thought at first of publishing 'an appeal to public opinion and to the Governments': but he quickly realized that without wider backing it would have little effect. One colleague suggested that he enter the French National Assembly, and there try to form a 'European Party'. The former suggestion he rejected. He liked the idea of a 'European Party', but not on a national basis. Why not, instead, form a broader 'European Front' by formalizing his international network of friends? If each were to bring in his own party or trade union, they would be a real political force.

It took time, but it succeeded. On 14 October 1955, Monnet was able to announce the formation of his 'Action Committee for the United States of Europe'. It comprised all the political parties and trade unions in France, Germany, Italy, and the Benelux countries, except for the Communists and the extreme Right – a new European party on a European scale.

As the Action Committee gradually took shape, so did its political programme. Three of Monnet's first ideas were unremarkable: extending the Schuman Plan to cover energy and transport; electing the Assembly by direct universal suffrage; forming a new *Ad hoc* Assembly to prepare further plans. A fourth proposal was more ambitious: to set up a new 'Community' organization to deal with armaments and the peaceful uses of nuclear energy.

The idea of an armaments pool risked arousing the same hostility as EDC, and Monnet soon dropped it. But the plan for an atomic energy Community seemed more promising. 'Automation and the atom are the future,' said Paul-Henri Spaak. The US Senate had recently amended the MacMahon Act, empowering the Administration to share nuclear secrets with its allies; and the astute Louis Armand, a close friend of Monnet's, saw at once how Europe might respond:

No country by itself, not even Britain, will benefit from this as much or as quickly as France, Britain, and their neighbours would if they acted together. The Americans are upset by the failure of EDC, and they will certainly welcome a European nuclear body and a Europe acting as one in negotiations for supplies and information.

It was Armand, a few months later, who nicknamed the proposed new Community 'Euratom'.

Its prospects seemed to improve in February 1955, when Pierre Mendès-France's Government was replaced by a more sympathetic Cabinet headed by Edgar Faure. It even began to look as if the programme that Monnet was drafting for the future Action Committee might stand a chance of adoption by governments themselves.

At first, Edgar Faure was reluctant to reopen the European debate. No sooner had he warmed to the idea than a fresh snag arose in Germany. On 5 April 1955, Hallstein telephoned Monnet from Bonn: the German Government was having second thoughts. To clarify matters, Monnet asked to talk with Carl Friedrich Ophüls, a German delegate to the Schuman Plan Conference who now headed the European desk at the Foreign Office in Bonn. Next day, Ophüls arrived. As Pierre Uri described the meeting –

Monnet was sure that the Germans would be delighted to be accepted as equals in the nuclear field. To his great surprise, Ophüls told him that the proposal would not be accepted by Germany, and that in particular Ludwig Erhard, the Minister of Economic Affairs, would oppose it.

It was then, according to Uri, that he and Monnet proposed what came to be known as 'the Common Market':

How would the Germans see things if the idea of forming Euratom among the six countries were justified by their preparing to pool the whole of their economy in a general integration effort? Ophüls replied that this would change everything. Monnet turned to me and said: 'Well, then, there's no other way.'

In essence, of course, the notion was not new. The Marshall Plan might have led to a European customs union; and two similar proposals had been made as early as June 1950. There had also been regional projects. In 1949, France and Italy had agreed, but failed, to form a customs union, 'Francita' – which some had proposed merging with Benelux under the name of 'Fritalux' or 'Finebel'. In 1953, the *Ad hoc* Assembly had envisaged a general 'common market'. In the same year, Johan Willem Beyen had proposed a 'tariff community'; and now, most recently, he had sent Paul-Henri Spaak a memorandum which suggested 'proceeding by means of a customs union to the establishment of an economic union.' If the Germans now backed such a venture, the way ahead seemed clear.

It seemed so; but there were still obstacles. In France, the Euratom idea was popular: cutting tariffs was not. And Edgar Faure, unlike his namesake Maurice, was not a man to take risks. At a press conference on 13 April 1955, he spoke vaguely of 'co-operation' on atomic power, and doubted whether energy and transport should be dealt with by the Schuman Plan. For once, Monnet was disheartened. He wrote to a colleague:

I myself don't know what to do. I sometimes wonder whether it wouldn't be preferable to leave the situation as it is and put off any action until later.

But events forced his hand. In a speech at The Hague on 21 April, Beyen made public the ideas he had put privately to Spaak. Within twenty-four hours, Monnet visited Spaak in Brussels. Next day, Spaak went to see Beyen in The Hague. Together, they asked Joseph Bech to agree on a joint Benelux memorandum to put to the Foreign Ministers of the Schuman Plan six. By 6 May, the final ᵗext was ready, based partly on Beyen's and partly on Monnet's drafts. It proposed further integration in transport, energy, and atomic power, and 'a European Economic Community' with 'a common authority endowed with the necessary powers of its own.' Spaak sent a copy to Monnet with an eloquent covering note: 'Herewith your child.'

On Wednesday 1 June 1955, the Foreign Ministers assembled in the Hotel San Domenico, a former monastery, at Taormina. Sicily in Spring was a bright, hopeful setting. In the comparative cool of the late afternoon, they drove some 25 miles along the coast to Messina, where their formal meeting was to be held.

Their host was Gaetano Martino, Foreign Minister of Italy and Rector of Messina University; their chairman was the avuncular Joseph Bech. The other participants were Spaak, Beyen, Pinay, and Hallstein. Their first task was to appoint René Mayer as Monnet's successor on the High Authority. Then they turned to broader questions. They had before them a paper from Italy, calling for social and regional development, and a German memorandum, inspired by Ludwig Erhard, proposing economic 'co-operation' on intergovernmental lines. Hallstein, the only non-Minister present, had the fretful task of presenting it: he looked uncomfortable, even in a lightweight suit. But before long the debate centred mainly on the Benelux text. When the Ministers parted in the early hours of 3 June, after a final candle-lit dinner in their monastery, they had approved a Resolution embodying most of the Benelux proposals, and establishing a Committee to see about putting them into effect. Its chairman was to be 'a political personality'.

'Isn't that all very vague?' asked a journalist. 'No,' replied the Ministers' Luxembourg Secretary-General, Christian Calmès. 'Proposing a statesman to run it is a guarantee that it will work, since he'll make it a point of honour to succeed.'

Calmès was right. Soon afterwards, the six Governments chose their 'political personality': it was Paul-Henri Spaak. He was no technical expert; but he had the bulldog physique, the common sense, and the energy needed to goad the experts on. Among them, alongside the national delegates, were two representatives of the High Authority: Dirk Spierenburg, a suave but proverbially stubborn Dutchman, and the ingenious, ubiquitous Pierre Uri.

The Committee held its first meeting on 9 July 1955, at the Belgian Foreign Office; thereafter, it met on the wooded outskirts of Brussels in the modest Château de Val Duchesse. When the talks had gone far enough,

Spaak sent Uri, with the German delegate Hans von der Groeben and one of his own Belgian assistants, to a quiet retreat in the South of France – the Grand Hotel at St-Jean-Cap-Ferrat – to draft what came to be called 'the Spaak Report'. On 21 April 1956, slightly retouched by the Committee, it was submitted to the Ministers. They adopted it as the basis for negotiations at a meeting in Venice at the end of May. Europe was not being made in night-clubs, but in beauty-spots.

In June, the delegates returned to Val Duchesse for the Treaty-making conference. Spaak was still in the chair, and his lively tactics proved their worth once again. On an occasion which later became famous, he deliberately lost his temper. The national experts had been wrangling about import duties on bananas. 'I give you two hours,' Spaak told them. 'If it's not settled by then, I shall call the press in and announce that Europe won't be built after all, because we can't agree about bananas.' Then he walked out. When he came back two hours later, the problem had been solved.

While Spaak and his colleagues toiled away at Val Duchesse, their efforts were spurred by two major events in the wider world. One was the Soviet invasion of Hungary. The other was Nasser's takeover of the Suez Canal. Meeting in Paris on 19 and 20 September 1956, Monnet's Action Committee commented:

The Suez crisis is a grave warning. Even if, as we hope, it is solved by peaceful means, this fundamental lack of balance, with its threat to peace, will remain: namely, the weakness and growing dependence of Western Europe as regards its supplies of power.

It went on to urge the Governments to appoint 'three wise men' to report on Europe's energy needs. Two months later, the Governments did so; and when the 'wise men' reported, in May 1957, their words had a prophetic ring:

As the quantity of oil imported from the Middle East increases, there will be a corresponding increase in the political temptation to interfere with the flow of oil from that region. A future stoppage could be an economic calamity for Europe. Excessive dependence of our highly industrialized countries on an unstable region might even lead to serious political trouble throughout the world. It is essential that oil should be a commodity and not a political weapon.

Meanwhile, the Val Duchesse negotiators had completed their task. It had taken them ten short months to produce two crucial Treaties: one for the European Atomic Energy Community, or Euratom; the other for the European Economic Community, the Common Market or EEC. Both provided for institutions modelled on – and partly to be shared with – those of the Schuman Plan: but in place of the High Authority each had an independent Commission. In Euratom, for which the Treaty could prescribe detailed rules, the Commission was an executant, like the High Authority. In the EEC, whose founding Treaty could set only general aims and procedures, the Commission's main role was to propose new agreements for governments to reach, if necessary by majority vote. The EEC Treaty established no 'Government of Europe'. But it was in effect the Constitution for an economic union still to be built.

On Monday 25 March 1957, in the vast Sala degli Orazi e Curiazi of the Capitol in Rome, amid mouldings and frescoes reminiscent of a Europe long since vanished, the representatives of the Six met to sign the Treaties that would weld their future. Spaak and Baron Snoy were there for Belgium; Adenauer and Hallstein for Germany; Christian Pineau and Maurice Faure for France; Antonio Segni and Gaetano Martino for Italy; Joseph Bech and Lambert Schaus for Luxembourg; Joseph Luns and Johannes Linthorst Homan for the Netherlands.

Britain, once more, was absent. For a time, at the Six's invitation, she had sent a representative to the Spaak Committee in Val Duchesse. Appointing him, Harold Macmillan had recalled the 'special difficulties for this country in any proposal for "a European common market"'. At the end of 1955, when Spaak had pressed for a firmer commitment, Britain's representative had withdrawn. Six months later, the British Government had proposed to link the future common market with an industrial 'free trade area', whose members would retain their own tariffs on imports from the rest of the world. Seen from London, this promised the best of both worlds: a market for manufactures in Europe, and continued cheap food from the Commonwealth. Seen from Paris, that looked unfair; and by seeming to offer France's partners free trade without the discipline of a common outer tariff, it threatened to dissolve the Community, as some said, 'like a lump of sugar in a British cup of tea'. At the end of 1958, the free trade area proposal was rejected by General de Gaulle. Three years were to pass before Britain applied to join the European Community – only to face De Gaulle's veto after fourteen months. Not until a decade later was the Community at last able to welcome the British in.

All this lay in the future. In Rome on that brisk March day in 1957, the bells rang out to mark a triumph. One long battle was over. Another was about to begin. One by one, the national Parliaments debated the Euratom and EEC Treaties. Monnet's Action Committee cajoled and prodded them. They were also spurred, in October 1957, by the Soviet Union's feat in launching Sputnik I. Finally, in December, the two Treaties cleared their last parliamentary hurdle, in the First Chamber of the Dutch States-General, where the Congress of Europe had met nearly ten years before. In all six Parliaments, they had won overwhelming support.

At the turn of the year, the Foreign Ministers met again, to appoint the new President of the High Authority, the Belgian trade unionist Paul Finet, and the Presidents of the two new Commissions – Louis Armand for Euratom, and Walter Hallstein for the EEC. 'We shall live in symbiosis,' announced Armand; and in future years the three executive bodies were indeed to merge. For the time being, the Governments failed yet again to agree on a permanent home for the Community institutions, and they provisionally straddled three cities: Brussels, Luxembourg, and Strasbourg. A generation later, the European Community still had no single resting-place. But already, by 1958, it had come a very long way.

Soon, well ahead of schedule, the frontiers were falling. For the first time in centuries, the citizens of Europe belonged to a wider Community than their nation-state. They were free to travel unhindered to another Community country, to take jobs there, to bring their families to live with them. They could buy and sell and move money across the borders without paying customs duties, almost as simply as from one province, department, or canton to another. The old barbed-wire barriers were disappearing; so, more slowly, were the bureaucratic controls. Within a few years of the Rome Treaty's signature, crossing Europe's frontiers had turned from an ordeal into a mere formality. Already in 1958, driving at night on a motorway, I even passed a frontier post without seeing it at all. Quite tangibly, Europe was beginning to be one.

The road to Europe had been hard going; and there was still trouble ahead. The Treaties had been in force less than five months when General de Gaulle returned to power in Paris, borne on the unruly tide of the Algerian War. Deeply nationalist, he fought Community Europe in the name of 'Europe of the States' – first barring the door to Britain, a potential rival, then once more attacking the majority vote. Even after De Gaulle's death – on Monnet's 82nd birthday – Europe was to face new setbacks: an international oil crisis and a world depression, rising prices, the loss of jobs. How would it survive these bitter storms? Would public opinion desert it?

Would extra recruits destroy its cohesion? How would it meet fresh challenges in foreign policy and defence?

The question marks were many, but the Community's early years suggested one answer: difficulties and disappointments were nothing new. Contrary to general belief, there had never been a golden age. The building of Europe had always been a suspense drama, and a battle against time. Europe was the best illustration of Oliver Wendell Holmes's maxim: 'The mode whereby the inevitable comes about is effort.'

Effort in many fields had made postwar Europe.

The victims of World War II had not died pointlessly. They had helped to defeat unimaginable evil. And their memory had not been betrayed.

Those who survived had built Europe afresh, and built better. They had come to terms with former enemies, purging guilt and offering amnesty. They had managed the great, painful transition from war to the arts of peace. With the United States, they had forged new bonds as the shadows had darkened over captive Eastern Europe. At home, they had improved their people's lot beyond recognition – at the cost of new conflicts and new demands. Overseas, they had slowly shed colonial pretensions. They had bequeathed to their children a new Europe. All this – in a bare thirteen years.

The men and women of postwar Europe had saved themselves by their exertions. Their example, like their achievement, still stands.

For Further Reading

The full bibliography of *Postwar* is unmanageably long. In selecting the following suggestions I have therefore omitted much scholarly and background reading, most of the books already mentioned in the text, many official documents, periodicals, newspapers, and any private material such as unpublished letters and diaries.

General

Useful general surveys include, in alphabetical order of their authors: Geoffrey Barraclough, *An Introduction to Contemporary History* (London, 1964); Michael D. Biddiss, *The Age of the Masses* (London, 1971); John Calmann (ed.), *Western Europe: A Handbook* (London, 1967); J. P. Cole, *Geography of World Affairs* (London, 1959); Gordon Connell-Smith, *Patterns of the Post-War World* (London, 1957); Maurice Crouzet, *The European Renaissance since 1945* (London, 1970); Stephen R. Graubard (ed.) *A New Europe?* (Boston, Mass., 1964); Stephen Holt, *Six European States* (London, 1970); H. Stuart Hughes, *Contemporary Europe: A History* (Englewood Cliffs, N.J., 1961); James Joll, *Europe Since 1870* (revised, London, 1976); Walter Laqueur, *Europe Since Hitler* (London, 1970); my own *The Recovery of Europe* (London, 1970); Roger Morgan, *West European Politics since 1945* (London, 1972); R. C. Mowat, *Ruin and Resurgence 1939–1965* (London, 1966); David Rees, *The Age of Containment* (London, 1967); David Thomson, *Europe Since Napoleon* (second edition, London, 1962); D. W. Urwin, *Western Europe since 1945* (London, 1968); and Charles Zorgbibe, *Le monde depuis 1945* (Paris, 1980).

Several American reporters have published vivid eye-witness accounts of the period, notably John Gunther, *Inside Europe Today* (revised, New York, 1962); Howard K. Smith, *The State of Europe* (London, 1950); C. L. Sulzberger, *The Last of the Giants* (London, 1972); and Theodore H. White, *Fire in the Ashes: Europe in Mid-century* (New York, 1953). From Britain, two of Anthony Sampson's reports are relevant here: *Anatomy of Britain Today* (London, 1965); and *The New Europeans* (London, 1968).

Autobiographers and diarists who belong in this section include Konrad Adenauer, *Erinnerungen 1945–53, 1953–55, 1955–59* (Stuttgart, 1965–7); George W. Ball, *The Discipline of Power* (Boston, Mass., 1968) and *The Past Has Another Pattern* (New York, 1982); Winston S. Churchill, *The Second World War* (paperback edition, London, 1964); Charles de Gaulle, *Mémoires de guerre*, vol. III, *Le salut 1944–1946* (Paris, 1959) and *Mémoires d'espoir*, vol. I, *Le renouveau 1958–1962* (Paris, 1970), André Gide, *Journal 1939–49* (Paris, 1954); Harold Macmillan, *Memoirs*, vol. II, *The Blast of War 1939–1945* (London, 1967), vol. III, *Tides of Fortune 1945–1955* (London, 1969), and vol. IV, *Riding the Storm 1956–1959* (London, 1971); Harold Nicolson, *Diaries and Letters 1939–45* (London, 1967) and *1945–62* (London, 1968); and Bertrand Russell, *Autobiography 1944–1967* (London, 1969).

On Britain, there are at least four entertaining and informative social histories: Harry Hopkins, *The New Look* (London, 1963); Peter Lewis, *The Fifties* (London, 1978); John Montgomery, *The Fifties* (London, 1965); and Michael Sissons and Philip French (eds.) *The Age of Austerity 1945–51* (paperback edition, London, 1964). British political history is well and briefly covered by Peter Calvocoressi, *The British Experience 1945–1975* (London, 1978); Alan Sked and Chris Cook, *Post-war Britain: A Political History* (London, 1979); and C. M. Woodhouse, *Post-War Britain* (London, 1966).

There is a mass of material on France. The best includes: Pierre Avril, *Politics in France* (London, 1969); Jean-Pierre Azéma, *De Munich à la Libération (1938–1944)* (Paris, 1979); Georgette Elgey, *Histoire de la IVe République*, vol. I: *La république des illusions* (Paris, 1965) and vol. II: *La république des contradictions* (Paris, 1968); Jacques Fauvet, *La France déchirée* (Paris, 1957) and *La IVe République* (Paris, 1959), Edgar S. Furness, *France, Troubled Ally* (New York, 1960); Catherine Gavin, *Liberated France* (London, 1955); Gilbert Guilleminault (ed.), *La France de Vincent Auriol* (Paris, 1970) and *Les lendemains qui ne chantaient pas* (Paris, 1969); Stanley Hoffmann and others, *France: Change and Tradition* (London, 1963); Jean-Pierre Rioux, *La Quatrième République (1944–1958)* (Paris, 1980); Alfred Sauvy, *De Paul Reynaud à Charles de Gaulle* (Paris, 1972); David Schoenbrun, *As France Goes* (London, 1957), Alexander Werth, *France 1940–1955* (London, 1956); and Philip Williams, *Crisis and Compromise* (London, 1964).

On other European countries, see mainly the specific references below. General works include: Margaret Carlyle, *Modern Italy* (London, 1957); Muriel Grindrod, *Italy* (London, 1964) and *The Rebuilding of Italy* (London, 1955); H. Stuart Hughes, *The United States and Italy* (Cambridge, Mass., 1953); Norman Kogon, *A Political History of Postwar Italy* (London, 1966); Eugene Davidson, *The Death and Life of Germany* (London, 1959); M. Dill, *Germany: A Modern History* (Michigan, 1961); J. F. Golay, *The Founding of the Federal Republic of Germany* (Chicago, 1958); Alfred Grosser, *La République Fédérale d'Allemagne* (Paris, 1963); Edgar McInnis and others, *The Shaping of Postwar Germany* (Toronto/London, 1960); John Midgley, *Germany* (London, 1968); Terence Prittie, *Germany Divided* (London, 1961); Bernard Pingaud, *Hollande* (Paris, 1954); H. Riemans, *Perspectief voor Nederland* (Amsterdam, 1957); Margot Lyon, *Belgium* (London, 1970).

On architecture, two books are most readily accessible: G. E. Kidder Smith, *The New Architecture of Europe* (London, 1962) and Nikolaus Pevsner, *An Outline of European Architecture* (seventh edition, London, 1963), On art, see especially Edward Lucie-Smith, *Movements in Art since 1945* (revised edition, London, 1975), and Herbert Read, *Contemporary British Art* (London,

1951). On films, Roy Armes, *French Cinema since 1946* (London, 1966); Penelope Houston, *The Contemporary Cinema 1945–1963* (London, 1963); Roger Manvell, *New Cinema in Britain* (London, 1969) and *New Cinema in Europe* (London, 1966); and Eric Rhode, *A History of the Cinema* (London, 1976). On literature, G. S. Fraser, *The Modern Writer and his World* (revised, London, 1964); Maurice Nadeau, *Le roman français depuis la guerre* (Paris, 1963); and Henri Peyre, *The Contemporary French Novel* (New York, 1955). These general works are chosen for their contemporary flavour, as is Joan Peyser, *Twentieth-century Music* (new edition, New York, 1980). More specific indications can be found below and in the text.

Chapter 1   Great Expectations

On the end of the war in Europe, see Norman Longmate, *When We Won the War* (London, 1977); Michel van der Plas, *Mooie Vrede* (Utrecht, 1966); Rene Cutforth, *Order to View* (London, 1969); and Harry C. Butcher, *My Three Years with Eisenhower* (New York, 1964). On war aims: Paul Addison, *The Road to 1945* (London, 1975); Raymond Ebsworth, *Restoring Democracy in Germany* (London, 1960); Pietro Malvezzi and Giovanni Pirelli (eds.) *Lettere di condannati a morte della Resistenza Italiana* (Milan, 1952). On Camus, Herbert R. Lottman, *Albert Camus* (London, 1979) and *The Left Bank* (London, 1982); Patrick McCarthy, *Camus* (London, 1982).

On postwar Italy, Domenico Bartoli, *La Fine della Monarchia* (Milan, 1947); Carlo Cattaneo, *I Problemi dello Stato Italiano* (Verona, 1966); Federico Chabod, *L'Italia Contemporanea 1918–1948* (paperback edition, Bari, 1967); Piergiovanni Permoli, *La Costituente e i Partiti Politici Italiani* (Rocca San Casciano, 1966); Elisabeth Wiskemann, *Italy* (London, 1947); Wayland Young, *The Italian Left* (London, 1949). On De Gasperi, Maria de Gasperi, *De Gasperi, Uomo Solo* (Milan, 1965).

On Christian Democracy, M. Einaudi and F. Goguel, *Christian Democracy in Italy and France* (Notre Dame, Indiana, 1952); M P. Fogarty, *Christian Democracy in Western Europe* (London, 1957); Giorgio Galli and Paolo Facchi, *La Sinistra Democristiana* (Milan, 1962); R. A. Webster, *Christian Democracracy in Italy* (London, 1961).

On Adenauer: A. T. Heidenheimer, *Adenauer and the C.D.U.*, (The Hague, 1960); Silvio Locatelli, *Konrad Adenauer* (Milan, 1965), Terence Prittie, *Konrad Adenauer 1876–1967* (London, 1972); Franz Rodens, *Konrad Adenauer* (Munich/Zurich, 1965).

On De Gaulle: Aidan Crawley, *De Gaulle* (London, 1969); Brian Crozier, *De Gaulle* (London, 1973); Anthony Hartley, *Gaullism* (London, 1972); Alexander Werth, *De Gaulle: A Political Biography* (third edition, London, 1969).

On Britain: Angus Calder, *The People's War* (London, 1969) and *The Common Wealth Party 1942–1945* (Sussex University Ph.D. thesis); Lord Moran, *Churchill: the Struggle for Survival* (London, 1966); J. E. D. Hall, *Labour's First Year* (London, 1947);

Kenneth Harris, *Attlee* (London, 1982); Francis Williams, *A Prime Minister Remembers* (London, 1961).

On Monnet: Jean Monnet, *Mémoires* (Paris, 1976). On refugees and UNRRA: Fred K. Hoehler, *Europe's Homeless Millions* (New York, 1945); Robert Kee, *Refugee World* (London, 1961); Malcolm J. Proudfoot, *European Refugees 1939–52* (London, 1957); George Woodbridge and others, *U.N.R.R.A.* (New York, 1950).

Chapter 2   There'll Always be a Deutschland

First impressions: Francesca Wilson, *Aftermath* (London, 1947); Stephen Spender, *European Witness* (London, 1946).

On the Nuremberg trials: R. W. Cooper, *The Nuremberg Trials* (London, 1946); Janet Flanner, *Janet Flanner's World* (London, 1980); G. M. Gilbert, *Nuremberg Diary* (New York, 1947); Whitney R. Harris, *Tyranny on Trial* (Dallas, 1954); J. J. Heydecker and J. Leeb, *Der Nürnberger Prozess* (Cologne, 1979); Robert A. Jackson, *Report* (Washington, 1949); Joseph Kessel, *L'heure des châtiments* (Paris, 1956); Airey Neave, *Nuremberg* (London, 1978) and *They Have Their Exits* (London, 1953); Bradley F. Smith, *Reaching Judgment at Nuremberg* (New York, 1977) and *The Road to Nuremberg* (London, 1981); Evelyn Waugh, *Diaries* (revised, London, 1979) and *Letters* (London, 1980).

On war guilt: Robert Aron, *Les grands dossiers de l'histoire contemporaine* (Paris, 1962), *Histoire de l'épuration* (Paris, 1967), and *Histoire de la libération de la France* (pocket edition, Paris, 1967); Tom Bower, *Blind Eye to Murder* (London, 1981); Richard Griffiths, *Marshal Pétain* (London, 1970); Karla Höcker (ed.), *Wilhelm Furtwängler* (Berlin, 1968); David Littlejohn, *The Patriotic Traitors* (London, 1972); W. Miles (ed.), *The Forrestal Diaries* (London, 1952); Henry Morgenthau, *Germany is our Problem* (New York, 1945); George Orwell, *Collected Essays, Journalism, and Letters* (London, 1968); Pascal Ory, *Les collaborateurs 1940–1945* (Paris, 1976); Jules Roy, *Le grand naufrage* (Paris, 1966); C. P. Snow, *Science and Government* (paperback edition, London, 1963); Iain Sproat, *Wodehouse at War* (London, 1981); Gudrun Tempel, *Speaking Frankly About the Germans* (London, 1963); Raymond Tournoux, *Pétain et de Gaulle* (Paris, 1964); Rebecca West, *The Meaning of Treason* (revised, London, 1965); P. G. Wodehouse, *Wodehouse on Wodehouse* (London, 1980); Gordon Young, *The Fall and Rise of Alfried Krupp* (London, 1960).

On Germany and its division: K. Bölling, *Republic in Suspense* (London, 1964); William Henry Chamberlin, *The German Phoenix* (London, 1964); Lucius D. Clay, *Decision in Germany* (London, 1950); Ralf Dahrendorf, *Gesellschaft und Demokratie in Deutschland* (Munich, 1965); Ernst Deuerlein (ed.), *Potsdam 1945* (Munich, 1963); F. S. V. Donnison, *Civil Affairs and Military Government: N.W. Europe 1944–1946* (New York, 1961); Herbert Feis, *Between War and Peace* (London, 1960); J. F. Golay, *The Founding of the Federal Republic of Germany* (Chicago, 1958); G. F. Hudson, *The Hard and Bitter Peace* (London, 1966); Richard Lukas, *Zehn*

Jahre Sowjetische Besatzungszone Deutschlands (Mainz/ Wiesbaden/Düsseldorf, 1955); F. Meinecke, *The German Catastrophe* (Cambridge, Mass., 1950); Peter H. Merkl, *Germany Yesterday and Tomorrow* (New York, 1965); Viscount Montgomery, *Memoirs* (paperback edition, London, 1960); Nicolas Nabokov, *Old Friends and New Music* (London, 1964); P. E. Schramm (ed.), *Die Niederlage 1945* (paperback edition, Munich, 1962); Tony Sharp, *The Wartime Alliance and the Zonal Division of Germany* (London, 1975); John Snell, *Wartime Origins of the East–West Dilemma over Germany* (New Orleans, 1959); Wolfgang Stolper, *Germany Between East and West* (Washington, 1960); Lord Strang, *At Home and Abroad* (London, 1956); Arnold Toynbee (ed.) *Four-Power Control in Germany and Austria 1945–1946* (London, 1956); Arnold and V.M. Toynbee, *The Realignment of Europe* (London, 1955); Thilo Vogelsang, *Das geteilte Deutschland* (Munich, 1966); D.C. Watt, *Britain Looks to Germany* (London, 1965); Daniel Yergin, *Shattered Peace* (London, 1977); Harold Zink, *American Military Government in Germany* (New York, 1947), and *The United States in Germany 1945–1955* (Princeton, 1957).

Chapter 3 Business as Usual

On Milan: Melton S. Davis, *Who Defends Rome?* (London, 1972); F.W. Deakin, *The Last Days of Mussolini* (London, 1962); Christopher Hibbert, *Benito Mussolini* (revised, London, 1965). On Toulouse, Pierre Bertaux, *La Libération de Toulouse* (Paris, 1973). On demobilization and repatriation: Joseph C. Goulden, *The Best Years* (New York, 1976); Henri Frenay, *La nuit finira* (Paris, 1973). On German housing, Alphons Silbermann *Vom Wohnen der Deutschen* (Frankfurt/Hamburg, 1966).

On the press: Abel Chatelain, *Le Monde et ses lecteurs sous la IVe République* (Paris, 1962); Jacques Thibau, *"Le Monde"* (Paris, 1978); Sefton Delmer, *Black Boomerang* (London, 1962). On Paris, Elizabeth Sprigge, *Gertrude Stein* (London, 1957); Françoise Gilot and Carlton Lake, *Life with Picasso* (London, 1964); André Maurois, *Mémoires* (Paris, 1970); Duff Cooper, *Old Men Forget* (London, 1953); Tom Hopkinson (ed.), *Picture Post 1938–50* (London, 1970). See also: Hermann Hesse, *Krieg und Frieden* (Zurich, 1946); Hans Schwab-Felisch (ed.), *Der Ruf* (Munich, 1962); Hugh Dalton, *High Tide and After* (London, 1962); H.S. Truman, *Memoirs* (paperback edition, New York, 1965).

Chapter 4 Westward, Look

There is a vast and still growing corpus of writing on and around the Marshall Plan. Of existing works, this selection may serve. Dean Acheson, *Present at the Creation* (London, 1970) and *Sketches from Life* (New York, 1961); Hervé Alphand, *L'étonnement d'être* (Paris, 1977); Hadley Arkes, *Bureaucracy, the Marshall Plan, and the National Interest* (Princeton, 1972); William Diebold, Jr., *Trade and Payments in Western Europe* (New York, 1952); Jacques Dumaine, *Quai d'Orsay*

1945–1951 (Paris, 1955); Howard S. Ellis, *The Economics of Freedom* (New York, 1950); Paul G. Hoffmann, *Peace Can Be Won* (New York, 1951); Joseph Marion Jones, *The Fifteen Weeks* (paperback edition, New York, 1964); George F. Kennan, *American Diplomacy 1900– 1950* (London, 1952) and *Memoirs 1925–1950* (London, 1968); David S. McLellan, *Dean Acheson: The State Department Years* (New York, 1976); René Massigli, *Une comédie des erreurs 1943–1956* (Paris, 1978); Merle Miller, *Plain Speaking: An Oral Biography of Harry S. Truman* (London, 1974); Robert Payne, *General Marshall* (London, 1952); Cabell Phillips, *The Truman Presidency* (New York, 1966); Harry Bayard Price, *The Marshall Plan and its Meaning* (Ithaca, N.Y., 1955); Arthur H. Vandenberg (ed.), *The Private Papers of Senator Vandenberg* (Boston, Mass., 1972); Ernst van der Beugel, *From Marshall Aid to Atlantic Partnership* (Amsterdam/London/New York, 1966); Barbara Ward, *Policy for the West* (New York, 1951) and *The West at Bay* (New York, 1948).

On transatlantic relations – political, economic, and psychological – see especially: H. C. Allen, *The Anglo-American Predicament* (London, 1960); Walter Allen, *The Urgent West* (London, 1970); Simone de Beauvoir, *La force des choses* (Paris, 1963); Crane Brinton, *The Americans and the French* (Cambridge, Mass., 1968); John C. Campbell, *The United States in World Affairs 1945–1947* (New York, 1947); Robert A. Dahl, *Congress and Foreign Policy* (New York, 1950); Christopher Frayling, *Spaghetti Westerns* (London, 1981); R. N. Gardner, *Sterling–Dollar Diplomacy* (Oxford, 1956); Christopher Isherwood, *A Single Man* (New York, 1964); George Lichtheim, *Europe and America* (London, 1963); Edward A. McCreary, *The Americanization of Europe* (New York, 1964); Cesare Pavese, *La letteratura americana e altri saggi* (Turin, 1959); Anthony Sampson, *The Arms Bazaar* (London, 1977); Stephen Spender, *Love–hate Relations* (London, 1974); Robert Penn Warren (ed.) *Faulkner* (Englewood Cliffs, N.J., 1966); Basil Wright, *The Long View* (London, 1974).

Chapter 5 Lost Horizons

The outstanding source for Jan Masaryk is Claire Sterling, *The Masaryk Case* (New York, 1969), supplemented in particular by Marcia Davenport, *Too Strong for Fantasy* (New York, 1967) and Sir Robert Bruce Lockhart, *Jan Masaryk: A Personal Memoir* (New York, 1956).

On the East European satellites: L. B. Bain, *The Reluctant Satellites* (New York, 1960); Enzo Bettiza, *L'altra Germania* (Milan, 1968); J. F. Brown, *The New Eastern Europe* (New York, 1966); Paolo Calzini (ed.), *Evoluzione delle economie orientali e prospettive degli scambi est-ovest* (Rome, 1968); Jan Ciechanowski, *Defeat in Victory* (New York, 1947); Tina Cosmin, *The Flight of Andrei Cosmin* (London, 1972); A. Cretzianu (ed.), *Captive Rumania* (New York, 1965); Vladimir Dedijer, *Tito Speaks* (London, 1953); Milovan Djilas, *Memoirs of a Revolutionary* (New York, 1973); M. R. D. Foot, *Resistance* (London, 1976); Karl Jech, *The Czechoslovak Economy 1945–1948* (Prague, 1968); Joseph

Mackiewicz, *The Katyn Wood Murders* (London, 1951); R. H. Markham, *Rumania under the Soviet Yoke* (Boston, Mass., 1949); Stanisław Mikołajczyk, *The Pattern of Soviet Domination* (London, 1948) and *The Rape of Poland* (New York, 1948); Ferenc Nagy, *The Struggle Behind the Iron Curtain* (London, 1970); John P. Nettl, *The Eastern Zone and Soviet Policy in Germany* (London, 1951); Hubert Ripka, *Czechoslovakia Enslaved* (London, 1950) and *Eastern Europe in the Postwar World* (London, 1961); Henry Roberts, *Eastern Europe* (New York, 1970); Gordon Schaffer, *Russian Zone* (London, 1947); Hugh Seton-Watson, *The East European Revolution* (third edition, New York, 1956) and *The Pattern of Communist Revolution* (London, 1953); Elisabeth Wiskemann, *Germany's Eastern Neighbours* (London, 1957); P. E. Zinner, *Communist Strategy and Tactics in Czechoslovakia 1914–1948* (London, 1963); and Anton Zischka, *The Other Europeans* (London, 1962).

On attitudes to Russia and the Soviet Union: A. Alvarez, *Under Pressure* (London, 1965); John Atkins, *Arthur Koestler* (London, 1956); Aleksandr Blok, *The Twelve and other Poems* (translated by Jon Stallworthy and Peter France, London, 1970); E. H. Carr, *The Soviet Impact on the Western World* (London, 1946); Iain Hamilton, *Arthur Koestler* (London, 1982); Tomáš Masaryk, *The Spirit of Russia* (London, 1919); Czesław Miłosz, *The Captive Mind* (London, 1953) and *Native Realm* (London, 1981); John Wain, *A House for the Truth* (London, 1972).

On the Soviet Union: C. E. Black, *The Transformation of Russian Society* (Cambridge, Mass., 1960); Jean Bruhat, *Histoire de l'U.R.S.S.* (seventh edition, Paris, 1964); Robert Conquest, *Common Sense About Russia* (London, 1961) and *The Great Terror* (revised, New York, 1973); Isaac Deutscher, *Stalin* (revised, London, 1966); Milovan Djilas, *Conversations with Stalin* (paperback edition, London, 1963); John Gunther, *Inside Russia Today* (London, 1958); N. Jasny, *The Soviet Economy during the Plan Era* (Stanford, 1951); Andrew Rothstein, *A History of the U.S.S.R.* (London, 1950); W. B. Walsh, *Russia and the Soviet Union* (Michigan, 1958).

On Soviet–American relations and the 'Cold War': W. Bedell Smith, *Moscow Mission 1946–1949* (London, 1950); Robert Paul Browder, *The Origins of Soviet–American Diplomacy* (Princeton, 1953); Arthur Conte, *Yalta ou le partage du monde* (pocket edition, Paris, 1965); Ludwig Dehio, *The Precarious Balance* (New York, 1962); Raymond Dennett and Joseph E. Johnson (eds.), *Negotiating with the Russians* (Boston, Mass., 1951); Herbert Feis, *Churchill, Roosevelt, Stalin* (Princeton, 1957); D. F. Fleming, *The Cold War and its Origins* (London, 1961); André Fontaine, *Histoire de la guerre froide* (Paris, 1965–7); Louis J. Halle, *The Cold War as History* (London, 1967); Martin Herz, *Beginnings of the Cold War* (Bloomington, Indiana, 1966); David Horowitz, *From Yalta to Vietnam* (London, 1967); Kenneth Ingram, *History of the Cold War* (London, 1955); George F. Kennan, *Russia and the West* (New York, 1962); Jean Laloy, *Entre guerres et paix* (Paris, 1966); Evan Luard (ed.), *The Cold War* (London, 1964); Philip E. Mosely, *The Kremlin in*

World Politics (paperback edition, New York, 1960); Thomas G. Paterson, *Soviet–American Confrontation* (Baltimore, 1973); W. W. Rostow, *The Division of Europe after World War II* (London, 1982); John L. Snell, *The Meaning of Yalta* (New York, 1956); Joseph V. Stalin, *Correspondence with Churchill, Attlee, Roosevelt, and Truman* (London, 1952) and *Problems of Leninism* (eleventh edition, Moscow, 1940); G. P. Tomaev, *Stalin Means War* (London, 1951).

On Berlin: William H. Conland, *Berlin: Beset and Bedevilled* (New York, 1963); W. Phillips Davison, *The Berlin Blockade* (Princeton, 1958); John Mander, *Berlin, Hostage for the West* (London, 1962); Hans Speier, *Divided Berlin* (London, 1961).

Chapter 6   Miracles and Corporation Men

On Erhard: Ludwig Erhard, *Deutschlands Rückkehr zum Weltmarkt* (Düsseldorf, 1953), *The Economics of Success* (London, 1963) and *Prosperity Through Competition* (second edition, London, 1959); Gerhard Schröder and others, *Ludwig Erhard: Beiträge zu seiner politischen Biographie* (Frankfurt/Berlin/Vienna, 1972). On the German 'miracle', less uncritically: Heinz Abosch, *The Menace of the Miracle* (London, 1962); Norman J. G. Pounds, *The Economic Pattern of Modern Germany* (London, 1963); Karl W. Roskamp, *Capital Formation in West Germany* (Detroit, 1965); Henry C. Wallich, *Mainsprings of German Revival* (New Haven, Conn., 1955).

On Europe's postwar growth generally: Jossleyn Hennessy and others, *Economic 'Miracles'* (London, 1964); Charles P. Kindleberger, *Economic Growth in France and Britain 1851–1950* (Cambridge, Mass., 1964) and *Europe's Postwar Growth* (Cambridge, Mass., 1967); Angus Maddison, *Economic Growth in the West* (New York/London, 1964); E. F. Penrose, *Economic Planning for Peace* (Princeton, 1953); M. M. Postan, *An Economic History of Western Europe 1945–1964* (London, 1967); Andrew Shonfield, *Modern Capitalism* (London, 1965).

On France: Jacques Guyard, *Le miracle français* (Paris, 1965); John and Anne-Marie Hackett, *Economic Planning in France* (London, 1963); Malcolm MacLennan, *French Planning: Some Lessons for Britain* (London, 1963); Pierre Maillet, *La croissance économique* (Paris, 1966). On Italy: L. P. Elwell-Sutton, *Persian Oil* (London, 1955); P. M. Frankel, *Mattei: Oil and Power Politics* (London, 1966); George H. Hildebrand, *Growth and Structure in the Economy of Modern Italy* (Cambridge, Mass., 1965); Libero Lenti, *Inventario dell'Economia Italiana* (Milan, 1966); Rudolfo Morandi, *Storia della Grande Industria in Italia* (Turin, 1966); M. V. Posner and S. J. Woolf, *Italian Public Enterprise* (London, 1967); Anthony Sampson, *The Seven Sisters* (London, 1975); Dow Votaw, *The Six-Legged Dog* (Berkeley, Calif., 1964). On Britain: Samuel Brittain, *The Treasury under the Tories 1951–1964* (London, 1964); Kevin Hawkins, *British Industrial Relations 1945–1975* (London, 1976); Andrew Shonfield, *British Economic Policy Since the War* (revised, London, 1959); G. D. N. Worswick and P. H. Ady (eds.), *The*

British Economy 1945–1950 (Oxford, 1952); Ferdynand Zweig, *The British Worker* (London, 1952).

On corporations, etc.: Raymond Aron, *Dix-huit leçons sur la société industrielle* (Paris, 1962) and *Trois essais sur l'âge industriel* (Paris, 1966); Graham Bannock, *The Juggernauts* (revised, London, 1973); Giorgio Bocca, *I Giovani Leoni del Neocapitalismo* (Bari, 1963); David Granick, *The European Executive* (New York, 1962); Jacques Lavrillère, *L'industrie des banquiers* (Paris, 1966); Henri Peyret, *La stratégie des trusts* (Paris, 1961); R. S. Sayers (ed.), *Banking in Western Europe* (Oxford, 1962).

Chapter 7   Easy Street

On Edith Piaf: Simone Berteaut, *Piaf* (Paris, 1969); on 'affluence', see suggestions for previous chapter. For statistics: John Burnett, *A History of the Cost of Living* (London, 1969); Alberto Cavallari, *L'Europa su Misura* (Florence, 1963); and above all J. Frederick Dewhurst and others, *Europe's Needs and Resources* (New York, 1961). On aviation, Bernard Dutoit, *L'aviation et l'Europe* (Lausanne, 1959); on television, Jacques Thibau, *Une télévision pour tous les français* (Paris, 1970); on consumers, Christina Fulop, *Competition for Consumers* (London, 1964) and Claude Quin and others, *Les consommateurs* (Paris, 1965); on retailing, James B. Jefferys and Derek Knee, *Retailing in Europe* (London, 1962). On Auden and Stravinsky, Charles Osborne, *W. H. Auden* (London, 1979); on DNA, James D. Watson, *The Double Helix* (London, 1968); on 'classlessness', Raymond Aron, *La lutte des classes* (Paris, 1964); on innovation, Christopher Booker, *The Neophiliacs* (London, 1969). On social and rural change, Margaret Scotford Archer and Salvador Giner (eds.), *Contemporary Europe* (London, 1971); S. H. Franklin, *The European Peasantry* (London, 1969); P. Lamartine Yates, *Food, Land, and Manpower in Western Europe* (London, 1960).

On Pasternak and the 'Thaw': Edward Crankshaw, *Khrushchev's Russia* (London, 1959) and *Russia Without Stalin* (London, 1956); Michael Glenny, *Novy Mir: A Selection 1925–1967* (London, 1972); H. Montgomery Hyde, *Stalin* (London, 1971); Boris Pasternak, *An Essay in Autobiography* (London, 1959) and *Safe Conduct* (London, 1959); Gerd Ruge, *Pasternak* (London, 1959); Hugh Seton-Watson, *From Stalin to Malenkov* (London, 1953); Simone Signoret, *La nostalgie n'est plus ce qu'elle était* (Paris, 1975).

Chapter 8   Strangers in Our Midst

On Samuel Beckett, etc.: Michel Butor, *Essais sur les modernes* (Paris, 1964); Martin Esslin, *The Theatre of the Absurd* (revised, London, 1968); Frank Kermode, *Modern Essays* (London, 1971); Alain Robbe-Grillet, *Pour un nouveau roman* (Paris, 1963); Alan Young, *Dada and After* (New York, 1981).

On poverty in Sicily: Danilo Dolci, *Conversazioni Contadini* (Turin, 1962) and *Inchiesta a Palermo* (Milan, 1956).

On John Osborne, etc.: Robert Hewison, *In Anger* (London, 1981); John Russell Taylor, *Anger and After* (revised, London, 1963); Simon Trussler, *The Plays of John Osborne* (London, 1969). On 'The Movement', Blake Morrison, *The Movement* (Oxford, 1980).

On modern frustrations: Michel Crozier, *Le monde des employés de bureau* (Paris, 1965); Georges Friedmann, *Le travail en miettes* (Paris, 1964); Anthony Hartley, *A State of England* (London, 1963); Bernice Martin, *A Sociology of Contemporary Cultural Change* (Oxford, 1981); Alain Peyrefitte, *Le mal français* (Paris, 1976); Michael Shanks, *The Stagnant Society* (London, 1961).

On environmental ills: Tony Aldous, *Battle for the Environment* (London, 1972); Robert Arvill, *Man and Environment* (London, 1967); Reyner Banham, *Megastructure* (London, 1976); John Barr, *Derelict Britain* (London, 1969); Jeremy Bugler, *Polluting Britain* (London, 1972); Nigel Calder, *The Environment Game* (London, 1967); Louis Chevalier, *L'assassinat de Paris* (Paris, 1977); Hermione Hobhouse, *Lost London* (London, 1971); Roy Worskett, *The Character of Towns* (London, 1969).

On espionage: E. H. Cookridge, *George Blake* (London, 1970) and *The Third Man* (London, 1968); Tom Driberg, *Guy Burgess* (London, 1956); Reinhard Gehlen, *The Gehlen Memoirs* (London, 1972); Heinz Höhne and Hermann Zolling, *Network* (London, 1972); Alan Moorehead, *The Traitors* (London, 1952); Bruce Page and others, *Philby* (revised, London, 1969); Oleg Penkovsky, *The Penkovsky Papers* (London, 1965); 'Kim' Philby, *My Silent War* (London, 1968); Chapman Pincher, *Their Trade is Treachery* (London, 1981); Patrick Seale and Maureen McConville, *Philby* (London, 1973); Charles Whiting, *Gehlen: Germany's Master Spy* (New York, 1972). On the hounding of homosexuals: Peter Wildeblood, *Against the Law* (London, 1955). On social problems: Wolfgang Abendroth, *Sozialgeschichte der Europäischer Arbeiterbewegung* (Frankfurt, 1965). On George Orwell: Bernard Crick, *George Orwell* (London, 1980) and T. R. Fyvel, *George Orwell* (London, 1982). On 'brinkmanship': John Foster Dulles, *War or Peace* (New York, 1950).

On drugs: Gordon Claridge, *Drugs and Human Behaviour* (London, 1970); Peter Laurie, *Drugs* (revised, London, 1971); Donald B. Louria, *The Drug Scene* (London, 1970); Michael Schofield, *The Strange Case of Pot* (London, 1971); David Solomon (ed.) *The Marijuana Papers* (London, 1969). On 'juvenile delinquents': T. R. Fyvel, *The Insecure Offenders* (revised, London, 1963). On 'admass': J. B. Priestley and Jacquetta Hawkes, *Journey Down a Rainbow* (London, 1955).

Chapter 9   The End of Empire

On Suez 1956: Henri Azeau, *Le piège de Suez* (Paris, 1964); Jacques Baeyens, *Un coup d'épée dans l'eau du canal* (Paris, 1976); A. J. Barker, *Suez: The Seven Days War* (London, 1967); André Beaufre, *The Suez Expedition 1956* (London, 1967); Russell Braddon, *Suez: Splitting of a Nation* (London, 1973); Serge and Merry

Bromberger, *Les secrets de l'expédition de Suez* (Paris, 1957); Erskine Childers, *The Road to Suez* (London, 1962); Anthony Eden, *Memoirs: Full Circle* (London, 1960); Paul Ely, *Mémoires: Suez ... le 13 mai* (Paris, 1969); Herman Finer, *Dulles over Suez* (London, 1964); Roy Fullick and Geoffrey Powell, *Suez: The Double War* (London, 1979); John Gunther, *Processional* (London, 1965); Robert Henriques, *One Hundred Hours to Suez* (London, 1957); Paul Johnson, *The Suez War* (London, 1957); Selwyn Lloyd, *Suez 1956* (London, 1978); Kennett Love, *Suez: The Twice Fought War* (London, 1970); Jacques Massu and Henri Le Mire, *Vérité sur Suez 1956* (Paris, 1978); Anthony Moncrieff (ed.), *Suez Ten Years After* (London, 1967); Robert Murphy, *Diplomat Among Warriors* (London, 1964); Anthony Nutting, *No End of a Lesson* (London, 1967); Christian Pineau, *1956 Suez* (Paris, 1976); Terence Robertson, *Crisis* (London, 1965); Hugh Thomas, *The Suez Affair* (London, 1967).

On decolonization generally: Stewart C. Easton, *The Twilight of European Colonialism* (London, 1961); Edward Grierson, *The Imperial Dream* (Newton Abbot, 1973); Arthur Creech Jones (ed.), *New Fabian Colonial Essays* (London, 1959); V.G. Kiernan, *European Empires from Conquest to Collapse 1815–1960* (London, 1982) and *The Lords of Human Kind* (revised, London, 1972); W.D. McIntyre, *Colonies into Commonwealth* (London, 1966); James Morris, *Farewell the Trumpets* (London, 1978); Patrick Gordon Walker, *The Commonwealth* (London, 1962).

On Africa, see especially W. Arthur Lewis and others, *Attitudes to Africa* (London, 1951), and W.M. Macmillan, *Africa Emergent* (revised, London, 1949). On Asia: Guy Wint, *Spotlight on Asia* (second edition, London, 1959). On India: Horace Alexander, *India Since Cripps* (London, 1944); Maulana Abdul Kalam Azad, *India Wins Freedom* (Bombay, 1959); Edward Behr, *Bearings* (New York, 1978); Michael Brecher, *Nehru: A Political Biography* (Oxford, 1953); Penderel Moon, *Divide and Quit* (London, 1962); Ronald Segal, *The Crisis of India* (London, 1965); Taya Zinkin, *India* (London, 1965). On North Africa: John Steward Ambler, *The French Army in Politics 1945–1962* (Columbus, Ohio, 1966); Edward Behr, *The Algerian Problem* (London, 1959); Pierre Rouanet, *Mendès-France au pouvoir 1954–1955* (Paris, 1965); C.L. Sulzberger, *The Test: De Gaulle and Algeria* (London, 1962); Alexander Werth, *The Strange History of Pierre Mendès-France* (London, 1957). On racial problems: W.W. Daniel, *Racial Discrimination in England* (London, 1968); Ronald Segal, *The Race War* (London, 1967).

On Eastern Europe: Noel Barber, *Seven Days of Freedom* (London, 1973); Nicholas Bethel, *Gomulka* (London, 1972); François Fejtö, *Budapest '56* (Paris, 1966).

Chapter 10   The Road to Rome

On the prehistory of European unification: Achille Albonetti, *Préhistoire des Etats-unis d'Europe* (Paris,

1963); René Albrecht-Carrié, *The Unity of Europe* (London, 1966); Henri Brugmans, *L'idée européenne 1918–1965* (Bruges, 1965); Federico Chabod, *Storia dell'Idea dell'Europa* (paperback edition, Bari, 1967); Richard Mayne, *The Community of Europe* (London, 1962) and *The Europeans* (London, 1972); Sidney Pollard, *European Economic Integration 1815–1970* (London, 1974); Bernard Voyenne, *Histoire de l'idée européenne* (Paris, 1964).

On Resistance antecedents: Jacques Bergier, *Agents secrets contre armes secrètes* (revised, Paris, 1964); Henri Bernard, *Histoire de la Résistance européenne* (Verviers, 1968); Blake Ehrlich, *The French Resistance* (London, 1966); R.R. Kedward, *Resistance in Vichy France* (Oxford, 1978); Walter Lipgens, *A History of European Integration 1945–1947* (Oxford, 1982); Henri Noguères, *Histoire de la Résistance en France juin 1940–juin 1941* (Paris, 1967); Peter Novick, *The Resistance versus Vichy* (London, 1968); Terence Prittie, *Germans Against Hitler* (Boston, 1964).

On the beginnings of the European Community: M. Margaret Ball, *Nato and the European Unity Movement* (New York, 1959); Max Beloff, *Europe and the Europeans* (London, 1957), *The Intellectual in Politics* (New York, 1971) and *The United States and the Unity of Europe* (London, 1963); Georges Bidault, *Resistance: The Political Autobiography* (New York, 1965); Merry and Serge Bromberger, *Les coulisses de l'Europe* (1968); Henri Brugmans, *L'Europe vécue* (Tournai, 1979); Don Cook, *Floodtide in Europe* (New York, 1965); William J. Diebold, Jr., *The Schuman Plan* (New York, 1959); Pierre Drouin, *L'Europe du marché commun* (Paris, 1963); Edward Fursdon, *The European Defence Community* (London, 1980); Ernst B. Haas, *The Uniting of Europe* (revised, Stanford, Calif., 1968); Walter Hallstein and Hans-Jürgen Schlochauer (eds.), *Zur Integration Europas* (Karlsruhe, 1965); Oliver Harvey, *Diplomatic Diaries* (London, 1970); Jean Lecerf, *Histoire de l'unité européenne* (Paris, 1965); Daniel Lerner and Raymond Aron, *France Defeats E.D.C.* (New York, 1957); J.E. Meade, *Negotiations for Benelux* (Princeton, 1957) and *Problems of Economic Union* (London, 1953); Jules Moch, *Histoire du réarmement allemand depuis 1950* (Paris, 1965); Jean Monnet, *Les Etats-unis d'Europe ont commencé* (Paris, 1955) – see also his *Mémoires*, cited under Chapter 1, above; R.C. Mowat, *Creating the European Community* (London, 1973); Robert Schuman, *Pour l'Europe* (Paris, 1963); Paul-Henri Spaak, *Combats inachevés* (Paris, 1969); Jacques Van Helmont, *Jean Monnet comme il était* (Lausanne, 1981); F. Roy Willis, *France, Germany, and the New Europe* (London, 1969); Arnold J. Zurcher, *The Struggle to Unite Europe* (New York, 1958).

On Britain and the nascent Community: Alan Bullock, *The Life and Times of Ernest Bevin* (London, 1960); Miriam Camps, *Britain and the European Community* (London, 1963); David Dilks (ed.), *Retreat from Power* (London, 1981); F.S. Northedge, *British Foreign Policy: The Process of Readjustment 1945–1961* (London, 1962); Neville Waites (ed.), *Troubled Neighbours* (London, 1971).

Index